GUANTÁNAMO AND BEYOND

The Military Commissions scheme established by President George W. Bush in November 2001 has garnered considerable national and international controversy. In parallel with the detention facilities at Guantánamo Bay, Cuba, the creation of military courts has focused significant global attention on the use of such courts as a mechanism to process and try persons suspected of committing terrorist acts or offenses during armed conflict. This book brings together the viewpoints of leading scholars and policy makers on the topic of exceptional courts and military commissions with a series of unique contributions setting out the current "state of the field." The book assesses the relationship between such courts and other intersecting and overlapping legal arenas including constitutional law, international law, international human rights law, and international humanitarian law. By examining the comparative patterns, similarities, and disjunctions arising from the use of such courts, this book also analyzes the political and legal challenges that the creation and operation of exceptional courts produce both within democratic states and for the international community.

Fionnuala Ní Aoláin is concurrently the Dorsey and Whitney Chair in Law at the University of Minnesota Law School and Professor of Law at the University of Ulster's Transitional Justice Institute in Belfast, Northern Ireland. Professor Ní Aoláin is the recipient of numerous academic awards and honors, including a Fulbright scholarship, the Alon Prize, the Robert Schumann Scholarship, a European Commission award, and the Lawlor fellowship. She has published extensively in the fields of emergency powers, conflict regulation, transitional justice, and sex-based violence in times of war. Her book *Law in Times of Crisis* (2006, with Oren Gross) was awarded the American Society of International Law's preeminent prize in 2007 – the Certificate of Merit for Preeminent Contribution to Creative Scholarship. She is also the author of *On the Frontlines: Gender, War, and the Post-Conflict Process* (2011). She was appointed to the Executive Council of the American Society of International Law in 2010 for a three-year term. She is Chair of the Board for the International Women's Program OSI.

Oren Gross is the Irving Younger Professor of Law and the Director of the Institute for International Legal and Security Studies at the University of Minnesota Law School. Professor Gross has received numerous academic awards and scholarships, including a Fulbright scholarship and British Academy and British Council awards. Between 1986 and 1991, Professor Gross served as a senior legal advisory officer in the international law branch of the Israeli Defense Forces Judge Advocate General's Corps. Professor Gross's work has been published extensively, and his articles have appeared in leading academic journals such as the *Yale Law Journal*, *Yale Journal of International Law*, *Michigan Journal of International Law*, *Minnesota Law Review*, and *Cardozo Law Review*. His book *Law in Times of Crisis* (Cambridge 2006, with Fionnuala Ní Aoláin) was awarded the American Society of International Law's preeminent prize in 2007 – the Certificate of Merit for Preeminent Contribution to Creative Scholarship. In 2008 he was elected as a member of the American Law Institute.

Guantánamo and Beyond

EXCEPTIONAL COURTS AND MILITARY COMMISSIONS IN COMPARATIVE PERSPECTIVE

Edited by

Fionnuala Ní Aoláin

University of Minnesota School of Law

Oren Gross

University of Minnesota School of Law

CAMBRIDGE
UNIVERSITY PRESS

CAMBRIDGE
UNIVERSITY PRESS

32 Avenue of the Americas, New York, NY 10013-2473, USA

Cambridge University Press is part of the University of Cambridge.

It furthers the University's mission by disseminating knowledge in the pursuit of education, learning, and research at the highest international levels of excellence.

www.cambridge.org
Information on this title: www.cambridge.org/9781107401686

First published 2013

Printed in the United States of America

A catalog record for this publication is available from the British Library.

Library of Congress Cataloging in Publication data
Guantánamo and beyond : exceptional courts and military commissions in comparative perspective / edited by Fionnuala Ní Aoláin & Oren Gross.
pages cm
Includes bibliographical references and index.
ISBN 978-1-107-00921-9 (hardback) – ISBN 978-1-107-40168-6 (pbk.)
1. Terrorism – Prevention – Law and legislation. 2. Courts of special jurisdiction. 3. Military courts. 4. Terrorism – Prevention – Law and legislation – United States. 5. Military courts – United States. I. Ní Aoláin, Fionnuala, 1967– II. Gross, Oren.
K5256.G83 2013
343′.0143–dc23 2013006439

ISBN 978-1-107-00921-9 Hardback
ISBN 978-1-107-40168-6 Paperback

Do Phádraig O' hAoláin

To Rina and Yehoshua Gross

Contents

Contributors

William C. Banks is recognized internationally as an expert on constitutional and national security law and counterterrorism. He is Board of Advisers Distinguished Professor at Syracuse University College of Law and Director of the Institute for National Security & Counterterrorism. Since 1987, when the Federation of American Scientists asked him to provide a legal perspective on first use of nuclear weapons, Banks has helped set the parameters for the relatively new field of national security law. Working with Steven Dycus, Arthur Berney, and Peter Raven-Hansen, Banks wrote the leading text in the field. *National Security Law* was first published in 1990 and is now in its fifth edition. Banks is also the author of numerous other books, book chapters, and articles including *Constitutional Law: Structure and Rights in Our Federal System*, Fourth Edition; "Troops Defending the Homeland: The Posse Comitatus Act and the Legal Environment for a Military Role in Domestic Counter Terrorism"; and "Targeted Killing and Assassination: The U.S. Legal Framework."

Carol L. Chomsky is a Professor of Law at the University of Minnesota Law School. Her scholarly work has focused on the history of women lawyers, American Indian legal history, and late-nineteenth-century American legal history. She has coauthored an innovative contracts casebook. She is a long-time board member of the Society of American Law Teachers (SALT) and served as co-president from 2000 to 2002.

She is past president of Minnesota Women Lawyers and is a member of the American Law Institute. Professor Chomsky served as Coordinator for the University of Minnesota's Early Career Teaching Program: Pursuing Excellence in Multicultural Education from 1999 to 2004 and as Co-Coordinator of the University's Multicultural Fellows Program from 2003 to 2008.

David Cole is a Professor of Law at Georgetown University Law Center. He is also a volunteer attorney for the Center for Constitutional Rights, the Legal Affairs Correspondent for *The Nation*, a regular contributor to the *New York Review of Books*, and a commentator on National Public Radio's "All Things Considered." He has published widely in law journals and the popular press, including the *Yale Law Journal*, *California Law Review*, *Stanford Law Review*, *New York Times*, *Washington Post*, *Wall Street Journal*, and *Los Angeles Times*. He is the author of six books including *Less Safe, Less Free: Why America Is Losing the War on Terror* (2007), which won the Palmer Civil Liberties Prize for best book on national security and civil liberties; *Enemy Aliens: Double Standards and Constitutional Freedoms in the War on Terrorism* (2003), which received the American Book Award in 2004; and *No Equal Justice: Race and Class in the American Criminal Justice System* (1999), which was named Best Non-Fiction Book of 1999 by the *Boston Book Review* and best book on an issue of national policy in 1999 by the American Political Science Association. His most recent book is *The Torture Memos: Rationalizing the Unthinkable* (2009). Professor Cole has litigated many significant constitutional cases in the Supreme Court, including, most recently, *Holder v. Humanitarian Law Project*. Professor Cole has received numerous awards for his human rights work, including from the Society of American Law Teachers, the National Lawyers Guild, the ACLU of Southern California, the ABA Section on Individual Rights and Responsibilities, and the American-Arab Anti-Discrimination Committee.

Alex Conte is the Director of the International Commission of Jurists' International Law & Protection Programmes and an Adjunct Professor at the Geneva Academy of International Humanitarian Law and Human Rights. Dr. Conte is a New Zealand–trained lawyer. He was a criminal law barrister for almost ten years, following which he entered academia as a professor of international law. Dr. Conte has acted as a consultant to the United Nations and the Organization for Security and Cooperation in Europe. He has led and participated in the training of judges, diplomats, practitioners, trial observers, and university undergraduate and postgraduate students and has been a key-note speaker at a number of conferences throughout the world. He holds undergraduate, masters, and PhD degrees in law and was the 2004 New Zealand Law Foundation International Research Fellow. His recent publications include the book *Human Rights in the Prevention and Punishment of Terrorism* (2010).

Fiona de Londras is a Professor of Law at Durham Law School and Co-Director of the Durham Human Rights Centre. Previously, she was a faculty member at the University College of Dublin School of Law. Widely published in the area of counterterrorism, human rights, and comparative constitutional law, her research is broadly concerned with mechanisms for maintaining constitutionalism – and particularly respect for rights – at times of strain. Professor de Londras is coeditor of the *Irish Yearbook of International Law* and an editor of *Legal Studies*, the journal of the Society of Legal Scholars of the UK and Ireland. Her latest book, *Detention in the War on Terror: Can Human Rights Fight Back?*, was published by Cambridge University Press in 2011. She is a Visiting Professorial Fellow of the University of New South Wales in Sydney.

David Glazier is a Professor of Law at Loyola Law School. Prior to joining Loyola Law School, he was a lecturer at the University of Virginia School of Law and a Research Fellow at the Center for National Security Law, where he conducted research on national security, military justice, and the law of war. He also served as a pro bono consultant to Human Rights First. Before attending law school, Professor Glazier served twenty-one years as a U.S. Navy surface warfare officer. In that capacity, he commanded the *USS George Philip*, served as the Seventh Fleet staff officer responsible for the U.S. Navy–Japan relationship, the Pacific Fleet officer responsible for the U.S. Navy–PRC relationship, and participated in UN sanctions enforcement against Yugoslavia and Haiti.

Steven Greer is Professor of Human Rights at the University of Bristol Law School and academician at the United Kingdom's Academy of Social Sciences. He has taught at several universities in the UK – and in Germany, France, and Australia – and acted as consultant/advisor to various organizations, including the Council of Europe and others in Northern Ireland, Palestine, and Nepal. He was a Nuffield Foundation Visiting Research Fellow at the Oñati International Institute for the Sociology of Law (Spain) and a British Academy Research Fellow at the University of Bristol. He has published widely, particularly in the fields of criminal justice, human rights, and law and terrorism. Two of his books have been short-listed for book prizes, and some of his published and other work has been translated into half a dozen languages. Current research projects include a book about human rights in the Council of Europe and the European Union (coauthored by Professor Andrew Williams, University of Warwick).

Emanuel Gross is a Professor of Law at the University of Haifa specializing in military law, law and morality, evidence, criminal procedure, criminal law, and law and terrorism. He is a member of the editorial board of *Ius Gentium* and served as a Deputy District Military Attorney, a Deputy Chief Judge, and a Chief Judge in the Israel Defense Force. His books include *The Struggle of Democracy against Terrorism: The Suicide Bombers – Do We Have Any Legal Answers for this Phenomenon?* (2009); *The Rule of Law and Terrorism* (2004); *The Crown Witness* (1989); and *The Struggling of Democracy against Terrorism: The Legal and Moral Aspects* (forthcoming).

Oren Gross is the Irving Younger Professor of Law and the Director of the Institute of International Legal & Security Studies at the University of Minnesota Law School. He has taught and held visiting positions at

Harvard Law School, Princeton University, the Institute for Advanced Studies at the Hebrew University of Jerusalem, Benjamin N. Cardozo School of Law, the Max Planck Institute for International Law and Comparative Public Law (Heidelberg, Germany), the Transitional Justice Institute (Belfast, Northern Ireland), Queen's University (Belfast, Northern Ireland), and the University of Santiago de Compostela (Spain). He has received numerous academic awards and scholarships, including a Fulbright scholarship and British Academy and British Council awards. Professor Gross's work has been published extensively. His articles have appeared in leading academic journals (including the *Yale Law Journal* and *Yale Journal of International Law*) and his book, *Law in Times of Crisis: Emergency Powers in Theory and Practice* (2006), was awarded the prestigious Certificate of Merit for Preeminent Contribution to Creative Scholarship by the American Society of International Law in 2007. In 2008 he was elected as a member of the American Law Institute.

Joseph C. Hansen is an associate at the law firm of Gibson, Dunn & Crutcher LLP. He graduated summa cum laude from the University of Minnesota Law School, where he studied a concentration in International Human Rights. He clerked on the U.S. Court of Appeals for the Third Circuit for the Honorable Ruggero J. Aldisert. He has published several articles on international humanitarian law and is the Vice Chair of the ABA International Refugee Law Committee.

John Jackson is presently Professor of Comparative Criminal Law & Procedure at the School of Law, University of Nottingham. He was Dean and Professor of Criminal Law of the School of Law, University College Dublin, from 2008 to 2011, and Professor of Public Law at Queen's University Belfast from 1995 to 2008. From 1998 to 2000 he was an independent assessor on the Northern Ireland Criminal Justice Review, established under the Belfast Agreement, and he is a Parole and Sentence Review Commissioner in Northern Ireland. His books include *Judge without Jury: Diplock Courts in the Adversary System* (1995) (with Sean Doran); *The Judicial Role in Criminal Proceedings* (2000) (coedited with Sean Doran); *Standards for Prosecutors: An Analysis of the United Kingdom National Prosecuting Agencies* (2006) (with Barry Hancock); *Crime, Evidence and Procedure in a Comparative and International Context: Essays in Honour of M R Damaska* (2008) (coedited with Maximo Langer and Peter Tillers); and, most recently, *The Internationalisation of Criminal Evidence: Beyond the Common Law and Civil Law Traditions* (2012). He is Book Review Editor of the *Criminal Law Review*, a member of the UK Arts and Humanities Research Council Peer Review College, and on the editorial board of the *International Journal of Evidence & Proof* and *The Irish Jurist*.

Jayanth K. Krishnan is the Charles L. Whistler Faculty Fellow and Professor of Law at the Indiana University Maurer School of Law. He teaches courses in property, comparative law, and immigration. In 2012 he received the Indiana University Trustees' Teaching Award. Professor Krishnan's academic research focuses on the legal profession, the behavior of lawyers, law and globalization, and legal education, with a special emphasis on how these areas intersect in India. He has written extensively on these subjects, and his work has appeared in both highly reputed law reviews and peer-reviewed journals. Professor Krishnan serves as the head of the India Initiative at Indiana Law's Center on the Global Legal Profession. He also serves as the Law School's representative to the O. P. Jindal Global University (in Haryana, India) and is codirector of the Law School's Center for Law, Society, and Culture.

Fionnuala Ní Aoláin is concurrently the Dorsey and Whitney Chair in Law at the University of Minnesota Law School and Professor of Law at the University of Ulster's Transitional Justice Institute in Belfast, Northern Ireland. Professor Ní Aoláin is the recipient of numerous academic awards and honors including a Fulbright scholarship, the Alon Prize, the Robert Schumann Scholarship, a European Commission award, and the Lawlor fellowship. She has published extensively in the fields of emergency powers, conflict regulation, transitional justice, and sex-based violence in times of war. Her book *Law in Times of Crisis* (2006) was awarded the American Society of International Law's preeminent prize in 2007 – the Certificate of Merit for Preeminent Contribution to Creative Scholarship. She is the author of *On the Frontlines: Gender, War, and the Post Conflict Process* (2011). She was appointed to the Executive Council of the American Society of International law in 2010 for a three-year term and is Chair of the Board for the International Women's Program of the OSI.

Kent Roach is a Professor of Law and Prichard-Wilson Chair of Law and Public Policy at the University of Toronto Faculty of Law, with cross-appointments in criminology and political science. Professor Roach has been Editor in Chief of the *Criminal Law Quarterly* since 1998. In 2002 he was elected a Fellow of the Royal Society of Canada. Professor Roach's books include *Constitutional Remedies in Canada* (winner of the 1997 Owen Prize for best law book); *Due Process and Victims' Rights: The New Law and Politics of Criminal Justice* (short-listed for the 1999 Donner Prize for best public policy book); *The Supreme Court on Trial: Judicial Activism or Democratic Dialogue* (short-listed for the 2001 Donner Prize); *September 11: Consequences for Canada* (named one of the five most significant books of 2003 by the *Literary Review of Canada*); (with Robert J. Sharpe) *Brian Dickson: A Judge's Journey* (winner of the 2004 J. W. Dafoe Prize for best contribution to the understanding of Canada); and *The 9/11 Effect: Comparative Counter-Terrorism* (winner of the 2012 Mundell Medal).

Gabor Rona the International Legal Director of Human Rights First, advises Human Rights First programs on questions of international law and coordinates international human rights litigation. He also represents Human Rights First with governments and intergovernmental and non-governmental organizations and the media and the public on matters of international human rights and international humanitarian law (the law of armed conflict). Before joining Human Rights First, Gabor was a Legal Advisor in the Legal Division of the International Committee of the Red Cross (ICRC) in Geneva. At the ICRC he focused on the application of international humanitarian and human rights law in the context of counterterrorism policies and practices. He represented the ICRC in intergovernmental, nongovernmental, academic, and public forums, and his articles on the topic have appeared in the *Financial Times*, the *Fletcher Forum on World Affairs*, and the *Chicago Journal of International Law*.

Yuval Shany is Dean and Hersch Lauterpacht Chair in International Law at the Law Faculty of the Hebrew University of Jerusalem. He also serves as a board member in the International Law Forum at the Hebrew University, a director in the Project on International Courts and Tribunals, and a Senior Research Fellow at the Israel Democracy Institute. Professor Shany has published a number of books and articles on international courts and arbitration tribunals and other international law issues such as international human rights and international humanitarian law. He is the recipient of the 2004 American Society of International Law book award (creative legal scholarship) and a 2008 recipient of a European Research Council grant awarded to pioneering research leaders. He currently coordinates a research group studying the effectiveness of international adjudication and is a member of a study group looking into the relationship between substantive national and international criminal law. He was appointed to the United Nations Human Rights Committee in 2012.

Viplav Sharma is a graduate of the National Academy of Legal Studies and Research University, Hyderabad. He clerked on the Supreme Court of India for Justice Arijit Pasayat and worked at the law firm of Amarchand Mangaldas. Since 2010, he has been practicing as an advocate in the Supreme Court of India.

Gary D. Solis is an Adjunct Professor of Law who teaches the laws of war at the Georgetown University Law Center and is an expert on the laws of war. He taught on the London School of Economics's law faculty for three years before joining the Department of Law at the United States Military Academy. For six years he headed West Point's law of war program, receiving Phi Kappa Phi's distinguished teaching award and, in 2005, the Apgar Award as the Military Academy's outstanding instructor. He retired from West Point in 2006. He is on the teaching faculty of the International Institute of Humanitarian Law in San Remo, Italy. Published monographs include *Marines and Military Law in Vietnam*; *Son Thang: An American War Crime*; and *The Law of Armed Conflict: International Humanitarian Law in War*.

Stephen I. Vladeck is a Professor of Law and the Associate Dean for Scholarship at American University Washington College of Law. His teaching and research focus on federal jurisdiction, constitutional law, national security law, and international criminal law. A nationally recognized expert on the role of the federal courts in the war on terrorism, he was part of the legal team that successfully challenged the Bush administration's use of military tribunals at Guantánamo Bay, Cuba, in *Hamdan v. Rumsfeld*, and has coauthored amicus briefs in a host of other major lawsuits, many of which have challenged the U.S. government's surveillance and detention of terrorism suspects. Professor Vladeck, who is a coeditor of Aspen Publishers's leading national security law casebook, has drafted reports on related topics for a wide range of organizations, including the First Amendment Center, the Constitution Project, and the American Bar Association's Standing Committee on Law and National Security. He is a senior editor of the peer-reviewed *Journal of National Security Law and Policy* and a senior contributor to the Lawfare blog.

Raha Wala is an Advocacy Counsel in the Law and Security Program at Human Rights First, where he advocates for U.S. counterterrorism and national security policies that are consistent with human rights norms. He graduated with honors from Georgetown University Law School, where he served as managing editor of the *Georgetown Journal of International Law*, co-president of Georgetown Law's Amnesty International chapter, and student co-director of the Iraqi Refugee Resettlement Fact-Finding Project. While at Georgetown Law, Mr. Raha undertook internships at Human Rights First, the Open Society Policy Center, the Human Rights Law Foundation, and the Institute for International Law and Human

Rights. Raha received his JD from Georgetown University Law School (2010) and his BBA in Finance and Political Science from the University of Wisconsin-Madison (2005).

Clive Walker is Professor of Criminal Justice Studies at the School of Law, University of Leeds. He was Director of the Centre for Criminal Justice Studies from 1987 to 2000 and Head of the Law School from 2000 to 2005 and again in 2010. He has researched and written extensively on terrorism issues. His books include *The Prevention of Terrorism in British Law* (1992), *Political Violence and the Law in Ireland* (1989), and *The Anti-Terrorism Legislation* (2009). His research has involved international publications and visiting professorships, and he is a regular contributor to governmental and Parliamentary inquiries. Arising from his appointment as a special adviser to a UK Parliamentary select committee is his book *The Civil Contingencies Act 2004: Risk, Resilience and the Law in the United Kingdom* (2006). His latest research, supported by the Arts & Humanities Research Council, is a comprehensive commentary, *Terrorism and the Law* (2011).

David S. Weissbrodt is a distinguished and widely published scholar of international human rights law. In 2005, he was appointed as the first Regents Professor at the University of Minnesota Law School. Since 1998 he has also been the Fredrikson and Byron Professor of Law. He was the Briggs and Morgan Professor of Law 1989–97 and the Julius E. Davis Professor of Law 1985–86. He established the University of Minnesota Human Rights Center and helped establish the University of Minnesota Human Rights Library online. He has represented and served as an officer or board member of the Advocates for Human Rights, Amnesty International, the Center for Victims of Torture, the International Human Rights Internship Program, Readers International, and the International League for Human Rights.

Acknowledgments

The completion of this book is the result of significant support from a number of institutions and individuals. They include the University of Minnesota Law School, which through the funding provided by the Robina Foundation generously supported the conference entitled *Exceptional Courts and Military Commissions: Comparative and Policy Perspectives*. This gathering enabled the editors and many of the scholars contributing to this volume to meet in Minneapolis in October 2009. The conference facilitated a rare discussion between legal scholars from numerous legal subfields on exceptional courts and military commissions and allowed fruitful analysis to take place. We both remain deeply indebted to Dean David Wippman for his ongoing support for this and other research projects we undertake individually and collectively. Professor Ní Aoláin would like to thank Dean Paul Carmichael and colleagues at the University of Ulster's Transitional Justice Institute in Belfast, Northern Ireland. Her interest in exceptional courts was sparked by long hours as a doctoral student spent observing Diplock Courts at the Antrim Road Courthouse on the northwest side of the city of Belfast, and lengthy hours of research observation spent in the Special Criminal Court in Dublin, Ireland. Portions of the introduction were presented at various conferences and roundtables including the LAPA reunion conference at Princeton University in October 2010, the National Security Forum at William Mitchell Law School in March 2009, and a Colloquium on Exceptional Courts at the University of Minnesota Law School in

March 2009. We undertook the final editing of this book at Harvard Law School in the autumn of 2012, and we appreciate the time in Cambridge to conclude the task.

Our collective debts are owed to the University of Minnesota Law School library, and in particular to Mary Rumsey, the Law School's foreign, comparative, and international law librarian. Mary has an uncanny capacity to locate the most obscure sources and give advice on research tangles big and small. John Berger has been an ever-patient editor and friend, and we thank him for his continued enthusiasm for the projects we undertake and his ongoing gentle prodding to keep us to our deadlines. A number of research assistants worked with us to check footnotes, sources, and keep us up to date on the various changes and adaptions to the military commission system in the United States and elsewhere. We thank Peter Anderson, Emily Hutchinson, Laura Matson, and Kristen Rau. Finally, we express gratitude to our three children – Aodhtan, Noa, and Malachi – for their patience in accommodating two parents completing a collective project such as this.

Introduction: Guantánamo and Beyond

Exceptional Courts and Military Commissions in Comparative and Policy Perspective

Fionnuala Ní Aoláin and Oren Gross

THE MILITARY COMMISSIONS SCHEME ESTABLISHED BY President George W. Bush on November 13, 2001, has garnered considerable national and international controversy.[1] The commissions' creation has focused significant global attention on the use of military courts as a mechanism to process and try individuals suspected of involvement in terrorist acts or offenses committed during armed conflict. As this book goes to press, the military commissions are still operational with President Obama indicating recently that he had asked the Department of Defense to designate a site in the United States where further military commissions' proceedings would be held.[2] Upon taking office in 2008, President Obama signed an executive order requiring the closure of the detention center at the U.S. Naval Base in Guantánamo Bay, Cuba, within a year. In the intervening twelve months various alternatives were explored including freeing those prisoners whose petitions for habeas corpus were successful, placing other prisoners on trial before military commissions or civilian courts, and seeking an alternative holding location for those individuals likely to remain incarcerated without trial. Despite substantial hand wringing nationally

1 Military Order of Nov. 13, 2001, 66 Fed. Reg. 57, 833 (Nov. 13. 2001).

2 President Barack Obama, Speech delivered at the National Defense University, Washington D.C. (May 23, 2013), retrieved from www.whitehouse.gov/the-press-office/2013/05/23/remarks-president-national-defense-university.

and internationally, a large group of individuals remains incarcerated at Guantánamo, and for some of them, operational progress to trial before a military tribunal continues.[3] The Obama administration relinquished its earlier position that indefinite detention without trial was not acceptable in a democratic society, and reinstated the full, if moderately amended, operation of the military commissions.

Framed by and against this political backdrop, this collection addresses the phenomena of what we broadly term "due process exceptionalism."[4] The essays included in this collection bring together the viewpoints of leading international, comparative, national security, and legal history experts from the United States and elsewhere. The collection also benefits from contributions by policy makers who offer policy-oriented analyses of the structural, legal, and political issues arising out of the use of exceptional courts and military commissions. These contributions include assessments of the relationship between exceptional courts and other intersecting and overlapping arenas in the context of U.S. domestic constitutional law, international law, international human rights law, and international humanitarian law; the patterns, similarities, and disjunctions that emerge as we view the process of resorting to such courts in comparative perspective; and the political and legal challenges that the creation or operation of such courts creates within states and for the international community.

The book focuses primarily on the role of exceptional courts and military tribunals in democratic polities, noting that courts are particularly relevant to the way in which democracies have responded to threats and crises, whether internal or external. Whereas the operation of such courts

3 When going to press six men face formal charges. In his May 23, 2013 speech on Terrorism, President Obama stated that the tension center at Guantánamo Bay "has become a symbol around the world for an America that flouts the rule of law," and opined that "there is no justification beyond politics for Congress to prevent us from closing a facility that should have never been opened." *Id.*

4 We note that some commentators use the term "national security exceptionalism." We view national security exceptionalism as being embraced by the concept of due process exceptionalism, but argue that the latter is a far wider term and has greater "catch."

in nondemocratic settings is noteworthy,[5] the precise challenges faced by democratic states are the ones that interest us the most as we draw out and explore the significance, patterns, and similarities that emerge in comparative assessment of due process exceptionalism. We use the term due process exceptionalism as an umbrella concept capturing a variety of state practices. It denotes the actions of executive and legislative branches in substantially modifying ordinary, well-accepted, and long-established due process practices and rules, particularly in the criminal justice area. The exceptionalism is derived from modifications to the requirement that the state must generally respect and uphold all of the legal rights that are owed to a person under its control. Justifications for due process exceptionalism are generally articulated as resulting from perceived challenge or threat, and they may be temporary or permanent. This is not a new phenomenon. With the fall of the monarchy in 509 BCE, the Roman republic moved to establish an executive branch of government that was headed by two chief magistrates, the consuls, who held immense power in their hands. In order to prevent reversion to a monarchical structure of government, the constitution of the republic based the executive offices of the republic on three fundamental principles: collegiality and equal power; limited, nonrenewable term of office; and the right of appeal (*provocatio*), which meant that any Roman citizen had the right to appeal any ruling by any other magistrate to a tribune.[6] This right of appeal – which assured Romans a core minimum of due process – was limited in several important ways. In addition to being limited to Roman citizens, the provocatio did not apply to matters pertaining to foreign affairs or decisions and actions taken by a dictator in times of extremely grave emergencies.

Then, as now, emergencies test the abilities of government to act vigorously and resolutely to overcome the crisis while not intruding

5 On the functioning of courts in nondemocratic settings, *see* LISA HILBINK, JUDGES BEYOND POLITICS IN DEMOCRACY AND DICTATORSHIP: LESSONS FROM CHILE (2007); TOM GINSBURG AND TAMIR MOUSTAFA (eds.), RULE BY LAW: THE POLITICS OF COURTS IN AUTHORITARIAN REGIMES (2008).

6 ANDREW LINTOTT, THE CONSTITUTION OF THE ROMAN REPUBLIC 152–57 (2003).

unnecessarily on established civil rights and liberties. The point was made by Attorney General Eric Holder in a speech delivered on March 5, 2012, in which he took pains to argue that, "both [federal civilian courts and the revised military commissions] incorporate fundamental due process and other protections that are essential to the effective administration of justice."[7] At the same time, discussing the targeted killing by the United States of an American citizen, the Attorney General argued:

> [T]he Due Process Clause does not impose one-size-fits-all requirements, but instead mandates procedural safeguards that depend on specific circumstances.... Where national security operations are at stake, due process takes into account the realities of combat.... "Due process" and "judicial process" are not one and the same, particularly when it comes to national security. The Constitution guarantees due process, not judicial process.... The Constitution's guarantee of due process is ironclad, and it is essential – but, as a recent court decision makes clear, it does not require judicial approval before the President may use force abroad against a senior operational leader of a foreign terrorist organization with which the United States is at war – even if that individual happens to be a U.S. citizen.[8]

The due process definition and its system management are uppermost in the minds of government decision-makers utilizing legal process to handle exigency. This book suggests that we should pay sustained and systematic attention to the sites and patterns of modification. By doing so we may more thoroughly understand the coping and adjustment patters of democratic states responding to violent challengers.

This collection is focused on modifications to courts, tribunals, and similar adjudicative bodies. In doing so, we explore how "normal" criminal justice responses may be deemed inadequate to the crisis or challenge at hand and, as a result, how states make adjustments to create new procedural mechanisms to prevent, contain, or punish the acts of those

7 Eric Holder, Speech delivered at Northwestern University School of Law (Mar. 5, 2012), retrieved from http://www.justice.gov/iso/opa/ag/speeches/2012/ag-speech-1203051.html.

8 *Id.*

challenging the state. The essays in this collection demonstrate, and critically assess, the phenomenon that when faced with acute violent challenges such as terrorism and armed conflict, democratic states make particular use of legal and judicial processes and institutions to manage such threats. This occurs in part because democratic states are constrained in their use of force to respond to such challenges, particularly when they manifest as internal armed conflicts or violence above a sporadic threshold.[9] Because democracies are particularly reluctant to cede the ground of combatant or armed conflict status to violent challengers, legal process becomes an important symbolic, expressive, communicative, and operational basis upon which to contain the effects and status of conflict.[10] Legal institutions and forms frame, and are framed by, the terms in which broader political responses to collective violence are shaped. Thus, the focus on democratic states and legal processes is significant, as it allows reflection on the restraints and limitations placed upon democratic states, and the extent to which there are consistent and comparative factors identifiable in such efforts. The reflection is particularly pertinent given

9 In a speech delivered on May 25, 2011, Harold Hongju Koh, the Legal Advisor to the U.S. Department of State, enumerated the "commitment to living our values by respecting the rule of law" as one of the four core commitments in what he called the emerging "Obama-Clinton Doctrine." Harold Hongju Koh, Legal Advisor to the Secretary of State, "The Obama Administration and International Law," speech before the American Society of International Law (May 25, 2011), retrieved from http://www.state.gov/s/l/releases/remarks/139119.htm. *See also* H.C. 5100/94, Pub. Comm. Against Torture in *Israel v. The State of Israel*, 53(4) P.D. 817, 845 (Barak, P.) (A democracy has "the upper hand" even though it "must sometimes fight with one hand behind its back." This is because "[t]he rule of law and the liberty of an individual constitute important components in its understanding of security. At the end of the day, they strengthen its spirit and this strength allows it to overcome its difficulties."). For critical review of what has been called "Lawfare" – the use of law as a weapon of war – see, e.g., Jack L. Goldsmith, The Terror Presidency: Law and Judgment Inside the Bush Administration 53–64 (2009).

10 The heated debate about the status of the individuals detained at Guantánamo Bay is a point in hand. *See, e.g.*, Benjamin Wittes, Detention and Denial: The Case for Candor after Guantánamo (2011). Another notable example pertains to the British government classification of captured IRA members as "criminals" and the insistence of the Republicans that they be accorded a political, or "special category," status. *See, e.g.*, Kieran McEvoy, Paramilitary Imprisonment in Northern Ireland: Resistance, Management, and Release (2001).

the heated political and legal debates surrounding the system of military commissions established by President Bush, and ongoing challenges concerning how best to process those detained in the aftermath of the terrorist attacks of 9/11 and the wars in Iraq and Afghanistan.

As noted previously, exceptional courts are not a new phenomenon. States have long used the legal process and courts as a means to manage and address exceptional threats and challenges. To achieve this, existing courts have been modified, new courts have been established, and jurisdiction for certain offenses moved from civilian criminal courts to military courts and commissions or were added to the roster of offenses with which the latter could deal. Arguably, the typifying of such military courts and commissions as exceptional is itself controversial, given that states have long established prerogatives to create various kinds of courts with variable jurisdictional and subject reach. A starting point in this introduction is to explore the meanings of due process exceptionalism, offering a spectrum of views that pertain to the uniqueness of court form, as well as the engagement of particular powers to establish or modify their operation.

A number of essays pay particular attention to the distinctions between civilian and military courts, including the operational and jurisdictional patterns that have historically framed their respective spheres of influence, probing the extent to which the rigidity of differences among such courts holds up to scrutiny. Military courts and commissions play a central role in any analysis of due process exceptionalism. However, as Gary Solis observes in Chapter 3, in many democracies, military courts in the form of courts-martial also have ongoing ordinary functions in implementing military codes of justice and regulating and enforcing military discipline. Equally, the resort by states to ad hoc military commissions has comparative and domestic pedigrees. Such commissions, in various forms, have been utilized by states as a means to process crimes and defendants deemed unsuitable for the ordinary courts. A number of the essays in this collection investigate the interplay between ordinary criminal courts, exceptional modified courts, military courts, and military commissions. Exploring the layered relationships between these institutions and providing an overview and analysis of how they complement, hinder, or reinforce one another gives a sense of the interplay between differing legal institutions as they respond to perceived political or military challenges. A number of contributions (Conte, Greer, Weissbrodt, and Hansen) also explore the relationship between exceptional courts and international oversight, particularly in the context of the United Nations Human Rights Committee, the Inter-American Court, the ad hoc international criminal tribunals, and the European Court of Human Rights. International judicial and quasi-judicial organs' standard setting on the meaning and forms of fair trial constrains the ways in which democratic states can utilize exceptional courts to try violent actors, and shapes broader rule-of-law understandings about the limits of legal exceptionalism for democracies.

1. Due Process Exceptionalism and Exceptional Discourses

What makes a court exceptional? Any definition of exceptionality must be sensitive to its own domestic system bias with its attendant and ever-present risk of identifying procedures and processes that appear different from those with which one is most familiar as procedurally or substantively deficient just because of that difference from the recognizable. We suggest that a number of factors and attributes must be considered when ascribing an exceptional or "extraordinary" character to a court:

- The authorization basis and context of a court's making;
- The limits articulated to such courts in their operation (time limits, geographical and jurisdictional limits);
- The range of offenses over which the courts have jurisdiction;
- Evidentiary and procedural rules used by and in the courts and the extent of their deviation from the rules applied in the ordinary courts' system;
- The judicial appointment mechanisms and processes to such courts;

- The perceived neutrality, impartiality, and independence of such courts from the other branches of government, with special focus on the executive branch;
- The limitations on due process rights ascribed to those subject to the courts' authority.

There are courts that satisfy some of these criteria even within the ordinary jurisdiction of the state, such as juvenile courts, immigration and asylum tribunals, and social security tribunals. Evidently, some courts meeting the criteria of exceptionalism encounter fewer criticisms than others. To pinpoint challenges to exceptional courts requires a nuanced and careful exploration of the various factors in the particular political, social, and legal contexts in which the courts are established and operate. However, based on the analyses presented across the contributions to this collection, we suggest that three characteristics have a particularly significant weight in assessing the legitimacy of exceptional courts. These are the areas that provoke the most resistance and challenge to exceptional courts: First, the range of offenses or regulatory terrain of the court; second, the procedural rules related to the introduction or exclusion of evidence; and finally, the perceived neutrality of the court and its distance from the other branches of government, including the mode of judicial appointment. The analyses provided by Conte, Weissbrodt and Hansen, and Greer strongly suggest that it is across these dimensions that democratic states are most likely to be found in breach of international treaty obligations when they opt to use exceptional courts.

It is generally conceded by proponents and defenders alike that exceptional and military courts make it easier to try a defendant than would be the case in an ordinary civilian court – no matter what state or legal system one operates within. Martin Scheinin, the former United Nations Special Rapporteur on Human Rights and Counterterrorism, has found that lower fair trial guarantees often characterize military and special courts due to prolonged periods of pre-charge and pretrial detention, with inadequate access to counsel, intrusion into attorney-client confidentiality, and strict limitations on the right to appeal and bail.[11] The consistency of modified rules about evidence, secrecy, legal access, and public access separately or in tandem lessen the burdens on those prosecuting and make the task for the defense more arduous. In particular, the procedural and evidentiary shifts deployed by exceptional courts and tribunals with a view to facilitating conviction, although much less discernible to the average observer than the gravity of the crimes charged or the status of the judicial officer presiding (military officer or civilian), may be far more distorting of the hitherto accepted "rules of the game" for criminal trials. Such rule changes, for example, may permit reliance on confessions in circumstances where reliance would normally be impermissible; burdens of proof may be reversed and rules pertaining to admissibility of evidence relaxed; abrogated pretrial procedures may substantially disadvantage the defendant during trial; definitions of the charged offenses may be "open textured" and "catchall," smoothing easier conviction; and the trial itself may be conducted in ways that adversely affect accountability and transparency.

Arguably, military commissions may fall into a singular category of perceived exceptionalism: when they are deployed by democratic states, and when they try civilians. A range of views on the permissibility, acceptability, and legitimacy of the commissions are reflected in this collection. Despite the general principle that military courts and commissions do not inherently violate the fair trial provisions of international law, Conte, Weissbrodt and Hansen all underscore the resistance by international courts as well as other mechanisms to accepting the legitimacy of trying civilians before military commissions. There are narrow formal exceptions to this bar: accepting that in extreme exigencies where regular trials before civilian courts are impossible, limited military jurisdiction might be undertaken. This reveals that civilian interface with judicial military oversight exposes core resistance to the seepage of military justice beyond

11 Protection of Human Rights and Fundamental Freedoms while Countering Terrorism, UN Doc. A/63/223, ¶¶ 27, 45(b) (2008). *See also*, UN General Assembly Res. 66/171 (Mar. 30, 2012), UN Doc. A/Res/66/171.

a narrowly defined remit, a position that allies democratic practice with express forms of judicial remit and demarcation. For some scholars the exceptionalism of military commissions cannot be detached from the continuum of modified arrest and detention practices that precedes trial before military officers. In this vein, Fiona de Londras argues in Chapter 5 that there is a continuum of exceptionalism pervading the preventive detention paradigm hazardously infected with a sweeping view of the scale of terrorist threat, in which military commissions play an auxiliary role. She charges that the preventive detention of suspected terrorists creates the conditions in which extraordinary courts and prosecutions are almost inevitable and whereby the detention process may itself constitute a type of extraordinary quasi-criminal procedure.

However, comparative analysis discloses that resort by states to ad hoc military commissions has comparative and long-standing domestic pedigree. Such commissions (in various forms) have been utilized by numerous democratic states as a means to process crimes and defendants deemed unsuitable for the ordinary courts. Ireland and Turkey offer two prominent European examples of such deployment.[12] The rich historical accounts provided by David Glazier and Gary Solis in Chapters 1 and 3, respectively, illuminate a narrative that captures elements of the routine use of U.S. military commissions and courts-martial in relatively straightforward and uncontentious ways, implementing military codes of justice and regulating military discipline, but also identifying stress points when military commissions operate as jurisdictional "gap fillers" for states looking to short circuit the usage of the ordinary courts.

One of the most trenchant critiques of exceptional courts in general and military courts in particular is their deviation from the ordinary processes of detention, pretrial process, and the conduct of the trial. The combined effects of prolonged (and, where courts are not involved, even indefinite) detention, coercive interrogation techniques, the particular

12 On the Irish Special Criminal Court *see, e.g.*, Fergal F. Davis, The History and Development of the Special Criminal Court – 1922–2005 (2007). On Turkey *see, e.g.*, Alastair Mowbray, *Military Judges and the Right to a Fair Trial*, 6 Hum. Rts. L. Rev. 176 (2006).

matrix of crimes alleged, and procedures and rules of evidence applied during trial makes the challenges to exceptional courts particularly salient. Separating out concerns about the structure and fairness of the eventual trials (if those take place at all) from the restrictions and indefinite detention of detainees may well be difficult.

2. Democratic States' Resort to Due Process Exceptionalism

The focus on democratic states and legal processes allows reflection on the restraints and limitations placed upon democratic states, and the extent to which there are consistent factors identifiable in such efforts. At the same time, using legal mechanisms is a means to enhancing the legitimacy of governmental responses to terrorism. We also suggest that democratic states gain some benefits precisely because of their status as "democracies" when they use legal mechanisms – particularly courts – to manage conflict. Law is simultaneously an enabling and a constraining tool and the intricate interplay between the two is explored in many of the essays in this book.

For democratic states the extent to which international fora have been willing to concede the legitimacy of domestic exceptional courts and accept or even affirmatively validate their usage has been an important feature in establishing, maintaining, and furthering the legitimacy of these courts and their capacity to become institutionally established over the long-term. International oversight has both enabled and constrained any exceptional measures taken by states. Interface with international judicial standard setting on the meaning and forms of fair trial theoretically constricts and shapes the ways in which democratic states can utilize exceptional courts to contend with violent actors, and contours broader rule-of-law understandings about the limits as well as the permissibility of legal exceptionalism. Thus, for example, as contributions by Conte and Weissbrodt and Hansen reveal, although due process rights were initially included in human rights treaties as derogable rights, international human rights oversight bodies have increasingly treated them as de facto non-derogable or have invoked limitations, thereupon narrowing – at least in theory – the range of action by the state. But democracies also utilize international oversight systems, taking advantage of oftentimes deferential attitudes and margins of appreciation that lead to decisions supportive of, or at least not adverse to, the state and conferring added legitimacy on the latter.[13] One counterargument to the leeway given to exceptional courts when deployed by democracies is that there is good reason to assume that there are countervailing pressures in the democratic setting that constrain the state and force a return to normality in ways that do not happen in illiberal systems.[14]

Courts have been particularly relevant to the way in which democracies have responded to threats and crises, whether internal or external. Parsing out the role of exceptional courts and military tribunals may lead to useful insights regarding the ability of democratic governments to deal successfully with terrorist threats while maintaining their own liberal values. A challenge unlocked by these essays is to promote further exploration of the significance, patterns, and similarities that emerge in comparative assessment of due process exceptionalism. A number of the essays illustrate how the road to exceptionalism is paved, across various jurisdictions, by perceptions that "normal," ordinary criminal justice responses may be inadequate to deal with the acute violent crisis or challenge at hand. The Indian case study presented by Jayanth Krishnan and Viplav Sharma in Chapter 13 exposes the fluidity of movement between ordinary and special courts. Their study tellingly reveals that the presumed benefits of the ordinary courts to persons charged with terrorist

13 Fionnuala Ní Aoláin, *The Emergence of Diversity: Differences in Human Rights Jurisprudence*, 19 Fordham Int'l L. J. 101 (1995); Oren Gross and Fionnuala Ní Aoláin, *From Discretion to Scrutiny: Revisiting the Application of the Margin of Appreciation Doctrine in the Context of Article 15 of the European Convention on Human Rights*, 23 Hum. Rts. Q. 625 (2001).

14 Aidan O'Neill, *The Lockerbie Bombing Case: A Miscarriage of Justice* (2010), retrieved from http://lapa.princeton.edu/hosteddocs/LAPA-Annual-Report.pdf (analysis of the Special Court created to try the Lockerbie bomber and the general perception of the unfairness of that Court at the local level arguing that a regular criminal court in Glasgow would have been fairer and that a jury would have likely acquitted).

offenses should not be assumed as an unqualified good. Rather paradoxically, the delays, inefficiencies, and procedural failings of the ordinary courts in India may make it a preferred site for the state to try its terrorism cases to the disadvantage of the defendant. Moreover, the ordinary courts have been infused with various exceptions and adjustments to due process protections that make it unclear how "ordinary" trial may in fact be conducted in these settings.

Several contributors discuss the apparent puzzle of state resort to exceptional courts when robust evidence exists that regular courts are adequate and capable of dealing with the exigency and its legal offshoots or can be, and frequently are, easily modified to achieve similar results. This is underscored where the "gap" between the ordinary courts and the exceptional courts is of a rather limited nature. The arguments in favor of exceptional courts are by now quite familiar: the need for secrecy, the difficulties of criminal prosecutions in open court, the potential expertise of specially selected judges, and so forth. An additional possible argument in these situations is that the use of exceptional courts is of mostly communicative and symbolic value, as it enables the relevant governments to signal that strong, tough measures are being pursued. Furthermore, exceptional courts may appear to permit the state to undertake certain measures that it may not otherwise be able to take, especially in connection with matters such as admissibility of evidence and the preservation of state secrets. There may also be an opportunity for the state to stigmatize or sanction the identified enemy in highly public ways while establishing a judicially approved narrative on the state's interaction with particular kinds of actors and groups. In his essay, David Cole closely examines the reasons given for the establishment of military commissions post-9/11 and finds them all to be wanting. Instead, he argues that the real rationale for using these exceptional bodies, rather than resorting to the established, functioning, and tested civilian court system or courts-martial, is to be found in the context of the more general "paradigm of prevention" that has characterized much of the War on Terror. Military commissions have persisted in the Bush and Obama administrations, Cole argues, because both – whether willingly or grudgingly – hope that by employing them, the United States may avoid "paying the costs of its imprudent resort to illegal tactics." Such tactics as illegal detentions; renditions; torture; and cruel, inhuman, and degrading treatment have been conceived of and utilized in the context of intelligence-gathering mindset and priorities. Whatever success they have achieved in that regard, they have, at the same time, tainted any evidence obtained from their deployment, making such evidence inadmissible in either civilian courts or courts-martial.

The challenges to such courts are manifold. They have both detractors and supporters. In capturing a range of views on exceptional courts and processes alike this collection airs the grievances that have mounted against such bodies, while addressing the complexities that democratic states encounter when tested by violent challengers. The book reveals various trade-offs for states facing exigency and relying on the courts to help navigate the regulatory terrain that follows. In doing so, there are valuable reflections on the interplay between the exceptional and the normal legal system that upend some of our presumptions about the complexities and costs of due process exceptionalism.

3. Exceptional Courts are not New

Exceptional courts are not a novel phenomenon. States have long used the legal process and the courts as means to manage and address exceptional threats and challenges, and historical examples – such as the use of the Star Chamber in Britain – abound.[15] A number of essays in this collection focus on the historical pedigree of military commissions in the United States. Carol Chomsky's nuanced study of the military

15 Edward P. Cheyney, *The Court of the Star Chamber*, 18 Am. Hist. Rev. 727 (1913). There is a long historical lineage carried by military justice systems, as they emerged in parallel with and sometimes before functional ordinary legal systems. For example, in the United Kingdom military justice mechanisms date back to the Norman conquest, institutionally established following the emergence of the Court of the Constable and the Marshall, a high (or perhaps low) point of trial modality for crimes against the crown in the creation of the Star Chamber, and ultimately the emergence of court of common law military justice in "General Courts Martial."

commissions used to try hundreds of Dakota who fought American soldiers in a brief frontier war in 1862 historicizes the precise locales of usage, and the complexity of their reception by the native communities whose members were tried by them. The use of these largely forgotten commissions, in which 392 combatants were tried, resulted in 323 convictions and the hanging of 38 – the largest mass execution in American history. This underscores some of the baggage with which any contemporary use may be saddled and against which it must be assessed. Indeed, the fact that convictions were often based exclusively on allegations of participation in the fighting and nothing more has an eerie resonance with the "participation in hostilities" argument that has been put forward by proponents of contemporary military commissions. David Glazier provides a comprehensive historical genealogy of the use of military commissions in the United States, demonstrating the variety of contexts and geographical locales in which they have been utilized. Commission usage is traced through various military engagements including the Mexican War (1846), the Civil War era, and the Philippine insurrection (1899–1902), as well as a detailed exposition of the usage in World War II in the Nazi saboteurs case.

If exceptional courts are not a new phenomenon, they are also not confined to the United States. They are found in numerous settings, and have long pedigrees of operation in multiple parts of the world. In offering a summary of the Indian criminal justice system, Jayanth Krishnan and Viplav Sharma illustrate the attractiveness of exceptional courts to successive governments in India. An effectiveness argument has framed the state construction of alternative forums to dispose of criminal matters – including terrorism-related cases – more expeditiously: a host of structural and political problems are viewed as rendering the regular courts incapable of providing justice in a timely manner. By providing a background on how special courts established under different antiterrorism statutes in India have evolved over the years, including a discussion of the Terrorism and Disruptive Activities (Prevention) Act (TADA) of 1985 and the 2002 Prevention of Terrorist Activities Act (POTA), Krishnan and Sharma illustrate the seductiveness of the exceptional. At the same time they demonstrate that the institutionally and formally special courts had, in fact, not been so special after all. Because lawyers, judges, norms, and even physical facilities were frequently the same as those found in the regular courts, the lines of demarcation between the various forums – the ordinary and the exceptional or special – had been blurred to a significant extent. Although both TADA and POTA had, eventually, been repealed, the 2008 Mumbai terror attacks reignited the call for sweeping measures to be enacted. The result was the passage of two statutes, the Unlawful Activities (Prevention) Act (UAPA) and the National Investigation Agency Act (NIAA), both of which helped establish the most recent set of NIAA special courts. Krishnan and Sharma assert that the operation of such courts presents fundamental challenges to India's regular judiciary and democratic system of government and suggest that in order for special terrorism courts to serve a constructive purpose in India their jurisdiction must be clearly clarified and denoted. This study illuminates a broader theme of this collection, namely the fluidity of movement between exceptional and ordinary systems within many democratic states and the persistence of the exceptional once it appears on the legal landscape.

A parallel comparative study by John Jackson discusses the use of nonjury Diplock courts in Northern Ireland during the modern phase of the conflict in the jurisdiction and further attests to the long pedigree of modified courts to address terrorist violence in common law systems. Jackson concentrates on the relationship between exceptional courts of various hues and the ordinary systems of criminal justice that parallel them. He demonstrates the relationship between what he terms a "vicious and virtuous cycle in prosecuting terrorism" in Northern Ireland. The fluidity between ordinary and extraordinary systems is revealed both positively and negatively. On the one hand, the transgressions and coercions that characterized the early stages of the conflict in Northern Ireland have, with time, given way to greater emphasis on the rule of law and a reversion to normal modalities. At the same time, normality has come at a price, as exceptional antiterrorism measures – including modifications to jury trial – have crept into the ordinary criminal justice system, leading to diminution in established rights that have long been a part of the criminal justice landscape.

Kent Roach explores the Canadian experience with exceptional courts and looks at the relationship between those and ordinary courts (a recurring theme in several of the essays in this collection). One such double-pronged interface between the regular system and the exceptional concerns security certificates issued under immigration law. First, specially designated judges of the Federal Court have been judicially reviewing those certificates. Second, the system of security certificates has itself been the subject of successful challenges under the Canadian Charter of Rights and Freedoms, which Roach identifies as an instance of "the law working itself pure." Another interface that Roach explores concerns the detention of a Canadian minor, Omar Khadr, in Guantánamo and his trial and conviction by a military commission, which has been the subject of protracted legal battles in Canada (including several decisions by the Canadian Supreme Court). His analysis leads Roach to conclude that the use of exceptional courts is likely to produce intractable legal and public relations quagmires, at least in healthy democracies committed to the rule of law, and is thus to be avoided for both due process and strategic reasons. The contribution underscores the pervasiveness of exceptional court form in multiple systems.

Emanuel Gross examines a unique set of military courts, those operating in the Occupied Territories in accordance with the international law of belligerent occupation. These courts, established after Israel occupied the West Bank and the Gaza Strip in 1967, have had substantial interface with the ordinary justice system in Israel proper. The essay sets out the operation of these courts and the judicial and legislative constraints imposed on their operation.

Yuval Shany suggests in his essay that domestic systems' resort to exceptional courts is not without parallel on the international plain. In Chapter 17 of this collection Shany addresses the phenomenon of special international courts, including the International Criminal Tribunal for the Former Yugoslavia and the International Criminal Court for Rwanda as well as other hybrid tribunals in Sierra Leone, Cambodia, Lebanon, East Timor, and Kosovo. In all of these cases, the international response had been exceptional in nature: institutions were created alongside the ordinary judicial system for a limited period of time in response to special catastrophic events for the purpose of handling a select category of past crimes, which were removed – fully or partly – from the ordinary criminal jurisdiction of national courts. This definition of exceptionality may also be relevant to how we conceptualize the International Criminal Court, which, although a permanent forum of criminal adjudication, also exercises its jurisdiction in an "episodic" manner. Thus, Shany challenges us to rethink the presumption that exceptionality is located exclusively within national legal systems. His methodical analysis also identifies a range of legitimacy and process concerns that arise from such exceptionality, some of which are uniquely characteristic to the supranational dimension of these judicial bodies; others mirror domestic concerns and practice.

These comparative analyses underscore the durability of exceptional courts and their capacity to persist long-term in highly functional and open democratic systems. The experiences are varied but point to the overlapping challenges posed by such courts, not least the osmosis that may occur with the systems of ordinary justice and the potential contamination that may follow.

4. The Exceptionalism of the Guantánamo System: A View from the United States

President Bush's years in the White House, and especially since the terrorist attacks of September 11, 2001, saw the revival of notions of American exceptionalism and the rise of unilateralism that had been directed both inward and outward. Domestically, the president made sweeping claims of constitutionally inherent executive powers to detain individuals (including U.S. citizens) who the president regarded as "enemy combatants," to order their interrogation without congressional regulation, and to try them before military commissions.

Invoking the imagery, frames, metaphors, and associative connections of "war" was a matter of conscious decision by President Bush and his team in the immediate aftermath of the 9/11 attacks. Immediately after the attacks took place administration spokespersons talked about the attacks in terms of a "crime." However, quickly recognizing the moment as "an opportunity," the president changed course.[16] "Make no mistake about it," he announced, "we are at war."[17] Objections from within the administration to the use of such terminology – voiced, for example, by the Chairman of the Joint Chiefs of Staff General Myers, who argued that, "if you call it a war, then you think of people in uniform as being the solution," and by Defense Secretary Rumsfeld, who preferred to speak of "global struggle against violent extremism"[18] – went unheeded. Using the language and rhetoric of war in framing the events of 9/11 allowed President Bush to cast himself in the role of a war president. This played directly to the tendency of presidents "to see themselves as the most immediate embodiments of a unitary popular will, standing above normal politics and in possession of super-mundane talents and a special aura."[19] As Richard Jackson comments, discourses in general, and the discourse of the war on terrorism in particular, set the logic and possibilities of policy formulation and help to create the wider legitimacy and social consensus that are required to enact policy.[20] That perceived legitimacy

16 Bob Woodward, Bush at War 32 (2002).

17 Richard W. Stevenson, *President Makes It Clear: Phrase Is "War on Terror,"* NY Times Aug. 4, 2005.

18 Eric Schmitt and Thom Shanker, *U.S. Officials Retool Slogan for Terror War*, NY Times July 26, 2005.

19 William E. Scheuerman, *Presidentialism and Emergency Powers*, in Emergencies and the Limits of Legality 258, 266 (Victor Ramraj ed., 2008); *see also* George Lakoff, The Political Mind: A Cognitive Scientist's Guide to Your Brain and Its Politics 148 (2009).

20 Richard Jackson, *Political Language, Policy Formulation and the Practice of Torture in the War on Terrorism: Implications for Human Rights* (2006), retrieved from http://cadair.aber.ac.uk/dspace/handle/2160/1944.

was suggested further by the use of the term "global" to describe the war. By suggesting multilateral action, despite the unilateralist undertones of American operations, the term global informed Americans that they were not alone in the fight. Others saw their cause as just and have joined it, much like they did ten years earlier when the "Coalition of the Willing" joined the United States in Operation Desert Storm. At the same time, global vocabulary was used to put pressure on other governments to do precisely that – join the United States in its war effort. The war frame also allowed for justifications of such actions to be more readily available and acceptable to the ordinary public. In practical terms this meant that the executive "[was] likely to latch onto more-or-less serious challenges to the political community and refashion them into life-or-death threats, or if the crisis at hand is indeed a dire one, milk it for everything it is worth politically even at the cost of undermining the rule of law."[21] Thus, by using the war frame, the president anchored the responses to the terrorist threats firmly in a war paradigm.[22] According to the Bush administration, the terrorist attacks of September 11, 2001, constituted acts of war against the United States, so that at least since that day the United States has been at war "both legally and in fact."[23] The war model and framing was then invoked to confer its own sense of legitimacy on, and justification to, a wide spectrum of presidential actions, including the establishment of military commissions to deal with suspected terrorists.

The Obama administration sought to soften its rhetoric away from the terminology of the "global war on terror." In March 2009, two months after assuming office, the Obama administration announced that it was abandoning two of the terms most closely identified with the former administration's policies and most sharply criticized: the "global war

21 Scheuerman, *supra* note 18, at 266.

22 *See, e.g.*, Elaine Tyler May, *Echoes of the Cold War: The Aftermath of September 11 at Home*, *in* SEPTEMBER 11 IN HISTORY: A WATERSHED MOMENT? 35 (Mary L. Dudziak ed., 2003).

23 William J. Haynes, *Enemy Combatants* (2002), retrieved from http://www.cfr.org/publication/5312/enemy_combatants.html.

on terror" and "enemy combatants."[24] In the National Security Strategy published in May 2010, President Obama stated that although the United States was waging a global campaign against al-Qaeda, this "[was] not a global war against a tactic – terrorism or a religion – Islam. We are at war with a specific network, al-Qa'ida, and its terrorist affiliates."[25] President Obama has also repeatedly stated his administration's commitment to multilateralism, engagement, and international cooperation, to "building new and deeper partnerships" and "strengthen[ing] international standards and institutions." He has emphasized that, "America has not succeeded by stepping outside the currents of international cooperation. We have succeeded by steering those currents in the direction of liberty and justice."[26]

Much of the anticipated change of course revolved around the system established in and around the detention center in the U.S. Naval base in Guantánamo, Cuba, which has been regarded by many in the United States and around the world as the most blatant manifestation of the Bush administration's disregard of international law and constitutional norms. In a strongly worded rebuke to the operation of the detention center at Guantánamo, the British judge Lord Steyn stated famously, "The most powerful democracy is detaining hundreds of suspected foot soldiers of the Taliban in a legal black hole at the United States naval base at Guantánamo Bay."[27] He called Guantánamo a place of "utter lawlessness,"[28] and answered the question of whether "the quality of justice envisaged for the prisoners at Guantánamo Bay complies with

24 Associated Press, *Obama Abandons Term "Enemy Combatant"* (Mar. 13, 2009), retrieved from http://www.msnbc.msn.com/id/29681819/ns/politics-white_house/; NPR, *US No Longer Using "War on Terror"* (Mar. 30, 2009), retrieved from http://www.npr.org/templates/story/story.php?storyId=102533451.

25 The White House, National Security Strategy 19–20 (2010), retrieved from http://www.whitehouse.gov/sites/default/files/rss_viewer/national_security_strategy.pdf (hereinafter NSS).

26 *Id.* at Letter from President.

27 Johan Steyn, *Guantanamo Bay: The Legal Black Hole*, 53 Int'l & Comp. L. Q. 1, 1 (2004).

28 *Id.* at 17.

minimum international standards for the conduct of fair trials" with "a resounding 'No.'"[29]

Executive Order 13,492 – the second of three executive orders signed by President Obama in his second day in the White House – ordered the closing of the Guantánamo Bay detention facility "as soon as practicable," but in no more than one year.[30] The Order recognized that a "prompt and appropriate disposition of the individuals detained at Guantánamo" ought to precede the closure of the detention facility, in order to "further the national security and foreign policy interests of the United States and the interests of justice." Thus, the president ordered an immediate review of the status of each individual detained at Guantánamo. Significantly, while that review was going on, no charges were to be referred to a military commission, and all proceedings of such military commissions to which charges have been referred but in which no judgment has been rendered, and all proceedings pending in the United States Court of Military Commission Review, were halted. The review process was designed to determine whether individual detainees were to be released, transferred, prosecuted, or otherwise lawfully disposed of. In case of prosecution, the review process was to identify "whether it [was] feasible to prosecute such individuals before a court established pursuant to Article III of the United States Constitution" (i.e., an ordinary civilian court rather than a military commission). As an "appropriate disposition" might not, after all, be that "prompt," the Order stated:

> [I]f any individuals covered by this order remain in detention at Guantánamo at the time of closure of those detention facilities, they shall be returned to their home country, released, transferred to a third country, or transferred to another United States detention facility in a manner consistent with law and the national security and foreign policy interests of the United States.

The Order also followed the 2008 ruling of the Supreme Court of the United States in *Boumediene v. Bush* – in which the Court held,

29 *Id.* at 14.

30 Exec. Order No. 13492, 74 Fed. Reg. 4897 (Jan. 22, 2009).

inter alia, that the Constitution granted habeas corpus rights to foreign nationals held at Guantánamo[31] – by explicitly recognizing that the Guantánamo detainees enjoyed the constitutional right of habeas corpus.

Efforts aimed at closing the detention center at Guantánamo Bay began in early 2009. But on September 28, 2009, the Obama administration acknowledged openly that it was unlikely to meet its self-imposed deadline for closing down Guantánamo. Indeed, despite the clear deadline stated in Executive Order 13,492, the detention facility remains open. As Peter Margulies notes, Guantánamo resembles "Humpty-Dumpty in reverse . . . alarmingly easy . . . to put together and . . . very difficult to take apart."[32] The major obstacle has been deciding what to do with the detainees. On February 20, 2009, Attorney General Eric Holder announced the formation of a special Guantánamo Review Task Force to review the cases of the detainees who remained in Guantánamo and decide how best to deal with them. The Task Force submitted its final report on January 22, 2010, precisely one year after the signing of Executive Order 13,492. The report, which was released on May 28, 2010,[33] found that the majority of the Guantánamo detainees were low-level fighters and identified only about 10 percent of the detainees as "leaders, operatives and facilitators involved in plots against the United States."[34] The report recommended that 126 of the 240 detainees be transferred either to their home country or to a third country; that 36 be prosecuted in either a federal court or a military commission; that a group of 30 Yemeni nationals be released "if security conditions in their home country improve"; and that 48 detainees be held indefinitely under the laws

31 *Boumediene v. Bush*, 553 U.S. 723 (2008).

32 Peter Margulies, *Putting Guantanamo in the Rear-View Mirror: The Political Economy of Detention Policy*, 32 W. New Eng. L. Rev. 339, 339 (2010).

33 Apparently, the reason for the delay was the administration's belief that in the wake of the attempted bombing by a Nigerian student of a Detroit-bound airliner on Christmas Day there would be little, if any, public or congressional support for even discussing the plan to close the detention center.

34 Peter Finn, *Most Guantanamo Detainees Low-Level Fighters, Task Force Report Says*, Wash. Post May 29, 2010.

of war.[35] It is worth pausing on this final proposal that forty-eight of the Guantánamo detainees would continue to be held without trial – potentially indefinitely – because they continued to pose a high level of threat, as they had significant roles in al-Qaeda or the Taliban and advanced training or expertise. It is noteworthy that the report was also at pains to clarify that obstacles to prosecution "typically did not stem from concerns over protecting sensitive sources or methods from disclosure, or concerns that evidence against the detainee was tainted." In a May 21, 2009, speech, President Obama stated that the eventual closing down of Guantánamo would not mean that the United States was going to release individuals if such release would endanger the country's national security. He also announced, for the first time, that closing Guantánamo would mean that some of the detainees held there might have to be held in what the president called "prolonged detention."[36]

On March 7, 2011, President Obama reversed his two-year policy halting new military charges against detainees at Guantánamo, permitting military trials to resume with revamped procedures.[37] The new rules required a review of status within a year and every three years thereafter to assess whether the individuals remained a threat, and whether they should be scheduled for a military trial or released. Critics have argued that these new procedures still fall short of the kind of legislative or congressional oversight one would expect in the context of an extraordinary detention regime. The oversight system is neither judicial

35 Since the detention center opened in Guantánamo in January 2002, 779 detainees have been held there. Of these, 530 individuals were released by the Bush administration. An additional 59 individuals were approved for release by the time Obama took office. The Obama administration released the 59 by repatriating 24 detainees to their home countries, resettling 33 in third countries, and sending two to Italy for prosecution. These 59 individuals were part of the 126 detainees identified in the Task Force's report as eligible to be released. See Guantánamo Review Taskforce, *Final Report* 1 (2010), retrieved from http://www.justice.gov/ag/guantanamo-review-final-report.pdf.

36 Peter Finn, *Obama Endorses Indefinite Detention Without Trial for Some*, WASH. POST May 22, 2009.

37 Scott Shane and Mark Landler, *Obama Clears Way for Guantánamo Trials*, NY TIMES Mar. 7, 2011.

nor legislative, but lodged directly within the executive branch. Executive Order 13,567 brings together senior officials from six government departments and offices – the Departments of State, Defense, Justice, and Homeland Security, and the Offices of the Director of National Intelligence and the Chairman of the Joint Chiefs of Staff – to determine whether the continued detention of each prisoner "is necessary to protect against a significant threat to the security of the United States."[38] It has been described as a "handcrafted parole procedure" controlled by political appointees whose capacity to decide each case independently and impartially remains questionable.[39] Whatever else it may be, the oversight system is not a trial, and the standards of proof and evidence that are applied are not those that ordinarily govern determinations of long-term imprisonment. The Executive Order further required compliance with the Geneva Conventions and the Convention Against Torture that bans both torture and inhumane treatment. Notably, the Order was limited to the 173 prisoners then held at Guantánamo and not extended to suspects caught in the future. Overall, although the "[p]eriodic review of the GTMO detainees . . . was more generous to the detainees than an analogous Bush program,"[40] a continuity of military detention and trial practices exists between the Bush and Obama administrations. The state retains substantial advantage with the commissions compared with civilian trials or courts-martial.

Given the significance of the Guantánamo system, including both detention practices and military commissions, the first part of this collection focuses mainly on the experience in the United States post-9/11,

38 Exec. Order No. 13567, 76 Fed. Reg. 13, 277 (March 7, 2011).

39 Owen Fiss, *Imprisonment without Trial* (2011), retrieved from http://www.law.yale.edu/documents/pdf/Faculty/Fiss_Cronista_en.pdf, at 17.

40 Jack Goldsmith, Power and Constraint: The Accountable Presidency after 9/11 7 (2012). Federal District Judge Reggie Walton has noted that the Obama refinements drew a "metaphysical difference" with the Bush position "of a minimal if not ephemeral character," *Gherebi v. Obama*, 609 F. Supp. 2d 43, 70 (D.D.C. 2009). Notably, more disqualifications were introduced disallowing evidence obtained by coercion, and detainees were given more leeway to choose attorneys.

with particular attention to the genealogy of military commissions. Gary Solis traces the evolution of military commissions to demonstrate that contemporary practices are out of sync with both historical precedents and the original intent for the establishment of such bodies. He outlines the transformation of military commissions from an American disciplinary "field expedient" to meet military necessity unaddressed by the Articles of War, to their place in contemporary law of war as a trial setting for enemies charged with law-of-war violations. The analysis reviews the military commissions that followed World War II, when they were employed by virtually all of the Allies, detailing how post–World War II multinational human rights and humanitarian law treaties – particularly the 1949 Geneva Conventions – had impacted the institution of the military commission. Solis argues convincingly that these interfaces changed military commissions from field tribunals with lowered procedural and evidentiary bars to trials closely reflecting U.S. courts-martial. He directly addresses the claims that post-9/11 changes implemented at Guantánamo have shifted the historical trajectory of their rules and procedures, turning them into a second-rate form of justice. The 2006 Military Commissions Act (MCA), the alterations it brought, and their reception in the Supreme Court of the United States are the main site of this assessment. Although the MCA of 2009 constitutes an improvement over its predecessor, Solis contends that it remains flawed.

The interplay between ordinary civilian criminal courts, exceptional modified courts, military courts, and military commissions is particularly relevant to any analysis of Guantánamo. The layered relationship between these entities, often functioning in tandem within the same legal system, demonstrates how they complement, hinder, or reinforce one another. In this vein, Stephen Vladeck's contribution focuses on the relationship between military commissions, Article III federal civilian courts, and courts-martial in the Article I system created by Congress, through examination of the U.S. courts-martial system and the system of military commissions. His close scrutiny of the evolution of the former demonstrates how it has been moving over time from an exceptional model toward a model that integrates the system of courts-martial within the larger structure of ordinary courts through the process of appellate review. Vladeck argues that the MCA of 2006 (as amended in 2009) has purported to create a similar system. However, according to Vladeck, it created an "inherently paradoxical" structure of new "exceptional" courts that are, in fact, partially integrated and interwoven into the ordinary judicial system by virtue of their being subjected to ordinary appellate review. This structure is, conceptually, unstable: it either weakens the underlying justification for the use of exceptional courts (by subjecting them to review that is governed by the rules that apply in ordinary courts) or the ordinary courts system by having them endorse rules designed specifically to not apply in those same ordinary courts.

Gabor Rona and Raha Wala's contribution complements these analyses by providing a careful articulation of the differences with respect to fairness, transparency, legitimacy, and outcomes between civilian courts and military commissions. They specifically note important distinctions between civilian and military courts pertaining to the operational and jurisdictional patterns that have historically framed their respective fields of operations. They conclude by making a cogent legitimacy- and policy-based argument to restore the jurisdiction of Article III courts in all post-9/11 cases.

With the undulating presence of military commissions now an entrenched part of the American legal response to terrorism, these debates are likely to continue. The analyses provided here give a robust comparative, historical, legal, and theoretical grounding within which to place those deliberations.

5. Spillover

A number of the essays included in this collection provide a further tantalizing glimpse of the variance in degrees of liberty protection for individual defendants who are processed through exceptional courts or military commissions. They also demonstrate the intricate interplay between normal and exceptional regimes illustrating how hard it is to cordon off and contain the exceptional to its own unique arena, regardless of firewalls that may be put in place to prevent a spillover from the exceptional to the normal. Two questions follow: the first one is an empirical question, whether the differences between civilian and military courts have narrowed over time. Looking at the essays in Parts I and II of this book we conclude that the answer ought to be a qualified yes. Assuming impermeable boundaries and clear demarcation lines between the ordinary and the exceptional systems underplays the growing convergence between the two systems. This leads, however, to the second and more critical inquiry, which is what are we to make of that convergence? Two competing narratives may be offered in this context. First, the breaking down of the "assumption of separation"[41] between the exceptional and the normal has resulted in the former spilling over and tainting the latter, using it, at minimum, to gain legitimacy and justification and in the process potentially subverting some of the rules and procedures that exist in the ordinary, normal sphere. In other words, the exceptional is becoming the new normal. Thus, for example, Clive Walker's analysis of the contemporary reinvigoration of the criminal-justice paradigm in the United Kingdom and the United States – following their medium-term flirtation with exceptional counterterrorism approaches – and his searching probe of certain salient features of British criminal justice finds clear evidence of exceptionality creeping into the regular system. Similarly, William Banks argues that because the factual predicate for gaining approval by the Foreign Intelligence Surveillance Court (FISC) – an exceptional court created by Congress to respond to a unique set of challenges related to foreign intelligence – to conduct surveillance or search is less exacting than what is required in traditional criminal cases, a spillover effect has developed. Criminal investigators and prosecutors rely significantly on the exceptional FISC procedures to gather evidence for later use in

41 Oren Gross and Fionnuala Ní Aoláin, Law in Times of Crisis: Emergency Powers in Theory and Practice 171–243 (2006).

criminal prosecutions. According to Banks, this spillover threatens Fourth Amendment protections for the accused. At the same time, recent revisions to the FISC essentially omit the case-by-case review of applications for surveillance and convert the FISC into an administrative clerk for executive officials.

An alternative reading regards the interaction between the two spheres as leading in a reverse direction, that is, toward the exceptional shedding off its extraordinary traits and assuming the rules and procedures of the normal legal system. However, as Vladeck suggests in his essay, this alternative understanding weakens the underlying justification for the use of exceptional courts by subjecting them to the rules that apply in ordinary courts.

The essays included in Part III of this collection examine the relationship between exceptional and normal judicial systems as it manifests itself on the international plain. Alex Conte's contribution suggests that the United Nations' adjudicative bodies and various special mechanisms including Special Rapporteurs are particularly attuned to the symbolic significance of departures from ordinary law. Their reports and jurisprudence demonstrate a strong preference for the ouster of military control of judicial and sentencing functions. Conte provides a thorough review of the international human rights apparatus, and the views of a substantial number of United Nations committee and juridical structures clustered on a thematic basis to reflect on issues of competence and jurisdiction, independence and impartiality, equality of arms, and procedural and matters of evidence. The conclusions and recommendations considered relate to universal fair trial obligations and standards, as well as their application to country-specific contexts. The general thrust of his argument is that the trial of civilians by military or special courts and tribunals "[s]hould only take place on an exceptional basis, limited to cases where the State can show that the trial of a civilian by a military or specialized court is necessary and justified by objective and serious reasons." Soft-law norms increasingly and trenchantly reiterate the position that even those suspected of serious terrorist offenses must be afforded the right to regular trial and due process of law, and that the recourse to military tribunals for civilians must only occur in the most restrictive circumstances when all other options are suspended. Similarly, Weissbrodt and Hansen underscore the regional and international reach of fair-trial protections. Surveying the rich jurisprudence of the Inter-American Court and Commission on Human Rights amply demonstrates the extent to which compromised protections of fair-trial provisions enabled the courts to play a critical role in expunging individual rights and liberties and turning the judicial system into part and parcel of the state's repressive architecture.

Conclusion

The term "exceptional court" is an oxymoron. The exceptional court holds a contradiction at its heart: to employ the designation court is to mark the institution out as a judicial vehicle for justice rather than for the convenient disposal of the state's detractors. But to be exceptional implies a departure, a derogation from the norm. The unspoken message is that the process itself as well as any outcome obtained is fraught with the possibility of greater opprobrium and potential punishment, messaging that what is made possible by such courts is outside the realm of the ordinary. But even in the creation of such exceptional entities caution is warranted for the democratic state: the creation of an exceptional court may carry within its folds seen and unseen risks for the polity, such as a legitimacy risk – namely that the resort to the exception may undercut the executive's basis of legitimacy or weaken the broader systemic appeal to the rule of law in situations where the state is under stress. The resort to exceptional substantive norms and trial procedures raises the specter of unfairness that undermines the legitimacy that is crucial for courts to function as the main instrumentalities and bastions of the rule of law. All meaningful understandings of the rule of law contain an irreducible core that rejects governmental lawlessness and arbitrariness and emphasizes the need for certainty, generality, clarity, and prospective effect of legal rules and norms. To be exceptional denotes deviations from that which is the natural providence of courts, and derogations from otherwise established norms.

Exceptional courts and military tribunals that are created in the context of acute violent threats to the state perform broad symbolic and communicative functions. In particular they are formed by, while themselves assisting in forming, a war/military model, rather than a law-enforcement model of counterterrorism management. This communicative aspect remains intact whether a "soft" or "harsh" version of the tribunals is in play for the detainees themselves. The existence of such bodies points to a broad menu of military and legal responses, as well as to the flexibility of moving between options to process violent challengers. Although the undulating attention to Guantánamo in the past decade may seem to suggest that exceptional tribunals occupy entirely new legal space, this collection clearly shows that is not the case. The resort to exceptional courts and tribunals is not a new departure for democratic states. Still, there is some newness; not all has been seen in all forms before. As Conor Gearty comments, "The repression of... past eras of anti-communism and anti-terrorism did not threaten to reconfigure liberal democracy's whole relationship with freedom in the way that the generality, pervasive effect, unendability, and international cohesiveness of the current 'war on terror' threatens to do."[42]

There exists a tension of "tragic dimensions" between democratic values and responses to acute violent crises.[43] Democratic nations faced with violence and legitimacy challenges must "maintain and protect life, the liberties necessary to a vibrant democracy, and the unity of the society, the loss of which can turn a healthy and diverse nation into a seriously divided and violent one."[44] At the same time, acute crises directly

42 Conor Gearty, *Rethinking Civil Liberties in a Counter-Terrorism World*, in FIELD DAY REVIEW 125 (Seamus Deane and Breandán Mac Suibhne, eds., 2007).

43 Pnina Lahav, *A Barrel Without Hoops: The Impact of Counterterrorism on Israel's Legal Culture*, 10 CARDOZO L. REV. 529, 531 (1988) (noting the "tragic dimensions of the tension between terrorism, counterterrorism, and justice in any democratic society").

44 PHILIP B. HEYMANN, TERRORISM AND AMERICA: A COMMONSENSE STRATEGY FOR A DEMOCRATIC SOCIETY ix (1998).

challenge the most fundamental concepts of constitutional democracy. The government's ability to act swiftly, secretly, and decisively against a threat to the life of the nation may push aside ordinary principles limiting governmental powers and individual rights. Two seemingly antithetical vectors are in a constant tug-of-war. Crises tend to result in the expansion of governmental powers, the concentration of powers in the hands of the executive, and the concomitant contraction of individual freedoms and liberties.[45] The existence of restrictions and limitations on governmental powers is a fundamental attribute of democratic regimes. The ideals of democracy, individual rights, legitimacy, accountability, and the rule of law suggest that even in times of acute danger, government is limited, both formally and substantively, in the range of activities that it may pursue in order to protect the state.

In the face of critical challenges, rule-of-law ideas of judicial impartiality, independence and equality of all in the administration and experience of justice harken to and have substantial purchase for democratic polities. Despite the stress provoked by violent challengers these values remain important and have undefinable traction even as the state is under stress. They are bolstered by an evolving international legal order committed to human rights that continues to emphasize obligations to protect these values. After the events of 9/11, the Security Council passed Resolution 1373 and established its Counter-Terrorism Committee (CTC). In its early years, the CTC and its executive directorate were ill informed, even hostile, toward any effort to sensitize them to the human rights consequences of counterterrorism measures. Some key states and human rights bodies fought an uphill battle in telling the same states that were reporting to the CTC that they should comply with human rights while countering terrorism. Gradually, reflecting on the salience of the values that seep through the international legal order, the CTC accepted that being briefed about human rights was, in fact, part of its counterterrorism

45 See Harold Hongju Koh, The National Security Constitution: Sharing Power After the Iran-Contra Affair 117–49 (1990); Clinton Rossiter, Constitutional Dictatorship: Crisis Government in the Modern Democracies 288–90 (1948).

mandate, and the Security Council confirmed that states (Resolutions 1456 and 1624) and even the Security Council itself (Resolutions 1822 and 1905) needed to comply with human rights while countering terrorism. Ultimately the 2006 Global Counter-Terrorism Strategy[46] came to acknowledge the benefits of human rights sensitivity, even compliance, in an effective and sustainable fight against terrorism. Lines of communication and institutional links have been developed between the counterterrorism and human rights worlds, underscoring that seepage works both ways. As we conceptualize the links between the ordinary and the exceptional, we need to consider similar two-way communication and effect, with values and norms moving in both directions.

There are mixed reviews in this collection for the resilience of the rule of law. Even the optimists bring caveats to the table. The contention that the rule of law has been resilient is true only to a degree. Despite the abandonment in Britain of Guantánamo "lite" (the Belmarsh prison regime) and several positive if rather formalistic U.S. Supreme Court decisions, there remains a parallel military-based system of counterterrorism that involves tactics (such as client state action, drones, and indefinite detention in conditions of inhumanity and discrimination) that still await substantive legal examination by the courts. So while in some quarters there are allusions to "retreat" or entrenchment to "normality," a sober assessment would leave more room for circumspection.

Much of the attention of lawyers has centered on law-enforcement agencies and the courts. We agonize over every phrase of every judgment. But as Clive Walker points out, courts are often a sideshow in the counterterrorism action.[47] Much more of the effort and expenditure of the executive has been on preemption and prevention through protective security measures that offer a more pervasive and insidious challenge to

46 The United Nations Global Counter-Terrorism Strategy, UN Doc. A/Res/60/288 (Sept. 20, 2006). *See also*, The United Nations Global Counter-Terrorism Strategy Review, UN Doc. A/Res/66/282 (July 12, 2012).

47 Clive Walker, *Keeping Control of Terrorists without Loosing Constitutionalism*, 59 Stanford L. Rev. (2007).

normality. There is some public notice taken of the impact at airports, but much else has remained covert, unquestioned, or outright accepted. Thus, we should also be wary of assuming that the courts are the exclusive, or indeed even the main, locale on which to direct our gaze when a protective security complex has grown up around us. This broader sense of the terrain in which responses to terrorism are being played out is evident in those jurisdictions that have started to work out interesting and broader strategies for living with the broad spectrum of internal and external threats. These policies seek to develop social and political – as well as security – programs to address the manifestation of terrorism but also to delve closely into the conditions conducive to its production.

Close attention to the broader political and legal context from which due process exceptionalism emerges is a first step. For democracies, courts remain significant to the legal responses to terrorism, and their processes, rules, oversight, modification, and review will continue to merit close and critical attention.

Part I MILITARY COMMISSIONS AND EXCEPTIONAL COURTS IN THE UNITED STATES

1 The Development of an Exceptional Court

The History of the American Military Commission

David Glazier

THE UNITED STATES'S CONTROVERSIAL GUANTÁNAMO MILItary commissions epitomize the common conception of "exceptional" courts: adopting a substandard level of justice for trials limited to foreign nationals suspected of terrorism-related offenses. The irony is that although these commissions are justified in large part on the basis of historical precedent, the original U.S. military commissions reflected the antonymic concept of exceptional, comporting to domestic U.S. legal standards, while exceeding the international norms of their day. Although there were some episodic exceptions, prior to World War II, properly conducted military commissions provided trials fully equivalent to conventional U.S. military justice. These commissions evenhandedly tried Americans and foreign nationals alike at a time when other nations generally accepted the summary execution of enemy law-of-war violators. The irony of the modern commissions' departure from traditional U.S. legal values is even greater given that the individual primarily responsible for it was Franklin D. Roosevelt's Attorney General Francis Biddle, a man otherwise noted as a civil libertarian who later sat as the U.S. judge on the International Military Tribunal at Nuremberg. The landing of eight Nazi saboteurs on U.S. soil was a rude shock to the American psyche and brought the war to the home front; that event led to the usage of military commissions, just as the traumatic events of 9/11 inspired the Bush administration to resurrect commissions after a half-century of dormancy.

Military commissions' creation can be traced to General Winfield Scott during the Mexican-American War of 1846–48, although the U.S. commitment to trying even its wartime enemies before inflicting punishment predates the Constitution. In August 1776, Congress adopted language providing that:

> [A]ll persons, not members of, nor owing allegiance to, any of the United States of America . . . who shall be found lurking as spies in or about the fortifications or encampments of the armies of the United States, or of any of them, shall suffer death, according to the law and usage of nations, by sentence of a court-martial.[1]

Whereas the British subjected captured spies – including, most famously, noted American patriot Nathan Hale – to summary execution based solely on the orders of senior commanders, George Washington's army tried at least twenty-five suspected enemy spies before regular general courts-martial.[2] However, even Washington was not immune to the pressures of extraordinary circumstances. In the public furor surrounding General Benedict Arnold's traitorous defection, Washington referred British Major John André (captured behind American lines carrying secret documents in Arnold's handwriting) to examination before a Board of General Officers, a high-level fact-finding and advisory panel, rather than the court-martial trial prescribed by Congress. Washington never explained this decision, which was not criticized at a time when public outrage saw Arnold and André burned in effigy at the seat of Congress in Philadelphia. Either Washington did not trust a court-martial to convict

1 Res. of the Cont'l Cong., August 21, 1776, 1 JOURNALS OF THE AMERICAN CONGRESS: FROM 1774 to 1778 450 (Way & Gideon eds., 1823).

2 *See* David Glazier, *Precedents Lost: The Neglected History of the Military Commission*, 46. Va J. Int'l L. 5, 20–22 (2005). Two other suspected spies, Thomas Shanks (an American falling outside the terms of the congressional resolution) and Major John André, were referred to Boards of General Officers for examination.

André, a conniving charmer who curried considerable sympathy among the American officer corps during his captivity, or he wanted the cover of the concurrence of his most senior generals before executing an officer who was, in addition, a personal favorite of the opposing British commander.

1. The Creation of the Military Commission

Given the United States's formal willingness to try its enemies before the same courts-martial as its own soldiers, it should not be surprising that the military commission was created not to try foreign nationals, as is commonly assumed, but rather to try America's own soldiers for offenses falling outside the statutory authority of the court-martial. Early American leaders implicitly assumed that the U.S. Army would only be used defensively inside the country. Although the navy was given authority to try criminal offenses such as murder, theft, or any maltreatment or abuse of persons outside the United States,[3] the Articles of War governing the army only provided for the trial of strictly military offenses such as desertion and disobedience of orders. They mandated that any soldier who "committed any offence against the persons or property of any citizen of any of the United States" be delivered to the appropriate civil magistrate for trial.[4] They made no provision whatsoever for punishing similar acts committed abroad.

General Zachary Taylor's army left Texas to conduct offensive operations south of the Rio Grande River at the start of the Mexican War in 1846, placing it outside the territorial jurisdiction of any U.S. civilian court. Following the deplorable conduct of some of his volunteer forces, Taylor discovered that he lacked any legal authority to punish them for depredations against the local populace. The secretary of war eventually

3 Rules and Regulations for the Government of the United States Navy, arts. XVII, XXI, XXVII, 2 Stat. 45, 47–48 (1800).

4 *See* Act for Establishing Rules and Articles for the Government of the Armies of the United States, 2 Stat. 359, 364 (1806) (known as the "Articles of War").

determined that all the Army could do to a soldier who murdered a Mexican national was to discharge the killer and send him home. General Scott, the U.S. Army's commanding general, was appalled. He was on the verge of departure for Mexico to lead what was intended to be the decisive campaign from Vera Cruz inland to the capital. Scott knew his forces would be substantially outnumbered, and he recognized that any chance of success demanded maintaining strict order among his men to get the Mexican population to at least acquiesce to the presence of his troops. He decided to draw on the law of war for authority to proclaim "martial law" in territory under his control. He did this through a series of general orders, promulgated initially to his troops and later to the local population, specifying offenses that he would punish, including such common crimes as murder, rape, robbery, and destruction of property. Because court-martial jurisdiction was expressly limited to the offenses and offenders specified in the Articles of War, Scott created a common-law tribunal that he called the "military commission" to try these crimes committed by, or against, his forces.[5] Scott let local civilian governments remain in place and left the trial of Mexican-on-Mexican offenses to their own courts.

The first individual ever tried by a military commission was Sergeant J. J. Adams of the Third Illinois Regiment. Adams was convicted of theft in April 1847, reduced to private, and confined for two months. Over the course of the war, at least 408 others were tried by military commissions; at least 302 of these were Americans.[6] Scott's military commissions closely followed court-martial practice, including their basic composition, procedural rules, and post-trial review. The commissions applied recognized principles of criminal justice, including requiring advance public

5 *See, e.g.*, General Winfield Scott, Gen. Order No. 20, *in* 41 1/2Orders and Special Orders, Headquarters of the Army, War with Mexico, 1847–48 140, *available at* Records Group 94, National Archives and Records Administration, Washington DC; *see also* Winfield Scott, 2 Memoirs of Lieut.-General Scott, LL.D 540–46 (1864) (reprinting a later version, General Order No. 287).

6 *See* Glazier, *supra* note 2, at 34, 37.

notice of punishable offenses and providing equal protection, evenhandedly subjecting American and foreign defendants to their jurisdiction.[7]

Scott established a separate tribunal, which he named the council of war, to try actual law-of-war violations. He permitted the councils to be more summary in form than the court-martial-based military commission, including the use of smaller trial panels. Scott justified this practice on the basis that the law of war at that time as applied by other nations permitted summary execution of guerillas upon capture. He thus concluded that providing any form of trial would be legally sufficient. Even the councils of war provided equal treatment regardless of nationality. Documented defendants included at least one American and a Belgian in addition to a modest number of Mexican nationals. The councils of war logically lacked meaningful precedential value as far as justifying lesser procedural standards for later war crimes trials. They were discontinued in favor of the court-martial–based military commission as the single "common law" military tribunal after the Mexican War. Moreover, authority for more summary treatment of law-of-war violators almost certainly runs contrary to the extensive fair trial standards now mandated by a host of treaties governing both the law of armed conflict and international human rights.[8]

The Mexican War experience demonstrates the necessity of distinguishing the legal foundation for each tribunal. Scott's martial law, on the basis of the authority of an occupying power referred to as military government today, is authorized by the law of war, but the substantive law being enforced is a form of domestic law. That law may be either the preexisting law of the occupied territory or rules promulgated by the occupying force commander (as Scott employed via his general orders).

7 For a more detailed history of the commissions' historic origins, *see* David Glazier, *Precedents Lost: The Neglected History of the Military Commission*, 46 VA. J. INT'L L 5, 31–40 (2005).

8 *See, e.g.*, Geneva Convention Relative to the Treatment of Prisoners of War, arts. 84 and 102, Aug. 12, 1949, 6 U.S.T. 3316, 75 U.N.T.S. 135 (hereinafter Geneva III). *See* David Weissbrodt and Joseph Hansen, *The Right to a Fair Trial in an Extraordinary Court* and Steven Greer, *Exceptional Courts and the European Convention on Human Rights*, in this volume.

Trials of actual law-of-war violations are the other legitimate use of military tribunals. However, these trials have subsequently been held by the U.S. Supreme Court to be strictly constrained by recognized limits of that corpus juris.[9]

2. The Civil War Era

The Civil War era saw approximately 6,000 military-commissions trials between the actual duration of the war itself and the Reconstruction years, according to the leading historian of this issue.[10] The U.S. Supreme Court also considered its jurisdiction over these tribunals for the first time. In Ex parte *Vallandigham*,[11] decided in 1863, the Court held that it lacked direct appellate review authority over military commissions. This was the same result the Court had reached with respect to courts-martial in *Dynes* v. *Hoover*[12] six years previously. However, U.S. federal courts have long had authority to consider challenges to military trials via various forms of collateral review. The most obvious form of these challenges were petitions for habeas corpus, to inquire into whether a military trial comprised "a court without jurisdiction over the subject-matter, or that of one which has neglected the forms and rules of precedure [sic] enjoined for the exercise of jurisdiction,"[13] in which case the courts would have to invalidate any convictions. This authority was highlighted at the end of the Civil War when the Supreme Court overturned the politically motivated Indiana military commission's conviction of Lambdin P. Milligan, which had been conducted as a purported exercise of domestic martial law. Milligan had clearly learned from Vallandigham's procedural error and brought a collateral habeas challenge to the tribunal's jurisdiction.

9 *See, e.g.*, Ex parte *Quirin*, 317 U.S. 1, 29 (1942).

10 *See* Mark E. Neely, Jr., The Fate of Liberty: Abraham Lincoln and Civil Liberties 168–73, 176–77 (1991).

11 68 U.S. (1 Wall.) 243, 252–54 (1863).

12 61 U.S. (20 How.) 65, 83–84 (1857).

13 *Id*. at 81.

All nine justices agreed that the commission could not try him. The majority opinion was based on constitutional grounds, holding that "a citizen in civil life, in nowise connected with the military service" could not be subjected to military trial when regular courts were open.[14] Four concurring justices believed the same result could have been reached on statutory grounds.

The overall Civil War military commission history is somewhat checkered. On the positive side, Scott's basic commission tenets were reinforced, as Congress implicitly called for commission convictions to receive the same post-trial review as courts-martial,[15] and a number of trials were overturned on technicalities when they departed from court-martial procedural rules. On the negative side, the rapid expansion of the Union Army resulted in large numbers of essentially unqualified individuals receiving direct commissions to senior ranks. Many military justice issues were thus decided by officers lacking meaningful understanding of military law, resulting in many injustices being perpetrated by both courts-martial and military commissions. This explains many of the issues noted by commentators with respect to specific commission trials. As discussed in this volume by Chomsky, the officer convening the controversial mass 1862 trials of more than 400 Dakota Sioux following an uprising in Minnesota, for example, was Colonel Henry H. Sibley, a politician who had been the first governor of that state but lacked any previous military experience. Sibley received a direct commission just weeks before he directed the Sioux trials and did not even know that military death sentences required higher authority review.[16] Another major issue was the resort to military commissions under the guise of martial law in Union territory to conduct trials of civilians suspected of aiding the Confederate cause, such

14 Ex parte *Milligan*, 71 U.S. (4 Wall.) 2, 121–22 (1866).

15 *See* Act of July 17, 1862, Ch. 201, § 5, 12 Stat. 597, 598 (1862) (calling for the Army Judge Advocate General to review both court-martial and military commission convictions).

16 *See* Rhoda H. Gilman, Henry Hastings Sibley: Divided Heart 168, 172–73 (2004); Carol L. Chomsky, *Military Commissions in Historical Perspective: Lessons from the United States – Dakota War Trials*, in this volume.

as Vallandigham and Milligan. Although these trials were not actually authorized by the Lincoln administration, they highlight how perceived national security threats can influence officials to rely on exceptional tribunals.

Lincoln's assassination in 1865 led to the use of another highly publicized military commission to try eight alleged surviving conspirators after the actual assassin, John Wilkes Booth, was chased down and killed by army troops. The actual motivation for employing the commission may well have been fear that a civilian jury in the nation's capital would harbor Southern sympathies and fail to convict. The government was careful to offer a legalistic justification, however; Attorney General Speed issued a formal opinion that Lincoln was killed in his military role as commander in chief by agents acting on behalf of the Confederacy, and a military trial was thus in keeping with law-of-war principles.[17] Nevertheless, the trial was and remains extremely controversial, highlighting the questionable long-term efficacy of resorting to exceptional tribunals when regular courts are available.

The February 1865 New York trial of Confederate naval officer John Y. Beall provides a straightforward example of valid Civil War military commission use. Discarding his uniform and operating in civilian dress, Beall led a group of Southern personnel who left the safety of neutral Canada and hijacked and robbed a Great Lakes steamboat. Beall later attempted, unsuccessfully, to derail a civilian passenger train to rob its express box. Although these acts would have constituted common crimes triable by an ordinary criminal court if carried out by a civilian, their conduct by military personnel in disguise behind enemy lines made them war crimes properly triable by a military commission. Curiously, Beall himself did not understand this fact. He wrote to friends in the South asking them to forward a copy of his officer's commission, which he presented to the tribunal, erroneously thinking it would entitle him to avoid trial and be treated as a prisoner of war. The reality, however, was that it supplied

17 Military Commissions, 11 Op. Att'y Gen. 297 (1869).

the prosecution with a required element of proof for establishing his acts as war crimes and confirming the military commission's jurisdiction over him. Beall was still ignorantly protesting the injustice of his treatment on the gallows, to no avail whatsoever.

Congress specifically authorized the use of military commissions in the South during the postwar Reconstruction era over concerns that regular civilian courts would not convict whites of crimes against recently freed slaves or accept the testimony of blacks against white defendants. Two more cases from these trials were heard by the Supreme Court, but neither reached the merits. The first, Ex parte *McCardle*,[18] was decided on the basis of congressional control over the Court's appellate jurisdiction; the second, Ex parte *Yerger*,[19] was mooted when the army decided to release the accused rather than give the Court the opportunity to strike down use of the commission.

Military commissions were mentioned in several Civil War–era laws, but were not explicitly required to conform to the procedural mandates specified for courts-martial in the Articles of War. This fact was noted by William Winthrop in his famous military law treatise, which is often cited by Guantánamo commission proponents as justifying legal shortcuts today. Despite Winthrop's statement of this legal fact, his detailed text clearly shows that the two tribunals closely conformed in actual practice.[20] Moreover, Winthrop's biographer writes that Winthrop believed that:

> [T]he two types of tribunal had to be substantially similar. He did not believe it lawful to prosecute civilians, or even enemy combatants, in a forum of lesser rights than found in a court-martial. To Winthrop, the test for efficacy of military commissions was whether United States soldiers were accorded similar treatment in terms of trial structure, procedure, and rights.[21]

18 74 U.S. (7 Wall.) 506, 515 (1869).
19 75 U.S. (8 Wall.) 85, 106 (1868).
20 William Winthrop, Military Law and Precedents (1896).
21 Joshua E. Kastenberg, The Blackstone of Military Law 139 (2009).

3. The Philippine Insurrection and Statutory Treatment of Military Commissions

The historical close conformity of military commissions to court-martial procedure was convincingly demonstrated again by U.S. Army practice during the Philippine Insurrection of 1899–1902, a period similar to the Mexican War, in which military justice was formally controlled by regular military officers. Army commanders and their judge advocates insisted on the close conformance of the two tribunals even while fighting a conflict against irregular insurgent forces contested with significant brutality on both sides. Despite this ferocity in conducting hostilities in what was essentially a remote third-world nation, both U.S. courts-martial and military commissions faithfully applied Anglo-American common-law rules of evidence from regular federal courts, including prohibitions on hearsay and the requirement that any confessions be both voluntary and supported by independent corroboration of the crime.[22] Several Americans were convicted by military commissions in the Philippines, so they did not discriminate on the basis of nationality.

Enoch Crowder served as the senior judge advocate in the Philippines from 1898 to 1901, and the experience clearly influenced his actions after his appointment as Army Judge Advocate General in 1911. Crowder personally oversaw a major rewrite of the Articles of War, which were then submitted to Congress for enactment. One potentially very important change was the statutory grant of general courts-martial jurisdiction over some crimes and offenders previously triable only by military commission, including, specifically, violations of the law of war. Crowder believed this statutory grant would implicitly strip the interstitial military commission of corresponding jurisdiction, so he drafted a "savings clause," which he explained to the Senate:

> Article 15 is new. We have included in article 2 as subject to military law a number of persons who are also subject to trial by military

22 *See* Glazier, *supra* note 2, at 54–55 (providing citations to individual cases).

> commission. A military commission is our common-law war court . . . [Article 15] just saves to these war courts the jurisdiction they now have and makes it a concurrent jurisdiction with courts-martial, so the military commander in the field in time of war will be at liberty to employ either form of court that happens to be convenient. Both classes of courts have the same procedure.[23]

This savings clause, which carried over into the modern Uniform Code of Military Justice (UCMJ) as Article 21,[24] would ultimately prove to be of far greater legal significance than its plain language would imply. Each time the Supreme Court was subsequently called on to consider the legality of military commission trials, ranging from Ex parte *Quirin*[25] in 1942 through its 2006 decision in *Hamdan* v. *Rumsfeld*,[26] it cited this language as implicit congressional delegation of its constitutional authority to define and punish offenses against the law of nations and regulate military justice to allow the executive to conduct these trials. Crowder's testimony has been given particular weight, which makes the last sentence about procedural conformance particularly noteworthy.

4. World War II

World War II saw the military commission's first deliberate downward departure from court-martial due process standards, during the trial of eight Germans covertly landed from two U-boats in June 1942 to sabotage U.S. war production. The men were rounded up by the Federal Bureau of Investigations (FBI) after one turned himself in and provided information on the others' identities and likely whereabouts. When J. Edgar Hoover unilaterally (and self-servingly) announced the arrests, a firestorm of outrage swept the nation, demanding their prompt execution. The FBI assumed that the saboteurs would be tried in regular federal

23 S. Rep. No. 64–582, at 40 (1916) (testimony of Brig. Gen. Crowder) (emphasis added).
24 10 U.S.C. § 821 (2006).
25 317 U.S. 1 (1942).
26 548 U.S. 557 (2006).

courts, however, and the agents working the case carefully followed accepted criminal procedure standards. All eight prisoners nevertheless made voluntary confessions including details about the Nazi sabotage school where they had trained and German plans for subsequent landings.

The situation highlighted the need to keep secret the porous nature of U.S. coastal defenses and the reality that the saboteurs' capture depended on the assistance of a turncoat rather than any U.S. penetration of the German intelligence services. It also called for severe sentences in an effort to deter the planned following attempts. It is true that this secrecy served Hoover's interests by covering up the fact that his FBI was unable to make headway on capturing the saboteurs until literally handed the details of the plot by the traitor. Dual motives do not, however, alter the core reality of compelling national security grounds for avoiding public disclosure of the details of the incident, at least for the duration of the war.

Security concerns aside, federal court trials proved problematic simply because the Nazis had not committed any serious crimes before their apprehension. Justice Department lawyers were literally considering offenses such as failing to register as foreign government agents and a general conspiracy statute to get even two to three years of prison time, providing no hope of meaningful deterrence. Roosevelt and his key legal advisors recognized the potential advantage of a military trial for the historically recognized offense of belligerents shedding their uniforms behind enemy lines to spy or carry out acts of violence. These defendants were effectively in the same legal position Beall had been in eight decades earlier.

Assistant Solicitor General Oscar Cox advised Biddle that a trial by court-martial or military commission on the basis of the law of war could be the solution. He noted that commissions were not statutorily required to follow court-martial procedure, but that it had been their practice to do so.[27] Biddle ignored Cox's observation about this traditional conformity and sent FDR a memo on June 30, 1942, recommending that the saboteurs

27 Louis Fisher, Nazi Saboteurs on Trial 48–49 (2003).

be tried by military commission. He also essentially called for the commission to make its own rules of procedure and admit any probative evidence. FDR sent Biddle a note that same day suggesting an actual court-martial for violation of the law of war and cited the executions of Nathan Hale and Major André as examples justifying that approach.

Biddle's memo included draft military orders implementing his recommendations and purporting to bar judicial review, which FDR promptly signed.[28] Roosevelt's signatures abruptly foreclosed any discussion of the comparative merits of the two trial fora or the appropriate legal standards that should guide them. The formal authorization Biddle drafted for the commission to dramatically depart from court-martial standards was both unprecedented and entirely unnecessary – the FBI had conducted interrogations and gathered considerable physical evidence with care to ensure that everything would be fully admissible in any regular court. Commission proceedings reflected trial panel bias against the defense, and statements by individual defendants were allowed to serve as evidence against the others (contrary to standard U.S. judicial practice of the day). These factors have fueled subsequent criticism, but do not undermine the basic validity of the overall verdicts given that each man had fully and voluntarily confessed their own role, supported by a substantial volume of admissible corroborating evidence. This evidence included secret writings; large amounts of otherwise inexplicable cash; and discarded uniform items, sabotage equipment, and explosives recovered from the landing beaches; as well as testimony from other eyewitnesses who had personal dealings with the defendants after their surreptitious arrival in the United States.

Although the military order FDR signed purported to bar judicial review, the Supreme Court agreed to convene for a special July term to hear the saboteur's habeas challenge to the commission's jurisdiction even before the defense had actually filed a petition in the district court. The subsequent Supreme Court decision, Ex parte *Quirin*,[29] has

28 Exec. Order No. 9185, 7 Fed. Reg. 5103 (July 7, 1942).
29 317 U.S. 1 (1942).

been subject to a great deal of criticism from across the political spectrum. Indeed, conservative Justice Antonin Scalia decried the holding as being "not this Court's finest hour" in his 2004 *Hamdi* v. *Rumsfeld* dissent addressing post-9/11 detention.[30] Justice Felix Frankfurter, for example, pressured his liberal colleague, Frank Murphy, to recuse himself because Murphy was serving as a uniformed military officer during the Court's summer recess. This proffered justification was almost certainly pretextual, and Frankfurter may have merely considered Murphy's vote unreliable.

After receiving hastily drafted briefs, the Court heard oral argument over two days before issuing a terse per curiam opinion upholding the trial. The commission promptly found all eight guilty, and six were quickly executed. The Court then faced the challenge of crafting its formal published opinion with no practical option of reconsidering its hasty per curiam decision. This proved easier said than done, and the final opinion is hardly a work of art. The Court gave in to political pressure, putting its formal sanction on an exceptional tribunal that departed from accepted standards of justice.

Despite frequent criticism, however, Quirin established a critical foundation for the Court's subsequent ability to constrain the Bush administration's post-9/11 conduct. The easiest thing for the Court to have done in 1942 would have been nothing. It was not in session during the military commission proceedings, and the justices could have deferred decision until the start of the October term when the issue might have been effectively mooted by the executions. The justices certainly could have delayed consideration until the defense had had a habeas petition considered by the district court and court of appeals.

Just by hearing the case, the Court implicitly rejected the idea that the president could foreclose judicial review of extraordinary trials. Chief Justice Harlan Fiske Stone privately stressed this aspect of the decision, noting that his opinion "flatly rejected (as unobtrusively as possible) the President's comment that no court should hear the plea of the saboteurs.

30 542 U.S. 507, 569 (2004) (Scalia, J. dissenting).

That, I thought, was going pretty far."[31] The Court's opinion did much more than that, however. It identified the fundamental issue as "whether any of the acts charged is an offense against the law of war cognizable before a military tribunal, and if so whether the Constitution prohibits the trial."[32] It thus made clear that the scope of offenses defined by the law of war serves as the outer limit on military-commission jurisdiction, but that there may be additional constraints posed by U.S. law. Equally important, the Court rejected broad claims of executive authority. It upheld the trial on the basis of finding an implied congressional delegation of authority in Crowder's Article 15, not inherent executive authority, concluding that Congress had validly exercised its authority under the "define and punish" clause.[33]

The United States made extensive use of military commissions to try law-of-war violations following the Axis surrender. Importantly, the 1942 model permitting departures from court-martial procedure and rules of evidence remained the basis rather than the historical practice of close conformity between military commission and court-martial standards. The Supreme Court heard several more cases from these trials, raising new jurisdictional issues.

The first post-hostilities case concerned the trial of General Tomoyuki Yamashita held in the Philippines in late 1945. The case raised questions of fundamental fairness including inadequate time for the defense to prepare for trial, admission of evidence of questionable reliability, and whether the commission retained jurisdiction after Japan's surrender. But it is best remembered for addressing the issue of command responsibility. The Court dodged procedural questions on the basis of technical interpretations of statutory and treaty language that are no longer in effect today, found that war ended not with surrender but when "peace has been officially recognized by treaty or proclamation of the political

31 Letter from Chief Justice Harlan Fiske Stone to Sterling Carr (Nov. 17, 1942), *quoted in* Alpheus Thomas Mason, Harlan Fiske Stone: Pillar of the Law 664 (1956).

32 317 U.S. at 29.

33 *Id.* at 25–29.

branch of the Government," and held that the charges did in fact "adequately allege a violation of the law of war."[34]

In a strongly worded dissent, Justice Murphy argued for the application of constitutional due process as a floor on any U.S. prosecution:

> The Fifth Amendment guarantee of due process of law applies to "any person" who is accused of a crime by the Federal Government or any of its agencies. No exception is made as to those who are accused of war crimes or as to those who possess the status of an enemy belligerent.... The immutable rights of the individual... belong not alone to the members of those nations that excel on the battlefield or that subscribe to the democratic ideology.[35]

The Court heard several additional challenges from Axis officials but rejected all of them.[36] The only military-commission trials actually overturned by the Court during the World War II period were those of two civilians conducted under martial law in Hawaii, decided as *Duncan v. Kahanamoku*[37] in February 1946. The Court gave Milligan only cursory mention, despite the obvious parallels between the two cases, before ultimately grounding its decision in a statutory interpretation of the Hawaiian Organic Act.[38]

Conclusion

The military commission has been an "exceptional" tribunal since its inception, when it was crafted to address gaps in the jurisdiction of regularly established U.S. civilian and military courts. But military

34 In re Yamashita, 327 U.S. 1, 12, 17 (1946).

35 *Id.* at 26 (Murphy, J., dissenting).

36 These cases were In re Homma, 327 U.S. 759 (1946) (challenging a military commission in the Philippines); *Hirota v. MacArthur*, 338 U.S. 197 (1948) (challenging the International Military Tribunal for the Far East – the Tokyo counterpart of the more famous Nuremberg Tribunal); *Johnson v. Eisentrager*, 339 U.S. 763 (1950) (challenging the trial of German civilians by the United States in China).

37 327 U.S. 304 (1946).

38 *Id.* at 309, 322, 324.

commissions were not intended to permit judicial shortcuts. Rather, by providing trials fully equivalent to those accorded similarly situated Americans, properly conducted military commissions exceeded the standards applied by other nations at the time. Although some individual commission trials clearly failed to measure up to accepted legal norms, these were concentrated in the Civil War era and their shortcomings equally plagued courts-martial of that period. Their deficiencies are thus explained by the wholesale influx of individuals from civilian life lacking knowledge of military law, rather than an accepted aspect of commission practice.

It was only in the mid-twentieth century that the military commission was first deliberately allowed a significant downward departure from the standards of regular courts-martial. The extensive controversy generated by the Guantánamo military commissions could have been avoided if the Bush administration had elected to employ either regular courts-martial or at least align current commissions more faithfully with court-martial procedure in accordance with original practice. To its credit, the Supreme Court has been true to its precedent, which clearly establishes that the federal judiciary can hear collateral challenges to exceptional courts, and its 2006 *Hamdan* decision repudiated unilateral executive claims of authority to conduct trials under rules it crafted. Instead, the *Hamdan* Court held that both the authority of Congress and the law of war (in the form of Common Article 3 to the Geneva Conventions of 1949) constitute checks on these exceptional courts. The precise limits remain to be established, however, and it is likely that years of litigation remain before any final resolution.

2 Military Commissions in Historical Perspective

Lessons from the United States – Dakota War Trials

Carol L. Chomsky

IN THE AFTERMATH OF SEPTEMBER 11, 2001, PRESIDENT BUSH declared that alleged perpetrators of terrorism against the United States would be brought to trial not in Article III federal courts, but instead before military commissions. It was commonly recognized that these would be distinct from military courts-martial, a form of dispensing justice familiar within the United States. But what kind of courts these would be and what challenges they would pose was far from clear. Throughout American history, military commissions had been used irregularly and rarely, most recently to try a handful of enemy combatants shortly after the end of World War II. Given the contemporary use of military commissions, it behooves us to consider what the historical use of such bodies can teach us about their risks and utility.

Created in a somewhat different guise as a structure for adjudication during the Mexican-American War and employed – although not without challenge – during the Civil War, the military commission was also the form of tribunal invoked in the trial of almost 400 Dakota who fought American soldiers in a brief frontier war in 1862. Of the 392 combatants who were tried, 323 were convicted, and 38 were hanged in the largest mass execution in American history. Bound up in the history of the new state of Minnesota and the relations between Americans and

American Indians, the significance of the events for American military and political history was long ignored. With the rising importance of military commissions and the continuing controversy over their legitimacy, it is enlightening to explore problems associated with their early use and reflect on the contemporary salience of those concerns.

1. Trial and Execution of the Dakota

The Dakota trials followed a brief war in Minnesota that began on August 17, 1862, reflecting accumulated Dakota grievances over treaty violations and trader abuses, worsening economic conditions, and pressures on the Dakota to assimilate.[1] As was typical in frontier warfare, the Dakota fought against both American mustered soldiers and "citizen-soldiers"; they also attacked settlers who had not yet taken shelter behind fortifications in towns or military forts, usually killing the men and taking women and children captive. The war ended abruptly on September 23, when Dakota who opposed continuation of the war took control and those who opposed surrender left the Dakota camp. In 37 days of fighting, an estimated 77 American soldiers, 29 citizen soldiers, 358 settlers, and 29 Dakota soldiers had been killed.

As soon as he took control of the Dakota camp, American military commander Colonel Henry Sibley appointed a three-member military commission to examine all captured Indian and mixed-blood men "so that if there are guilty parties among them they can be arrested and properly dealt with."[2] Perhaps initially Sibley was proposing a court of inquiry, a military tribunal designed to collect information for later use in prosecution or other proceedings but with no authority to enter judgments and sentences. Sibley's September 28 order went further, however, appointing

1 *See generally* Carol Chomsky, *The United States-Dakota War Trials: A Study in Military Injustice*, 43 Stan. L. Rev. 13 (1990).

2 Letter from Col. Henry Sibley to Maj. Gen. John Pope (Sept. 27, 1862), *reprinted in* 13 United States Department of War, The War of the Rebellion: A Compilation of the Official Records of the Union and Confederate Armies, Series I, at 679–80 (Gov't Printing Office. 1885) (hereinafter War of the Rebellion, Ser. I).

a five-member military commission composed of men who had fought in the just-concluded war and authorizing it to "try summarily the... Indians, or mixed bloods, now prisoners, or who may be brought before them... and pass judgement upon them, if found guilty of murders or other outrages upon the Whites, during the present State of hostilities of the Indians."[3] He planned to have the guilty executed immediately, although he expressed some uncertainty about the extent of his authority.[4] There seemed little question that Sibley's actions would be approved by Major General Pope, who had already written to Sibley that the actions of the Dakota "call for punishment beyond human power to inflict. There will be no peace in this region by virtue of treaties and Indian faith. It is my purpose utterly to exterminate the Sioux if I have the power to do so."[5]

The trials[6] began immediately, on September 28. The transcripts show the commission trying sixteen men on that first day: ten were convicted and sentenced to be hanged; six were acquitted and released. On October 7, although he had not yet reviewed the commission proceedings, Sibley informed Pope that he would probably approve the results and "hang the villains" although the proceedings might not be "exactly in form."[7] In the next 36 days, the commission tried 392 Dakota, as many as 42 listed in a single day. Although a few were charged with robbery or rape, most were charged with murder, often based exclusively on an allegation of participation in the fighting between August 19 and September 28. All defendants found to have participated in any fighting, whether against soldiers or settlers, whether in a battle or a raid, were convicted

3 Order No. 55, issued at Camp Release (Sept. 28, 1862), *reprinted in* Trial Transcripts (contained in each transcript).

4 Letter from Col. Henry Sibley to Maj. Gen. John Pope (Sept. 28, 1862), *reprinted in* 13 War of the Rebellion, Ser. I, *supra* note 2, at 687.

5 Letter from Maj. Gen. John Pope to Col. Henry Sibley (Sept. 28, 1862), *reprinted in* 13 War of the Rebellion, Ser. I, *supra* note 2, at 685–86.

6 *See generally* Trial Transcripts.

7 Letter from Col. Henry Sibley to Maj. Gen. John Pope (Oct. 7, 1862), *reprinted in* 13 War of the Rebellion, Ser. I, *supra* note 2, at 717.

and sentenced to be hanged. Those found to have participated only in plundering were found guilty and sentenced to terms of imprisonment ranging from one to ten years. Of the 392 men tried, the commission convicted 323 and sentenced 303 to be hanged; it acquitted the remaining 69 prisoners.

Meanwhile, on October 14, General Pope's report on the trials and planned executions was read at President Lincoln's cabinet meeting in Washington. Disturbed by the report, Lincoln sent word through Pope that no executions should be carried out without his sanction.[8] Prevailing federal statutes required the president's personal approval before the death sentences could be carried out, although Sibley and his immediate superiors – and President Lincoln – appeared unaware of that requirement. On November 15, Pope forwarded the transcripts and a letter in which he urged the president to execute all of the condemned, claiming that "the only distinction between the culprits is as to which of them murdered most people or violated most young girls."[9] He warned that the people of Minnesota, perhaps combined with some of the soldiers, would take matters into their own hands and kill "all the Indians – old men, women, and children" if the president did not allow all the executions to go forward. If the president proved reluctant to decide, he suggested, the condemned could be turned over to the state government. Minnesota Governor Ramsey left no doubt what decision he would make if given the opportunity, writing to Lincoln to urge execution of all the condemned.[10]

A great public outcry arose in Minnesota in response to reports that Lincoln might not carry out the full sentence of the military commission. Mob violence erupted against the Dakota, with crowds seriously injuring shackled prisoners and their guards with hurled bricks. The army foiled

8 Letter from Pres. Abraham Lincoln to Maj. Gen. John Pope (Nov. 10, 1862), *reprinted in* 13 War of the Rebellion, Ser. I, *supra* note 2, at 787.

9 Letter from Maj. Gen. John Pope to Pres. Abraham Lincoln (Nov. 11, 1862), *reprinted in* 13 War of the Rebellion, Ser. I, *supra* note 2, at 788.

10 Letter from Gov. Alexander Ramsey to Pres. Abraham Lincoln (Nov. 10, 1862), *reprinted in* 13 War of the Rebellion, Ser. I, *supra* note 2, at 787.

one attack by civilians armed with clubs, hatchets, and knives and warned of a "general, fearful and bloody demonstration" if the prisoners were moved or a general pardon issued.[11]

Lincoln was apparently torn between the cries for vengeance, potential injustice to the accused, and possible political fallout from a decision to commute any of the sentences. He considered leaving the ruling to an "officer on the ground," but was told he could not delegate the decision.[12] On December 6, Lincoln finally issued his decision in a message to the Senate: "Anxious to not act with so much clemency as to encourage another outbreak, on the one hand, nor with so much severity as to be real cruelty, on the other,"[13] Lincoln drew the line by ordering the execution of thirty-nine men who he said had participated in "massacres," as distinguished from those who had participated in "battles." On December 23, the president suspended the execution of one of the condemned men after Sibley telegraphed that new information led him to doubt the prisoner's guilt.[14] Meanwhile, the troops constructed a scaffold large enough to hang all thirty-eight at one time, and the commander of the local forces declared martial law to help troops control the expected crowds.[15] The executions were carried out on December 26, watched by a large but orderly crowd.[16]

Over the next several years, President Lincoln pardoned some of the prisoners convicted but not executed, with some of those decisions made

11 Letter from Col. Stephen Miller to Ass't Adj Gen. Rollin Olin (Dec. 9, 1862), *in* Letters Rec'd, NARG 393 (Entry 346).

12 Letter from Pres. Abraham Lincoln to J. Adv. Gen. Joseph Holt (Dec. 1, 1862), *reprinted in* 5 COLLECTED WORKS OF ABRAHAM LINCOLN 537–38 (R. Basler ed. 1954); Letter from J. Adv. Gen. Joseph Holt to Pres. Abraham Lincoln (Dec. 1, 1862), *in* Letters Sent-JAG, NARG 153 (Entry 1).

13 S. Exec. Doc. No. 7, 37th Cong., 3d Sess. 1 (1862).

14 Telegram from Brig. Gen. Henry Sibley to Pres. Abraham Lincoln (Dec. 22, 1862), *in* Letters and Telegrams Sent, NARG 393 (Entry 343); Letter from Brig. Gen. Henry Sibley to Col. Stephen Miller (Dec. 23, 1862), *in* Letters and Telegrams Sent, NARG 393 (Entry 343).

15 Gen. Order No. 21 (Dec. 24, 1862), *reprinted in* ISAAC V.D. HEARD, HISTORY OF THE SIOUX WAR AND MASSACRES OF 1862 AND 1863, at 277 (1864 and photo. reprint 1975).

16 HEARD, *supra* note 15, at 287–90.

at Sibley's request or with his concurrence. For example, local minister Reverend Riggs, who had earlier assisted the prosecution, requested pardons for four prisoners he believed had not participated in the fighting.[17] Sibley agreed, noting that there was "reasonable doubt of the guilt of the prisoners named from circumstances that have transpired since their trial by the Military Commission, and . . . they are entitled to the benefit of that doubt."[18] Lincoln pardoned a convicted prisoner at the recommendation of the judge advocate general because the record "was altogether too imperfect to justify the government in carrying the sentence into execution,"[19] although there was little to distinguish that individual's record from those of executed defendants.[20] At Sibley's request Lincoln also pardoned one mixed blood who had testified against many other defendants, noting his claim that he participated in the fighting under duress,[21] an assertion made by many others.

The Army convened additional military commissions in 1863 and 1864 to try three more Dakota captured well after the fighting ended. The first to be tried was Wowinape, the sixteen-year-old son of tribal chief Taoyateduta. He was convicted on September 28, 1863, and was sentenced to death by hanging. Sibley, as the officer convening the commission, approved the sentence.[22] Subsequent review took a surprising turn, however. The secretary of war and the judge advocate general required Major General Pope to confirm or disapprove the proceedings rather than simply "refer" the result, as he had uniformly done in all

17 Letter from Rev. Stephen Riggs to Brig. Gen. Henry Sibley (Apr. 7, 1864), *in* Court Martial Cases, NARG 153, File NN3132.

18 Notation by Brig. Gen. Henry Sibley (Apr. 8, 1864), *in* Court Martial Cases, NARG 153, File NN3132.

19 Gen. Order No. 120 (May 11, 1863), *in* Military Orders, NARG 94.

20 *Compare* Trial Transcripts, Case No. 105 *with* Cases No. 106, 111, 190, 191.

21 Letter from Brig. Gen. Henry Sibley to Pres. Abraham Lincoln (Jan. 26, 1863), *accompanied by* endorsement of J. Adv. Gen. Joseph Holt (Feb. 16, 1863); pardon by Pres. Abraham Lincoln (May 11, 1863), *in* Letters and Telegrams Sent, NARG 393 (Entry 343).

22 *See* Endorsements to Wowinape Trial Transcript (Oct. 1, 1863) (Sibley's approval), *in* Court Martial Cases, NARG 153, File NN3132.

previous cases. Unexpectedly, General Pope discovered a technical difficulty that he said might prevent him from approving the sentence: in contravention of Article 65 of the Articles of War, Colonel Sibley was both Wowinape's "accuser," because he had originated the commission charge, and the convener of the military commission that tried him for the accused offenses. Although Article 65 referred by its terms only to courts-martial, Pope concluded that it might apply by analogy to military commissions, a ruling confirmed by Judge Advocate General Holt.[23] Not surprisingly, Sibley objected, accurately noting that "a precisely similar condition of things existed in 1862, when nearly four hundred Indian warriors, taken prisoners by the forces under my command, were tried and the greater number condemned to death by a Military Commission ordered by me upon charges and specifications preferred by myself."[24]

After being kidnapped from Canada and returned to the United States surreptitiously, tribal chiefs Wakanozanzan and Shakopee were tried by military commission in 1864, both charged with participating in massacres and murdering whites "whose names are unknown." For the first time in any of the Dakota trials, the defendants were identified as "Sioux Indian[s] ... under the protection ... of the United States," signaling a belated recognition of sovereignty and jurisdictional issues in the military commission trials. The defendants successfully petitioned to introduce counsel, but had to rely on written statements from counsel when a continuance to accommodate the attorney's schedule was denied. Both defendants were convicted and sentenced to be hanged,[25] and

23 *See id.* at Oct. 8, 1863 (Pope's referral to President); *id.* at Oct. 11, 1863 (General-in-Chief Halleck to Sec'y of War Stanton); *id.* at Oct. 12, 1863 (referred to J. Adv., Gen. Holt by Sec'y of War); *id.* at Oct. 13, 1863 (returned to Sec'y of War with Holt's remarks on requiring confirmation); *id.* at Oct. 16, 1863 (returned to General Pope by Sec'y of War); J. Adv. Gen. Joseph Holt to Maj. Gen. John Pope (Nov. 3, 1863), inscribed on back of letter from Maj. Gen. John Pope to J. Adv. Gen. Joseph Holt (Oct. 29, 1863), in Court Martial Cases, NARG 153, File NN3132.

24 Letter from Brig. Gen. Henry Sibley to J. Adv. Gen. Joseph Holt (Dec. 7, 1863), *in* Sioux War Trials, MHS P1423.

25 Transcripts of the Commission Proceedings in the Trials of Tahtaechashnahmanne and Shakopee, *in* Court Martial Cases, NARG 153, File NN3132.

the sentences were confirmed by Sibley, Pope, and President Andrew Johnson,[26] ignoring the defect that had caused Pope to disapprove Wowinape's trial. The two chiefs were hanged at Fort Snelling on November 11, 1865.

2. Procedural and Jurisdictional Injustice

Even a cursory familiarity with the story of the hastily conducted Dakota military-commission trials reveals significant defects in the trial process. Isaac Heard, the recorder for the commission, attempted to justify the extraordinary rapidity of the proceedings: "The trials," he said, "were elaborately conducted until the commission became acquainted with the details of the different outrages and battles, and then, the only point being the connection of the prisoner with them, five minutes would dispose of a case."[27] As one observer commented, however, the commission "could not and did not make a careful examination."[28]

Other procedural defects are less obvious but no less problematic. In early cases, convictions were based on eyewitness testimony to attacks on individual settlers.[29] As the trials progressed, however, there was less and less of such evidence. Many later convictions were based solely on defendants' admission to being present at a battle or with a group when another Dakota killed a settler. Testimony from witnesses was brief, serving merely to identify that the prisoner was present at particular battles or attacks. In many cases, the only evidence was testimony that the

26 Endorsement to Transcript of the Commission Proceeding in the Trial of Shakopee, *in* Court Martial Cases, NARG 153, File NN3132; Letter from Sec'y of the Interior James Harlan to Sec'y of War Edwin Stanton (Oct. 10, 1865), *in* Court Martial Cases, NARG 153, File NN3132; Letter from Pres. Andrew Johnson to Sec'y of War Edwin Stanton (Oct. 10, 1865), *in id.*

27 HEARD, *supra* note 15, at 254–55.

28 Letter from Bishop Henry Whipple to Ass't Sec'y of the Interior John Usher (Apr. 21, 1863), *in* Whipple Papers, MHS.

29 See, e.g., Trial Transcripts, Case No. 2 (Tehehdonecha), Case No. 3 (Wechankwashtodopee).

defendant had appeared to go willingly into battle, "whooping around" with the rest, and had boasted afterward about the number killed.[30]

Some procedural problems evident in the Dakota trials are unlikely to be reproduced in modern military-commission trials, which will not be held in haste immediately after the events at issue and will be governed by procedures specified by Congress and the Justice Department rather than administered at the discretion of military men untrained in dispensing military justice. But some of the stresses and circumstances that led to irregularities in 1862 continue today. Members of the 1862 military commission and those who reviewed the convictions acted amid fears of continuing violence and were under great public pressure to quickly punish the accused, leading to hasty determinations and undermining the quality of justice. Similar pressures and possible consequences exist today. In 1862, defendants understood little about the nature and purpose of the trials, given linguistic and cultural differences, and were given no assistance in navigating the proceedings. Today's prisoners are entitled to representation by counsel, but significant restrictions on their access to and the functioning of their attorneys place limits on counsels' ability to protect client interests. Deep cultural divisions between accusers and accused, counsel and client, and captors and captives undermine and perhaps defeat the understanding necessary for proceedings to be both legitimate and perceived as such.

Credibility of evidence against the defendants is a problem today as it was in 1862. In the Dakota trials, much testimony consisted of repetition of incriminating statements made by defendants and overheard by the witnesses, many of whom were white women held in the Indian camp after being captured in the fighting. Such statements by the Dakota about their exploits in the fighting should have been understood in the context of the culture and circumstances in which they were made. Even a truthful report of responsibility for a killing might have had a different meaning as spoken by a Dakota than as understood by the American witnesses and

30 *See, e.g.*, Trial Transcripts, Case No. 1 (Godfrey).

trial judges. In Dakota tradition, special acts of bravery, such as touching an armed soldier during battle or sneaking into an enemy camp to steal or release horses, might have been boasted of in a manner suggesting that killings had occurred.[31] The first four men to touch an enemy killed in fighting were entitled to claim responsibility for the act, even if the individual died before they reached him.[32] The man who first touched an enemy was also credited with having killed him, even if the actual killing was done by another, and the one who first entered a house where people were later killed by any of the group was given credit for all the killings. Thus, defendants' descriptions and boasting of their own acts in battle may not have reflected the act of killing and criminal culpability as understood by the commission. Moreover, the defendants' claims, made in the midst of the fighting, may have been exaggerated to prove loyalty to the Dakota community in the midst of a controversial war. It is noteworthy, too, that much of the testimony in the Dakota trials came from individuals who were themselves on trial for their lives, accused of participating in the war and attempting to prove their own innocence.

Such evidentiary concerns exist with respect to the contemplated contemporary prosecutions. Given the cultural specificity of the conflicts in Iraq and Afghanistan one can speculate on the effects of political and cultural contexts that would result in some individuals exaggerating complicity in violent acts, only to have their statements later reported as fact. Suspicion that some of the charges against detained prisoners are politically motivated or inept has proven justified, with some prisoners released after long detention as "dangerous terrorists" when the cases against them collapsed for lack of hard evidence.[33] Whether cultural

31 *See, e.g.*, Trial Transcripts, Case No. 383 (witness testified that defendant said he killed two boys with his war lance in house near Traveller's Home; defendant testified only that he might have "done it" – he touched one with his "flute" but did not use his lance).

32 Samuel W. Pond, The Dakota or Sioux in Minnesota as They Were in 1834 128 (1986).

33 *See, e.g.*, *Boumedienne v. Bush*, 579 F.Supp.2d 191 (D.D.C. 2008) (finding insufficient evidence to hold five of six detainees as enemy combatants); *Fouad Mahmoud Al Rabiah v. United States*, 658 F.Supp.2d 11 (D.D.C. 2009); Carol Rosenberg and

and political differences between the sides threaten understanding of the "true" facts, as it did in 1862, has yet to be explored.

Possible bias of decision-makers also remains a concern. The Dakota faced a panel convened and reviewed by the very commander who led opposing forces and who was the defendants' formal accuser. As already noted, Article 65 formally forbade such conflicts of interest with respect to courts-martial; the military determined that the same rule should also apply to military commissions. Sibley's pretrial and post-trial correspondence shows that he had precisely the mindset that inspired the rule prohibiting the playing of dual roles. The problem of bias was heightened by the attitudes of panel members, men who had fought in the recent battles and some of whom later admitted they acted with predisposition toward conviction, in part from animus against the Dakota. With our contemporary American military commissions, it is reasonable to express similar concern about the risk of prejudgment of the accused based on conflict of interest and possible racial or ethnic prejudice, in substance or appearance.

The status of those tried and the nature of offenses with which they could legitimately be charged should have been considered in 1862; similar questions must be addressed today. In a public war, those who fight are considered justified when they act within the bounds of "proper" warfare, whether or not the war itself is considered "just." Individuals who act for their own private gain or operate without authorization from their government, even if their government is at war, are considered marauders, robbers, and murderers and may be punished as such. Questions of combatant status went unexplored in 1862; the Dakota were treated as private actors on trial for murder and other civil offenses when they should have been considered soldiers subject to punishment only for violating the laws of war. The status of the Dakota was complicated by their unusual position as a group considered sovereign for many purposes

Jonathon S. Landay, *Young Afghan Sent Home from Guantánamo*, MIAMI HERALD, Aug. 24, 2009 (noting that U.S. District Judge Ellen Segal Huvelle declared the Pentagon's case against Mohammed Jawad a "shambles").

but existing within U.S. borders and over which Congress was granted "plenary power" in the Constitution. Different but comparable complications exist with respect to those who may be tried by today's military commissions. Defining what constitutes a government for purposes of fighting a public war – a group of bands or a tribe in 1862, al-Qaeda today – and what constitutes a declaration of war – a consensus decision of tribal councils in 1862, a declaration of jihad today – are questions that have yet to be resolved. Certainly, combatant status has been one of the most contested aspects of the current controversy surrounding military-commission authority over the Guantánamo prisoners.

The legitimacy of the military commission itself was uncertain in 1862, and questions about legitimacy continue. As discussed by David Glazier elsewhere in this volume,[34] military commissions were originally used not to try enemy combatants, but to provide justice in occupied territory in both the Mexican-American and Civil Wars. Tribunals akin to military commissions but called "councils of war" were convened to try combatants for violations of the laws of war in the Mexican-American War. The first statutory mention of military commissions was an off-hand reference in a July 1862 enactment establishing the position of judge advocate general of the Army and stating that the person holding that position would review proceedings from both courts-martial and military commissions.[35] Military commissions were formalized by General Order 100 in April 1863,[36] but still without statutory authority. In 1864, a law authorized commanders to execute sentences imposed by military commissions, permitting such sentences to be carried out without the delay caused by having to seek presidential approval but conferring no new authority on military tribunals.[37]

Presumably responding to inquiries about the validity of military commissions, the highest-ranking judicial officer in the Army, Judge

34 David Glazier, *The Development of an Exceptional Court: The History of the American Military Commission*, Ch. 1 in this volume.

35 *See* Act of July 17, 1862, ch. 36, § 5, 12 Stat. 597, 598.

36 Gen. Order No. 100, ¶ 13 (Apr. 24, 1863), *reprinted in* Richard Shelly Hartigan, Lieber's Code And The Law Of War 45 (1983).

37 Cong. Globe, 38th Cong., 1st Sess. 3030, 3416–17 (1864).

Advocate John F. Lee, told the secretary of war in March 1862 that military commissions lacked validity.[38] In June, Lee reiterated that opinion, but bowing to reality, noted, "Still, it is done."[39] Just three months later, the issue was still under advisement by the president, but Lee's successor, former Secretary of War Joseph Holt expressed his own view that military commissions' "[l]ong uninterrupted usage" had rendered them "part and parcel of the common military law."[40] Despite the fact that commissions' usage had been anything but long and uninterrupted, the practice continued.

On November 13, 2001, when President Bush declared by military order that the secretary of defense should create and use military commissions,[41] there was still no definition of what that might mean. Statutory references were still limited to statements that military commissions could exist and procedures could be established for them. The absence of authority led the Supreme Court in *Hamdan v. Rumsfeld*[42] to invalidate the military-commission system established by Bush's order. In response, Congress passed the Military Commissions Act of 2006 (amended in 2009) to provide authorization of and establish procedural rules for military commissions. Military commissions no longer depend on fictional long and uninterrupted usage, but questions remain about whether executive declarations about the contours of the military tribunals are within statutory mandates and whether specific provisions regulating post-9/11 military commissions conform to due process, constitutional, and international legal norms.

Two final parallels exist. First, military authorities and the public no doubt aimed both to punish the Dakota for what they viewed as unlawful

38 Letter from J. Adv. John Lee to Sec'y of War (Mar. 1862), *in* Letters Sent-JAG, NARG 153 (Entry 1), at 289.

39 Letter from J. Adv. John Lee to Sec'y of War (June 8, 1862), *in* Letters Sent-JAG, NARG 153 (Entry 1), at 312.

40 Letter from J. Adv. Gen. Joseph Holt to Sec'y of War Edwin Stanton (Sept. 8, 1862), *in* Letters Sent-JAG, NARG 153 (Entry 1).

41 *See* Press Release, White House, President Issues Military Order (Nov. 13, 2001), retrieved from http://georgewbush-whitehouse.archives.gov/news/releases/2001/11/20011113-27.html.

42 *Hamdan v. Rumsfeld*, 548 U.S. 557, 634 (2006), *rev'g* 415 F.3d 33 (D.C. Cir. 2005).

conduct and to declare to the Dakota the bounds of appropriate behavior. But because of the wide cultural and juridical gulf separating the accusers and the accused, the Dakota in 1862 did not – and many still do not – fully understand why trials were held, some men were convicted and some were not, or why forty men and not others were executed. We risk creating the same dynamic today if we do not address widely divergent understandings held by the multiple communities represented in contemporary prosecutions. A fundamental and unexplored divide remains when acts are viewed by some as legitimate acts of war and by others as terrorism. Bravado and acts of violence may be considered legitimate by one community and criminal by another. Conflicting frames of reference mean that the accused are left little room to defend themselves without conceding the legitimacy of the prosecution's conceptualization of the war context.

The injustices of the 1862 military-commission trials went largely unchallenged at the time, in part because of the absence of judicial review. In the case of Wowinape, the procedural nicety requiring General Pope to approve, not simply refer, the conviction provided the opportunity for him to discover a difficulty with the validity of the entire proceeding. The events of 1862 – indeed, the entire history of the use of military commissions[43] – demonstrate the critical role of courts in setting limits on the use of commissions if defendants and the public are to be assured of their legitimacy.

3. Liability of Enemy Combatants

Because of the procedural and jurisdictional errors made in the Dakota trials, no participants asked the crucial and fundamental questions about liability that remain unanswered today. Were any of the combatants in fact guilty of violating the laws of war, making them subject to

43 *See generally* Michal R. Belknap, *A Putrid Pedigree: The Bush Administration's Military Tribunals in Historical Perspective*, 38 CAL. WEST. L. REV. 433 (2002).

conviction by a military commission actually authorized to try combatants for such offenses? If an individual acts as a legitimate belligerent in warfare, what acts of aggression are permitted and which are not? When does a noncombatant become sufficiently engaged in hostilities to lose the protections accorded civilians by international humanitarian law and principles? When does connection with those who violate the laws of war, or presence when such unlawful acts are committed, become a criminally sanctioned act?

Answers to these questions were unclear in 1862, early in the development of international standards of warfare. General Order 100, issued in 1863 to guide the United States Army in its fight against the Confederacy, stated that the citizen of a hostile country is an enemy and is subject to the hardships of war, but introduced the principle that civilians warranted protection "as much as the exigencies of war will admit."[44] But General Order 100 and contemporary treatises failed to detail what those exigencies were, and when injury to civilians would be considered "unavoidable" and therefore tolerated. Perhaps the only certainty was that violence from both sides was often directed at civilians, especially in fighting between the United States and the Indian nations, and was seldom punished.[45] Moreover, the Dakota traditionally fought with methods substantially different from those of Americans and Europeans. In intertribal Indian wars, almost all members of the enemy nation – including women and children – were legitimate targets of attack, and captives were rarely taken.[46] These practices were largely dictated by circumstances: Indians had no prison camps in which to confine captives;

44 General Order No. 100, *supra* note 36, § 1, ¶ 22.

45 *See, e.g.*, Donald A. Wells, War Crimes and Laws of War 3–4 (1984); Geoffrey Best, *Restraints on War By Land Before 1945*, *in* Restraints on War 29–31(Michael Howard ed. 1979); Michael Howard and Temperamenta Belli, *Can War Be Controlled*, *in* Restraints on War 1, 9–11(Michael Howard ed. 1979); Donald Cameron Watt, *Restraints on War in the Air Before 1945*, *in* Restraints on War 657–58 (Michael Howard ed. 1979).

46 *See* William W. Warren, History Of The Ojibway People 102–07, 183–87, 224–27, 327–29, 352–53, 367 (1885 and photo. reprint 1984).

women and older children, if taken, were likely to escape and bring vital information back to their own tribes; fighting men could not effectively transport the younger children, and infants would likely die on the way. This raises a broader question about the cultural distinctiveness of war as an enterprise, and the extent to which the developing rules of war took and should take account of indigenous and non-Western modalities of warfare.

Moreover, the 1862 military commission may have convicted some defendants merely because they were present when civilians were killed by others in a manner that itself could have been a violation of the laws of war, although nothing in General Order 100 or customary international law affirmatively established such "group" liability. Whether association with or general assistance to those engaged in unlawful acts of war is grounds for liability remains highly contested; the Military Commissions Act defines conspiracy as a war crime, but neither the Geneva Conventions nor the Uniform Code of Military Justice do so, a definitional matter that remains under judicial dispute at the time of writing. Violence against and humiliating or degrading treatment of civilians is prohibited, but we still struggle with defining when a civilian loses that status.[47] What constitutes murder "in violation of the law of war" and whether "material support for terrorism" is a war crime are far from settled questions,[48] although both have been included among the charges against Guantánamo prisoners.

Conclusion

The Dakota War trials provide no direct guidance about how to handle today's challenges, but it is instructive to consider how many of our own seemingly new questions about military commissions were reflected in

47 *See generally*, Nils Melzer, Int'l Comm. Red Cross, Interpretative Guidance on the Notion of Direct Participation in Hostilities Under International Humanitarian Law (2009).

48 *See* Jennifer K. Elsea, Cong. Research Serv., The Military Commissions Act of 2009: Overview and Legal Issues 11–13 (2010).

the events of 150 years ago. The failure to answer those questions then – indeed, the failure to even ask many of them – was an added source of injustice to the Dakota. If today's defendants and the rest of the world are to respect verdicts and the punishment that follows, if those outcomes are to be seen as just responses to unlawful acts of violence, we must hope for more thorough questions and answers this time.

Appendix

Documents at the National Archives

Court Martial Cases, NARG 153, File NN3132	Court Martial Case Files; Records of the Immediate Office of the Judge Advocate General; Records of the Office of the Judge Advocate General (Army), 1808–1942; Record Group 153, National Archives, Washington, DC.
Letters Rec'd, NARG 393 (Entry 346)	Letters Received, 1862–1869; District of Minnesota, Nov. 1862–June 1873; Geographical Districts and Subdistricts; United States Army Continental Commands, 1821–1920, Record Group 393 (Entry 346); National Archives, Washington, DC.
Letters and Telegrams Sent, NARG 393 (Entry 343)	Letters and Telegrams Sent, Nov. 1862–Oct. 1873; District of Minnesota, Nov. 1862–June 1873; Geographical Districts and Subdistricts; United States Army Continental Commands, 1821–1920, Record Group 393 (Entry 343); National Archives, Washington, DC.
Letters Sent, JAG, NARG 153 (Entry 1)	Letters Sent, 1842–1889; Records of the Immediate Office of the Judge Advocate General; Records of the Office of the Judge Advocate General (Army), 1808–1942, Record Group 153 (Entry 1); National Archives, Washington, DC.
Military Orders, NARG 94	Orders and Circulars, 1797–1910; Orders, 1797–1939; General Records of the Adjutant General's Office, Record Group 94; National Archives, Washington, DC.
Trial Transcripts	Senate Records 37A–F2, Original Transcripts of the Records of Trials of Certain Sioux Indians Charged with Barbarities in the State of Minnesota; National Archives, Washington, DC.

Documents at the Minnesota Historical Society

Sioux War Trials, MHS P1423	U.S. Army; Military Commission, Sioux War Trials, 1862; Trial Transcripts; File P1423, Minnesota Historical Society, St. Paul, Minnesota.
Whipple Papers, MHS	Henry Benjamin Whipple Papers, 1833–1934; File P823, Minnesota Historical Society, St. Paul, Minnesota.

3 Contemporary Law of War and Military Commissions

Gary D. Solis

TODAY, "MILITARY COMMISSION" IS A TERM OFTEN SPOKEN with derision, associated with torture and Star Chamber proceedings. It was not always so, and it need not be so today. In democratic societies, there remains a legitimate place for military commissions. As long as there are armed conflicts, there will likely be military commissions in one form or another. Their misuse, however, negates both their moral legitimacy and legal utility.

This chapter outlines the evolution of military commissions from an American disciplinary "field expedient" to meet a military necessity unaddressed by the Articles of War, to their place in contemporary law of war as a trial setting for enemies charged with violation of the laws and customs of war. Section 1 sets the stage in the U.S.-Mexican War (1846–48), and explains the genesis of military commissions. Section 2 traces their transformation from disciplinary tool to a Civil War trial forum for U.S. enemies, while section 3 reviews the military commissions that followed World War II, when they were employed by virtually every Allied country. Section 4 details post–World War II issues that had an impact on military commissions – human rights, multinational human rights treaties, and particularly, the 1949 Geneva Conventions. These interfaces changed military commissions from field tribunals with lowered procedural and evidentiary bars to trials closely reflecting U.S. courts-martial practice. Since the 9/11 attacks, many argue that commission changes implemented at Guantánamo have shifted the historical arc of their rules and procedures, making them a second-rate form of justice. This alleged progression is briefly discussed in Section 5. Section 6 looks at one of those changes – the 2006 Military Commissions Act (MCA) – the alterations it brought, and their reception in the Supreme Court of the United States. Finally, Section 7 examines a later change, the MCA of 2009. Although an improvement over its 2006 predecessor, it remains flawed in regard to the legal efficacy of some offenses it authorizes. This and other issues do not lend confidence to a process that, before 9/11, enjoyed 150 years of relative success and legal utility.

1. Military Commissions: A Beginning

"Military tribunal" is the unifying term for all military proceedings of a judicial nature. Courts-martial, employed in virtually all military legal systems, are a form of military tribunal, as are courts of inquiry, which investigate serious military incidents such as the loss of ships at sea. Provost courts, another form of military tribunal, convene in occupied territory to try offenses alleged against civilians. Military government courts and Provisional Courts are additional American forms of military tribunal, both now disused.

Military commissions should not be confused with their tribunal brethren, courts-martial. Courts-martial try offenses committed by members of the armed forces against the State's military criminal code. Today, in the United States and many other countries, they employ rigorous procedural rules and evidentiary standards.[1] Military commissions, on the other hand, are traditional wartime tribunals that try captured enemies

1 Court-martial procedure and rules of evidence are mandated by Congress, publically reviewed, updated annually, and printed in the *Manual for Courts-Martial*. They largely mirror rules of evidence and procedure found in federal courts. See entry *Courts Martial*, in THE OXFORD COMPANION TO INTERNATIONAL CRIMINAL JUSTICE 283, 284 (Antonio Cassese ed., 2009) ("Like many social institutions, courts-martial have benefitted from the modern shift toward the recognition of human rights.").

accused of violating the laws and customs of war.[2] In keeping with their utilitarian in-the-field nature, they have employed less stringent rules of procedure and evidence than are found in either domestic courts or courts-martial.

The so-called War on Terror brought a new version of military commission. Unlike pre-9/11 commissions, the Guantánamo version differs in significant ways from court-martial rules and procedures. For example, under jurisdictional rules for current military commissions, offenses must be "violations of the law of war [or] other offenses triable by military commission."[3] In the past, commission jurisdiction simply included war crimes, espionage, and sabotage. Current charges have included passing information between terrorist cells, serving as an al-Qaeda accountant, being a bodyguard to Osama bin Laden, and assisting bin Laden in avoiding capture.[4] These are not violations of the law of war as they are usually considered. After World War II, Hitler's accountant, driver, or bodyguard were not tried. Other novel procedural issues: current commissions may be closed for the usual reasons relating to classified matters and for the safety of participants. Today, they may also be closed to the press and public to meet unspecified "national security interests" and "for any other reason necessary for the conduct of a full and fair trial."[5] In courts-martial, the defense may view any prosecution document related to the charges. In current military commissions, however, that right is circumscribed.[6] Other current procedures that differ from courts-martial

2 See David Glazier, *The Development of an Exceptional Court: The History of the American Military Commission*, in this volume.

3 See, e.g., U.S. Dep't of Def., Military Commission Order No. 1: Procedures for Trials by Military Commissions of Certain Non-United States Citizens in the War Against Terrorism § 3(B) (Mar. 21, 2002) (hereinafter Military Commission Order No. 1).

4 Office of Military Commissions, Charge Sheet, *U.S. v. Ibrahim Ahmed Mahmoud al Qosi* (Feb. 8, 2006), retrieved from http://www.defense.gov/news/d20080305-alqosi charges.pdf.

5 Military Commission Order No. 1, §6(D)(5); Jennifer Elsea, Cong. Research Serv., The Department of Defense Rules for Military Commissions: Analysis of Procedural Rules 7 (2003).

6 Military Commission Order No. 1, §6(D)(5).

include review and appeal procedures, the right to face one's accuser, and protections against unlawful command influence.

Military commissions, born of military necessity, were first raised in 1847 during the United States's War with Mexico (1846–48). The American commander, General Winfield Scott, faced lawlessness among his troops and the Mexican populace. The 1806 Articles of War were considered to not apply extraterritorially, leaving Scott with no means of punishing his own soldiers or Mexican nationals. His solution was to create military commissions out of whole cloth. Scott's commissions tried 400 U.S. soldiers for what would otherwise have been Article of War violations. It was during America's Civil War (1861–65), however, that military commissions took the shape we recognize today.[7]

2. Military Commissions Transformed

Today's military commission is a descendant of the Civil War–era Lieber Code, adopted in 1863 as Union Army General Orders 100. The Lieber Code was the first codification of the rules and customs of war written for soldiers in the field. It was fathered in small but critical part by General Henry W. Halleck, but written by Columbia University Professor Francis Lieber. Halleck recognized in General Scott's earlier military commissions a vehicle by which Confederate soldiers and their civilian sympathizers who took a direct part in hostilities could be prosecuted for violations of the laws of war. Seeking a route to the trial of rebel civilians by military tribunal, Halleck urged Lieber to include in his Code provisions for the prosecution of "war traitors."

In domestic courts, civilians could be tried for treason under Article III of the Constitution. Halleck, however, wanted captured civilians who took active roles on behalf of the Confederacy tried by the military, rather than civilian courts sympathetic to the rebel cause, of which there were many. But the offense of treason was not included in the 1806

7 For an excellent history of Civil War military commissions, see generally, Gideon M. Hart, *Military Commissions and the Lieber Code: Toward a New Understanding of the Jurisdictional Foundations of Military Commissions*, 203 Mil. L. Rev. 1–69 (2010).

Articles of War. In any event, absent martial law, civilians were not subject to military jurisdiction while the civilian courts were open. Halleck correctly foresaw, however, that military commissions would look to the Lieber Code for guidance in charging and trying civilians brought before them, were jurisdiction available – for example, during periods of martial law. For that reason, he was eager to have war traitors included in the Lieber Code and urged its author to do so. Lieber did, in Articles 90 and 91:

> A traitor under the law of war, or a war-traitor, is a person in a place or district under martial law who... gives information of any kind to the enemy, or holds intercourse with him... If his offense consists in betraying to the enemy anything concerning the condition, safety, operations, or plans of the troops holding or occupying the place or district, his punishment is death.[8]

With these charging provisions, the door was opened for a military commission metamorphosis from a simple disciplinary tribunal of Union soldiers to a forum for the prosecution of enemy law-of-war violators, be they combatants or civilians.

In September 1863 – five months after the Lieber Code was adopted – President Lincoln, with congressional concurrence, declared martial law in areas where hostilities were ongoing. Halleck, now General-in-Chief of the Union Armies, seized the opportunity to urge subordinate commanders to bring civilians charged with anti-Union acts before military commissions, despite open domestic courts. Military commissions flourished.

In a significant 1864 opinion, the Supreme Court ruled that it had no appellate jurisdiction over military-commission convictions, and commissions were soon seen as the accepted venue for the trial of enemies charged with violation of the laws and customs of war.[9] Throughout the Civil War and during Reconstruction, more than 2,000 were convened,[10]

8 Francis Lieber, Instructions for the Government of Armies of the United States in the Field, arts. 90–91 (1863) (hereinafter Lieber Code).

9 *Ex parte* Vallandingham, 68 U.S. 243, 251 (1864).

10 William Winthrop, Military Law and Precedents 834 (2d ed. 1920).

and they were not kangaroo courts. By 1864, military-commission convictions were reviewed by the newly formed Bureau of Military Justice. "Of the 341 files [cases] reviewed, forty-eight were reversed entirely, and 169 sentences were mitigated to some lesser punishment (rates of about fifteen and fifty percent respectively)."[11]

3. World War II Military Commissions

By World War II (1939–45), military commissions had become a congressionally enacted Article I trial forum in U.S. practice, validated by long use and appellate court approval.[12] They exist only in time of armed conflict, their subject-matter jurisdiction extends only to violations of the laws and customs of war, and their personal jurisdiction reaches only enemy fighters.

The four years following World War II were the apogee of commission proceedings. After Germany's surrender the Nuremberg International Military Tribunal convened, followed by Nuremberg's twelve "subsequent trials," conducted under Control Council Law #10, all of them military commissions. Commissions were conducted by all Allied States. Great Britain, Australia, France, the Netherlands, Poland, Norway, Canada, China, and Greece conducted a combined 1,166 proceedings. The number of Russian commissions has never been released, but is known to have been very large. The United States conducted about 500 in the European Theater of Operations and another 450 in the Pacific Theater.[13]

For some, the lasting impression of World War II military commissions is the dissent of Supreme Court Justice William F. Murphy in the

11 Hart, *supra* note 7, at 60.

12 An Article I court is raised by Congress under its authority in Article I, §8, of U.S. Constitution, as opposed to those courts authorized under Article III of the U.S. Constitution. The military commissions raised immediately after the 9/11 attacks were Art. II courts, established on the authority of the president. With Congress's passage of the Military Commissions Act of 2006, they were transformed into Art. III courts.

13 John A. Appleman, Military Tribunals and International Crimes (1954).

case of Japanese General Tomoyuki Yamashita: "[P]etitioner was rushed to trial under an improper charge," Murphy wrote, "given insufficient time to prepare an adequate defense, deprived of the benefits of some of the most elementary rules of evidence and summarily sentenced to be hanged."[14] A more accurate valedictory is found in the opening statement of Supreme Court Justice Robert H. Jackson, the American chief prosecutor at the Nuremberg IMT:

> The wrongs which we seek to condemn and punish have been so calculated, so malignant and so devastating, that civilization cannot tolerate their being ignored, because it cannot survive their being repeated. That four great nations, flushed with victory and stung with injury, stay the hands of vengeance and voluntarily submit their captive enemies to the judgment of the law, is one of the most significant tributes that Power has ever paid to Reason.[15]

By 1946, military commissions were recognized by all nations. Their broad customary use ensured there would be no repetition of the post–World War I Leipzig war crime trials. In those unsatisfactory 1921 proceedings, the Allies charged 895 former enemy individuals with war crimes, but allowed the defeated Germans to try their own citizens at Leipzig. Of the twelve actually tried, six were acquitted and six received light sentences.

Military commissions have no standing rules – no constant rules of procedure or evidence, no normative charges. That is because they may potentially be created by different senior commanders at differing times and locations. Each military commission iteration writes its own rules and raises its own charges. In 1942, this lack of mandated rules allowed for unsatisfactory procedures that saw captured Nazi saboteurs tried in secret and executed five days after their military commission ended. The Supreme Court affirmed the outcome three months after the petitioners

14 *Yamashita v. Styer*, 327 U.S. 1, 27–28 (1946).

15 International Military Tribunal, The Trial of German Major War Criminals: Opening Speeches of the Chief Prosecutors 3 (1946).

had been executed.[16] A lack of standing rules or charges similarly allowed General Douglas MacArthur to authorize rules of evidence permitting double and triple hearsay in the Yamashita military commission. An absence of standing rules also allowed for the reasonably fair conviction of nineteen senior Nazis at Nuremberg, on the basis of internationally agreed-on charges and procedural rules.[17]

In 2006, the Supreme Court wrote that military commissions were "not born of a desire to dispense a more summary form of justice than is afforded by courts-martial," but were instead, "tribunal[s] of necessity to be employed when courts-martial lacked jurisdiction over either the accused or the subject matter.... Exigency lent the commission its legitimacy, but did not further justify the wholesale jettisoning of procedural protections."[18] Domestic courts, with finely balanced rules of procedure and evidence, are not always equipped to deal with every aspect of enemy misconduct. In combat, evidence of war crimes is often collected, if at all, in an ammunition box or body bag that is heaved into a momentarily grounded medevac helicopter under enemy fire, and off-loaded at a tactical refueling point, to be damaged or lost at many stops between the scene of the offense and a judge advocate's office. Soldiers in contact with the enemy lack the legal luxury of a chain of custody for seized evidence. Marines in a 360-degree defensive position cannot take witness statements. Military commissions admit hearsay evidence because too often the maker of the statement is captured, wounded, or dead. There are valid reasons of military necessity a commission judge may find that "evidence having probative value to a reasonable person is admissible."[19]

16 *Ex parte* Quirin, 317 U.S. 1 (1942). The case also affirms the law of war as a basis for military-commission jurisdiction, eliminates citizenship as a factor in law-of-war prosecutions (two of the eight saboteurs were naturalized U.S. citizens), and narrows the application of *Ex Parte Milligan*. 71 U.S. (4 Wall.) 2 (1866).

17 The Legacy of Nuremberg 102–15 (David A. Blumenthal and Timothy L.H. Comstock eds., 2008).

18 *Hamdan v. Rumsfeld*, 548 U.S. 557, 624 (2006) (plurality opinion).

19 U.S. Dep't of Def., Manual for Military Commissions, United States pt. III, § IV, r. 402 (rev. ed. 2010) (hereinafter Manual for Military Commissions).

4. Postwar Developments Impact Military Commissions

Following World War II, the international community sought to strengthen legal regimes to avoid prosecutorial issues and abuses seen in some postwar commissions. The most significant innovation was the 1949 Geneva Conventions. Article 3, common to all four of the 1949 conventions, remains particularly important. Of the 429 articles in the 4 conventions, common Article 3 is the sole article applicable to internal armed conflicts – uprisings, sustained insurrections, civil wars, and insurgencies within the borders of a State. Article 3 outlines principles of humane treatment for those taking no part in the conflict and for those who are hors de combat. Although by its wording it applies only in internal armed conflicts, so basic are its humanitarian norms that today it is the minimum yardstick of international humanitarian law, applicable across the spectrum of all armed conflicts.[20] It also seeks to ensure that captured rebels are not subject to summary justice but are tried by regularly constituted courts. In 2006, it was common Article 3 to which the U.S. Supreme Court looked in determining the illegitimacy of American military commissions as then formed.

Article 102 of the 1949 Prisoners of War (POW) convention, applicable in international armed conflicts, portends significant change to trials of future POWs charged with pre-capture war crimes. Article 102 mandates that POWs can validly be tried only if their sentence is pronounced by the same courts, following trial by the same procedures, as members of the armed forces of the capturing State. Thus, if there were American-held POWs in the "war on terror," Article 102 would require they be tried just as U.S. military personnel would be: that is, by court-martial, subject to the charges and rules of procedure and evidence required by the *Manual for Courts-Martial*. These high standards certainly provide no motivation to designate captured al-Qaeda and Taliban fighters POWs, because in numerous cases pretrial detention and interrogation

20 *Prosecutor v. Delalić et al.*, Case No. IT-96–21-A, Judgment, ¶ 143 (Feb. 20, 2001).

techniques, the admissibility of incriminating pretrial statements, and other trial issues, would be ripe for attack by the defense.

The atrocities of World War II also gave birth to the human rights movement, another postwar development affecting today's military commissions. Geneva Convention IV, relating to the protection of civilians, was the first multinational treaty devoted exclusively to civilian victims of armed conflict. The 1949 Conventions also brought human rights-related changes to contemporary law of war. Convention IV's Articles 64–77, for example, detail trial procedures applicable to civilians in occupied territory. Although the term is not found in the Geneva Conventions, an unlawful combatant is a civilian who takes up arms and directly participates in armed conflict.[21] Unlawful combatants, such as Taliban and al-Qaeda fighters in Iraq and Afghanistan, lose their protected status as civilians and may be lawfully targeted while they are engaged in unlawful acts. Very early in the Afghan conflict, a few captured unlawful combatants were transported to Guantánamo Bay and confined there contrary to Article 49 of Convention IV.[22]

International human rights law, largely unknown until after World War II, burgeoned in the postwar years, complementing advances in the law of war represented by the 1949 Conventions. The growth of human rights law is evidenced in the 1948 Universal Declaration of Human Rights, the 1950 European Convention for the Protection of Human Rights, the 1966 International Covenant on Civil and Political Rights, and the 1969 American Convention on Human Rights – all human

21 The term "unlawful combatant," originating in a 1951 British Yearbook of International Law article, is obliquely alluded to in Article 51.3 of the 1977 Additional Protocol, referring to international conflicts.

22 "Individual... forcible transfers, as well as deportations of protected persons from occupied territory to the territory of the Occupying Power or to that of any other country... are prohibited, regardless of their motive." Geneva Convention Relative to the Protection of Civilian Persons in Time of War art. 49, Aug. 12, 1949, 6 U.S.T. 3516, 75 U.N.T.S. 287. The few Taliban and al-Qaeda fighters captured during periods of occupation, during which the Geneva Conventions applied in their entirety, were "protected persons." Their movement to Guantánamo constituted "deportation."

rights treaties. The battlefield effects of such treaties have been less direct than those of the 1949 Geneva Conventions. Still, an unintended fusion of international human rights law and international humanitarian law – the law of war – is a consequence of the late-twentieth-century concern for the protection of victims of armed conflict. Contrary to the European position, the United States insists that, on the battlefield, the law of armed conflict is the controlling *lex specialis* and that human rights law is applicable only to address the infrequent gaps in that *lex specialis*. Despite that frequently enunciated position, human rights law has assumed increasing relevance in U.S. combat zones. In Afghanistan today, U.S. combatants routinely photograph evidence of enemy bomb making and other violations of the law of armed conflict. They sometimes photograph enemy bodies to forestall abuse charges. Soldiers initiate evidentiary chains of custody, and take written statements for use at trial, all these procedures being related to human rights standards rather than mandated by the law of war. Applied to military commissions, the infusion of human rights concepts emphasizes their changed nature from informal field tribunals to more traditional criminal trials by another name; soldiers become policemen collecting evidence for the prosecution almost as much as they are fighters seeking enemy targets.

The two 1977 Additional Protocols to the 1949 Geneva Conventions are also significant. The 1977 Protocols were an effort to modernize the 1949 Conventions, influenced by nationalistic "freedom movements" of the 1970s and a widespread anticolonial mood. Although not ratified by the United States, Additional Protocol I has been ratified by 173 states; Additional Protocol II by 167 states. Both protocols contain numerous provisions now considered customary law. Article 75 of Additional Protocol I, "Fundamental guarantees," provides a list of prisoners' rights that sound in human rights law. These due process provisions have altered the way U.S. war fighters treat captured enemy fighters, requiring, for instance, that detainees be advised in their language of the reasons for their detention. Procedures specified for the prosecution of pre-capture offenses have reshaped military commission evidentiary rules and evidence-gathering procedures. No past conflict has seen such concern by combatants for the legal niceties of later prosecutions. Other Additional Protocol articles add a further suggestion of human rights' influence. Article 82 of Additional Protocol I requires that trained legal advisors be available to tactical commanders. Article 88 mandates cooperation between High Contracting Parties in the prosecution of individuals suspected of committing grave breaches. Article 6 of Additional Protocol II specifies procedures for "penal prosecutions" in non-international conflicts. These provisions, plus emergent human rights treaties combined with a greater international willingness to enforce international humanitarian law, have altered how prisoners are treated, confined, and tried.

5. 9/11: Post–World War II Developments Applied

There were no military commissions following the Korean and Vietnam conflicts because the United States held no suspects prisoner. The results of the juxtaposition of military commissions and post–World War II changes in the law of armed conflict would wait for the conflicts in Iraq and Afghanistan.

The 9/11 attacks on American soil were found to be armed attacks prohibited by the United Nations Charter, justifying armed response in self-defense under Article 51. A week after the attacks, the congressionally legislated Authorization for Use of Military Force (AUMF) was issued. It authorizes armed force "against those nations, organizations, or persons [the President] determines planned, authorized, committed, or aided the terrorist attacks that occurred on September 11, 2001, or harbored such organizations or persons." The broadly worded AUMF all but invited trials by military commission, which were initiated by President George W. Bush's Military Order of November 2001.[23] Those military commissions initially bore little resemblance to U.S. courts-martial.

23 Military Order, Detention, Treatment, and Trial of Certain Non-Citizens in the War against Terrorism, 66 Fed. Reg. 57,833 (Nov. 16 2001).

The first prisoners arrived at Guantánamo in January 2002, shortly after the U.S.–Afghanistan international armed conflict concluded and the occupation phase began. Six months later, Salim Ahmed Hamdan joined the Guantánamo "detainees." Meanwhile, several individuals designated "illegal enemy combatants" were held in U.S. military confinement facilities on the U.S. mainland, as well. Several of these early cases set the tone for much of the Byzantine military commission process that followed through the next decade.

In November 2005, shortly before Salim Hamdan's military commission was to convene at Guantánamo, the Supreme Court granted his petition for certiorari to decide military-commission jurisdiction and Geneva Convention applicability. The Court noted that common Article 3 of the 1949 Geneva Conventions is applicable to the war on terrorism:

> [T]here is at least one provision of the Geneva Conventions that applies here even if the relevant conflict is not one between [State] signatories. Article 3, often referred to as Common Article 3 . . . prohibits "the passing of sentences and the carrying out of executions without previous judgment pronounced by a regularly constituted court affording all the judicial guarantees which are recognized as indispensable by civilized peoples."[24]

The Court further found that the commissions established by the AUMF and President Bush's Military Order were unauthorized by law, were inconsistent with the Uniform Code of Military Justice, and were in violation of common Article 3 because they were not "regularly constituted courts."

With the *Hamdan* decision, it was clear that the post–World War II Geneva Conventions would significantly affect not only individuals seeking their protections, but also contemporary law of war. Other matters were decided by the *Hamdan* decision, but the applicability of common Article 3 to military commissions involving non-State-accused persons was a landmark ruling.

24 *Hamdan v. Rumsfeld*, 548 U.S. 557, 629–30 (2006) (plurality opinion).

6. The Military Commissions Act of 2006

The initial version of military commissions having been found unlawful in *Hamdan*, President Bush and Congress rushed to cure the deficiencies specified by the Court. The 2006 MCA,[25] enacted by Congress three months after *Hamdan*, was the new legislative blueprint for U.S. military commissions. Like its Military Order predecessor, the 2006 MCA remained a long step away from courts-martial.

The MCA incorporated a disturbingly broad definition of who constituted an enemy combatant – one that significantly exceeded any recent definition. It also held that no court, justice, or judge had jurisdiction to hear detainee habeas corpus applications. (With regard to pending habeas applications, the Supreme Court sidestepped the jurisdictional roadblock in *Boumediene v. Bush*.[26]) The MCA had no speedy trial requirement, although it did provide for an appeals procedure much like that for courts-martial. Conspiracy, without reference to an underlying criminal act, and material support of terrorism were made triable charges, although legally questionable. Classified "sources, methods, or activities" were protected from inquiry – a blow to defendants – although evidence derived from them would be admissible – a boon to prosecutors. Evidence obtained through cruel, inhuman, or degrading treatment was admissible if found to be probative and reliable. As with habeas petitions, no court, justice, or judge had jurisdiction to hear any action against the United States relating to any aspect of the detention or treatment of a detainee. The president could interpret the meaning and application of non-grave breach violations of the Geneva Conventions, effectively allowing him to define away such violations, including common Article 3 breaches.

One academic charged that the 2006 MCA contradicted the law of war by lowering the legal standard for the trial and treatment of detainees, redefining combatancy, creating new law-of-war offenses, and conflating

25 Military Commissions Act of 2006, Pub. L. No. 109–366, 120 Stat. 2600 (codified in scattered sections of 10, 18, 28, and 42 U.S.C. (2006)).

26 Boumediene v. Bush, 553 U.S. 723 (2008).

the law governing international and non-international armed conflicts.[27] Another commentator described it as "Orwellian."[28] Critics notwithstanding, Guantánamo military commissions began trying detainees. It was the 2006 MCA under which Salim Hamdan was tried.

U.S. federal courts beat the military to the initial prosecution punch, however. From the outset, there was confusion as to whether the war on terror should follow the military model or the law-enforcement model. Did the law of armed conflict's "kill or capture" ethos apply to the conflict, or did human rights law apply? Ultimately, both models were pursued: some prisoners held inside U.S. borders would be tried in federal courts; others, most of them captured on the battlefield and held in Guantánamo, would be tried by military commission.

John Walker Lindh, the "American Taliban," was captured in Afghan combat but tried in a federal court. In a 2002 plea agreement, Lindh pleaded guilty to supplying services to the Taliban and carrying explosives during the commission of a felony. He was sentenced to twenty years' confinement.[29] The trials of others accused of being or aiding terrorists followed. Yaser Hamdi, a dual citizen of Saudi Arabia and the United States, was captured in Afghanistan and transferred to military brigs where he was held in solitary confinement, without charges, for three years. He was designated an "illegal enemy combatant." After the Supreme Court ruled he must be allowed a trial, in 2004 Hamdi was simply released to return to Saudi Arabia.[30] In 2006, Zacarias Moussaoui, arrested in Minnesota in 2001, pleaded guilty to terrorism-related charges in his federal trial and was sentenced to six life terms without possibility of parole.[31] José Padilla, another illegal enemy combatant, was arrested

27 Jack M. Beard, *The Geneva Boomerang: The Military Commissions Act of 2006 and U.S. Counterterror Operations*, 101 Am. J. Int'l L. 56–64 (2007).

28 Michael C. Dorf, *The Orwellian Military Commissions Act of 2006*, 5 J. Int'l Crim. Just. 10, 12 (March 2007).

29 U.S. v. John Walker Lindh, 212 F. Supp. 2d 541 (E.D. Va. 2002).

30 Hamdi v. Rumsfeld, 542 U.S. 507 (2004).

31 *See* Neil A. Lewis, *Moussaoui Given Life Term by Jury over Link to 9/11*, N.Y. Times, May 4, 2006, at A5.

in Chicago in 2002 and held in military brigs for more than four years. In 2007, in a Virginia federal courtroom, Padilla was convicted of conspiracy to murder, kidnap, and maim, and was sentenced to seventeen years and four months' confinement.[32] Other civilian federal court cases followed, some involving Guantánamo detainees, some involving prisoners arrested in the United States, and others involving suspects captured on the battlefield. The logic of trial sites, military or civilian, was as confusingly inconsistent as were decisions of who would be tried in which system.

At Guantánamo in March 2007 – after Hamdi and Moussaoui had been tried and sentenced by federal courts – Australian David Hicks pleaded guilty to material support of terrorism as part of a plea agreement. His was the first military commission held since World War II commissions concluded. Captured in Afghanistan in 2001, Hicks was sentenced by a military jury to seven years' confinement, all but seven months suspended. He was released to serve his brief post-conviction confinement in Australia.

In 2008, Salim Hamdan, whose earlier Supreme Court case established the applicability of common Article 3 in military commissions, was re-charged and tried under the 2006 MCA. Convicted of material support of terrorism, he was sentenced to five and a half years. He received credit for sixty-one months of pretrial confinement, in keeping with U.S. court-martial practice. He was transferred to his native Yemen to serve his brief remaining confinement. (Immediately after Hamdan's trial, commission rules were changed to preclude sentencing credit for time served.) A series of Guantánamo military commissions followed with similar results: Ali al-Bahlul (the accused stood mute and, in 2008, was sentenced to imprisonment for life); Ibrahim al-Qosi (a 2010 guilty plea, he was sentenced to fourteen years' confinement with a secret pretrial agreement for release within two years and repatriation to

32 *See* Abby Goodnough & Scott Shane, *Padilla is Guilty on All Charges in Terror* Trial, NY Times, Aug. 17, 2007, at A1. Padilla, a lawful permanent resident of the U.S., was not subject to military commission jurisdiction under the Military Order of 2002 or the 2006 MCA.

Sudan); Omar Khadr (another 2010 guilty plea with a pretrial for eight years, seven to be served in his native Canada).

Stymied by domestic political opposition from either closing Guantánamo or trying detainees in federal courts within the United States, the president directed the resumption of military-commission trials at Guantánamo, the only other forum available.[33] The initial cases, few as they were (three prosecutions in the first seven years), might have smoothed commission processes and established precedents. Instead, they revealed troublesome legal and philosophic issues, as well as systemic flaws.

7. The Military Commissions Act of 2009 and Other Issues

In October 2009, under a new political administration, Congress revised the 2006 MCA,[34] enhancing an accused's rights, somewhat. The use of statements made under torture or cruel, inhuman, or degrading treatment was explicitly prohibited, and the circumstances under which hearsay evidence is admissible were more closely defined. Revisions also provide, however, that no accused may invoke the Geneva Conventions as a basis for a private right of action. The 2009 MCA was not the major course correction that the 2006 MCA was, but neither is it as aggressively contentious. It also brought military commissions a step closer to U.S. court-martial procedure, although retaining questionable 2006 MCA charges.

(a) Questions Regarding Military Commission Charges

The 2009 MCA reads: "The provisions of this subchapter codify offenses that have traditionally been triable by military commission. This

33 New Actions on Guantánamo and Detainee Policy (March 7, 2011), available at: www.whitehouse.gov/the-press-office/2011/03/07/fact-sheet-new-actions-guantanamo-and-detention-policy

34 The revision was part of the 2010 National Defense Authorization Act. Military Commissions Act of 2009, Pub. L. No. 111–84, 123 Stat. 2190 (codified as amended in scattered sections of 10 U.S.C.).

chapter does not establish new crimes that did not exist before the date of the enactment."[35] Nevertheless, there are questions regarding the legal legitimacy of some commission charges.

Murder in violation of the law of war, providing material support for terrorism, and conspiracy (three of the thirty-two charges prosecutors may bring)[36] remain troublesome. They certainly are not "traditionally" triable by military commissions. In fact, in 2012, a Federal Court of Appeals set aside Salim Hamdan's 2008 military commission conviction for material support for terrorism, finding that "the international law of war did not proscribe material support for terrorism as a war crime"[37] and, as to Hamdan, it was an ex post facto application of that 2006 MCA offense. Although an analysis of each controversial charge is beyond the scope of this chapter, there are well-reasoned arguments that the questioned charges are not internationally recognized violations of the laws and customs of war, and they should not be triable by military commission. Clearly, Congress may make such charges domestic crimes punishable in domestic courts, as some European states have.[38] A Military commission, however, is a forum for the prosecution of violations of the law of armed conflict, not domestic crimes. As the Supreme Court has opined, to constitute an offense under the laws and customs of war "the precedent must be plain and unambiguous. To demand any less would be to risk concentrating in military hands a degree of adjudicative and punitive power in excess of that contemplated either by statute or the Constitution."[39] More than a century ago the Court wrote, "Whether the offense as defined is an offense against the law of nations depends on the thing done, not on any declaration to that effect by Congress."[40]

35 10 U.S.C §950p(d).

36 MANUAL FOR MILITARY COMMISSIONS, *supra* note 19, pt. IV.

37 Salim Ahmed Hamdan v. United States, No. 11-1257 (D.C. Cir., Oct. 16, 2012).

38 ERLING JOHANNES HUSABØ & INGVILD BRUCE, FIGHTING TERRORISM THROUGH MULTILEVEL CRIMINAL LEGISLATION 97–192, 381 (2009).

39 Hamdan v. Rumsfeld, 548 U.S. 557, 601–02 (2006) (plurality opinion) (footnote omitted).

40 United States v. Arjona, 120 U.S. 479, 488 (1887).

The legitimacy of the Guantánamo charges will likely be settled only after years of litigation.

(b) Guantánamo's Internal Problems

As a trial forum, military commissions are consistent with international law and supported by American constitutional law and precedent, although civilian court proceedings have a greater legitimacy in the eyes of some. Recent U.S. practice demonstrates that civilian courts are equal to the most complex terrorist trials. Even in light of their excellent record in terrorism cases, however, federal courts are not always well configured for the prosecution of high-profile enemy fighters who encourage violence and seek martyrdom. Federal evidentiary rules regarding witness availability, chains of custody, the safeguarding of evidence, self-incrimination, and the disclosure of sensitive or classified information – among other issues – can raise problems easily resolved by military commissions. The current commissions clearly have their own stumbling blocks. As conceived by the 2001 AUMF, the 2001 Military Order, and the 2006 and 2009 MCAs, they are widely seen to be ill-conceived vehicles too often functioning outside both U.S. and international law. They have proved cumbersome, opaque in their operation, and excruciatingly slow. Beside persistent allegations of torture, signs of their ethical hollowness have been all too frequent.

In 2007, Marine Corps Lieutenant Colonel Colby Vokey, a Guantánamo defense counsel, charged that Bush administration officials abused the military-commission system, and called them "disgraceful" and "a sham." Also in 2007, Army Lieutenant Colonel Stephen Abraham, tasked with reviewing the status of Guantánamo detainees, alleged that exculpatory evidence was possibly withheld by the government from Combatant Status Review Boards – the panels that at that time decided detainees' suitability for trial – resulting in "fundamentally flawed" reviews. Army Lieutenant Colonel Darrel Vandeveld resigned as a military prosecutor in 2008, citing ethical concerns about failures to turn over exculpatory material to defense attorneys. A fellow prosecutor, Air Force

Major David Frakt, publicly charged "gross government misconduct" in a detainee case. Also in 2008, Guantánamo's chief prosecutor, Air Force Colonel Morris Davis, resigned his office and testified for the defense in the *Hamdan* case. He charged "that Pentagon officials interfered with prosecutors, exerted political pressure and approved the use of evidence obtained by torture."[41] Later, the judge in the *Hamdan* case, disqualified Guantánamo's legal advisor to the convening authority from acting in the case, ruling that Air Force Brigadier General Thomas Hartmann had exerted improper influence over prosecutors. In 2009, Guantánamo's military commission convening authority, civilian Susan Crawford – formerly a judge on the United States Court of Appeals for the Armed Forces – refused to refer to trial the case of Mohammed al-Qahtani. "'We tortured Qahtani,' said Crawford.... 'His treatment met the legal definition of torture. And that's why I did not refer the case.'... Crawford said detainee interrogation practices are a blot on the reputation of the United States and its military judicial system."[42] In late 2012, shortly after Hamdan's conviction for material support for terrorism was vacated, Brigadier General Mark Martins, Guantánamo's sixth chief prosecutor in ten years, refused to sign a Justice Department brief in another case because it charged the same material support charge that had already been found legally deficient. Time has not lessened the serious legal and ethical issues Guantánamo has raised and its future appears little brighter.

The war on terror forced difficult decisions on an unprepared government. Gaming the legal system, warping commission practice to achieve government goals, raising questionable offenses and calling them war crimes, and violating international law in the name of the law have harmed the nation, as well as future military commissions. Denunciations of the commissions by government lawyers and commission officials suggest a corruption of Guantánamo's trial process that renders it a sham in the

41 William Glaberson, *Ex-Guantánamo Prosecutor to Testify for Detainee*, N.Y. TIMES, Feb. 28, 2008, at A14.

42 Bob Woodward, *Detainee Tortured, Says U.S. Official*, WASH. POST, Jan. 14, 2009, at A1.

eyes of much of the international community and the American public. The often-heard response that all has been done in the name of national security is an insult to Americans. After all, a nation is what it stands for, at the time when standing for something is most difficult.[43]

Conclusion

What is the future of military commissions? As long as there are armed conflicts, simple utility and military necessity for such forums will mandate their use. Efforts have been made to bring increased fairness to Guantánamo proceedings, bending them away from overbearing governmental influences encountered in the past. Military and civilian men and women of unquestioned ethics and professionalism continue to labor to make the system fair and effective; to make it a relatively swift trial process with evidentiary and procedural standards that may be lowered, but are not hollow. Francis Lieber, Nuremberg prosecutors Justice Robert Jackson and Telford Taylor, and many others created and implemented military commissions that were firm but essentially fair to captured enemies. They can be so again.

In his 1945 opening statement to the Nuremberg International Military Tribunal, Justice Jackson said, "We must never forget that the record on which we judge these defendants is the record on which history will judge us tomorrow. To pass these defendants a poisoned chalice is to put it to our own lips as well."[44] His words remain true today.

43 Abby Mann, Judgment at Nuremberg 171 (1961).

44 International Military Tribunal, *supra* note 19, at 5.

4 Military Commissions and the Paradigm of Prevention

David Cole

WHY MILITARY COMMISSIONS? THAT IS THE CENTRAL question posed by President George W. Bush's decision to create the commissions in the first place, Congress's to authorize them twice in statutes enacted in 2006 and 2009, and President Barack Obama's to continue their use under his administration, notwithstanding his criticisms of them as a candidate. There is, no doubt, historical precedent for military commissions – but for the most part, that historical precedent involved materially different situations, in which military commissions were a matter of necessity, not discretion. Military commissions were employed, for example, where the military had ousted the existing government, and had to provide some venue for the enforcement of law as an occupying force. Moreover, their procedures have generally conformed to those of courts-martial. In the current circumstances, by contrast, there seems to be little or no necessity for military commissions. Most of the conduct charged and tried as war crimes in military commissions could be charged and tried in civilian criminal courts, under ordinary terrorism laws. If it is thought that a military court is particularly appropriate for the trial of war crimes, the preexisting and established system of courts-martial could have been employed.

Both the civilian criminal court and the court-martial are preferable venues for many reasons. They both have established track records. The United States has a robust civilian criminal justice system, in which many individuals have been tried successfully for terrorist crimes, both before and after September 11, 2001. The United States has an equally strong court-martial system, with rules of evidence that largely track those of civilian criminal courts, and in which thousands of criminal trials have been successfully conducted. The rules governing civilian criminal proceedings and courts-martial are clear, well settled, and have been subjected to and survived repeated constitutional testing. The judges are experienced in conducting trials. There is substantial precedent to guide their decisions, which decreases the likelihood of erroneous or arbitrary decision making, and in turn reduces the likelihood of long and costly appeals and retrials.

Perhaps most significantly, civilian criminal trials and courts-martial enjoy the imprimatur of legitimacy. American criminal procedure has its flaws, to be sure, but apart from its reliance on the death penalty, its criminal trial practices are not generally subject to criticism for the denial of basic human rights.[1] Both the civilian justice system and the court-martial proceedings afford defendants the right to: be notified of the charges, confront and rebut the evidence against them, a trial by a jury of one's peers, independent appellate review; the assistance of counsel; the privilege against compelled self-incrimination; and a panoply of other rights. Moreover, at least as a formal matter, the rules apply equally to all defendants. A foreign national being tried for a criminal offense in a civilian court or a court-martial has all the same trial rights that a U.S. citizen does. As a result, when an individual is convicted in either a civilian criminal court or a court-martial, there is a presumption that his conviction was warranted. Injustices occur, of course; but the burden is on the individual convicted to demonstrate that in his case injustice was done.

Military commissions, by contrast, are largely untested; the few military-commission proceedings that have been conducted at Guantánamo thus far have been rife with errors, misfires, and embarrassments. Military commissions are discriminatory on their face, as they

1 For a discussion of the many flaws of the American criminal justice system, in particular as it disparately affects racial minorities and the poor, *see* David Cole, No Equal Justice: Race and Class in the American Criminal Justice System (1999).

apply only to foreign nationals, not U.S. citizens accused of the very same conduct. In large part because the Bush administration's initial version of military commissions was patently invalid, their procedures are widely perceived as illegitimate. The military commissions have already gone through at least three separate iterations, and every attempt to proceed has been beset by countless problems. The initial post-9/11 commissions were created by a summary presidential order, supplemented by barely more detailed military orders. They allowed the introduction of testimony obtained through torture, permitted defendants to be tried effectively in absentia, and contemplated no judicial review. The president supervised the prosecution, judges, and defense, and was the final stage of appeal. When the Supreme Court ruled in 2006 that the original commissions violated the laws of war and the Uniform Code of Military Justice, in *Hamdan v. Rumsfeld*,[2] Congress responded with the 2006 Military Commissions Act (hereinafter 2006 Act). That act did relatively little to correct the procedural deficiencies in the military commissions, still permitted the introduction of coerced testimony, and treated conduct as "war crimes" that had never before been so recognized, including "material support" to terrorism and "conspiracy."

The few attempts to pursue military charges in military commissions under the 2006 Act were beleaguered by legal problems. Several military lawyers involved in the process resigned because of ethical concerns regarding interference with the process, the use of evidence obtained by torture, and attempts to conceal exculpatory evidence from defense counsel. Practically the only convictions obtained were through guilty pleas that effectively granted defendants a short fixed term and release from Guantánamo, a better deal than the indefinite detention they otherwise faced as "enemy combatants."[3] None of those tried were central

2 *Hamdan v. Rumsfeld*, 548 U.S. 557 (2006).

3 *See* Ben Wizner, Op-Ed, *Tribunals of the Absurd*, L.A. Times, Apr. 5, 2007, retrieved from http://articles.latimes.com/2007/apr/05/opinion/oe-wizner5. ("In an ordinary justice system, the accused must be acquitted to be released. In Guantánamo, the accused must plead guilty to be released – because even if he is acquitted, he remains an 'enemy

figures; more often than not, they were drivers or foot soldiers. When President Obama took office, Congress enacted the Military Commissions Act of 2009 (hereinafter 2009 Act), which improved the procedures substantially – but still fell short of providing the guarantees available in military courts-martial, continued to apply exclusively to foreign nationals, and still authorized charges for conduct that the rest of the world had never viewed as a war crime. As of this writing, the Obama administration has restarted military-commission proceedings against Khalid Sheikh Mohammed (KSM), the alleged mastermind of the 9/11 attacks. After an aborted military-commission proceeding brought against KSM by the Bush administration, the Justice Department under Obama initially decided to try him in a civilian criminal court in New York City. When political opposition mounted and Congress tied its hands by barring the expenditure of funds to bring Guantánamo detainees to the United States, even for a criminal trial, the Obama administration indicted KSM again before a military commission. Those proceedings have only begun, but if recent history is any indication, the new proceedings will again be tied up in knotty problems, for which there will be little if any precedent to guide the military judges who preside.

Why invite such trouble? If Guantánamo detainees have committed terrorist offenses, they can be tried in civilian criminal courts. If the president believes that some should be prosecuted for war crimes in a military venue, courts-martial could be employed for that task. In his May 2009 speech on national security at the National Archives, President Obama expressed a strong preference for civilian criminal trials, stating that "wherever feasible," those held at Guantánamo would be tried in civilian criminal court.[4] He retained the option of trials in military commissions, explaining:

combatant' subject to indefinite detention. Only by striking a deal does a detainee stand a chance of getting out.")

4 President Barack Obama, Remarks by the President on National Security (May 21, 2009) (transcript retrieved from http://www.whitehouse.gov/the_press_office/Remarks-by-the-President-On-National-Security-5-21-09/).

> Military commissions have a history in the United States dating back to George Washington and the Revolutionary War. They are an appropriate venue for trying detainees for violations of the laws of war. They allow for the protection of sensitive sources and methods of intelligence-gathering; they allow for the safety and security of participants; and for the presentation of evidence gathered from the battlefield that cannot always be effectively presented in federal courts.[5]

Do these justifications warrant the use of military commissions? In this chapter, I maintain that they do not. In the end, the impetus behind the military commissions is the hope – in my view, unsupported – that the commissions may permit easier convictions of individuals, and may allow prosecutors to avoid confronting the consequences of the United States's systemic reliance on torture and cruel, inhuman, and degrading tactics in its interrogations of detainees. In this respect, the commissions are best understood not as a legitimate forum for trying war crimes, but as an avenue for short circuiting legal processes that might hold us accountable for our wrongs.

The military commissions are a by-product of the "paradigm of prevention," a term coined by then-Attorney General John Ashcroft for the post-9/11 emphasis on aggressively preventing future terrorism, rather than responding to crime after the fact. That approach stressed early intervention and aggressive gathering of intelligence about future threats, and therefore led government officials to sweep broadly, presume guilt without substantial evidence, detain innocents, and adopt "enhanced interrogation techniques" to coerce detainees into talking. Those choices, in turn, have greatly complicated and compromised the task of holding terrorists accountable, because such illegal shortcuts on investigatory rules taint any evidence obtained therefrom, and make it inadmissible in a criminal trial.

The military commissions reflect an ill-advised effort to avoid paying the price for the paradigm of prevention. That goal is an illegitimate one,

5 *Id.*

and will in the end leave the commissions – and any convictions obtained in them – fundamentally tainted. Absent a willingness both to reckon candidly with the United States's own past wrongs, and to proceed in the future under fundamentally fair trial procedures, the military commissions are likely to disserve our security interests and undermine our constitutional principles.

1. The Asserted Justifications for Military Commissions

President Obama offered four justifications for the use of military commissions: (1) they are an appropriate forum for trying war crimes; (2) they "allow for the protection of sensitive sources and methods of intelligence-gathering"; (3) they are more secure; and (4) their evidentiary rules are more tolerant, recognizing that evidence gathered from the battlefield cannot be expected to meet the requirements we impose in civilian criminal courts. These rationales are not frivolous, and may well justify military commissions in certain circumstances. But they do not suffice to justify the military commissions in the form they take under the 2009 Act and as they have been and are being employed by the military at Guantánamo.

Military commissions have been used to try individuals for war crimes, but they are generally restricted to situations of necessity, where other courts are unavailable. Thus, for example, the United States first employed military commissions during the Mexican War, in order to maintain order in occupied territory where neither U.S. civilian courts nor courts-martial had jurisdiction.[6] They were used during the Civil War with mixed results, sometimes properly employed to try war crimes subject to procedures equivalent to those provided in courts-martial, but other times used, it appeared, to ensure convictions.[7] When President Lincoln sought to use a military commission to try a civilian accused of

6 *See* David Glazier, *The Development of an Exceptional Court: The History of the American Military Commission*, in this volume.

7 *Id.*

supporting the rebel forces, the Supreme Court held that he had overstepped his authority, and that civilians could not be tried in a military commission where the civilian courts were open and ready for business.[8] Military commissions were used during the Philippines Insurrection of 1899–1902, but their procedures conformed to those in courts-martial, and they used the same rules of evidence used in civilian courts.[9] Thus, military commissions are most legitimate when used as a matter of necessity, and without departing significantly from the procedural practices in other courts.

There are exceptions to this pattern, to be sure. The most prominent – and the most dubious – is the military commission that President Franklin D. Roosevelt created to try Nazi saboteurs who landed in the United States in a German U-boat, crossed the border wearing civilian clothes, and planned to blow up munitions factories. The saboteurs could have been tried in civilian courts for their crimes, and civilian courts were certainly open for business. Roosevelt had them tried in a military commission, empowered to create its own rules, with an appeal only to him, because he feared that a civilian criminal trial would not lead to a sufficient penalty. There is also evidence that the government did not want it known that the men were discovered only because one of the saboteurs chose to turn on his partners and reveal the conspiracy to the Federal Bureau of Investigation (FBI).[10] The trials were held behind closed doors in the Justice Department, and most of the saboteurs were sentenced to death. The Supreme Court took up an extraordinary habeas review of the tribunal while it was underway, affirmed the tribunal's jurisdiction in a summary order one week later, and did not write its decision justifying its result until after the defendants had been executed.

It is far from clear that military commissions are a matter of necessity for trials of most of those held at Guantánamo. In the case of KSM,

8 *Ex Parte* Milligan, 71 U.S. (4 Wall.) 2 (1866).

9 *Id.* at 16.

10 Louis Fisher, *Military Commissions: Problems of Authority and Practice*, 24 B. U. Int'l L. J. 15, 34–39 (2006).

for example, the United States was fully prepared to try him and his coconspirators in a civilian criminal court in Manhattan; in fact, the Justice Department determined that a civilian criminal trial was the more appropriate forum. If they can be tried in a civilian criminal court, however, it is not even clear that we should be able to resort to military commissions, because in that context, the commissions are evidently not a matter of necessity. Most war crimes are also a federal crime prosecutable in civilian criminal court.[11] The most frequent charge thus far in the military commissions has been the provision of material support to terrorism, but federal criminal law also prohibits material support to terrorist groups, including Al Qaeda, as well as material support for terrorist acts.[12] In some instances, these domestic laws may not have had a sufficient extraterritorial reach at the time Guantánamo detainees engaged in the conduct for which they might be charged. If their conduct was nonetheless a war crime, then a military forum might be the only venue in which they could be tried; but in that case, military courts-martial would be available. In many instances, in any event, individuals could be tried in civilian criminal court for violating federal laws. If a detainee's conduct could be prosecuted in civilian criminal court, or even in a court-martial, the administration must point to some rationale other than the appropriateness of military commissions for war crimes to justify proceeding in a military commission.

The second rationale President Obama advanced – the need to protect sensitive sources and methods of intelligence-gathering – also provides little support for using military commissions. Federal civilian courts are well acquainted with classified information and maintaining secrecy where warranted. Under the Foreign Intelligence Surveillance Act, federal judges hear classified requests for orders authorizing wiretapping and searches for foreign-intelligence and counterterrorism purposes.[13] Under

11 18 U.S.C. § 2441 (2006).

12 18 U.S.C. §§ 2339A, 2339B, 2339C (2006).

13 50 U.S.C. § 1801 (2007). *See* William C. Banks, *Exceptional Courts in Counterterrorism: Lessons from the Foreign Intelligence Surveillance Act (FISA)*, in this volume.

the Classified Information Procedures Act (CIPA), federal courts handle and assess classified information related to criminal trials.[14] In the habeas corpus proceedings reviewing Guantánamo detentions that federal courts in the District of Columbia have been conducting, the federal courts routinely consider classified information, and attorneys for both sides have access to the information and may rely on it in their briefs, as long as they are filed under seal. Thus far, there have been no reports of mishaps or leaks. By contrast, virtually all of the military's secret intelligence assessments of Guantánamo detainees were disclosed to WikiLeaks, allegedly by a military intelligence operative, and then released by WikiLeaks and several news outlets to the general public. Thus, it is far from clear that the military process has any distinct advantage over civilian courts when it comes to keeping secrets.

If President Obama meant that trials in military commissions might permit individuals to be tried and convicted on evidence without disclosing its source, it is not clear that the military commission rules make that possible. The treatment of classified evidence in military commissions under the 2009 Act is closely modeled on the CIPA rules that govern civilian criminal trials, and those rules appear to provide no advantage to using military commissions. Moreover, any such shortcut would very likely deprive the defendant of the fundamental elements of a fair trial. If due process applies to the Guantánamo military commissions – and it is likely to, given the extension of habeas corpus there – the prosecution will not be able to conceal sources and methods of evidence gathering wherever access to those sources and methods is necessary to confront the evidence used against the defendant. As a matter of due process and fundamental fairness, defendants would presumably be entitled to know, for example, whether any evidence used against them was obtained from coerced testimony, or from a lead generated through coerced testimony. They would also presumably be entitled to know the identity of their accusers, because without that information one cannot meaningfully

14 18 U.S.C. app. §§ 1–16 (2011).

challenge the reliability of what has been said. Any trial in which such information was denied to the defense would very likely be viewed as illegitimate – and properly so. Thus, it is simply not evident that military commissions, if they are to be fair, will be able to protect sensitive sources and methods any more robustly than civilian criminal trials.

The third rationale President Obama offered for military commissions is that the proceedings can be made more secure for the participants, presumably because they can be held on a military base, far from a civilian population, and subject to the security measures the military can provide. It is certainly plausible that it would be easier to hold a secure trial at Guantánamo than in the heart of Manhattan, but the difference is really a geographic one and has nothing to do with the difference between a military and civilian trial. A civilian trial at Guantánamo would be easier to make secure than a military trial in Manhattan. Congress could presumably authorize a federal civilian court to conduct trials at Guantánamo, just as a federal civilian court conducted certain legal proceedings in Berlin after the war.[15]

Fourth, President Obama reasoned that military commissions might admit and consider evidence gathered from the battlefield that could not satisfy the rigorous requirements that apply to evidence in a civilian criminal court. There may well be some situations in which this will prove a salient difference. But courts-martial have for years dealt with situations that arise on or near battlefields, and they apply largely the same evidentiary rules as civilian criminal trials. Moreover, many of the detainees at Guantánamo were not picked up on a battlefield at all, but were captured far from any battlefield, or were turned over by bounty hunters. For the vast number of detainees not captured on the field of battle, Obama's fourth rationale would be inapplicable, and the administration has offered no reason why the government should be permitted to avoid ordinary evidentiary requirements in such cases. Those requirements, after all, are designed only to ensure the accuracy and reliability

15 *United States v. Tiede*, 86 F.R.D. 227 (1979).

of evidence; they were not created simply to impose meaningless obligations on government. Short circuiting them comes at a cost to reliability – a cost that may arguably be warranted in some battlefield situations, but not otherwise.

Finally, and perhaps most importantly, the fact that military commissions are applicable only to foreign nationals accused of war crimes, and not to U.S. citizens accused of the same crimes, undermines all of the above arguments. If a military commission is appropriate to try foreign nationals for war crimes, why would it not be equally appropriate to try U.S. nationals? Concerns about sources and methods, the security of the proceedings, and the difficulties of evidence gathering on the battlefield are exactly the same whether the defendant is a U.S. citizen or a foreign national. But we have committed to trying U.S. citizens accused of war crimes in civilian criminal courts. John Walker Lindh, the so-called American Taliban, captured on the battlefield in Afghanistan, was tried in a civilian criminal court for material support, not in a military commission. If the civilian criminal court system is sufficient for trying U.S. citizens, it is sufficient for trying foreign nationals, as well.[16]

2. Military Commissions as an Outgrowth of the Preventive Paradigm

The poverty of the asserted justifications for military commissions suggests that what is really at stake is some other, unstated interest. Some advocates of using military commissions appear to be driven by an ideological commitment to military commissions as a fundamental feature of the "war paradigm." The view that the struggle with Al Qaeda is properly understood as a war, and that therefore civilian criminal law measures are inappropriate, no doubt motivates some of the commentators who insist on the use of military tribunals. But that is not President Obama's view, and does not accurately reflect President Bush's practice. Both President

16 *A (FC) and Others v. Secretary of State for the Home Department*, (2004) UKHL 56.

Bush and Obama's administrations have prosecuted Al Qaeda-related would-be terrorists in civilian criminal court; neither took the position that civilian criminal measures were inappropriate ab initio for terrorism cases, or for Al Qaeda terrorism cases.[17]

What seems a more likely motive for the persistence of military commissions is the hope that by employing such commissions, the United States might avoid paying the costs of its imprudent resort to illegal tactics in pursuing the paradigm of prevention. In a meeting on September 12, 2001, at the White House recounted by Bob Woodward in *Bush at War*, FBI Director Robert Mueller was briefing the National Security Council on the events of the day before, and stressing the need to investigate in a manner that did not taint the evidence. At that point, Woodward reports, Ashcroft interrupted: "'Let's stop the discussion right here. The chief mission of U.S. law enforcement,' he added, 'is to stop another attack and apprehend any accomplices or terrorists before they hit us again. *If we can't bring them to trial, so be it.*'"[18]

In the days that followed, the Bush administration followed Ashcroft's advice, not Mueller's. But whereas the administration readily adopted Ashcroft's prescription for prevention, it was less willing to accept his "so be it" with regard to prosecution. The military commissions can be understood as an attempt to act preventively *and* bring those captured to trial, to avoid the trade-off that Ashcroft suggested was necessary and warranted.

The Bush administration wholeheartedly embraced the paradigm of prevention. In the first days, months, and years after 9/11, it used a variety of mechanisms to detain individuals before they committed an act of terrorism. By definition, this meant sweeping broadly, because the government could not, of course, predict who would actually commit a terrorist act if left free. In the United States, Ashcroft oversaw an aggressive deployment of immigration law, the "material witness" statute, and

17 *See, e.g.*, *United States v. Padilla*, 508 U.S. 77 (1993); *United States v. Lindh*, 212 F.Supp. 2d 541 (E.D.Va. 2002); *United States v. Ghailani*, 761 F.Supp.2d 167 (S.D.N.Y. 2011).

18 Bob Woodward, Bush at War 42 (2002) (emphasis added).

pretextual prosecutions in the first two years after 9/11 that led to the detention of more than 5,000 foreign nationals suspected, often on the slimmest of reeds, of possibly being involved in terrorism.[19] Nearly all were Arab or Muslim men. Of the 5,000 detained, none were actually charged and convicted of any act of terrorism. Most were held on immigration charges, often exceedingly technical. Many were held without any evidence that they actually posed any danger to the community, much less of terrorism.

Beyond our borders, the Bush administration followed a similar policy of sweeping detention. It brought 779 "terror suspects" to Guantánamo. The administration insisted initially that these detainees were the "worst of the worst," and claimed that they had been carefully screened, but by the time the Bush administration had left office it had released more than 500 of them. It had little or no reliable evidence that many of these individuals were in fact dangerous, and when the Supreme Court ruled that the detainees were entitled to review the legality of their detentions in court, the Bush administration started releasing many of those it had once claimed were the worst of the worst. The majority were not captured by U.S. forces, but were turned in by others, often to obtain bounties that were equivalent to a year's salary in Afghanistan. Secret military intelligence assessments of the risk posed by each detainee, disclosed by WikiLeaks in 2011, revealed that the military classified many as "high risk" but released them anyway, and that the assessments were often on the basis of unreliable statements obtained through coercion, without any acknowledgment by the military that the statements might be unreliable.[20]

19 *See* David Cole, Enemy Aliens: Double Standards and Constitutional Freedoms in the War on Terrorism (2003); David Cole and Jules Lobel, Less Safe, Less Free: Why America Is Losing the War on Terrorism (2007).

20 Charlie Savage, William Glaberson, and Andrew Lehren, *Classified Files Offer New Insight into Detainees*, NY Times, Apr. 24, 2011, at A1; Scott Shane and Benjamin Weiser, *Judging Detainees' Risk, Often with Flawed Evidence*, NY Times, Apr. 24, 2011, retrieved from http://www.nytimes.com/2011/04/25/world/guantanamo-files-flawed-evidence-for-assessing-risk.html?_r=1&pagewanted=all.

The administration's broad-brush preventive approach in turn placed tremendous pressure on using interrogation as an intelligence-gathering mechanism. Law enforcement and intelligence agents generally prefer not to detain suspects prematurely, because once one does so, the suspect and his accomplices know that the government is aware of their activities. In the absence of imminent danger, it is far better to maintain surveillance, both from an intelligence perspective and from the standpoint of gathering admissible evidence to prosecute. Such surveillance is more likely to provide a better understanding of the scope of the conspiracy or illegal scheme. If, in the name of prevention, suspects are detained prematurely and on scant information, then the only way to gather intelligence from them may be interrogation.

At the same time, if one sweeps broadly, many of those detained are likely to be innocent and may well lack any information regarding true threats. If so, interrogation will often prove frustrating, as interrogators confront "suspects" who actually have nothing to tell them. Moreover, an ideologically driven opponent is likely to be less willing to share information than an ordinary criminal defendant, so it will be difficult to distinguish those genuine suspects who have information and are not sharing it from mistaken suspects who simply have nothing to share.

These circumstances quickly led the Bush administration to entertain the possibility of employing harsh interrogation tactics. In August 2002, the Justice Department – with the approval of President Bush and Vice President Cheney – authorized the Central Intelligence Agency (CIA) to use "enhanced interrogation techniques," including slamming suspects into walls, sleep deprivation of up to eleven days straight, painful stress positions, confinement in small boxes, and waterboarding in order to obtain information from "high-value detainees" who had been "disappeared" into CIA secret prisons. A few months later, Defense Secretary Donald Rumsfeld authorized interrogators at Guantánamo to use similar, although somewhat less extreme, tactics. These tactics were used for more than 100 days straight on one Guantánamo detainee, Mohammed al Qahtani, to such an extent that the military's own prosecutor, Susan

Crawford, determined that she had to dismiss a war crimes case against him because al Qahtani had been tortured. After the officer in charge at Guantánamo visited Abu Ghraib, similar tactics "migrated" there. The administration also adopted a policy of "extraordinary rendition," in which suspects were kidnapped and delivered to security officials in countries such as Syria, Egypt, and Jordan, to be interrogated using the very torture tactics that the United States State Department has long condemned in those countries.

The Bush administration justified all of these tactics in the name of preventing the next attack. There is no evidence that the tactics actually preempted any actual attacks. As noted previously, none of the 5,000 foreign nationals preventively detained in the United States was convicted of a terrorist offense. The CIA's own inspector general, in a study of the enhanced interrogation tactics, found no evidence that the coercive tactics obtained information that lawful interrogation could not have obtained. Indeed, in many instances the inspector general could not disentangle information obtained from legal and coercive tactics. President Bush and Vice President Cheney claimed repeatedly that the tactics had "saved lives," but never identified a single specific instance in which that claim could be verified. After a naval special-operations team killed Osama bin Laden in May 2011, some of those who authorized torture argued that their tactics had led to the discovery of bin Laden's hiding place by helping identify the courier that eventually led investigators to bin Laden, but the facts do not support their self-interested claim. KSM and Abu Faraj al-Libi were subjected to enhanced interrogation tactics, but neither is reported to have identified the courier. In fact, both provided affirmatively misleading information regarding the courier after they were subjected to enhanced interrogation techniques. Neither provided any information at all about the courier in direct response to the enhanced interrogation techniques, but only long afterward, in response to ordinary questioning.[21]

21 *See* Dan Froomkin, *Torture May Have Slowed Hunt for Osama, not Hastened It*, Huffington Post (May 6, 2011, 4:48 PM), retrieved from http://www.huffingtonpost.com/2011/05/06/torture-may-have-slowed-h_n_858642.html; Andrew Sullivan, *The Big Lie,*

Whether or not such tactics – illegal detentions, renditions, torture, and cruel, inhuman, and degrading treatment – resulted in useful information is at best debatable. It is indisputable, however, that because they are illegal, they taint any evidence obtained from their deployment. As a result, such information would plainly be inadmissible in a civilian criminal court – or a court-martial, where similar rules of exclusion apply. Moreover, even if the government attempts to make its case without relying affirmatively on any tainted evidence, defendants who have been subjected to such tactics are almost certain to seek to use it in their defense. It might support a claim that as a result of their mistreatment, they are no longer mentally competent to stand trial. The use of such tactics on a systemic basis calls into question virtually any evidence the government gathers subsequently, as much of it may be linked back, through some chain of leads or "mosaic," to the use of torture or coercive interrogation. Defense lawyers would be ineffective if they did not aggressively pursue discovery of potentially exculpatory evidence regarding these practices and their potential impact on any evidence the government sought to introduce.

As anyone with foresight would have predicted, the administration could not really accept the consequences of Ashcroft's "so be it" statement of bravado. There are substantial moral, political, and legal pressures to bring to justice those who have perpetrated acts of terrorism. The United States cannot responsibly leave unprosecuted those who attacked it on September 11 and killed 3,000 innocent civilians. But how, for example, does the United States try KSM after he has been disappeared into a secret prison for years, and waterboarded 183 times?

Military commissions were the Bush administration's answer. As initially formulated by the executive branch, the commissions would permit defendants to be tried on the basis of coerced testimony. When the Supreme Court declared President Bush's military commissions to be in violation of the Uniform Code of Military Justice and Common Article 3

Ctd, The Daily Beast (May 4, 2011, 11:29 AM), retrieved from http://andrewsullivan.thedailybeast.com/2011/05/the-big-lie-.html.

of the Geneva Conventions, Congress enacted the MCA of 2006. This act prohibited admission of statements acquired through torture, but permitted statements coerced through mistreatment short of torture so long as a military judge deemed it "reliable."[22]

In 2009, Congress again amended the rules governing military commissions, and tightened the rules for admissibility of an accused's statements. The 2009 Act categorically prohibits the introduction of any statement obtained through torture or cruel, inhuman, or degrading treatment.[23] It generally requires that an accused's prior statements can be introduced only if deemed voluntary – which is what the Supreme Court has long ruled that due process requires in civilian criminal trials.[24] But it still makes an exception, permitting even involuntary statements if the military judge finds that "the statement was made incident to lawful conduct during military operations at the point of capture or during closely related active combat engagement, and the interests of justice would best be served by admission of the statement."[25] This exception appears to be narrow, and presumably would not apply to statements obtained at CIA "black sites" or at Guantánamo, as these would not meet the requirement that they be at the point of capture or during closely related active combat engagement. Thus, although the commission rules were initially designed to permit the introduction of coerced testimony, thereby allowing the government to avoid paying the cost of its illegal interrogation tactics, under the current rules that particular loophole has largely been closed.

The military commissions, however, continue to seek to further the government's paradigm of prevention in still another way – they permit prosecution for conduct that was in fact not a crime when it took place, and that is not a war crime at all. The 2009 Act, like the 2006 Act, makes it a crime, for example, to provide "material support or resources to an

22 Military Commissions Act of 2006, 10 U.S.C. §§948(a)–(d) (2006).

23 Military Commissions Act of 2009, 10 U.S.C. § 948r(a) (2009).

24 *Rogers v. Richmond*, 365 U.S. 534 (1961); *Ashcraft v. Tennessee*, 322 U.S. 143 (1944).

25 10 U.S.C. § 948r(c)(2)(A).

international terrorist organization engaged in hostilities against the United States."[26] The international laws of war, however, have never recognized material support as a war crime. The statute also permits prosecution for conspiracy to engage in any other war crime, including material support. In *Hamdan*, the Court's four-Justice plurality concluded that conspiracy was not a war crime under the laws of war.[27] Justice Kennedy, the fifth vote, deemed it unnecessary to reach the issue. If these "crimes" are not recognized internationally by the laws of war, two issues arise: (1) may Congress, pursuant to its authority to define offenses against the law of nations, enact war crimes that in fact have no foundation in the laws of war; and (2) even if Congress has the power to expand the scope of war crimes, if these acts were not recognized as war crimes by the laws of war, application of the 2009 Act to acts committed prior to its enactment constitutes ex post facto punishment.

The administration's interpretation and enforcement of other war crimes has also raised serious legal questions about its misuse of the law of war. David Glazier argues convincingly, for example, that the United States has effectively sought to make fighting for the other side itself a war crime.[28] Thus, in its prosecution of Omar Khadr, a young Canadian captured on the battlefield after shooting an American soldier, the government argued that Khadr had committed murder and attempted murder in violation of the laws of war by merely engaging in battle against the United States military on behalf of Al Qaeda.[29] The United States's theory appears to be that because Al Qaeda does not have the privilege of belligerency, any fighting anyone engages in on its behalf, even when targeted at combatants, is a war crime. In this view, it is a war

26 10 U.S.C. § 950t(25)(A).

27 *Hamdan v. Rumsfeld*, 548 U.S. 557 (2006).

28 David Glazier, *Still a Bad Idea: Military Commissions under the Obama Administration* 9–11 (Loyola-LA Legal Studies Paper No. 2010–32), pp. 65–86.

29 *See*, Kent Roach, *The Law Working Itself Pure? The Canadian Experience with Exceptional Courts and Guantánamo*, in this volume. *See also* David Glazier, *A Court Without Jurisdiction: A Critical Assessment of the Military Commission Charges against Omar Khadr* (Loyola-LA Legal Studies Paper No. 2010–37).

crime for Al Qaeda to fight, and the law of war would become a sword under which the United States can shoot to kill their combatants, but they can't shoot back at U.S. combatants. The government's approach, Glazier argues, "repudiates the functional equivalence between the conflict parties which is a core element of the [law of armed conflict], and endeavors to transform it into a unilateral shield for one side."[30]

As Glazier explains, the law of war does not make killing combatants a war crime, unless it is done in particularly egregious ways.[31] An unprivileged belligerent may be tried for murder if he kills a combatant, or attempted murder for trying to do so, but only as a domestic law matter, in a civilian court – not as a war crime in a military commission. Glazier quotes law-of-war expert Yoram Dinstein, who writes in his treatise on the law of armed conflict: "With unlawful combatants, [the law of armed conflict] refrains from stigmatizing the acts as criminal. It merely takes off a mantle of immunity from the defendant, who is therefore accessible to penal charges for any offense committed against the domestic legal system."[32] The International Committee of the Red Cross takes the same view.[33]

In October 2012, the administration faced yet another roadblock to prosecution in the military commissions, when the U.S. Court of Appeals for the D.C. Circuit reversed the military-commission conviction of Yasir Hamdan, Osama bin Laden's driver, on the ground that providing material support to terrorism was not a war crime under the international laws of war when Hamdan engaged in the conduct charged.[34] Under the court's rationale, it is also possible that charges of "conspiracy" to commit

30 Glazier, *supra* note 28, at 77.

31 It is a war crime, for example, to use a prohibited weapon, such as poison or to kill by means of treachery or perfidy. Glazier, *supra* note 28, at 70–71.

32 Glazier, *supra* note 28, at 72 (quoting Yoram Dinstein, The Conduct of Hostilities Under the Law of International Armed Conflict 200 [2004]).

33 Glazier, *supra* note 28, at 72–73 (quoting International Committee of the Red Cross, Interpretive Guidance on the Notion of Direct Participation in Hostilities Under International Humanitarian Law 83–84 [2009]).

34 *Hamdan v. United States*, 696 F.3d 1238 (D.C. Cir. 2012).

war crimes will not be triable in the military commissions. The government has petitioned for rehearing en banc. If the decision stands, the military will be able to try far fewer Guantánamo detainees in military commissions.

The United States's attempt to stretch the concept of war crimes in these ways is particularly telling in light of the fact that Al Qaeda fighters' status as unprivileged belligerents means that they have no "privilege of belligerency" and are therefore subject to ordinary domestic prosecution. It suggests a strong incentive to try detainees in military commissions. That incentive, it seems, cannot be explained by any of the rationales President Obama has set forth. Even if military commissions were especially appropriate for the trial of war crimes, as opposed to courts-martial, the fact that many of the crimes defined by Congress and charged by the executive are not in fact legitimate war crimes directly undermines that rationale. It appears that the real motive for employing military commissions is a sense that convictions will be easier to obtain – and that is hardly a legitimate justification for affording second-class justice. That motive, in turn, may be driven by the preventive rationale; one way to make the law more effectively "preventive" is to reduce or eliminate safeguards for criminal defendants while expanding the scope of conduct subject to criminal prosecution. The military commissions do just that.

Conclusion: Transparency, Accountability, and Fair Process

Even the physical design of the Guantánamo courtroom where military commission trials are conducted is shaped by the desire to conceal the government's own abuses. A soundproof glass wall separates the onlookers from the trial participants, so that the only way an observer can hear what is going on is through headphones with a forty-second delay. The reason, according to Denny LeBoeuf – an ACLU lawyer advising on the defense of several detainees – is "the Rule: detainees are forbidden from speaking about their torture."[35] Even in pretrial proceedings, the wall

35 Mark P. Denbeaux and Jonathan Hafetz, eds., The Guantanamo Lawyers: Inside a Prison Outside the Law (2009), p. 196.

has been employed to block public transmission of information the military wants to keep secret – and the central secrets they seek to preserve are the details of the defendant's mistreatment and torture at U.S. hands. Remarkably, the U.S. government has declared "classified" anything that the detainees say about their torture, and has required the lawyers, as a condition of access to their clients, to keep secret all details of their clients' treatment. But of course, the United States cannot compel the detainees themselves not to speak of the unspeakable. The only way it can keep them from telling their stories is by keeping them detained, behind bars, behind glass, silenced.

That soundproof wall is an apt symbol for the United States's choice to use military commissions at all. It was and remains driven not by necessity, as war crimes may be tried in courts-martial, and most acts of terrorism that target or affect the United States or its citizens are crimes prosecutable in civilian criminal court. Rather, the choice to employ military commissions is driven by a sense that in some cases, we want to hold individuals responsible even where we lack admissible evidence establishing their guilt. The military commissions originally permitted reliance on statements obtained by torture. Today, tortured testimony is excluded, but the commission procedures still fall short of those provided in courts-martial. If they didn't, there would be no need for them, as they would be entirely duplicative. The government has yet to offer any legitimate rationale for seeking an easier avenue to convictions. None of the justifications President Obama advanced withstand scrutiny. One is left feeling that the commissions are, in the end, nothing more than a way to get around the deal John Ashcroft advocated, and the Bush administration accepted, on September 12, 2001: "If we can't bring them to trial, so be it." That deal no longer looks so good, and the military commissions are an attempt to bring them to trial notwithstanding our own violations of law.

That strategy, however, is not sustainable. Any convictions obtained through military commissions are exceedingly likely to be viewed as illegitimate by much of the world. As such, they are likely to play into Al Qaeda's hands, much as our interrogation tactics at Abu Ghraib, the CIA black sites, and Guantánamo itself offered Al Qaeda the best propaganda it could find. Military-commission convictions will support the terrorists' narrative, in which they are martyrs for a cause, fighting injustice – not brutal criminals who targeted innocent and defenseless civilians.

The fact that the United States employed a paradigm of prevention, and in some instances violated basic principles of international and domestic law in doing so, does not mean that terrorists must go free. The fact that a suspect has been tortured does not excuse his crimes, nor does it bar any prosecution. Torture taints subsequent evidence, but if the government can meet its burden of demonstrating that all of its evidence has an independent source, it may proceed with its trial. Much like the prosecution of a tortured defendant, the United States's efforts at bringing terrorists at Guantánamo to justice through the military system are tainted, not only by torture and mistreatment of defendants, but more broadly by the history of the military commissions themselves. This does not mean that alleged terrorists cannot be brought to justice. But it does mean that the United States bears a heavy burden of proving to the world that it has not profited from its illegal actions, and that it has cleared up the taint of the past. That burden is unlikely to be met in a military-commission process that provides second-class justice only to foreign nationals. The best way forward would be to abandon the military commissions, and to commit to a principle of equality, in which foreign nationals accused of terrorism have the same rights as U.S. citizens accused of terrorism, whether in a civilian criminal court or a military court-martial.

5 Prevention, Detention, and Extraordinariness

Fiona de Londras

THE REPORT OF THE 9/11 COMMISSION STATES THAT "[c]ountering terrorism has become, beyond any doubt, the top national security priority for the United States."[1] This is reflected in the high priority given to counterterrorism in the National Security Strategies that followed 2001[2] and, indeed, in the way in which the United States responded more directly to the devastating attacks of 9/11. In policy, word, and deed prevention became a dominant concern, particularly in states' approaches to noncitizen (or foreign) suspected terrorists.[3] This both reflects and constitutes an intensification of contemporary preventative approaches to risk management and security.[4] The

1 COMM'N ON TERRORIST ATTACKS UPON THE U.S., THE 9/11 COMMISSION REPORT 361 (2004).

2 THE WHITE HOUSE, NATIONAL SECURITY STRATEGY (2010), retrieved from http://www.whitehouse.gov/sites/default/files/rss_viewer/national security strategy.pdf; THE WHITE HOUSE, NATIONAL SECURITY STRATEGY (2006), retrieved from http://georgewbush-whitehouse.archives.gov/nsc/nss/2006/; THE WHITE HOUSE, NATIONAL SECURITY STRATEGY (2002), retrieved from http://nssarchive.us/NSSR/2002.pdf.

3 *See* John Jackson, *Vicious and Virtuous Cycles in Prosecuting Terrorism: The Diplock Court Experience* and Clive Walker, *Terrorism Prosecution in the United Kingdom: Lessons in the Manipulation of Criminalization and Due Process* in this volume, setting out the approach in the United States and the United Kingdom toward "domestic" terrorism. Although there are some commonalities (such as the applicability of preventive orders in the UK to citizens and noncitizens alike), this paper is concerned with these states' approaches to foreign terrorists.

4 *See, e.g.*, DAVID GARLAND, THE CULTURE OF CONTROL: CRIME AND SOCIAL ORDER IN CONTEMPORARY SOCIETY (2001); Tamar Pitch, PERVASIVE PREVENTION: A FEMINIST READING OF THE RISE OF THE SECURITY SOCIETY ch. 1 (2010).

prominence of prevention as a concern is important because a strategy and approach that is focused on preventing future attacks is of a different hue to one that is committed to prosecuting past ones. Rather than evidence gathering states are intelligence gathering; rather than prosecuting, prejudging; rather than innocent before proven guilty, suspects are dangerous until proven otherwise. In this kind of system prosecution is not front and center; it is ancillary and perhaps even extraneous. It is also almost invariably extraordinary.

The detention of suspected terrorists has been core to the United States' preventative counterterrorism strategy over the past decade. Whereas the United Kingdom has tended to prioritize deportation as a means of dealing with noncitizen suspected terrorists – with detention being a second-place option for situations where an individual suspected of terrorist activity cannot be deported for legal reasons (especially because it would breach Article 3 of the European Convention on Human Rights) – during the Bush Administration the United States focused on disabling suspected terrorists by depriving them of liberty. Whereas the Obama administration has greatly expanded the targeted killing program and focused less attention on detention, hundreds of suspected terrorists remain in preventative detention, held around the world. Although detention has been a less dominant element of the United Kingdom's approach, detention and quasi-detention measures continue to be used in the jurisdiction against suspected terrorists to a significant degree. In both cases, detention is not necessarily intended to act as an antecedent to prosecution; rather, it is intended to prevent further terrorist activity either by removing that individual from the capacity to engage directly in terrorism or by enhancing the state's capacity to acquire intelligence from the detainee to prevent terroristic activity by others. Detainees might well be prosecuted at some point, but that is not universally the case.

In this chapter, I undertake a comparative exploration of the relationships between prevention, detention, and prosecution in the United States and United Kingdom since 9/11. I argue that the prominence of prevention as a counterterrorist paradigm from which a concentration on detention might be said to have flowed made it almost inevitable that any prosecutions that followed would be extraordinary in some way. However, even in cases where detention is not strictly administrative (as it is in Guantánamo Bay, for example) but rather grounded on some kind of order, the matter of extraordinariness in procedures is germane. This is because, as I argue, the detention order is itself a quasi-conviction; it is, in Lucia Zedner's terms, "pre-punishment,"[5] and it is created through processes that are extraordinary when compared with conventional criminal procedures and convictions. In these first two sections, the chapter argues that so-called preventative detention of suspected terrorists either creates conditions where extraordinary courts and prosecutions are almost inevitable or itself constitutes a type of extraordinary quasi-criminal procedure, depending on the circumstances. There is, however, a further – and somewhat more positive – relationship between detention and prosecution that is explored in the third part of the chapter; namely, the use of proceedings by which detention has been challenged (such as habeas corpus proceedings) to "due processize" extraordinary counterterrorist proceedings in a way that asserts the continuing significance for democratic states of a constitutionalist commitment to limited power and individual rights, even in a situation of exigency.

1. Prevention as a Core Concern in the "War on Terror"

Although the phrase "War on Terror" has fallen into official disuse at this point, it was certainly the dominant frame for virtually all political and indeed legal conversations in the immediate aftermath of the attacks of September 11, 2001. It is clear that a core concern of the United States and, shortly thereafter, other states was the prevention of further acts of terrorism. The preventative agenda is reflected in various strands of contemporary counterterrorism including UN-mandated

5 Lucia Zedner, *Preventive Justice or Pre-Punishment? The Case of Control Orders*, 60 CURRENT LEGAL PROBS. 174 (2007).

intelligence sharing,[6] disruption of terrorist financing,[7] and the disruption of terroristic uses of the Internet and other broadcast and communication media.

The dominance of a prevention paradigm over the past decade or so has meant that protecting "the People" against further attacks, removing key terrorist leaders from operation, steadily trying to erode state support for terrorist activities and organizations, and disrupting terrorist organizations' capacity to operate coherently have all been marked as key counterterrorist priorities. Meanwhile, the possibility that the risk of terrorist attacks might simply be incapable of eradication has taken on the character of the politically unspeakable. This is neither entirely new in the context of counterterrorism nor easily divisible from the emergence of a hyper-regulated society, in which the state imposes coercive measures and structures (either through criminal law or "general" regulatory measures) to govern everything and suggest the manageability of risk. Part of the prevention agenda has, of course, been the removal of individuals from terrorist activity. Realistically speaking there are three ways in which one can prevent particular individuals from continuing their suspected involvement in terroristic activity: kill them, turn them, or detain them. Although all three strategies have been employed in the past decade, the third – detention – was particularly high profile during the Bush management of the war on terrorism. The specificity of detention practices might be loosely described as "preventative detention," rather than detention designed or intended to lead to a prosecution. Preventative detention has a number of functions beyond simply removing individuals from active involvement in terroristic activity; it also offers the opportunity for interrogation and intelligence gathering and creates a powerful semiotic of state supremacy or eroded values (or perhaps both).

Preventative detention in the United States and the United Kingdom has taken a number of forms. In the United States there has been what

6 S.C. Res. 1373, U.N. Doc. S/RES/1373 (Sept. 28, 2001).

7 *Id.*

we might call "open" non-battlefield preventative detention (detention that is not denied or hidden but rather is undertaken relatively publicly, almost always outside of the strict territory of the United States); closed detention (detention that is not publicly admitted or known of, also known as ghost detention or detention in "black sites"), and battlefield detention (detention of individuals captured during "traditional" warfare in Afghanistan and Iraq). In the United Kingdom preventative detention has largely been by means of an order and, since 2005, has comprised a kind of quasi-detention, albeit still imposing significant limitations on people's liberty.

In its first incarnation under s. 23 of the Anti-Terrorism, Crime and Security Act 2001 such detention was limited to non-UK citizens certified by the Home Secretary as suspected international terrorists whose presence within the UK constituted a risk[8] to national security.[9] In its second guise – the control order – preventative detention was not in a prison; rather, it was a quasi-detention whereby individuals could have their freedom to leave their homes, communicate, and even worship in a place of their choosing restricted by means of an order imposed "for purposes connected with protecting members of public from a risk of terrorism."[10] For the purposes of the Act, "involvement in terrorism-related activity" was expansively defined as committing, preparing, or instigating terrorist acts,[11] engaging in conduct that facilitated or was intended to facilitate or encouraged, supported, or assisted the commission, preparation, or instigation of terrorist acts.[12] The most recent form of quasi-detention – the Terrorism Prevention and Investigation Measure (TPIM) – is imposed by

8 In this context risk is interpreted in line with *Secretary of State for the Home Department v. Rehman*, [2001] 3 W.L.R. 877 [16] (Wales), in which Lord Slynn defined risk as engaging in activities aimed at the overthrow of the government of the national concerned by illegal means, or activities directed at a foreign government that may result in a serious threat of intervention against the government concerned (citing Atle Grahl-Madsen, 1 The Status of Refugees in International Law: Refugee Character [1966]).

9 Anti-Terrorism, Crime and Security Act 2001, c. 24, § 21(1) (U.K).

10 Prevention of Terrorism Act 2005, c. 2, § 1(1) (U.K.).

11 *Id.* § 1(9)(a).

12 *Id.* § 1(9)(b), (c), and (d).

the Secretary of State where she "reasonably believes that the individual is, or has been, involved in terrorism-related activity,"[13] at least some of which is "new"[14] and the Secretary "reasonably considers" that the Measure is necessary to protect the public from terrorism[15] and to prevent or restrict the individual's involvement in terrorism-related activity.[16] Once these conditions have been met a court can permit the imposition of the Measure or, where the urgency of the situation requires it, the Secretary can impose the Measure without the permission of a court.[17] When imposed, the Measures can quite significantly limit individuals' capacity to choose where to reside, travel, communicate with particular individuals, enjoy privacy and freedom relating to financial transactions, and so on.[18] As with other preventative measures, such as antisocial behavior orders, this reflects "the way in which governments, particularly in the United Kingdom, have been trying to devise preventative measures that are coercive and yet avoid the safeguards established for the criminal justice paradigm,"[19] either sidestepping courts entirely or giving them minimal involvement.

All of these kinds of detention or quasi-detention are clearly focused on prevention as a primary concern, and this preventative focus is significant in comparing such detention to the kinds of detention to which we are more accustomed in democratic states. In the ordinary course of events, we do not generally permit the indefinite detention of individuals for the purposes of preventing unlawful behavior.[20] Rather, in the wake

13 Terrorism Prevention and Investigation Measures Act 2011, c. 23, § 3(1).

14 *Id.* § 3(2).

15 *Id.* § 3(3).

16 *Id.* § 3(4).

17 *Id.* § 3(5).

18 *Id.* sch. 1.

19 Andrew Ashworth, *Criminal Law, Human Rights and Preventative Justice*, *in* REGULATING DEVIANCE: THE REDIRECTION OF CRIMINALISATION AND THE FUTURES OF CRIMINAL LAW 87, 95 (Bernadette McSherry et al. eds. 2008).

20 It is important to note that this really is a generalization. In many states people are voluntarily or involuntarily detained in, for example, mental health detention for many years, ostensibly for their own protection but also for public order reasons. Similarly,

of a criminal event taking place investigations are undertaken by law enforcement officials for the purposes of building a case against someone; the presumption of innocence means that there is an imperative for the state to build an admissible and compelling case against an individual for the purposes of prosecution. The "end point" dictates the state's behavior toward the individual in question to a large extent. In liberal democratic states, evidence that is tainted by illegality is generally inadmissible, which effectively constrains the types of behavior the state is willing to engage in relative to detained individuals. Failure to act within these accepted behavioral constraints will almost certainly result in the collapse of a trial and the failure of the investigative process. Thus, the prosecutorial orientation helps regulate state action.

In contrast, when a state proceeds with a detention policy that is oriented toward prevention rather than prosecution there is an inevitable risk that these standard behavioral constraints might become relatively less effective than is usually the case; they might even become disregarded altogether for reasons of perceived necessity, frustration, ill-discipline, or even spectacularism. The intervention of the Court to constrain state behavior through evidential rules is essentially designed out. When what is sought is intelligence rather than evidence the perspective of the state in which preventative detention is normalized changes, and actions are undertaken that might ordinarily rid the information acquired of evidential capacity. Thus, interrogations might take place after an unduly long period of detention, without access to legal counsel or medical supervision, after a period of sleep deprivation or sensory manipulation, and after or contemporaneous with acts of physical and mental force that constitute torture or at the very least render the information offered up involuntary. Standard elements of fair trial rights such as equality of arms and the privilege against self-incrimination are arguably abandoned because of the preventative mission. The extraordinariness of the

disciplinary governance has at times taken the form of long-term (effectively indefinite) de facto detention in both private and public institutions such as convents and industrial schools for both preventive and disciplinary reasons.

detention, in effect, crafts an extraordinary context if and when trials come about.

Thus, although extraordinary or special courts are frequently rationalized by reference only to security concerns and presented as being necessary in order to prevent jury intimidation, safeguard sensitive information, and deprive suspected terrorists of the "oxygen of publicity," thinking about the ways in which a focus on prevention rather than prosecution might influence a state's treatment of detainees reveals another rationale: quarantine. Our focus in this volume is on democratic states for which the rule of law and integrity of the criminal justice system are paramount. Such systems recognize when wrongs have been done. Put another way, democratic states are capable of holding simultaneous but contradictory positions whereby they profess the strategic desirability of preventative detention without trial on the one hand but want to maintain the generally applicable principles of due process, equality of arms, the prohibition of torture, and the presumption of innocence on the other. Standing in such a torn position, "quarantining" cases or scenarios in which preventative detention has resulted in violations of those core legal and constitutionalist values to extraordinary courts or extraordinary processes holds a certain attraction. Any attempt to try such individuals in civilian courts and, as part of that trial, admit evidence tainted by illegality would either draw the ordinary courts into the disreputable process of implicitly approving of such techniques (by admitting the evidence) or writing bare the constitutionalist ruptures that preventative detention brought about (by refusing to admit such evidence). The risk in either context is substantial. Should the evidence be admitted, the integrity of evidentiary rules may be called into question; should the evidence not be admitted, the government finds itself confronted with a judicially pronounced accusation of deeply undemocratic behavior by a detainee who must either be released or returned to indefinite detention in spite of a collapsed ordinary trial.

Extraordinary court procedures can take a number of different forms. There is precedent for the establishment and use of special courts oriented entirely toward the prosecution of terrorist activity (such as the Diplock Courts in Northern Ireland and the Special Criminal Court in the Republic of Ireland), the use of specialized courts with other foci for quasi-prosecutorial tasks (such as the use of the Special Immigration Appeals Commission in the United Kingdom), and the establishment and use of military commissions (such as those in operation in Guantánamo Bay). Furthermore, the "ordinary courts" might be rendered extraordinary in the context of trying terrorist offenses by introducing special rules for such cases, such as the use of special advocates[21] to represent the interest of the suspected terrorist or the implementation of so-called secret-justice processes to avoid any sensitive materials being disclosed.[22] Although all of these approaches can be justified on security-related grounds, they also all have some potential quarantining rationale, and that rationale is linked to the preventative policy of detention and intensity and type of interrogation that accompanied it.

2. Preventative Detention as a Quasi-Prosecutorial Phenomenon

Proceedings relating to preventative detention might themselves be considered a type of extraordinary prosecutorial exercise, particularly when such detention and quasi-detention are based on relatively formalized procedures culminating in administrative orders or measures such as the control orders and TPIMs described previously. Lucia Zedner argues that we ought to dismantle the concept of prevention as generally understood and look instead at the actual processes and standards applied when deciding that someone ought to be subjected to this kind of liberty deprivation.[23] In doing that, she argues, it becomes evident that rather than being merely preventative these kinds of measures are in fact a kind of "pre-punishment"; they are an effective finding of guilt with an

21 Further considered later.

22 Adam Tomkins, *National Security and the Due Process of Law*, 64 Current Legal Probs. 215 (2011).

23 Zedner, *supra* note 5.

attendant punishment but without the kinds of safeguards, procedures, and guarantees we conventionally associate with the levying of sentences. In the counterterrorist context we can see that imposing an order of this kind serves a declaratory function that we normally associate with the full process of the criminal law ("you are a terrorist/criminal"), which in turn creates the rhetorical justification for imposing coercive measures intended to govern the individual-as-risk. The person is deemed sufficiently dangerous to be subjected to more coercion than the rest of "us" by means of what is effectively a governance decision undertaken by those perceived to have the expertise in appropriate risk management to make this determination more or less without question. Those governors are not courts, which we deem the appropriate governance agents in the ordinary criminal justice system, but rather "socially accredited experts"[24] such as politicians, intelligence officers, and law enforcement. If we conceptualize the measures imposed as punishing rather than "merely" preventative the means of their imposition is marked as clearly extraordinary.

Zedner's focus is on the control order, which – as considered – is now being replaced by TPIMs in the United Kingdom. Although control orders may not constitute detention as conventionally understood, they certainly imposed serious limitations on liberty by means of a process that was either exclusively (in the case of non-derogating orders) or heavily (in the case of derogating control orders) executive in nature.[25] TPIMs are to be imposed with the permission of a court or, where the situation is of so urgent a nature that court proceedings cannot be taken, by the Home Secretary acting alone. Even when imposed with the permission of a court the standard to be met in order for such permission to be granted is nowhere near as high as the "beyond a reasonable doubt" standard required for a criminal conviction.[26] For Zedner, control orders

24 Stanley Cohen, Folk Devils and Moral Panics 1 (3d ed., 2002).

25 Anti-Terrorism, Crime and Security Act 2003, 2003 c. s. 23.

26 Rather it is a "reasonable belief" standard. *See* Terrorism Prevention and Investigation Measures Act 2011, c. 23, §§ 3 & 6.

were properly considered as penal (rather than preventative) measures because "the alleged activities that may give rise to Control Orders are in the main serious criminal offences; the burdens imposed by the orders are punitive in effect; and the provision for breach is a long period of imprisonment."[27]

Although Zedner's focus is firmly on the UK in her critique, the principled argument she makes seems transferrable to detention in Guantánamo Bay. Let us recall that preventatively detaining someone as a suspected terrorist in Guantánamo Bay in effect comprises three important claims: (a) the detainee is involved in terrorist activity, (b) the detainee is too dangerous to be released, and (c) the detainee is an enemy combatant relative to the United States or its allies. Although there is no "provision for breach," as what is in question here is detention conventionally understood, the other two elements of Zedner's penal characterization (the serious criminal nature of alleged activities and punitive nature of the burden imposed) are present. Furthermore, the processes surrounding detention in Guantánamo Bay are unquestionably deficient.

While they operated in Guantánamo Bay, the Combatant Status Review Tribunals (CSRT) offered only inadequate review. Every Guantánamo Bay detainee was presumptively classified as an enemy combatant (and therefore subject to detention) before the CSRT,[28] which then conducted a relatively shallow review asking only whether that presumptive classification remained appropriate on "the preponderance of evidence." In addition to this relatively low standard of proof, evidence adduced by the government enjoyed a rebuttable presumption of being genuine and accurate.[29] The CSRT was not bound by standard rules of

27 Zedner, *supra* note 5, at 196.

28 Memorandum from Gordon England, Sec'y of the Navy, Enc. (1), § B, (July 29, 2004) (regarding "Implementation of Combatant Status Review Tribunal Procedures for Enemy Combatants detained at Guantánamo Bay Naval Base, Cuba"), retrieved from www.defenselink.mil/news/Jul2004/d20040730comb.pdf.

29 *Id.*

evidence,[30] but rather could consider any evidence deemed to be both relevant and helpful to the matter under consideration.[31] There was no disclosure requirement as to evidence between the parties, and although detainees could call witnesses their appearance was limited to those who were "reasonably available"[32] to appear.

Characterizing detention in Guantánamo Bay as a type of pre-punishment within Zedner's categorization reveals the fact that such review was problematic. This is because it not only fell substantially short of international standards relating to the right to challenge the lawfulness of one's detention, but also because it comprised a process through which something analogous to a finding of guilt could be made (the determination that one was properly detained), but without any of the due process guarantees that attend criminal prosecutions. In this way preventative detention in Guantánamo Bay as reviewed by the internal processes operative there can itself be conceptualized as a type of extraordinary process before a type of extraordinary tribunal. Here the proceeding was extraordinary not only because of its bespoke nature, limited remit, and physical location but also because it was effectively a sentence-bearing process without the procedures and safeguards we would normally associate therewith, even in a time of emergency when some modifications might be said to have been justifiably required.

3. Challenging and "Due Processizing" Preventative Detention

One of the core areas of legal activity in the War on Terror has involved mounting challenges to the lawfulness of suspected terrorists' detention or subjection to quasi-detention orders. In the United States these claims

30 Memorandum from Paul Wolfowitz, Deputy Sec'y of Def., to the Sec'y of the Navy (July 7, 2004) (regarding "Order Establishing Combatant Status Review Tribunal"), retrieved from http://www.defense.gov/news/Jul2004/d20040707review.pdf.

31 *Id*

32 *Id*.

have primarily taken the form of habeas corpus applications; in the United Kingdom multiple challenges to the various types of detention (or quasi-detention) orders used since 2001 have been based on the Human Rights Act 1998. These challenges have played an important legal and politico-legal role. In relation to the latter they have tended to ratchet-up popular pressure for some kind of normality to be injected into the status quo, no matter how abnormal that apparent normality turns out to be. In the context of Guantánamo Bay, for example, the pressure that built through a combination of nongovernmental organization (NGO) activity, journalistic attention, strategic litigation, and international outrage contributed to the construction of some kind of prosecutorial structure there, even though in fact it was an extraordinary structure taking the form of military commissions. Of course, the extent to which this kind of pressure contributed to the establishment and execution of a prosecution strategy of some kind is difficult to quantify, and any attempt to do so requires one to take into account the likelihood that such pressure is more likely to (a) build; and (b) be effective as time passes from the traumatic event bringing on the crisis (such as an attack). That said, the dominance of a preventative paradigm with minimal (if any) attention being paid to prosecution and normal criminal justice processes arguably creates a momentum toward advocacy of this kind, which in turn may result in some kind of prosecutorial approach being crafted, albeit it one that may need to be extraordinary for the quarantining reasons considered earlier.

In legal terms, these challenges have created the conditions for an important judicial intervention that has had at least some kind of normalizing effect on procedures related to detention;[33] they have allowed for superior courts to make it clear that even in a time of exigency at least some core constitutionalist principles continue to apply. The fact that superior courts have in fact asserted this rather than being purely

33 David Cole, *Military Commissions and the Paradigm of Prevention*, in this volume.

deferential as might have been expected in advance is a matter of some significance.[34] It is trite to remark that in times of crisis, and especially violent crisis, there is a tendency to suggest that extraordinariness is the order of the day and that this extraordinariness ought even to determine the extent to which constitutionalist principles are applicable to limit state power. This is a fundamental matter that, at a fairly simplified level, demands of us a consideration of what constitutes law in a situation of crisis. For democratic states it seems anathema to suggest that the answer to this could be something as bare as sovereignty, necessity, or unchecked executive power, but to some extent that is indeed the answer that was offered in the wake of September 11, 2001. Stripped to their barest bones, "unitary executive theory" and the demand for absolute deference to the executive in assessing what is necessary and justifiable in order to counter terrorism are claims that I perceive as characterizing law as nothing more complex or constitutionalist than judgment untethered by principle. This then fundamentally challenges the concept of law's autonomy.[35] The detention cases that came before the U.S. Supreme Court and the UK House of Lords (and later the UK Supreme Court) have resisted such characterization.

In a series of Guantánamo Bay cases,[36] the U.S. Supreme Court rejected claims that the detention center's physical location outside of the mainland United States (although within the exclusive jurisdiction of the United States) would prevent those detained there from making a habeas corpus application either on statutory[37] or, eventually, constitutional bases[38] in the absence of express jurisdiction stripping and

34 Deference would have been the expected judicial position on the basis of former performance in times of war or emergency, exemplified by well-known decisions such as *Korematsu v. United States,* 323 U.S. 214 (1944) and *Liversidge v. Anderson*, [1942] A.C. 206 (H.L.).

35 Fiona de Londras, Detention in the "War on Terror": Can Human Rights Fight Back? Ch. 4 (2011).

36 *See Boumediene v. Bush*, 553 U.S. 723 (2008); *Hamdan v. Rumsfeld*, 548 U.S. 557 (2006); *Rasul v. Bush*, 542 U.S. 466 (2004).

37 *See Hamdan*, 548 U.S. at 557; *Rasul*, 542 U.S. at 466.

38 *Boumediene*, 553 U.S. at 723.

suspension of habeas corpus by Congress. Furthermore, although the crisis-ridden context within which such a claim might be made would be weighed in the balance when deciding on whether or not to grant habeas corpus in any particular case, it could not in itself preclude such applications or writs.[39] The writ would run, as has been the case since the founding of the United States, as a fundamental check on governmental power within the complex separation and balance of powers through which the principle of constitutionalism is structured in that jurisdiction.[40] These cases made it quite clear that executive primacy could not override constitutional limitations, even in a situation of (perceived) grave threat to the state. Constitutional and constitutionalist principles of limited and accountable power could not easily be evaded by geographical location or executive power. To allow that would strip law of its autonomous capacity to limit the state.

In the United Kingdom any suggestion that the Human Rights Act 1998 – a constitutionalist statute enshrining in domestic law rights and obligations transposed from the European Convention on Human Rights (hereinafter Convention) – could somehow be brushed aside by exigent circumstances was resisted at the highest judicial level. The first major challenge – in the form of *A (FC) and others; (X) FC and another v. Secretary of State for the Home Department* (hereinafter *Belmarsh*)[41] – was individuals detained under s. 23 of the Anti-Terrorism, Crime and Security Act 2001 claiming that the detention regime was incompatible with the Convention because (a) there was no emergency as required for a valid derogation; and (b) that notwithstanding a valid derogation, s. 23 was incompatible with the Convention, as it was not limited to that which was strictly required by the exigencies of the situation.[42] Part of the

39 *See Boumediene*, 553 U.S. at 723; *Hamdan*, 548 U.S. at 557; *Hamdi v. Rumsfeld*, 542 U.S. 507 (2004); *Rasul*, 542 U.S. at 466.

40 *See Boumediene*, 553 U.S. at 723.

41 *A (FC) and others*; *(X) FC and another v. Secretary of State for the Home Department*, (2004) UKHL 56, (2005) 2 AC 68 (appeal taken from Eng.).

42 *See, e.g.*, David Harris et al., Law of the European Convention on Human Rights ch. 16 (2d ed. 2009) (discussing the derogation test under Article 15 of the Convention).

government's case was to claim that both the judgment that an emergency requiring derogation existed and the measures taken pursuant to that derogation were matters within the competence of the executive to which courts ought to show substantial deference. Although the House of Lords was very deferential in respect of the threshold question of whether an emergency exists per se, it was far less deferential in relation to the latter, and in fact concluded that there was a breach of the Convention because the detention regime was applicable only to non-UK citizens and this discrimination was not objectively justifiable. This case was a monumental one in the United Kingdom; it made very clear a judicial approach that considered the Human Rights Act to be a substantial constitutionalist barrier to counterterrorist action notwithstanding executive claims of necessity that had previously more or less determined legality in that jurisdiction.[43]

I do not mean, here, to overstate the case. There are certainly flaws in how the courts have responded to the claims made by the executive in these cases, and indeed, in others. Fenwick and Phillipson have convincingly argued that courts in the UK have, perhaps inadvertently, created "covert derogations" by lowering the standards considered appropriate and permissible even while being non-deferential when degrees of deference are judged against past performance.[44] In the United States the vague and underconstructed concept of de facto sovereignty outlined in *Boumediene* was in fact so loosely articulated as to allow it to be interpreted almost beyond usefulness by lower courts.[45] However, I remain of the view that these decisions are important assertions of constitutionalism in the context of a terroristic crisis and, to that extent,

43 *See generally* Tom Bingham, The Rule of Law (2011) (discussing the changing conceptualization of the Rule of Law as including compliance with human rights obligations including the Human Rights Act 1998 in the United Kingdom).

44 Helen Fenwick and Gavin Phillipson, *Covert Derogations and Judicial Deference: Redefining Liberty and Due Process Rights in Counterterrorism Law and Beyond*, 56 McGill L. J. 864 (2011).

45 Christina Duffy Burnett, *A Convenient Constitution? Extraterritoriality after* Boumediene, 109 Colum. L. Rev. 973 (2009).

core elements in maintaining the democratic commitment to an autonomous law.[46]

If constitutionalism represents the belief that law has a core that limits governmental action, then its manifestation in the prosecutorial context is surely in the democratic commitment to due process and the right to a fair trial. The precise requirements of a fair trial may vary from situation to situation, but at a minimum one would suggest that access to legal counsel and the capacity to respond effectively to the case put against you (which necessarily requires disclosure of the case against the accused) are core elements.[47] So, too, it seems sensible to suggest, is the enforcement of rules of evidence that either exclude or treat with extreme caution any evidence that emanates from unlawful or suspicious behavior, including torture or other forms of illegality.[48] It seems unsustainable to claim that the fact that a prosecutorial process is extraordinary means that it cannot offer due process and a fair trial.[49] It is quite conceivable that some kind of structures would be put in place in order to ensure that due process can occur in a situation of extraordinary trials, and the detention-related cases adjudicated on in the United States and United Kingdom have gone some way toward this. In the United States it was the detention-related case of *Hamdan* that ensured that Common Article 3 of the Geneva Convention would be marked as the minimum acceptable level of rights protection applicable in Guantánamo Bay, including in the conduct of military commissions there. Furthermore, the decision in *Boumediene* that at least some constitutional rights can be enjoyed by those detained in Guantánamo Bay suggests the possibility that some constitutional due process rights would be applicable to the military commissions, although the scope of that decision is far from clear. Regrettably, its application is

46 de Londras, *supra* note 35, at ch. 6.

47 John Jackson and Sarah Summers, The Internationalisation of Criminal Evidence: Beyond the Common Law and Civil Law Traditions (2012).

48 *Id.* ch. 6.

49 *Id.*; *see also* Fergal F. Davis, The History and Development of the Special Criminal Court, 1922–2005 (2007); John Jackson, Many Years On in Northern Ireland: The Diplock Legacy, 60 N.I.L.Q. 213 (2009).

essentially determined by a discursive process of political constitutionalism, showing the importance of the interplay between judicial pronouncements, legislative interpretation, and administrative enactment.

In the United Kingdom the challenge to due process and fair trial that has arisen in the context of contemporary counterterrorism is very much encapsulated by the term "secret justice,"[50] used to describe increasing situations in which individuals can be subjected to certain orders (including detention and quasi-detention) on the basis of a case made up substantially of closed evidence. At present the clear challenges to individual rights posed by reliance on closed evidence are largely met through the use of special advocates: lawyers paid from the public purse with significant security clearance who are shown the case against a suspected terrorist and then act for the benefit of that individual.[51] This is a difficult system to operationalize in a realistic sense, as once the special advocate has seen the case against her client, her capacity to consult meaningfully is greatly constrained by the fact that the details of the closed materials cannot be revealed to the individual in question. However, the European Court of Human Rights has confirmed that the special advocates system can in fact satisfy the requirements of a fair trial enshrined in Article 6 of the Convention provided that the open case consists of more than general and unsubstantiated assertions and that the "thrust" of the closed case is revealed to the individual concerned.[52] Although special advocates and closed-materials hearings are extraordinary, they are not necessarily devoid of due process or unfair.[53] Indeed, one might argue that although suboptimal from a rights-based perspective these extraordinary types of

50 In 2011 the UK Government released its Green Paper on Justice and Security, 2011, Cm. 8194, at 3 (U.K.), suggesting the continued and indeed increased reliance on closed materials in order to mediate between the "twin imperatives" of justice and security. This then crystallized into the Justice and Security Bill, 2012–2013, H.L. Bill [27].

51 The Special Immigration Appeals Commission (Procedure) Rules, 2003, S.I. 2003/1034.

52 *A and others v. United Kingdom*, Eur. Ct. H.R. 301, ¶ 220 (2009), retrieved from http://www.echr.coe.int. *See also Secretary of State for the Home Department v. AF* (No. 3), (2010) 2 A.C. 269 (H.L.) (appeal taken from Eng.) (suggesting that in fact more than the mere thrust/gist of the evidence should be revealed).

53 *C.f.* Tomkins, *supra* note 22.

approaches are intended to – and to a substantial extent do – uphold the constitutionalist principle of fair trial and due process of law reflected in the Human Rights Act 1998, and operationalized largely because of the knowledge that failure to meet those minimum standards will result in judicial condemnation along the lines of that expressed in *Belmarsh*.

Conclusion

The material considered in this chapter suggests that the relationship between detention and prosecution or other forms of quasi-prosecutorial processes since 2001 is one that can clearly be related to two things: the primacy of prevention and the resilience of law. On the one hand, giving priority to prevention within the planning and execution of a counterterrorism strategy has clear implications for the ways in which processes around challenge, liberty, and ultimately conviction end up being designed and implemented. On the other, judicial commitment to constitutionalism has created a context in which even extraordinary tribunals and processes can be injected with due process and fairness of procedures to at least some extent.

The suggestion here is not that the military commissions currently operating in Guantánamo Bay offer fair trials. Indeed, one might question whether any trial following such protracted detention, not to mention ill-treatment and media coverage, could ever be fair. Nor is it suggested that secret justice is a desirable approach. Rather, it is that the prominence of prevention in the War on Terror, reflected in the commitment on both sides of the Atlantic to preventative detention, created conditions in which measures of this kind were the only viable approach to prosecutorial and quasi-prosecutorial procedures. This suggests both that we ought to beware of prevention masquerading as cure if we truly want to maintain democratic principles while countering terrorism, and that the extraordinary can be injected with fairness and process where courts demonstrate a willingness to reject absolute deference in pursuit of the democratic value of constitutionalism. It also suggests that law's resilience in counterterrorist contexts may be demonstrated (if at all) by judicial intervention, albeit subject to political interpretation and implementation. Thus, the extraordinariness of courts' engagement, or indeed deliberate marginalization, as well as courts' insistence on acting in a constitutionalist manner in the conceptual and legal spaces in which they were "allowed in" to act at all, is vitally connected to law's capacity to demonstrate resilience in a climate of preventative action.

6 In Defense of Federal Criminal Courts for Terrorism Cases in the United States

Gabor Rona and Raha Wala

DEBATE OVER THE USE BY THE U.S. GOVERNMENT OF MILITARY commissions rather than federal criminal courts for terrorism cases is ultimately about how best to situate and respond to the threat of international terrorism as a matter of law and policy. After the terrorist attacks of September 11, 2001, it was thought by many, including top policy makers in the Bush administration, that the United States had experienced a paradigm-shifting event that created a new post-9/11 legal world. The old paradigm – pre-9/11 thinking – was one in which terrorists were generally considered common criminals, subject to law-enforcement action. After 9/11 arguments began to take shape favoring a law of armed-conflict paradigm for detention and prosecution of terrorism suspects.

The Bush administration's new modified war paradigm was extraordinary, indeed, revolutionary in two respects. First, its breadth was unprecedented. The war spanned the globe and construed "terror," "terrorism," and "terrorists" as the enemy. Second, the administration asserted all the powers of wartime law, including the right to detain without charge or trial. Notably, suspected terrorists were considered unlawful combatants who did not merit the rights typically afforded to either combatants or civilians detained in armed conflict.

International law considers armed conflict to be an extraordinary state of affairs, where otherwise universally applicable human rights law is partially displaced by the laws of war, international humanitarian law. But the Bush war paradigm invoked the supposedly novel aspects of the terrorist threat to claim that neither international humanitarian law nor international human rights law nor American constitutional or statutory law could limit the state's conduct. Although rhetorically asserting that suspected terrorists were war criminals, the Bush administration denied them the protections of both the laws of war and domestic criminal law. The military commissions at the U.S. Naval Base in Guantánamo Bay, Cuba are fundamentally a by-product of this Bush war paradigm, as are the legal and policy debates over the continued use of military commissions for terrorism trials.

Shortly after 9/11, on November 13, 2001, President Bush signed an executive order creating military commissions to try terrorism suspects detained at Guantánamo. The Guantánamo project, including the military commissions, is a direct outgrowth of the Bush administration's intent to create a legal black hole.[1] Guantánamo was the ideal location – perhaps the only place on earth – where it was thought that individuals could be detained beyond the jurisdiction of either U.S. or any other nation's courts. Ultimately however, the Supreme Court not only affirmed a judicial role in determining the legitimacy of both detention and military commissions, but also ruled that the first generation of military commissions failed to meet applicable international legal standards.[2]

Had the architects of Guantánamo detention predicted correctly that domestic courts would not give the administration carte blanche, there might be no Guantánamo today, and no post-9/11 military commissions. That alone should undermine any assumption that these military commissions and traditional federal criminal court trial mechanisms are entitled to an equal measure of presumptive validity. Military commissions

1 *See* Daniel F. McCallum, *Why GTMO?* (unpublished seminar paper, National Defense University, National War College), retrieved from http://www.pegc.us/archive/Authorities/McCallum_why_gtmo.pdf. *But cf. Rasul v. Bush*, 542 U.S. 466 (2004) (rejecting the Bush Administration's argument that Guantánamo detainees could not challenge their detention because they were outside of the territorial jurisdiction of the United States).

2 *See Hamdan v. Rumsfeld*, 548 U.S. 557 (2006).

are, as a practical matter, irrelevant to anyone beyond the small cadre of select Guantánamo detainees. The Obama administration does want to close Guantánamo and will not likely be considering additions to its detainee population. All this suggests that military commissions are, at best, a vestigial organ of a failed species. But in spite of Obama's derision of them, military commissions persist, in no small part because of their talismanic role in the "tough on terrorism" political sweepstakes. And so, the "federal courts versus military commissions" debate also persists.

In striking down the first military commissions, the Supreme Court rejected a fundamental tenant of the Bush war paradigm in holding that at a minimum Common Article 3 of the Geneva Conventions applies to the armed conflict against al Qaeda. Moreover, according to the Court, the military commissions, with their subpar procedural protections, could not be considered "regularly constituted" courts under Common Article 3. The administration and Congress went back to the drawing board to create new military commissions, first under the Military Commissions Act of 2006, later replaced by the Military Commissions Act of 2009. The Supreme Court has yet to rule on the validity of the newly constituted military commissions.

Despite foreswearing some of the more objectionable aspects of the Bush war paradigm, the Obama administration has accepted the basic premise that responding to international terrorism requires the use of extraordinary war powers. Accordingly, the Obama administration has hedged its bets on terrorism trials by resuming the use of military commissions while arguing that civilian courts play an important – even preferred – role in trying terrorist suspects. Proponents of the continued use of military commissions for terrorism trials, including some within in the Obama administration, argue that federal court trials may not be an appropriate conceptual or practical fit for terrorism trials, given the realities of counterterrorism policy and practice. The conceptual and practical objections go hand in hand, and have largely focused on the purported mismatch between the militarized response to international terrorism and the law-enforcement approach presented by civilian trials.

According to this line of thought, civilian courts are not an appropriate forum to mete out justice to "combatants," "the enemy," or others captured "on the battlefield," despite the fact that the War Crimes Act in the U.S. federal criminal code provides jurisdiction against all such individuals. Moreover, civilian trials are thought to present unnecessary logistical burdens and national security risks, and generally undermine the government's ability to incapacitate terrorists.[3]

In this essay, we make the case that critics of civilian trials have it backward: federal courts established under Article III of the U.S. Constitution, referred to as Article III courts – not military commissions – are a better fit for terrorism trials. Large, complex, international terrorism cases have been tried in Article III courts for over two decades now, and U.S. domestic law provides a host of tools for ensuring fair trials and protecting national security interests. The government has secured nearly 500 convictions against al-Qaeda or related groups in Article III court prosecutions since 9/11.[4] According to one study, these cases have resulted in convictions or guilty pleas more than 90 percent of the time, and there have been few, if any, security breaches.[5] Moreover, federal judges have generally been successful at safeguarding constitutional protections with careful, creative jurisprudence built on more than 200 years of criminal

3 *See, e.g.*, Michael B. Mukasey, *Civilian Courts Are no Place to Try Terrorists,* WALL ST. J., Oct. 19, 2009, retrieved from http://online.wsj.com/article/SB10001424052748704107204574475300052267212.html.

4 Letter from Ronald Weich, Assistant Att'y Gen., to Senator Leahy and Senator Sessions, Regarding Statistics Relating to the Prosecution of Terrorism, Terrorism-Related Crimes and Incarceration of Terrorists by the Bureau of Prisons (Mar. 26, 2010), retrieved from http://www.justice.gov/cjs/docs/terrorism-crimes-letter.pdf; DEP'T OF JUSTICE, NATIONAL SECURITY DIVISION STATISTICS ON UNSEALED INTERNATIONAL TERRORISM AND TERRORISM-RELATED CONVICTIONS 9/11/2001–06/06/2012 (2012) (retrieved from http://www.humanrightsfirst.org/wp-content/uploads/DOJ-Terrorism-Related-Convictions.pdf).

5 *See* RICHARD Z. ZABEL AND JAMES J. BENJAMIN, JR., IN PURSUIT OF JUSTICE: PROSECUTING TERRORISM CASES IN FEDERAL COURTS, 2009 UPDATE AND RECENT DEVELOPMENTS 6–9 (2009); RICHARD Z. ZABEL AND JAMES J. BENJAMIN, JR., HUMAN RIGHTS FIRST, IN PURSUIT OF JUSTICE: PROSECUTING TERRORISM CASES IN FEDERAL COURTS, 2008 UPDATE AND RECENT DEVELOPMENTS (2008).

law precedent. Many of these cases arose from terrorist acts that were planned and carried out overseas, and the government has nonetheless been able to prosecute them by using a wide variety of evidence gathered by law enforcement and intelligence methods alike.

Unlike the proven track record of federal courts with terrorism trials, military commissions have little history with terrorism trials and pose unique legal and national security concerns. The current military commissions system in Guantánamo Bay, Cuba, is the third try since 9/11. The original post-9/11 military commissions were established pursuant to executive order and struck down by the Supreme Court in *Hamdan v. Rumsfeld*. Congress and the president responded with the Military Commissions Act of 2006, which was then replaced by the Military Commissions Act of 2009. Unsurprisingly, only seven convictions have come from this cumbersome, stop-and-go process and only one of those seven was the result of a contested trial.[6] Meanwhile, the legal framework undergirding the current system – the Military Commissions Act of 2009 – remains shaky and untested, calling into question whether the commissions even have jurisdiction to try suspected terrorists under the laws of armed conflict. Moreover, military commissions, with their subpar procedural safeguards and inextricable ties to the Guantánamo project, are broadly seen – rightly or wrongly – as a second-class system of justice.[7] This has devastating national security consequences, serving as a propaganda tool for al Qaeda and like-minded organizations and undermining the ability of the United States to work with allies to suppress terrorist and insurgent activities.[8]

Part I of this chapter discusses in some detail the major flaws in the current military commissions system. Parts II through V address the most common arguments advanced against trying terrorism suspects in civilian

6 *Hamdan*, 548 U.S.

7 *See, e.g.*, Walter Pincus, *Powell Calls for Closure of Military Prison at Guantanamo*, Wash. Post, June 11, 2007; *Gates Defends Decision to Close Guantanamo*, Ass. Press, May 22, 2009.

8 *Id.*

courts. Part II describes how domestic criminal law has been effective in reaching extraterritorially to disrupt terrorist plots before they are carried out. Part III describes the various tools that civilian courts use to protect sensitive national security information in terrorism cases. Part IV dispels a common myth that granting suspected terrorists due process rights will hamper counterterrorism efforts. Part V describes how civilian courts have capably handled difficult evidentiary issues associated with terrorism trials.

1. Military Commissions and Terrorism Trials: Enduring Problems

The use of military commissions to try terrorism suspects is problematic in several ways that only reinforce the shadow cast on them by the Supreme Court in *Hamdan v. Rumsfeld*.[9] An initial problem is that most common acts of terrorism, although crimes under domestic law, are not war crimes, and thus military commissions are inherently limited in their ability to incapacitate terrorists by asserting jurisdiction over their criminal acts. Most of the terrorism prosecutions in U.S. military commissions have relied on a conspiracy charge – a charge held not to be a war crime by the post–World War II war crimes tribunals and modern international law of war conventions and jurisprudence.[10] The *Hamdan* decision itself cast doubt on the validity of conspiracy as a war crime.[11] Similarly, "material support for terrorism," another commonly charged crime in the military commissions, is not a traditional war crime, as the Obama administration has admitted.[12] A federal appeals court recently overturned two military

9 *Hamdan*, 548 U.S.

10 Raha Wala, *From Guantanamo to Nuremberg and Back: An Analysis of Conspiracy to Commit War Crimes under International Humanitarian Law*, 41 Geo. J. Int'l L. 683 (2010).

11 *Hamdan*, 548 U.S., slip op. at 48. ("Far from making the requisite substantial showing, the Government has failed even to offer a 'merely colorable' case for inclusion of conspiracy among those offenses cognizable by law-of-war military commission.")

12 *Military Commissions: Hearing Before the S. Comm. on Armed Services*, 111th Cong. (2009) (statement of David Kris, Assistant Att'y Gen. of the Dep't of Justice).

commission convictions – in the *Hamdan* and *al Bahlul* cases – because it held that material support and conspiracy could not be considered war crimes at the time the offenses were codified in the Military Commissions Act.[13]

Whereas the crimes of material support for terrorism and conspiracy are of dubious legitimacy in military commissions, that of "murder by an unprivileged belligerent in violation of the laws of war," another prominent military commission crime, is clearly improper under the laws of war. Prosecutions of this crime are a legacy of the Bush war paradigm, which held that those who "wear no uniform, do not carry arms openly, and fail to distinguish themselves from the civilian population" are not protected by the laws of war.[14] As charged against Omar Khadr, the Canadian child soldier accused of killing a U.S. soldier, "murder by an unprivileged belligerent" attempted to render the very act of unprivileged belligerency a war crime.[15] In fact, the laws of war contain no such prohibition.[16] What they do prohibit is the targeting of civilians and the use of perfidious means to target even legitimate military objectives. Simply put, for civilians to target enemy combatants is not a violation of the laws of war, and attempts to prosecute such acts have created intractable legal problems.

Even if states can create new classes of war crimes – such as material support for terrorism, conspiracy, and murder by an unprivileged

13 *Salim Hamdan v. United States of America*, No. 11-1257 (D.C. Cir. Oct. 16, 2012); *Ali Hamza Ahmad Suliman al Bahlul v. United States of America*, No. 11-1324 (D.C. Cir. Jan. 25, 2013).

14 Memorandum from the Office of Legal Counsel, Dep't of Justice to Counsel to the President on Status of Taliban Forces Under Article 4 of the Third Geneva Convention of 1949 (Feb. 7, 2002), retrieved from http://www.fas.org/irp/agency/doj/olc/taliban.pdf.

15 Although the relevant military commission offense does not suggest that any killing by an unprivileged belligerent is murder, it has been applied in such fashion, for example, in *United States v. Khadr*. *See* Military Commissions Act of 2009, 10 U.S.C. § 950t (15) (2009); Amended Charge Sheet, *United States v. Khadr* (Mil. Com. 2010); Dep't of Def., Manual for Military Commissions IV-11 (2010) (providing examples and commentary regarding the crime of murder in violation of the laws of war).

16 Jelena Pejic, *"Unlawful/Enemy Combatants," Interpretations and Consequences, in* International Law and Armed Conflict: Exploring the Fault Lines, Essays in Honor of Yoram Dinstein, 335, 338 (Michael Schmitt and Jelena Pejic eds., 2007).

belligerent – they cannot apply them retrospectively, as the military commissions have done. Most of the alleged criminal acts undertaken by defendants sitting before the military commissions occurred years before the Military Commissions Act of 2006 codified these crimes. To punish such acts would be a violation of the international legal principle of legality, an aspect of which is the prohibition against ex post facto punishment. These and other jurisdictional issues are likely to compromise ongoing attempts to bring terrorists to justice in military commissions.

Moreover, the current military commissions system is plagued by both actual and perceived deficiencies of due process, or "judicial guarantees." This has created a legitimacy crisis with serious consequences for U.S. national security. First, although the inadmissibility of evidence gained through torture is thought to be the rule in military commissions and federal courts alike, hearsay remains more broadly admissible in military commissions than in federal courts, so there will be instances in which it is never known if the evidence was the result of torture.[17] In one prominent example, a military commission judge admitted statements made by the defendant after he – just fifteen years old at the time – was threatened with murder and gang rape. Second, although evidence gained through lesser forms of abuse is also theoretically inadmissible, the military commission rules leave plenty of room for the introduction of involuntary statements.[18] Third, it is unclear that the military commissions will strike a proper balance between the need to protect national security information and the need to disclose both exculpatory and inculpatory evidence to the accused, as is provided for by the Classified Information Procedures Act in federal courts.[19] Finally, the military commissions process is notorious

17 *See* David Kris, Assistant Att'y Gen., Nat'l Sec. Div., Dep't of Justice, Remarks at The Brookings Institution (June 11, 2010).

18 *See* 10 U.S.C. § 948(r)(c)(2).

19 *Compare* Military Commissions Act 2009, 10 U.S.C. § § 949 *with* Classified Information Procedures Act, 18a U.S.C. §§ 1–16 (2011). The Military Commissions Act of 2009 by and large adopts the structure provided for in Classified Information Procedures Act. However, the differences allow for further exclusion of the defendant and defense

for impeding defendants from effectively accessing and communicating with their counsel, undermining their ability to lodge a vigorous defense.

These procedural defects are legacy effects of a broader pattern of institutional incompetence and abuse within the post-9/11 military commissions system that calls into question the legitimacy of military commissions to try terrorism suspects. U.S. military commissions in their present form lack a jurisprudential or institutional history to rely on. They have been marred by challenges under international and U.S. constitutional law. Whereas, as of this writing, the United States has been able to conclude only seven military commissions cases since 9/11, an equal number of military commissions prosecutors have resigned amidst ethical concerns regarding the military commissions process. Unsurprisingly, the international community, including many strong allies of the United States, sees the military commissions system as inextricably linked to the abuses of Guantánamo. The military commission prosecution of Omar Khadr, the first prosecution of a child soldier by a Western power since World War II, only served to reinforce this perception.

The perception of military commission trials as an extension of the Guantánamo project has serious national security consequences. State Department and Pentagon officials have said that even close allies are uncomfortable with Guantánamo, making it more difficult in some cases to coordinate efforts in counterterrorism, intelligence, and law enforcement.[20] In 2010, President Obama's top counterterrorism advisor said, "Some of our most important allies will not hand over terrorists, or the evidence needed to convict them, unless we commit to only using it in . . . federal courts [as opposed to military commissions]."[21] Military leaders and intelligence officials alike have warned that the second-class

counsel from proceedings, which potentially disrupts the delicate balance struck by Classified Information Procedures Act in the first place.

20 Tom Shanker and David E. Sanger, *New to Job, Gates Argued for Closing Guantánamo*, NY Times, Mar. 23, 2007, retrieved from http://www.nytimes.com/2007/03/23/washington/23gitmo.html?_r=1.

21 John O. Brennan, Assistant to the President For Homeland Sec. and Counterterrorism, Remarks at Brennan Center for Justice, NYU School of Law (Mar.18, 2010),

system of justice at Guantánamo only serves as a recruitment tool for al Qaeda and its affiliates. One experienced military interrogator called Guantánamo the number-one recruitment tool for al Qaeda, and U.S. officials have noted that al Qaeda and its affiliates have used Guantánamo almost sixty times in promotional materials since 9/11.[22]

All of these problems associated with military commissions – the legal uncertainty, legitimacy deficit, national security costs – might be worth it if there were other substantial benefits for holding trials in extraordinary courts rather than regular Article III federal courts. However, as will be shown, the ordinary criminal justice process has a long history of handing complex international terrorism cases without posing serious risks to national security.

2. U.S. Domestic Law is Well Suited to Handling Complex International Terrorism Cases: Extraterritorial Scope and Preventive Capacity

Notwithstanding the common criticisms of civilian terrorism trials, Article III federal courts are capable of handling complex international terrorism cases. Critics of civilian terrorism trials claim that the civilian criminal justice system is ill suited to ensuring that individuals who plan terrorist attacks can be prosecuted without endangering counterterrorism efforts. One specific criticism is that the civilian criminal justice system is designed to punish and deter common criminals in the United States, but not incapacitate international terrorists before they undertake large-scale, deadly acts.[23] In practice, two features of domestic criminal law have allowed for successful prosecutions against terrorists who plot attacks

transcript retrieved from http://www.brennancenter.org/content/resource/remarks_by_john_brennan_at_brennan_center_symposium/.

22 David Edwards and Joe Byrne, *Gitmo Recruited Thousands of Terrorists, Says US Interrogator*, The Raw Story (Jan. 27, 2009), retrieved from http://rawstory.com/news/2008/Gitmo_recruited_thousands_of_terrorists_says_0127.html.

23 *See* Mukasey, *supra* notc 3.

abroad: (1) the extraterritorial application of criminal jurisdiction; and (2) the availability to prosecutors of criminal offenses that prohibit planning and supporting terrorist activities.

A number of terrorism-related federal criminal statutes apply extraterritorially, and have served as the foundation for dozens of prosecutions of terrorist activity planned, initiated, or carried out overseas since September 11, 2001.[24] Indeed, modern international-terrorism prosecutions are built on more than two decades of international application of domestic counterterrorism law, beginning with the successful overseas apprehension and domestic prosecutions of several airplane hijackers in the 1980s. In the early 1990s, federal prosecutors brought charges against twenty-five defendants for the 1993 bombing of the World Trade Center and related plots, which were in large part planned overseas. All twenty-five were convicted for their involvement in these plots, including the leader of the World Trade Center bombing, Ramzi Yousef, who was apprehended in Pakistan before being transferred to the United States for trial. The August 7, 1998, bombings of the U.S. embassies in Kenya and Tanzania were planned and executed overseas, but U.S. law-enforcement officials worked with their foreign counterparts to interrogate and transfer many of the coconspirators for federal civilian trials, which resulted in convictions and life sentences for four individuals associated with al Qaeda. Since 9/11, international cooperation on domestic terrorism prosecutions has only increased as the U.S. government continues to build on existing law-enforcement relationships in the international arena. In total, nearly 500 individuals

24 Two recent cases involving terrorism suspects apprehended overseas and brought to U.S. federal courts exemplify this point. *See* Mosi Secret, *Man Charged with Plotting Against U.S. Abroad*, NY Times, Mar. 20, 2013, retrieved from http://www.nytimes.com/2013/03/21/nyregion/man-accused-of-plotting-terrorism-abroad.html?r=0; Mark Mazzetti and William K. Rashbaum, *Bin Laden Relative With Qaeda Past to Have New York Trial*, NY Times, Mar. 7, 2013, retrieved from http://www.nytimes.com/2013/03/08/world/middleeast/bin-laden-son-in-law-is-being-held-in-a-new-york-jail.html?ref=osamabinladen.

affiliated with al Qaeda or other organizations with international terrorism ties have been convicted in federal courts since 9/11.[25]

In addition to a long history of dealing with international terrorism, U.S. criminal law also has an established history of incapacitating individuals before they undertake terrorist acts. U.S. federal criminal law prohibits a variety of acts associated with planning, attempting, or assisting in terrorism plots. Individuals can be prosecuted for merely conspiring to commit a terrorist act – that is, agreeing to commit terrorism and taking some overt act in furtherance of that agreement. Moreover, conspiracy applies whether or not the act of terrorism is ultimately undertaken and, if the terrorist act is undertaken, conspiracy holds all coconspirators liable. Federal criminal law also makes it an offense to provide material support to terrorists and terrorist organizations, even absent the intent to further their illegal activities.

In Article III courts, these material support and conspiracy charges are thought to have disrupted a number of potential terrorist attacks. Omar Abdel Rahman, for example, was convicted not only for his role in encouraging the 1993 World Trade Center bombing, but also for taking a leadership role in plots to bomb several New York landmarks. Similarly, convictions were obtained in a series of post-9/11 "sleeper cell" cases, where individuals had trained for an attack, but not yet put into motion any specific terrorist plot. In total, material support and conspiracy charges have led to convictions of hundreds who played supporting roles in terrorist activity since 9/11, even when no terrorist acts were ultimately committed.[26] Whatever critics may legitimately claim about prosecutorial power in civilian terrorism cases, it is certainly not the case that the government is prevented from incapacitating would-be terrorists.[27]

25 *See* Dep't of Justice, National Security Division Statistics on Unsealed International Terrorism and Terrorism-Related Convictions 9/11/2001–06/06/2012 (2012) (retrieved from http://www.humanrightsfirst.org/wp-content/uploads/DOJ-Terrorism-Related-Convictions.pdf); Weich, *supra* note 4.

26 *See* Zabel & Benjamin, *supra* note 5, at 17.

27 In fact, some claim that federal crimes of material support and conspiracy are too broad, and may at times reach individuals who are not sufficiently connected to criminal

The benefits of the ordinary counterterrorism law-enforcement model over the military commission process should be immediately apparent. Whereas conspiracy and material support for terrorism are subject to legal challenge in military commissions, they remain staple counterterrorism tools in ordinary federal courts. The exact nature of charges aside, the civilian criminal justice system has developed expertise in uncovering incipient plots through the use of informants and "turning" low-level operatives to assist in the capture and prosecution of higher-ups.[28] Such methods are well-understood law-enforcement techniques employed by the Federal Bureau of Investigation (FBI) that soldiers cannot be expected to routinely administer. Putting the well-documented practices of torture and abuse aside, military interrogations of terrorist suspects have typically not yielded evidence appropriate for prosecutions.[29] It is not surprising then that military commissions have attempted to secure convictions through lax evidentiary standards and other procedural shortcuts that continue to haunt the military commissions system to this day.

3. Protecting Sensitive Information in Article III Courts

Despite the claims of critics,[30] the longstanding record of civilian terrorism trials shows that Article III federal courts, under applicable domestic law, are well positioned to protect sensitive national security information from exposure. Allegations that the government may be required to choose between pursuing a terrorism prosecution or protecting the sources, methods, and content of national security intelligence are likely exaggerated.

conduct. *See, e.g.*, Center for Constitutional Rights, Fact Sheet: Material Support, retrieved from http://ccrjustice.org/learn-more/faqs/factsheet:-material-support.

28 *See* Kris, *supra* note 17. See also Kelly Anne Moore, Op-Ed, Take al Qaeda to Court, NY Times, Aug. 21, 2007, retrieved from http://www.nytimes.com/2007/08/21/opinion/21moore.html?oref=slogin.

29 *See* Kris, *supra* note 17, at 18–20.

30 *Cf.* Mukasey, *supra* note 3.

On the contrary, well-established legal precedents have allowed the government to use such intelligence in prosecutions without compromising national security interests. The Classified Information Procedures Act (CIPA) is the backbone of federal protection against national security intelligence disclosures in civilian criminal trials. CIPA was enacted in 1980 to protect against "graymailing" – attempts by defendants to gain leverage by threatening to disclose classified information during trial.[31] To address this and related issues, CIPA imposes protection measures when either the defendant or the government seeks to introduce classified information at trial. Under CIPA, the judge first reviews any such classified evidence to assess its relevance. On finding the evidence relevant, the judge may order redactions or substitute unclassified or summarized versions that protect any sensitive national security information. CIPA also allows the government to accept court sanctions instead of disclosing information to the defendant pursuant to a disclosure order. Moreover, the government is entitled to immediate, interlocutory appeal of any disclosure order. Administrative rules established pursuant to CIPA also ensure that classified information is stored securely and only handled by individuals with security clearances. Although CIPA litigation can be cumbersome, it is broadly seen as an effective tool for protecting sensitive national security information. According to one study that analyzed more than 100 international terrorism cases against almost 300 defendants, the government has never experienced a security breach when it has used the protection measures that U.S. law provides.[32]

CIPA has also been influential in shaping the federal courts' approach to prosecutorial obligations of disclosure to the defense before trial. Normally in a civilian criminal case, the prosecutor is required to disclose all materials that may be relevant for mounting an effective defense. In terrorism cases, these materials often include classified information,

31 *See* Larry M. Eig, Congressional Research Service, Classified Information Procedures Act (CIPA): An Overview, CRS Report for Congress (1989); Serrin Turner and Stephen J. Schulhofer, Brennan Ctr. for Justice at NYU Sch. of Law, The Secrecy Problem in Terrorism Trials (2005).

32 *See* Zabel and Benjamin, *supra* note 5, at 9.

creating some tension between the disclosure obligations and the government's national security interests. CIPA operates at this pretrial phase, as well as at trial, enabling federal courts to address this tension by providing redacted documents, unclassified summaries, or other substitutes to ensure that defendants can mount a vigorous defense without compromise to national security.[33] Given CIPA and the federal courts' twenty-year record of successfully handling terrorism cases, it is unsurprising that the military commissions system has emulated CIPA – albeit without the established jurisprudence – in developing its information protection measures.[34]

4. The False Dichotomy between Rights and National Security in Civilian Terrorism Trials

Article III federal courts have also built from established constitutional precedents to advance the proper balance between national security interests and procedural protections. Critics of holding civilian terrorism trials in Article III courts often assert that it harms national security to give suspected terrorists the enhanced procedural protections of civilian trials.[35] According to these critics, it does not make sense to extend such protections to the battlefield and require soldiers to comply with criminal procedure requirements.[36] Despite the rhetorical appeal, arguments of this kind are ultimately unhelpful in assessing the impact of procedural

33 *Id.* at 93–95.

34 *Compare* Military Commissions Act of 2009, 10 U.S.C. § 949 *with* Classified Information Procedures Act, 18a U.S.C. §§ 1–16 (2011). Although there are some differences, the Military Commissions Act of 2009 classified information disclosure provisions are substantially similar in form and substance to Classified Information Procedures Act. Indeed, in hearings on the Military Commissions Act of 2009 before it was passed, witnesses commented that it would be prudent if the military commissions adopted these well-established procedures.

35 John Yoo, *The KSM Trial Will Be an Intelligence Bonanza for al Qaeda*, WALL ST. J., Nov. 15, 2009, at A23.

36 Stephen F. Hayes, *Miranda Rights for Terrorists*, THE WKLY. STANDARD, June 19, 2009, retrieved from http://www.weeklystandard.com/weblogs/TWSFP/2009/06/miranda_rights_for_terrorists.asp.

protections on military operations or the effectiveness of civilian terrorism trials; no one suggests that soldiers should read combatants Miranda warnings such as the right to remain silent or the right to an attorney, or obtain warrants before conducting searches and seizures on the battlefield. More generally, a close look at the way federal courts have handled procedural protections in terrorism cases reveals an intuitive and largely successful approach of balancing rights with legitimate national security interests – the ordinary criminal justice process has worked in ways that military commissions – extraordinary courts – have not been able to.

One common objection to the procedural protections afforded to defendants in civilian terrorism trials is that such protections may foreclose criminal prosecutions because crucial evidence cannot be admitted in trial because of the manner in which it was collected.[37] According to this line of thinking, once the government gathers valuable national security intelligence of a criminal plot, the fact that it did so pursuant to a warrantless search or seizure may prohibit prosecution in civilian federal court even if the evidence is otherwise reliable. However, the way in which the U.S. Constitution's Fourth Amendment protections against unreasonable search and seizure actually apply in these contexts reveals such objections to be largely theoretical. In a number of international terrorism cases, the government has been able to introduce vast amounts of foreign intelligence against the defendant, Fourth Amendment protections notwithstanding.[38]

The government's broad power to introduce foreign-intelligence evidence in civilian terrorism trials arises under the Foreign Intelligence Surveillance Act (FISA), which permits warrantless searches, electronic or physical, pursuant to the foreign-intelligence exception to the Fourth

37 Richard Bernstein, *Balancing Civil Liberties and Warfare*, N.Y. Times, Oct. 20, 2010, retrieved from http://www.nytimes.com/2010/10/21/us/21iht-letter.html (citing Andrew McCarthy's arguments that the Ghailani prosecution will be defeated because key evidence obtained from torture is inadmissible).

38 *See* Zabel and Benjamin, *supra* note 5, at 77–78 (describing several terrorism cases in which wiretap and physical evidence was admissible under FISA despite Fourth Amendment protections).

Amendment's probable cause and warrant requirements.[39] In contrast to the typical process, where the government would need probable cause of criminal activity to conduct a search, FISA allows the government to conduct foreign-intelligence surveillance by merely showing that the target is a terrorist suspect located abroad.[40] To invoke FISA, the government petitions the Foreign Intelligence Surveillance Court, which meets secretly, for permission to undertake the surveillance consistent with statutory guidelines. FISA also makes emergency procedures available when immediate surveillance is necessary. Considered as a whole, and contrary to common misconceptions, FISA's procedures have provided broad authority to the government to conduct foreign surveillance while preserving the ability to use foreign-intelligence evidence to facilitate federal civilian terrorism prosecutions. In fact, the government has been able to successfully introduce a variety of foreign-intelligence evidence – including recorded telephone conversations, e-mails, and documents – in at least eight international terrorism cases since 9/11.[41]

As with concerns over the Fourth Amendment's probable cause and warrant requirements, concerns about the Fifth Amendment's Miranda requirement undermining civilian terrorism trials have not panned out. Admittedly, case law is sparse on the extraterritorial applicability of the Miranda requirement, but what case law is available suggests that Miranda will not be a substantial obstacle to terrorism prosecutions in Article III courts. Importantly, several cases have held that Miranda requirements do not apply where statements are made to foreign interrogators without the involvement of U.S. officials; such statements have been admitted in civilian terrorism trials in many instances.[42] Even where

39 *See* FISA Amendments Act of 2008, Pub. L. No. 110–261; also *see* William C. Banks, *Exceptional Courts in Counterterrorism: Lessons from the Foreign Intelligence Surveillance Act (FISA)*, in this volume.

40 *Id.* § 702(a).

41 *See* Zabel and Benjamin, *supra* note 5, at 77–78.

42 *See United States v. Yousef*, 327 F.3d 56, 145 (2d Cir. 2003); *United States v. Suchit*, 480 F. Supp. 2d 39, 54 (D.D.C. 2007); *United States v. Abu Ali*, 395 F. Supp. 2d 338, 373–74 (E.D. Va. 2005).

U.S. interrogators are involved, Miranda's applicability is likely to be limited. In the "East African Embassy Bombings Case," the judge held that although Miranda warnings were required in the context of overseas interrogations involving U.S. officials, the Miranda requirements in this case were met even though the U.S. officials in question did not precisely read the Miranda statement.[43] In *United States v. Abu Ali*, the Fourth Circuit rejected the defendant's assertion that Miranda applied to statements he made to the Mabahith – the Saudi counterterrorism agency – during questioning that was in part at the behest of the FBI.[44] Future cases are likely to flesh out the exact contours of the Miranda requirement's applicability to overseas interrogations, but the embassy bombings and *Abu Ali* cases suggest that federal judges are reluctant to strictly impose Miranda requirements in ways that might hamper counterterrorism efforts.

Even where the Miranda requirements could apply, they would not substantially impair the ability to conduct civilian terrorism prosecutions for a number of reasons. First, the government may elect to simply read suspected terrorists Miranda warnings, as doing so has not been shown to harm law enforcement efforts, and may even increase law-enforcement and intelligence-gathering opportunities.[45] Second, where Miranda warnings are not issued before an interrogation, statements made in subsequent interrogations after Miranda warnings are issued can still be considered admissible, if sufficiently attenuated from the initial interrogation.[46] Finally, even in the improbable scenario of battlefield statements made

43 *See United States v. Bin Laden*, 132 F. Supp. 2d 168, 192–93 (S.D.N.Y. 2001).

44 *See United States v. Abu Ali*, 528 F.3d 210, 227–28 (4th Cir. 2008).

45 *See* Robert Mueller, Director, Fed. Bureau of Investigation, Statement to the Bipartisan Policy Center (Oct. 6, 2010) ("I do believe that if you look at the number of recent cases we've had, Miranda has not stood in the way of getting extensive intelligence."); Letter from Jim Clemente, Jack Cloonan, and Joe Navarro, Retired Special FBI Agents, to President Barack Obama (May 13, 2010) (on file with author). *See also* Stephen J. Schulhofer, *Miranda's Practical Effect: Substantial Benefits and Vanishingly Small Social Costs in* The Miranda Debate: Law, Justice, and Policing (Richard A. Leo and George Conner Thomas eds., 1998).

46 *See Missouri v. Seibert*, 524 U.S. 600, 615 (2004); Oregon v. Elstad, 470 U.S. 298, 324 (1985).

to soldiers, it is likely that courts will extend application of the public safety exception to hold that Miranda does not apply.[47] In sum, the Fifth Amendment's Miranda requirement has yet to pose a serious problem for prosecuting terrorism trials in Article III courts, and there is little reason to believe that it will.

Critics of civilian terrorism trials also claim that the need to delay prosecutions because of prolonged detention and intelligence-gathering may lead to scuttled prosecutions when a terrorist suspect asserts the right to a speedy trial, as embodied in the Sixth Amendment and Speedy Trial Act. But in international terrorism cases to date, speedy trial challenges have not barred the government from moving forward with prosecutions. In the 2010 trial of Ahmed Ghailani for his role in the East Africa embassy bombings, the trial judge rejected the defendant's speedy trial objection despite the fact that the accused had been indicted for more than ten years and detained for more than five years by both the Central Intelligence Agency (CIA) and the Department of Defense before the trial began.[48] According to the judge, because the United States detained Ghailani for intelligence-gathering purposes and did not seek any prosecutorial advantage, it had sufficient justification for delaying the trial.[49] In *United States v. al-Arian*, the government withstood speedy trial objections because the case was a complex, international terrorism case that involved substantial pretrial issues associated with classified information and discovery.[50] The Court conceded that delays were to be expected in such cases, and would not be considered violations of the defendant's right to speedy trial.[51] The government withstood similar objections in several other terrorism cases,[52] and in our view, there is no indication

47 *See* Zabel and Benjamin, *supra* note 7, at 103–05 (discussing the applicability of the public safety exception articulated in *New York v. Quarles* to battlefield interrogations).

48 *See* United States v. Ghailani, 743 F. Supp. 2d 261 (S.D.N.Y. 2010).

49 *Id.*

50 *See United States v. al-Arian*, 267 F. Supp. 2d 1258 (M.D. Fla. 2004).

51 *Id.* at 1262–64.

52 *See* Order Denying Defendant's Motion to Dismiss Indictment, *United States v. Padilla*, No. 04–60001, *2007 U.S. Dist. LEXIS 26077* (S.D. Fla. Apr. 3, 2007); *United States v. Abu Ali*, 395 F. Supp. 2d 338, 384–85 (E.D. Va. 2005); *United States v. Moussaoui*, No. 01-CR-00455, 2001 WL 1887910 (E.D. Va. Dec. 27, 2001) (holding that the seven-day

that speedy trial issues will pose a significant challenge to international terrorism prosecutions in Article III courts.

In sum, ordinary Article III federal courts have, as a general matter, properly balanced national security considerations with constitutional requirements in a way that allows terrorism trials to proceed without the negative baggage associated with the military commissions.

5. Evidentiary Issues

Contrary to the claims of critics of civilian terrorism trials,[53] Article III federal courts are adept at handling the difficult evidentiary issues presented by international terrorism trials. In particular, critics claim that authentication requirements, the rule against admitting hearsay, and the defendant's constitutional right to confront witnesses make it prohibitively difficult to admit testimony from individuals who may be overseas or otherwise unable or unwilling to testify in court. However, an examination of relevant civilian terrorism trials shows that these evidentiary rules have not posed insurmountable burdens for terrorism prosecutions. Where federal judges have encountered difficult evidentiary issues, creative solutions have almost always paved the way for successful terrorism prosecutions. In short, when considering evidentiary issues, the case for resorting to an extraordinary process like military commissions is far from clear.

Although authenticating evidence obtained overseas can be challenging, applying the Federal Rules of Evidence – with a deferential authentication standard and at least ten different ways to authenticate evidence[54] – has generally not proven to be a barrier to admitting crucial evidence at trial. *United States v. Padilla* illustrates how overseas

time limit between arraignment and trial normally required under the Speedy Trial Act does not apply); *United States v. Resaq*, 899 F. Supp. 697, 704–06 (D.D.C. 1995).

53 *See* Mukasey, *supra* note 3.

54 Fed. R. Evid. 902. There are an additional twelve categories of self-authenticating documents that do not need to meet the authentication standard to be admitted. Some of these categories include foreign reports and public records. *Id.*

evidence – even evidence obtained in an armed-conflict setting – can be authenticated despite these challenges. In *Padilla*, the prosecution sought to authenticate and introduce a key piece of evidence recovered by U.S. personnel abroad: an application form to attend an al Qaeda training camp.[55] The government was able to authenticate the form and establish a chain of custody by putting on testimony of a disguised CIA agent who possessed the form in Kandahar, Afghanistan, and later delivered it to the FBI.[56] Although problems in authenticating evidence were overcome in *Padilla*, in some cases authentication has proven to be more challenging because of lack of established interagency evidence-handling guidelines. Increasingly though, these problems are being addressed as agencies within the U.S. government work together and with their foreign counterparts to facilitate international terrorism prosecutions.

As with evidence authentication issues, difficulties in securing overseas witness testimony have not been a substantial roadblock to civilian terrorism prosecutions in Article III courts. In many cases, government witnesses – including members of the armed services – will be willing and able to testify, even if such testimony requires suspension of normal duties and travel from overseas. For example, in *United States v. al-Moayad*, the Department of Justice coordinated with the Department of Defense to arrange for a Marine captain, who was deployed to Iraq at the time, to travel back to the United States to testify as a government witness.[57] Similarly, active-duty military personnel, including Special Forces officers, were reportedly ready, willing, and able to testify against John

55 Government's Motion in Limine Regarding Proposed Procedures for One Chain of Custody Witness, *United States v. Padilla*, No. 04–60001, 2007 U.S. Dist. LEXIS 26077 (S.D. Fla. Mar. 22, 2007); Adam Liptak, *Padilla Case Offers New Model of Terrorism Trial*, NY Times, Aug. 18, 2007, retrieved from http://www.nytimes.com/2007/08/18/us/nationalspecial3/18legal.html.

56 Government's Motion in Limine Regarding Proposed Procedures for One Chain of Custody Witness, *United States v. Padilla*, No. 04–60001, 2007 U.S. Dist. LEXIS 26077 (S.D. Fla. Mar. 22, 2007).

57 *See* Zabel and Benjamin, *supra* note 5, at 109.

Walker Lindh – an American who joined the Taliban – before he accepted a plea deal, obviating the need for such testimony.[58]

In some cases, witnesses are either unwilling or unable to testify, presenting challenges to having statements from these witnesses admitted in court. These challenges have nonetheless been successfully addressed in several international terrorism cases. In *United States v. Ressam*, for example, the court rejected the defendant's Confrontation Clause challenge to the admission of testimony from witnesses who were unwilling to travel to the United States but agreed to be deposed and cross-examined via video conference.[59] Testimony by two-way videoconferencing has been upheld by several circuits where a witness is unavailable for good reasons.[60] Where witnesses are reluctant to testify in terrorism trials for security reasons, courts have ordered protective measures such as the use of an alias.[61] Where financial hardship may prevent a defendant from accessing overseas witnesses, courts have approved travel costs or allowed deposition via videoconferencing.[62]

Moreover, in many international terrorism cases, live witness testimony has been unnecessary in a variety of common scenarios where hearsay prohibitions do not apply. Statements not offered for the truth of the matter asserted therein – statements to show a defendant's intent or motive, for example – do not constitute inadmissible hearsay.[63] The defendant's own statements constitute an exception to the hearsay rule when they are made voluntarily, and prosecutors can freely admit

58 *Id.*

59 *See United States v. Ressam*, 221 F. Supp. 2d 1252 (W.D. Wash. 2002).

60 *See United States v. Gigante*, 166 F.3d 75, 19–82 (2d. Cir. 1999); *United States v. Weekley*, 130 F.3d 747, 754 (6th Cir. 1997); *United States v. Quintero*, 21 F.3d 885, 892–93 (9th Cir. 1994); *United States v. Carrier*, 9 F.3d 867, 869–71 (10th Cir. 1993).

61 *See United States v. Holy Land Foundation for Relief and Development*, No. 04-CR-00240, 2007 WL 1308383 (N.D. Tex. May 4, 2007).

62 *See* United States v. al-Moayad, No. 03-CR-01197 (E.D.N.Y. Jan. 28, 2005). Admittedly, using videoconferencing to secure testimony in criminal cases is controversial, but judges have found the method to be acceptable in narrow circumstances where witnesses are unavailable.

63 Fed. R. Evid. 801.

statements of coconspirators that are made in furtherance of the conspiracy.[64] Indeed, the Federal Rules of Evidence contain a broad range of exceptions to the hearsay prohibition, which could obviate the need to secure difficult-to-obtain live testimony in some international terrorism cases.[65]

In sum, there is little evidence that procedural protections afforded to defendants have, as a general matter, impeded or prevented international terrorism prosecutions in Article III courts. Hundreds of international terrorism cases have gone forward, with critics lodging largely theoretical objections to the role procedural protections could play in disrupting battlefield operations or otherwise jeopardizing national security. As has always been the case, judges interpret rights in ways that account for national security interests. Where tensions do arise, creative solutions – such as the use of two-way videoconferencing to admit witness testimony – have made prosecutions possible. Indeed, we are aware of no international terrorism case that has been scuttled by factors unique to international terrorism prosecutions.

Conclusion

Given the long history of international terrorism cases, hundreds of prosecutions since 9/11, high conviction rate of suspected terrorists, and lack of serious security breaches, the burden rests on critics of terrorism trials in Article III courts to make the case for why military commissions – extraordinary courts – are necessary. This is not to say that civilian terrorism trials are not without problems. Any trial with significant international components and national security ramifications will pose some challenges. Civil liberties advocates have also rightly expressed concern over the extent to which national security interests may be trumping traditional procedural protections in terrorism trials. Although more thought

64 *Id.*
65 *Id.* at 803, 804.

needs to be given to the proper way to approach terrorism trials in Article III courts, simply pointing out these challenges is not a case against civilian terrorism trials. The alternative to Article III courts – military commissions – must stand up to scrutiny, as well.

In contrast, the military commissions cannot stand up to meaningful scrutiny. Two of the staple crimes used in domestic counterterrorism prosecutions – material support for terrorism and conspiracy – are not war crimes despite claims by the commissions system to the contrary. Attempts to make unprivileged belligerency a war crime, a legacy effect of the Bush war paradigm, is equally problematic under the laws of war. Nearly all military commissions prosecutions would violate the principle of legality for attempting to punish conduct that was not illegal when committed. Not only are these features an affront to the rule of law, but they risk undermining what might otherwise be legitimate attempts to bring terrorists to justice.

Substantive legal problems aside, military commissions lack legitimacy because of perceived and actual defects in procedural due process. It remains an open question, one that is not open in Article III courts, regarding whether – and to what extent – evidence obtained from torture and abuse will be admitted in military commissions prosecutions. More broadly, the world views the modern-day military commissions not as a product of the significantly improved Military Commissions Act of 2009, but as the legacy of the infamous Guantanamo Project. As a result, the perception of military commissions as a system of second-class justice is impossible to shake, and threatens to bolster al Qaeda recruitment and undermine much needed American cooperation with its allies. Even if there were substantial security benefits to holding terrorism trials in military commissions – and we've tried to make the case that there are not – they would not be worth these costs.

Post-9/11 military commissions were conceived in the sin of intent to avoid judicial scrutiny. There is a direct link from the flawed logic of that desire to the continued failure of military commissions to provide the minimal judicial guarantees required by applicable international humanitarian law: Common Article 3 of the Geneva Conventions. The drafters' knowledge that they were promulgating second-class justice may also be inferred by the highly suspicious timing of two events: Congress removed the war crime of subjecting individuals to unfair trials from the federal War Crimes Act at the same time that it passed the Military Commissions Act of 2006. Although this change may prevent prosecution of those responsible for the military commissions, the use of commissions that fail to comply with Common Article 3's judicial guarantee requirements could still remain a war crime under international law.

Federal courts, on the other hand, enjoy a reputation for legitimacy and comply with the requirements of Common Article 3. Moreover, federal courts have a track record of efficacy that puts the current military commissions to shame; federal court prosecutions have a proven ability to disrupt incipient terrorist behavior, unlike military commission prosecutions, and have a longstanding record of moving forward while protecting national security information.

An abiding faith in American notions of justice suggests the application of Winston Churchill's observation that America always does the right thing, once it exhausts all other possibilities. One hopes that the point of exhaustion with the military commission experiment is reached sooner rather than later.

7 Exceptional Courts and the Structure of American Military Justice

Stephen I. Vladeck

MOST DISCUSSIONS OF "EXCEPTIONAL" COURTS TEND TO focus on the specific nature of adjudication before such tribunals. Whether directed to the jurisdiction of these ersatz bodies or the procedural, evidentiary, or substantive rules by which they operate, analyses of such institutions necessarily presuppose that the relevant comparison is horizontal, that is, that the question to ask is how the rules differ as between the extraordinary and the ordinary. Once one understands the full extent of the differences, one can better assess whether these variances, to the extent that they are permissible in the abstract, can be squared with the proffered justifications for departing from the norm.

In the U.S. context, virtually all of the debate over the military commissions at Guantánamo Bay has focused on myriad respects in which proceedings before those tribunals differ from the preexisting baseline, be it criminal trials in the Article III federal civilian courts or courts-martial in the Article I system created by Congress. Those who defend the commission process tend to emphasize how it can accommodate the government's interests in ways that the civilian courts and courts-martial cannot; those who attack it typically assert that such accommodations are either unnecessary, unconstitutional, or both. The same goes for arguments for and against proposals for hybrid "national security courts" that mesh elements of each system.

As interesting as the differences between these sets of courts, though, is the relationship between them. Remarkably, the Military Commissions Act (MCA) of 2006 (as amended in 2009) vests appellate review of the commissions in the Article III U.S. Court of Appeals for the DC Circuit, and ultimately, the U.S. Supreme Court. To be sure, the MCA interposes a new intermediate military court – the Court of Military Commission Review (CMCR) – between the military trial court and the ordinary federal courts. Nevertheless, it simultaneously creates a new system of courts that are generally understood to be exceptional, and then subjects them to what appears at least superficially to be entirely ordinary appellate review.[1]

In this chapter, I suggest that this structure is inherently paradoxical. However we are to understand what defines the category of exceptional courts, it should follow that one of their characteristics is existence wholly apart from the ordinary. After all, the analytical justification for exceptional courts invariably includes an account of why it would be inefficient, inappropriate, or just unwise to have the same category of disputes resolved by ordinary judicial processes. Thus, avoiding the rules that would apply in the ordinary courts – and their consequences – is the goal of most exceptional courts. As a result, inasmuch as ordinary appellate review of such purportedly exceptional courts – especially to the extent that it is de novo – may help obviate criticisms of such bodies, it should to at least the same degree weaken the underlying justification for the exception. And to the extent that appellate review is not de novo

1 Indeed, the "ordinary" nature of the appellate process under the MCA has prompted two different district judges to decline to resolve pretrial challenges to the commissions, holding that any such claims could properly be resolved on post-conviction review. *See Khadr v. Bush*, 587 F. Supp. 2d 225, 230–31 (D.D.C. 2008); *Hamdan v. Gates*, 565 F. Supp. 2d 130, 132–33, 136–37 (D.D.C. 2008); *see also Khadr v. Obama*, 724 F. Sup. 2d 61, 64–68 (D.D.C. 2010). These holdings are telling, given that the Supreme Court had specifically declined to abstain from deciding such a pretrial challenge to the commissions prior to the enactment of the MCA. *See, e.g.*, *Hamdan v. Rumsfeld*, 548 U.S. 557, 584–90 (2006). In other words, abstention in the later cases rested at least formally on the existence of a statutory appellate process.

either formally or practically, such a structure is even more problematic, for it risks enlisting the ordinary courts in the work of the exceptional courts by promoting tacit (or even overt) endorsement by the ordinary system of rules designed specifically to not apply there.

In short, my thesis is that, at least in the criminal context, it is difficult – if not impossible – to split the difference. Ordinary appellate review has the effect of converting exceptional courts into ordinary ones, whether for the better (by exerting top-down pressure on the exceptional lower courts to adhere to ordinary rules) or worse (by exerting bottom-up pressure on the ordinary appellate courts to endorse the exceptional rules as a general matter). To be sure, there is still a distinct role for trial courts to play as compared to their appellate counterparts, especially with regard to the development of the factual record. But at least where procedural, evidentiary, and substantive rules are concerned, it is ultimately self-defeating to have both an exceptional and ordinary court interpret and apply the same principles unless, in reality, that's not what they're doing.

To illustrate this phenomenon, I focus in the first part of this chapter not on the commissions themselves, which are – remarkably – still in their formative stages, but on the U.S. court-martial system. This system has moved over time from a true exceptional model toward the model of which the MCA is intentionally evocative – with courts-martial now subject to increasingly ordinary appellate review by an intermediate appellate military court, and then two civilian courts – the U.S. Court of Appeals for the Armed Forces (CAAF) and, ultimately, the U.S. Supreme Court. As I explain, it wasn't always so. Instead, the evolution of the structure of military justice in the United States may have a lot to teach us about how ordinary appellate review turns exceptional courts into regular ones.

In the second part of this chapter, I turn to the current structure of U.S. military commissions, and demonstrate the ways in which the structure of review in the commission system both mirrors and departs from the review of courts-martial. Although it largely remains to be seen how appellate review functions in practice under the MCA, if the court-martial example is any guide, the results will only serve to undermine the normative desirability of the project, one way or the other.

1. The U.S. Court-Martial System

Since before the Constitution was written, the United States has had a separate system of military justice. As the Supreme Court explained in 1983, "The need for special regulations in relation to military discipline, and the consequent need and justification for a special and exclusive system of military justice, is too obvious to require extensive discussion."[2] Such a separate system was wholly divorced from the ordinary civilian courts, so much so that, through the end of World War II, U.S. military courts were not subject to any direct appellate review by civilian courts. Instead, the only judicial means available for challenging a conviction by court-martial was the collateral review provided by habeas corpus, and even that review was limited to "jurisdictional" challenges – claims that the military lacked the power to prosecute either the defendant or the charged offenses.[3] To be sure, concerns over the "rough form of justice"[4] thought to be dispensed by World War II–era military courts may have been responsible for a series of contemporaneous Supreme Court decisions identifying constitutional constraints on both the offenders and offenses that such tribunals could prosecute.[5] Whether the military justice system was otherwise depriving those properly subject to its jurisdiction of their constitutional rights was largely thought to be a matter best left for the political branches.

Two developments precipitated a fundamental change in that understanding: the first came in 1950, with the creation of a statutory appellate

2 *Chappell v. Wallace*, 462 U.S. 296, 300 (1983).

3 *See, e.g.*, *Hiatt v. Brown*, 339 U.S. 103, 111 (1950).

4 *Reid v. Covert*, 354 U.S. 1, 35 (1957) (plurality opinion).

5 *See, e.g.*, *O'Callahan v. Parker*, 395 U.S. 258, 272 (1969) (courts-martial may only exercise jurisdiction over "service-connected" offenses).

structure for courts-martial – including the Article I Court of Military Appeals, later renamed CAAF – as part of the larger codification of the Uniform Code of Military Justice (UCMJ). As Harvard law professor Edmund Morgan (who chaired the committee that proposed the UCMJ) would later note, the UCMJ was designed as a "complete repudiation of a system of military justice conceived of only as an instrument of command," but was also intended to negate "a system designed to be administered as the criminal law is administered in a civilian criminal court."[6]

Thus, after review by the Convening Authority, the UCMJ created a two-tier appellate process that would apply to most defendants: The accused could first appeal to their service branch's "board of review" (later the Court of Criminal Appeals or CCA), which would be able to review the conviction de novo both as to the law and – unlike in the civilian courts – the facts. If the board affirmed the conviction, the accused could then seek discretionary review in the Court of Military Appeals, which, unlike the board, was empowered to act only as to questions of law.

The second major development came three years after the UCMJ in *Burns* v. *Wilson*, in which a fractured Supreme Court widened the scope of collateral Article III review of courts-martial to include claims that the military courts had failed to give "full and fair consideration" to the defendant's constitutional claims.[7] Thus, in addition to claims that the military courts had acted without jurisdiction, *Burns* opened the door to arguments that the military courts had not meaningfully provided an opportunity for the vindication of defendants' constitutional rights. At roughly the same time, Congress thus began to expand the availability of meaningful appellate review within the military justice system (and, eventually, in the U.S. Supreme Court), and the Court itself began to expand the scope of collateral review in the Article III courts for cases in

6 Edmund M. Morgan, *The Background of the Uniform Code of Military Justice*, 6 Vand. L. Rev. 169, 174 (1953).

7 346 U.S. 137, 144 (1953) (plurality opinion).

which the (increasing) safeguards within the military justice system had failed.

Little has changed in the past half-century with regard to the scope of collateral review in the Article III courts, even as Congress has made a series of tweaks (large and small) to the structure of military appeals, culminating with the 1983 provision authorizing at least some appellate review of CAAF in the U.S. Supreme Court. As a matter of statute, CAAF today may grant review in:

> (1) all cases in which the sentence, as affirmed by a Court of Criminal Appeals, extends to death; (2) all cases reviewed by a Court of Criminal Appeals which the Judge Advocate General orders sent to the Court of Appeals for the Armed Forces for review; and (3) all cases reviewed by a Court of Criminal Appeals in which, upon petition of the accused and on good cause shown, the Court of Appeals for the Armed Forces has granted a review.[8]

Additionally – so long as CAAF granted review – the U.S. Supreme Court may exercise jurisdiction over CAAF in cases falling within these three enumerated categories, as well as in "Cases . . . in which the Court of Appeals for the Armed Forces granted relief."[9] In other words, except in cases in which CAAF denies discretionary review outright, most military defendants today are entitled to post-conviction review that is largely comparable to that available to criminal defendants in the federal civilian courts.[10]

In addition to statutory innovation, the military courts themselves have increasingly interpreted their jurisdiction to resemble their civilian counterparts. Although many of these decisions have involved hyper-specific questions of interlocutory appellate jurisdiction, perhaps the most significant development has been CAAF's increasing use of its

8 10 U.S.C. § 867(a) (2006).

9 28 U.S.C. § 1259(4) (2006).

10 Even this distinction may be short-lived. Several bills have been introduced in recent sessions of Congress to extend the Supreme Court's appellate jurisdiction to encompass all cases resulting in a grant or denial of review by the CAAF.

power to fashion extraordinary relief to effect a form of collateral review within the military justice system. That is, although there is no separate statutory post-conviction remedy within the military justice system, CAAF has repeatedly rested on the All Writs Act[11] to allow it to provide various forms of collateral relief. Although the Supreme Court rebuffed CAAF's expansive assertion of All Writs Act authority in *Clinton* v. *Goldsmith*,[12] CAAF has since read into that same statute the more modest authority to issue writs of habeas corpus and writs of error coram nobis in appropriate cases. Notwithstanding *Goldsmith*, the Supreme Court in *United States* v. *Denedo* upheld the CAAF's power to provide such relief. As Justice Kennedy there explained:

> We hold that Article I military courts have jurisdiction to entertain *coram nobis* petitions to consider allegations that an earlier judgment of conviction was flawed in a fundamental respect. That conclusion is consistent with our holding that Article III courts have a like authority. The result we reach today is of central importance for military courts. The military justice system relies upon courts that must take all appropriate means, consistent with their statutory jurisdiction, to ensure the neutrality and integrity of their judgments. Under the premises and statutes we have relied upon here, the jurisdiction and the responsibility of military courts to reexamine judgments in rare cases where a fundamental flaw is alleged and other judicial processes for correction are unavailable are consistent with the powers Congress has granted those courts under Article I and with the system Congress has designed.[13]

In effect, *Denedo* recognized that the military courts have reached adolescence – that far from reflecting a rough form of justice, they have evolved to operate in much the same manner as the Article III civilian courts, and should therefore be able to exercise comparable authority, at

11 28 U.S.C. § 1651(a) (2006) ("The Supreme Court and all courts established by Act of Congress may issue all writs necessary or appropriate in aid of their respective jurisdictions and agreeable to the usages and principles of law.").

12 526 U.S. 529, 531 (1999).

13 556 U.S. 904, 917 (2009).

least absent a clear indication that Congress meant for them not to do so.[14] The unintended consequence of this line of cases may be to reduce the number of circumstances in which collateral review is available in the Article III courts, as the military courts will have additional opportunities to provide the "full and fair consideration" that *Burns* and its progeny require. But such a result would only prove the underlying point – that the military justice system is increasingly able to dispense justice without frequent oversight by the Article III courts.

As all of these developments were taking place, they produced a stark and decisive effect: the "civilianization" of the military justice system.[15] Although many of the trial procedures in the military justice system differ from those that are observed in the civilian courts, the past half-century has seen an ever-shrinking set of distinctions between the substantive law that applies in the two forums, especially when it comes to the constitutional rights of those subjected to trial. As CAAF explained in *United States* v. *Marcum*:

> The Supreme Court and this Court have long recognized that [m]en and women in the Armed Forces do not leave constitutional safeguards and judicial protection behind when they enter military service. Our citizens in uniform may not be stripped of basic rights simply because they have doffed their civilian clothes. As a result, this Court has consistently applied the Bill of Rights to members of the Armed Forces, except in cases where the express terms of the Constitution make such application inapposite.[16]

To be sure, "these constitutional rights may apply differently to members of the armed forces than they do to civilians."[17] It may also be

14 Chief Justice Roberts' dissent invoked the rough form of justice language of previous opinions to describe the contemporary military courts. *Id.* at 2225 (Roberts, C.J., concurring in part and dissenting in part). This language drew a rebuttal even from CAAF judges who agreed with him on the merits.

15 Karen A. Ruzic, Note, *Military Justice and the Supreme Court's Outdated Standard of Deference:* Weiss v. United States, 70 Chi.-Kent L. Rev. 265, 273 & n.78 (1994). *See generally* Peter Rowe, The Impact of Human Rights Law on Armed Forces (2006).

16 60 M.J. 198, 205 (CAAF 2004) (citations and internal quotation marks omitted).

17 *Id.*

happenstance that the proliferation of ordinary appellate review coincided with a series of cases holding the military courts to most provisions of the Bill of Rights. But, as was true for federal post-conviction relief for state convictions in the civilian federal courts, it seems far more likely that the availability of Article III oversight exerted both direct and indirect pressure on the military courts to bring their decisions increasingly into line with their civilian counterparts. Such developments may well have happened in any event, but it strains credulity to think that they would have transpired so quickly. Regardless of which was the cause and which the effect, the combination of ordinary appellate review and the general applicability of ordinary constitutional protections has unquestionably regularized the military process, such that the U.S. court-martial system today is consistently held out as a model of fairness – a far cry from the flawed, problematic system that Justice Black decried a half-century ago.

2. The Structure of U.S. Military Commissions

Superficially at least, the history of appellate and collateral review of military commissions has largely mirrored the history of such review of courts-martial. Military commissions, like courts-martial, were not traditionally subject to ordinary appellate review, as the Supreme Court emphasized in *Ex parte Vallandigham* in 1864.[18] Instead, like courts-martial, the only means of obtaining judicial review of a military commission was a collateral challenge, usually in the form of a habeas petition.[19]

Whereas the codification of the UCMJ in 1950 changed that pattern for courts-martial, it still held true for commissions when President Bush, in November 2001, promulgated an Executive Order creating new tribunals to try certain noncitizens in conjunction with the war on terrorism. And although the Order itself purported to bar judicial review of any sort, in *Hamdan* the Supreme Court found no barrier to the use of a habeas

18 68 U.S. 243, 251–54 (1864).

19 See David Glazier, *The Development of an Exceptional Court: The History of the American Military Commission*, in this volume.

petition to collaterally attack the legality of these new commissions.[20] Indeed, without any available means of obtaining direct review, habeas presented the only vehicle through which the civilian courts could entertain even the most fundamental challenges to military commissions.

It was the Court's grant of certiorari in *Hamdan*, however, and not its decision on the merits, that precipitated a critical statutory development. In the Detainee Treatment Act of 2005 (DTA), enacted one month after the Court decided to hear *Hamdan* (and largely in response thereto), Congress provided for the first time for statutory appeals from military commissions in at least some circumstances. In particular, section 1005(e)(3) of the DTA authorized appeals to the DC Circuit "to determine the validity of any final decision rendered pursuant to Military Commission Order No. 1, dated August 31, 2005 (or any successor military order),"[21] and made the appeal as of right "with respect to a capital case or a case in which the alien was sentenced to a term of imprisonment of 10 years or more."[22] The Act also circumscribed the scope of the DC Circuit's review, limiting it to:

(i) whether the final decision was consistent with the standards and procedures specified in the military order referred to in subparagraph (A); and
(ii) the extent the Constitution and laws of the United States are applicable, whether the use of such standards and procedures to reach the final decision is consistent with the Constitution and laws of the United States.[23]

20 Indeed, the government never even argued that the Order deprived the federal courts of the habeas jurisdiction that the Supreme Court had previously recognized elsewhere.
21 Detainee Treatment Act of 2005, Pub. L. No. 109–148 § 1005(e)(3)(A), 119 Stat. 2680, 2743 (codified as amended at 28 U.S.C. § 2241[e] [2006]).
22 *Id.* § 1005(e)(3)(B)(i), 119 Stat. 2680, 2743 (codified as amended at 28 U.S.C. § 2241[e] [2006]). Appeals in other cases were left to the DC Circuit's discretion. *Id.* § 1005(e)(3)(B)(ii), 119 Stat. 2680, 2743 (codified as amended at 28 U.S.C. § 2241[e] [2006]).
23 *Id.* § 1005(e)(3)(D), 119 Stat. 2680, 2743 (codified as amended at 28 U.S.C. § 2241[e] [2006]).

Although the DTA provided for a similar appeal from a final decision of a Combatant Status Review Tribunal, it otherwise purported to preclude all judicial review of claims arising out of Guantánamo, a provision that the Supreme Court in *Hamdan* held to be inapplicable to "pending cases."[24] Had it applied, it would have presented a series of difficult questions as to its scope, as among other defects, it only allowed challenges to the August 31, 2005, military order (and subsequent directives), and not to the earlier orders establishing the commissions; defining their jurisdiction; or delineating the offenses that could be tried.

Undeterred by the Supreme Court's decision in *Hamdan*, Congress effectively reenacted the same scheme in the Military Commissions Act of 2006, albeit (1) emphasizing that it did apply to pending cases; (2) creating an intermediate appellate court – the CMCR; (3) making all appeals to both the newly created CMCR and the DC Circuit as of right; and (4) cleaning up some of the textual flaws in the DTA's appellate review that had been highlighted during the *Hamdan* litigation.[25] And whereas the Supreme Court in *Boumediene* invalidated the jurisdiction-stripping provision of the MCA as applied to the Guantánamo detainees, the decision both explicitly and logically left the post-conviction review scheme wholly intact.[26]

Added together then, the DTA and the 2006 MCA produced the following scheme for appeals in the context of military commissions: the government – but not the defendant – could take interlocutory appeals at various stages during the pretrial and trial proceedings; the defendant could appeal a conviction (once confirmed by the Convening Authority) as of right to the CMCR, which "may act only with respect to matters of law."[27] From there, an appeal would lie to the DC Circuit, which, as under the DTA, could consider "(1) whether the final decision was

24 *Hamdan v. Rumsfeld*, 548 U.S. 557, 572–84 (2006).

25 For example, the MCA removed language limiting the statute to cases arising out of Guantánamo.

26 *Boumediene v. Bush*, 553 U.S. 723, 795 (2008).

27 10 U.S.C. § 950f(d) (2006).

consistent with the standards and procedures specified in this chapter; and (2) to the extent applicable, the Constitution and the laws of the United States."[28] Finally, the Supreme Court could exercise certiorari jurisdiction "pursuant to section 1257 of title 28."[29]

Congress left this basic structure intact in the 2009 MCA, but made four important amendments at the behest of the Obama Administration. First, it dramatically expanded the scope of appellate review in the CMCR, providing:

> [The intermediate appellate court] may act only with respect to the findings and sentence as approved by the convening authority. The Court may affirm only such findings of guilty, and the sentence or such part or amount of the sentence, as the Court finds correct in law and fact and determines, on the basis of the entire record, should be approved. In considering the record, the Court may weigh the evidence, judge the credibility of witnesses, and determine controverted questions of fact, recognizing that the military commission saw and heard the witnesses.[30]

Second, the 2009 MCA expanded the scope of the DC Circuit's review on appeal from the CMCR to encompass all "matters of law, including the sufficiency of the evidence to support the verdict."[31] Third, the 2009 MCA clarified that the Supreme Court's jurisdiction, were it to be invoked, would be analogous to its review of federal courts under 28 U.S.C. § 1254, rather than the state-court provision (28 U.S.C. § 1257) cited in the 2006 MCA.[32] Fourth, although there is no question that individuals convicted by courts-martial may pursue collateral relief in either the military or civilian court system (especially to the extent that their claims did not receive "full and fair consideration" in the military system), the 2006 MCA attempted to bar such review of military

28 § 950g(c) (2006).
29 § 950g(d) (2006).
30 § 950f(d) (2009).
31 § 950g(d) (2009).
32 § 950g(e) (2009).

commissions. In particular, language initially codified at 10 U.S.C. § 950j(b) specified:

> Except as otherwise provided in this chapter and notwithstanding any other provision of law (including section 2241 of title 28 or any other habeas corpus provision), no court, justice, or judge shall have jurisdiction to hear or consider any claim or cause of action whatsoever, including any action pending on or filed after the date of the enactment of the Military Commissions Act of 2006, relating to the prosecution, trial, or judgment of a military commission under this chapter, including challenges to the lawfulness of procedures of military commissions under this chapter.[33]

To the extent that this provision precluded individuals from collaterally attacking military commissions via habeas petitions, it may well have been unconstitutional.[34] That issue never squarely arose, however, and the 2009 MCA, which otherwise left the 2006 MCA's appellate structure entirely unchanged, deleted § 950j(b) without any comment or explanation. As a result, collateral review of military commissions in the civilian courts is available today to the exact same extent that it was available before the 2006 MCA was enacted.

The net effect of the 2009 amendments is to produce a structure that closely (and intentionally) mirrors the current structure for direct and collateral review of courts-martial.[35] As of today, the scope of the CMCR's post-conviction review is a word-for-word copy of the scope of the CCAs' authority under Article 66 of the UCMJ, and the DC Circuit's power is as broad as the authority that Article 67 gives to CAAF – if

33 Military Commissions Act of 2006, Pub. L. No. 109–366, § 3(a), 120 Stat. 2600, 2623–24 (formerly codified at 10 U.S.C. 948a[1][A] [2006]).

34 *See* Stephen I. Vladeck, *Military Commissions, the Right not To Be Tried, and the Suspension Clause after* Boumediene, Hum. Rts. Brief, Fall 2008, at 6.

35 Perhaps the only significant difference in the structure is that appeals from the CMCR go to the DC Circuit, rather than CAAF. As for why Congress would have chosen to both (1) create an intermediate appellate court in a system with so few cases; and (2) have appeals go to judges other than the experienced military jurists who comprise CAAF, see Eugene R. Fidell and Stephen A. Saltzburg, *Military Justice*, *in* Am. Bar Ass'n, The State of Criminal Justice 133, 134–35 (2010).

not broader. Moreover, unlike CAAF, the DC Circuit can't decline to review an appeal from the CMCR, which also means that there are no such appeals that fall outside the scope of the Supreme Court's power. In short, then, despite some key differences with regard to the evidentiary and procedural rules at trial, the appellate review provided by the present-day MCA is no stricter – and in some cases, significantly less restrictive – than the review available to most accused under the current court-martial system.

To be sure, it took a series of revisions – from the DTA process to the 2006 MCA to the 2009 MCA – to end up at this point, and there were serious reasons to doubt whether the post-conviction review provided by the 2006 MCA would have been sufficient. Nevertheless, one is hard-pressed to find meaningful textual differences in the scope of appellate review in the military-commission system today as compared to courts-martial. There may remain serious and substantial questions about who can be tried by such tribunals, and for which offenses.[36] There may also be serious questions about the procedures that the trial courts apply, but for those properly subject to the jurisdiction of these commissions, those questions can be addressed in similar fashion to the way comparable issues would be resolved in the court-martial system.

Instead, the real problem to date has been practice. As of this writing, the DC Circuit is still resolving issues raised in the appeals of two different convictions – *Hamdan* and *Al-Bahlul* – that were first argued to the CMCR in January 2010. Until and unless the civilian courts decide these cases (let alone others that might come through the pipeline), it is impossible to evaluate what effect the "ordinary" appellate process provided by the DTA and MCA (as amended) will have on the work of the military commissions. Further complicating things, the first round of appeals raise (and will raise) a number of critical questions of first impression, including whether the Constitution limits the jurisdiction of

36 *See, e.g., Hamdan v. United States*, 696 F.3d 1238 (D.C. Cir. 2012); *Al-Bahlul v. United States*, No. 11-1324 (D.C. Cir. to be argued en banc Sept. 30, 2013).

the commissions, commission defendants may invoke the Bill of Rights in their defense, various of the prescribed Rules for Military Commissions are consistent with both the MCA and Constitution, and so on.

It is entirely possible that these courts will conclude that, as noncitizens held outside the territorial United States, military-commission defendants are not entitled to the same protections as defendants in civilian courts or courts-martial.[37] However, if the court-martial experience is any guide, it is just as likely that there will be pressure on the CMCR and the DC Circuit to reconcile the jurisprudence of the military commissions with preexisting principles "except in cases where the express terms of the Constitution make such application inapposite."[38] Whereas the 2006 MCA purported to bar such cross-fertilization by banning courts-martial from relying on any "findings, holdings, interpretations, and other precedents of military commissions under this chapter," that provision, too, was deleted by the 2009 MCA.

Indeed, this pressure may already have prompted one significant change in the government's legal position: In the *Hamdan* and *Al-Bahlul* appeals currently pending before the DC Circuit, one of the central questions is whether the MCA violates the Constitution's Ex Post Facto Clause to the extent that the defendants were convicted of offenses – conspiracy and providing material support for terrorism – that were not recognized as war crimes prior to the MCA's 2006 enactment.[39] In the trial court and CMCR, the government's central argument, and the one on which both courts seized, was that these offenses were recognized as war crimes under customary international law at the time of their commission. In its briefing before the Article III DC Circuit, however, the

37 *See, e.g.*, *United States v. Ali*, No. 12–0008 (CAAF July 18, 2012) (holding that the Fifth and Sixth Amendments do not apply to a noncitizen civilian contractor court-martialed outside the territorial United States for offenses committed overseas), *Cert. denied*, No. 12-805 (U.S. May 13, 2013).

38 *United States v. Marcum*, 60 M.J. 198, 205 (CAAF 2004).

39 *See United States v. Hamdan*, 801 F. Supp. 2d 1247 (Ct. Mil. Comm'n Rev. 2011), *rev'd*, 696 F.3d 1238.

government shifted tack, conceding that material support is not recognized as a violation of customary international law, arguing instead that it is a well-established offense under the "U.S. common law of war," which if true would obviate ex post facto concerns.[40] Whether or not the en banc DC Circuit ultimately accepts this alternative theory, it is telling that the government shifted focus out of an apparent belief that the civilian court of appeals would be unsympathetic to the argument that had prevailed in the military courts. Even before the ordinary appellate review took place, its mere specter had a substantial effect in forcing the government to shift to an argument ordinary civilian appellate judges were more likely to accept.

Conclusion

In 2006, the United Nations Commission on Human Rights issued Draft Principles Governing the Administration of Justice through Military Tribunals, known as the Decaux Principles after Emmanuel Decaux, the special rapporteur of the Sub-Commission on the Promotion and Protection of Human Rights. Most relevant here, Principle No. 17 provides:

> In all cases where military tribunals exist, their authority should be limited to ruling in first instance. Consequently, recourse procedures, particularly appeals, should be brought before the civil courts. In all situations, disputes concerning legality should be settled by the highest civil court. Conflicts of authority and jurisdiction between military tribunals and ordinary courts must be resolved by a higher judicial body, such as a supreme court or constitutional court, that forms part of the system of ordinary courts and is composed of independent, impartial and competent judges.[41]

40 *See* Brief for the United States, *Hamdan*, No. 11–1257 (DC Cir. argued May 3, 2012), retrieved from http://www.lawfareblog.com/wp-content/uploads/2012/01/Hamdan-Brief-for-US-As-Filed.pdf.

41 United Nations Economic and Social Council, Commission on Human Rights, 62nd Sess., Civil and Political Rights, Including the Question of Independence of the Judiciary, Administration of Justice, Impunity: Issue of the Administration of Justice

The concerns animating Principle No. 17 are reflected in the current structure of military justice in the United States, both in the court-martial and military-commission contexts. However, if the former class of tribunals is any guide, the existence of such ordinary appellate review may well undermine the need for two distinct systems in the first place.

Ultimately, we can't yet know whether the courts in these cases will lean toward imposing constraints on the commissions that resemble civilian trials or courts-martial, or whether, in the alternative, the accommodations that the courts endorse in the commission context will spill over into these more established systems. If either scenario unfolds,[42] however, the point will have been made – the equalization of the two systems will have undermined the case for exceptionalism. All that will remain to be seen is whether the end result is for the better or worse compared to that which came before.

through Military Tribunals, UN Doc. E/CN.42006/58, ¶¶ 55–57, at 21–22 (Jan. 13, 2006).

42 The third possibility, of course, is that the courts recognize a wholly distinct and unique set of substantive and procedural standards in the context of military commissions. The court-martial experience surveyed in Part I in this chapter, however, suggests that this is the least likely scenario.

8 Exceptional Courts in Counterterrorism

Lessons from the Foreign Intelligence Surveillance Act (FISA)

William C. Banks

THE FOREIGN INTELLIGENCE SURVEILLANCE COURT (FISC) IS an exceptional court created by Congress to respond to a unique set of challenges related to foreign intelligence. On the one hand, U.S. presidents had on occasion authorized electronic surveillance and physical searches in pursuit of foreign intelligence without any prior judicial authorization, raising concerns that executive officials were violating the free expression and privacy rights of affected persons. On the other hand, many experts agreed that the need for speed and secrecy in collecting foreign intelligence in the face of threats of terrorism and espionage rendered traditional judicial warrant procedures ill-suited for foreign-intelligence surveillance. The FISC responded effectively to these challenges, but this exceptional court has also generated new problems. Because the factual predicate for gaining FISC approval to conduct surveillance or search is less demanding than what is required in traditional criminal cases, there has developed a considerable spillover effect, where criminal investigators and prosecutors rely on the exceptional FISC procedures to gather evidence for later use in criminal prosecutions. As a result, Fourth Amendment protections for the accused may be threatened by use of the exceptional procedures. At the same time, recent revisions to the FISC authorize the exceptional court to grant blanket approval to wholesale collection of foreign intelligence through issuance of directives to telecommunications companies and Internet service providers.

In this new role, the authorization for programmatic surveillance omits the case-by-case review of applications for surveillance and converts the FISC into an administrative clerk for executive officials.

This chapter first describes the history leading to the original creation of the FISC in 1978. Next, the role of this exceptional court in implementing the special scheme for foreign-intelligence collection is assessed, focusing on its overlap with law-enforcement objectives and the challenges of keeping up with changing technologies of surveillance and evasion. These challenges to the court's role are evaluated, as is the changing role of the FISC in the era of programmatic surveillance. In the concluding section, reforms are suggested that could help shore up the FISC in the face of the civil liberties threats posed by the continuing operation of this special court.

1. The Original FISA Scheme

Following the Watergate scandal and collapse of the Nixon presidency, congressional investigations discovered that, without seeking judicial approval, the federal government had engaged in widespread domestic surveillance for decades. The National Security Agency (NSA) had collected millions of telegrams sent from the United States abroad, and the Federal Bureau of Investigation (FBI) maintained watch lists of U.S. citizens involved in political protests. In 1976, the Senate investigatory Church Committee found that "too many people have been spied upon by too many Government agencies and [too] much information has been collected. The Government has often undertaken the secret surveillance of citizens on the basis of their political beliefs, even when those beliefs posed no threat of violence or illegal acts on behalf of a hostile foreign power."[1]

After the congressional investigators and media reports detailed the surveillance abuses targeting innocent civil rights and antiwar protestors in violation of their First and Fourth Amendment rights, members of

1 S. Rep. No. 94–755, AT 5 (1975).

Congress worked to devise a new law that would limit the surveillance powers of the federal law-enforcement and intelligence agencies. Although presidents had long asserted inherent authority to conduct warrantless electronic surveillance in furtherance of national security interests, congressional and White House negotiators enacted legislation that relied heavily on the unprecedented role of a new exceptional court.

Beginning in 1978, the Foreign Intelligence Surveillance Act (FISA)[2] authorized the means for electronic collection of foreign intelligence that served the nation well for many years. Before FISA, courts in the United States had extended Fourth Amendment judicial warrant requirements at two different times and in two different contexts: to government wiretapping in the law-enforcement setting in 1967; and to electronic surveillance in a case involving a domestic security investigation in 1972.[3] In the latter case, the Supreme Court rejected the government's argument that security matters are "too subtle and complex" for judicial evaluation, and the Court obliquely recommended that Congress consider regulating security investigations separately from its scheme for law enforcement, including applications to a "specially designated court."[4] The basic idea behind FISA was simple. Government may conduct intrusive electronic surveillance of Americans or others lawfully in the United States without traditional probable cause to believe that surveillance targets committed a crime so long as it can persuade a special Article III court – the FISC – that there exists a different kind of probable cause: reason to believe that targets of surveillance are acting on behalf of foreign powers.[5]

The FISC meets in secret, in ex parte proceedings where the targets of surveillance do not appear and have no notice of the proceedings or eventual surveillance. The court consists of eleven U.S. district court judges designated by the Chief Justice for staggered, nonrenewable terms

2 Foreign Intelligence Surveillance Act of 1978, Pub. L. No. 95–511, 92 Stat. 1783 (codified as amended in scattered titles of the U.S.C.) (hereinafter FISA).

3 *Katz v. United States*, 389 U.S. 347, 353, 358–59 (1967); *United States v. U.S. Dist. Court*, 407 U.S. 297, 313, 327 (1972).

4 407 U.S. at 320, 323.

5 FISA § 105(a) (codified at 50 U.S.C. § 1805[a] [2010]).

of up to seven years. There are no special requirements that the judges have expertise in national security or counterterrorism; all district court judges are presumptively eligible. FISA also provides for designation by the Chief Justice of three district or court of appeals judges to sit as a special court of review to hear appeals by the government from denial of an application by one of the FISC judges. The government may then appeal to the Supreme Court.

Electronic surveillance can capture movements and conversations about plans to commit a terrorist act and thus allows the government to step in before the act occurs. At the same time, electronic surveillance imposes a heavy cost in threats to personal privacy and expressive freedoms if it reaches innocent persons. Threats to civil liberties are especially acute when national security reasons are invoked to monitor political activities, as the convergence of First and Fourth Amendment values is not present in cases of ordinary crime. The government may have strong interests because of the threat of terrorism, but those targeted also have important interests to be taken into account.

FISA governed the electronic surveillance only of persons in the United States and only for the purpose of collecting foreign intelligence. It did not apply to surveillance conducted outside the United States or to foreign-to-foreign telephone communications intercepted within the United States. "Probable cause" required that a target of the surveillance be a "foreign power," an "agent of a foreign power," or since 2004, a "lone wolf" terrorism suspect – a person believed to be preparing for terrorist activities who is not shown to be affiliated with a terrorist organization. Applications to the FISC for approval of a search or surveillance had to specify "facilities" where the surveillance would be directed[6] and procedures to "minimize" the acquisition, retention, and dissemination of information not relevant to an investigation.[7]

6 *Id.* § 105(b)(1)(B).

7 *Id.* § 101(h); see also Intelligence Authorization Act for Fiscal Year 1995, Pub. L. No. 103–359, sec. 807, § 301(4), 108 Stat. 3423, 3443–44 (codified at 50 U.S.C. § 1821[4] [2006]) (amending FISA to include a new definition for "minimization procedures").

Before the FISC issued an order approving electronic surveillance involving a U.S. person, a FISC judge had to find probable cause that the target was an agent of a foreign power, on the basis of meeting one of four conditions: (1) the target knowingly engaged in clandestine intelligence activities on behalf of a foreign power, which "may involve" a criminal law violation; (2) the target knowingly engaged in other secret intelligence activities on behalf of a foreign power pursuant to the direction of an intelligence network, and those activities involved or were about to involve criminal law violations; (3) the target knowingly engaged in sabotage or international terrorism or was preparing for such activities; or (4) the target knowingly aided or abetted another who acted in one of the above ways.

The process undertaken by the government before going to the FISC (and before any wiretap is turned on) was elaborate and multilayered. FBI lawyers oversaw FBI agents who wanted to carry out the surveillance, and Department of Justice lawyers oversaw the FBI lawyers. Then, an application for FISA surveillance had to be approved by the Attorney General before presentation to the FISC: the department had to provide detailed information, including the identity of the target, a description of the information sought, and certifications that the information sought was believed to be foreign-intelligence information that could not reasonably be obtained by normal investigative techniques. The FISC may grant orders approving electronic surveillance anywhere within the United States.

However, what most of us think of as the judicial role in authorizing surveillance was limited by Congress in FISA in several important respects. From the beginning, FISA has allowed warrantless surveillance of non-U.S. persons for as long as one year, and another provision authorized electronic surveillance without judicial approval in an emergency situation.[8] The special court's review of FISA applications is also limited. Unlike deciding the reasonableness of surveillance in a criminal case, or

8 50 U.S.C. §§1802(a)(1),1805(e) (2010).

compliance with probable cause standards, FISC judges simply certify that a purpose of the surveillance is to collect foreign intelligence. The FISC does not determine whether there is probable cause that the electronic surveillance will result in acquisition of foreign intelligence, even where the principal objective of government investigators is to build a case for prosecution. In essence, the FISC decides that the government's paperwork is complete and in order. The legal standard requires only that the FISC find that the government certifications are not clearly erroneous.[9]

Once the statutory findings are made by the FISC, it must issue the surveillance order. The order must describe the target, the information sought, and the means of acquiring the information. The order must also determine that the government has set *minimization procedures* – mechanisms to assure that collected information is not stored or disseminated beyond the scope of what the FISC approved. The order must also set a period of time during which the surveillance may occur. The government may apply to renew the order on the same basis as the original application, and following the same procedures. More than 20,000 applications for surveillance or searches have been approved by the FISC since 1979. Less than 1 percent have been denied, and most of those denied applications were later approved after revision of the application.

To some observers, the FISC serves as a rubber stamp for executive branch officials who lack the traditional probable cause required by a magistrate in criminal cases. Some counter that the FISC is an unnecessary impediment as the executive branch strives to become nimble in collecting necessary intelligence. To others, the FISC has been a neutral arbiter necessary to ensure government accountability and legitimacy in furtherance of the narrow objectives for collecting foreign intelligence prescribed by FISA. At a minimum, the FISC provides assurances to Congress and the public that the government is meeting its statutory

9 *Id.* §1805(a).

obligations before undertaking surveillance of suspected terrorists or foreign agents.

Although the FISA scheme was complex, the legislation struck a fundamental balance. Those who worried most about the abuses of past presidents and their subordinates took comfort in the regulation of foreign-intelligence surveillance that involved Article III judges, albeit to a limited extent. The secrecy, ex parte proceedings, and corresponding lack of notice to targets was troubling, but at least applicable procedures had been prescribed by law. From the executive branch and intelligence investigators' perspectives, what was done in the past on the basis of supposed inherent constitutional authority was now subject to rules imposed by Congress. The rules lent legitimacy to secret surveillance.

The process worked well for several years as a mechanism to regulate surveillance of known intelligence targets. The FISA process and its eventual orders were always limited in two respects, however. First, whereas FISA demanded that "the purpose" of any surveillance or search be the gathering of foreign intelligence, a FISC judge in each case granted approval of the surveillance or search and found its primary purpose to be the pursuit of foreign intelligence or foreign counterintelligence information. In other words, although judicial review of FISC orders was limited, the reviewing courts used the discretion possessed by all Article III judges to require that collection of foreign intelligence was the primary purpose of the FISA investigation. Moreover, FISA was concerned with acquisition of information, not with the uses government might have for that which was collected. Second, FISA assumed that officials knew where the target was and what facilities the target would use for his communications. FISA did not authorize intelligence collection for the purpose of identifying the targets of surveillance, or of collecting aggregate communications traffic and then identifying the surveillance target. In other words, FISA envisioned case-specific surveillance with prior review by the special court, not a generic surveillance operation, and its approval architecture was accordingly geared to specific, narrowly targeted applications. FISA also recognized that persons lawfully in the

United States have constitutional privacy and free expression rights that stand in the way of unfettered government surveillance.

Although the volume of FISA applications increased gradually through the 1990s, after 9/11 the pace of electronic intelligence collection quickened. Bush administration officials argued that traditional FISA procedures interfered with necessary "speed and agility."[10] As the pre-9/11 annual FISA applications doubled to more than 2,000 a few years later, the Director of National Intelligence (DNI) complained that more than "200 man hours" were required to prepare an application "for one [phone] number."[11] The system was, it seemed, grinding along, but it was carrying a lot of weight.

2. Challenges to the FISA System

In the years after 9/11, the FISA scheme and the role of the special court were stretched well beyond their case-specific focus on gathering foreign intelligence. Two developments placed special stresses on the FISC. Increasingly, terrorism-related activities had been criminalized, leading to frequent intersections of law enforcement and intelligence investigations. The FISC became the favored venue for seeking authorization to conduct surveillance in anticipation of prosecution in terrorism cases. As a result, the traditional law-enforcement warrant was often bypassed, and attendant Fourth Amendment interests of the targets and those on the other end of the phone line were compromised through incidental collection of communications. Second, digital communications technologies were at once exploited by foreign agents and suspected terrorists and relied on by government. The development of data-mining techniques for

10 Administration Defends NSA Eavesdropping to Congress, CNN.com (Dec. 23, 2005), retrieved from http://articles.cnn.com/2005-12-23/politics/justice.nsa_1_security-and-privacy-national-security-agency-letter%_s=PM:POLITICS (last visited Mar. 29, 2012).

11 Chris Roberts, Transcript: Debate on the Foreign Intelligence Surveillance Act, El Paso Times (Aug. 22, 2007, 1:05AM), retrieved from http://www.clpasotimcs.com/ncws/ci_6685679 (last visited Mar. 29, 2012).

use by the government enabled investigators to depersonalize electronic surveillance and focus on gathering massive quantities of communications data to mine for further indications of terrorist activities.

Meanwhile, the Bush Administration decided to obtain what it viewed as the necessary speed and agility by tasking the NSA to undertake a massive electronic surveillance program on its own, in secret, and without involvement of FISA processes or the FISC. Within weeks of 9/11, although not reported until the December 2005 publication of an article in *The New York Times*,[12] the NSA began intercepting communications where one party was located outside the United States and the other party inside the United States. The collection occurred without gaining orders from the FISC. Instead of seeking new investigative authorities from Congress, the Bush administration simply ignored the requirements of FISA. The White House vigorously defended what it called the Terrorist Surveillance Program (TSP) after the story broke, but its legal arguments were weak and unpersuasive. Although details of the TSP remain secret, the NSA apparently would sweep up large quantities of data and then sift through it using data-mining processes. If the sifting produced information about specific individuals or groups that could be targeted for further surveillance, the NSA would then approach the FISC with a traditional FISA application.

Through statutory amendments to FISA since the September 11 attacks – in the 2001 USA Patriot Act, the 2007 Protect America Act, and the 2008 FISA Amendments Act (FAA) – the executive branch and Congress have tasked the FISC to endorse government efforts to build criminal prosecutions without following traditional Fourth Amendment rules, and to permit sweeping programmatic surveillance orders without review of the individual facts of potential targets. Even before the September 11 attacks, the United States moved to criminalize more terrorism-related activities. Although FISA and the FISC were designed

12 James Risen and Eric Lichtblau, *Bush Lets U.S. Spy on Callers without Courts*, NY Times, Dec. 16, 2005, at A1.

as preventives – to help the government forestall terrorism and espionage by learning about it in advance – increasingly, the investigations for foreign-intelligence and law-enforcement purposes had begun to blend and their objectives merge. Meanwhile, the FISA Court of Review approved executive branch practices that might sacrifice Fourth Amendment values and threaten the independence and legitimacy of the FISC. In the USA Patriot Act, Congress amended FISA to dismantle the wall between law enforcement and intelligence investigations by permitting the use of FISA procedures when there is "a significant" foreign-intelligence purpose to an investigation designed at the outset to build a criminal case. In other words, instead of coming to the FISC only when the primary purpose is collecting foreign intelligence, the government could launch its law-enforcement investigation with the FISC so long as some significant foreign intelligence could be collected. After the FISC objected to new Justice Department guidelines that dismantled the wall on the basis of the statutory change, the FISA Court of Review overturned the FISC and ruled that the Criminal Division of the Department of Justice could submit an application to the FISC so long as there was some significant foreign intelligence that could be collected. As a result, the role of the FISC diminished. The Court no longer questions the dominant prosecution objectives of government investigators who come before it, so long as there is some foreign-intelligence objective connected to the investigation. Similarly, its role in the new era of programmatic surveillance – to be described – is simply to approve and then occasionally monitor the suspicionless targeting procedures developed by the investigators.

3. Programmatic Surveillance and the Special Court

Under FISA as amended by the temporary Protect America Act in 2007 and the FAA in 2008, a significant portion of the FISC role has been transformed into performing a clerking function for the executive branch. Before Congress and in the context of the secret NSA surveillance program, the Bush administration successfully emphasized the need to amend FISA to account for changes in technology and thus enable it to conduct surveillance of foreign digital communications from within the United States. But providing statutory access to U.S. digital telecommunications switches would enable NSA to access e-mail traffic traveling to or from U.S. servers, opening up a vast swath of U.S. person communications for government scrutiny. In effect, the FAA authorized the TSP. The FISA architecture was changed to accomplish this neat trick in a simple way. The definition of electronic surveillance was amended so as not to apply to surveillance of a person reasonably believed to be outside the United States. Under the new legislation, the DNI and the Attorney General were authorized to collect foreign intelligence "directed at" persons reasonably believed to be outside the United States, without obtaining an order from the FISC, even if one party to the communication was a U.S. citizen inside the United States. The predicate for collection thus became the location of the target, not his status in relation to a foreign power or terrorist organization.

Under the FAA, the role of the FISC is narrowly circumscribed. The Attorney General submits procedures to the FISC by which the government will determine that acquisitions conducted under the program meet the program targeting objectives and satisfy traditional FISA minimization procedures. After a FISC judge approves the program targeting procedures, executive branch officials authorize the surveillance of persons reasonably believed to be outside the United States and issue directives compelling communications carriers to assist. Although details of the implementation of the program authorized by the FAA remain classified, a best guess is the government uses a broad vacuum cleaner-like first stage of collection focusing on transactional data in which wholesale interception occurs following the development and implementation of filtering criteria. Targeting might be directed at a terrorist organization or telephone number or e-mail address. Then NSA engages in a more particularized collection of content after analyzing mined data.

Although traditional FISA orders are still required for "intentional acquisition" of domestic communications, and they are also required for the first time for a U.S. person targeted as a foreign power or agent of a foreign power outside the United States, accidental or incidental acquisition of communications of U.S. persons inside the United States surely occurs, especially in light of the difficulty of ascertaining a target's location. Following a periodic review of the directives issued after enactment of the FAA, the Justice Department and DNI reported to the FISC in April 2009 that the NSA had been engaging in significant and systematic over-collection of the domestic e-mail messages of Americans. After investigations had been launched, intelligence officials told *The New York Times* that the NSA exceeded its statutory authority in implementing eight to ten separate orders issued by the FISC since enactment of the FAA. Because each order could permit collection of hundreds or thousands of phone numbers or e-mail addresses, millions of individual communications could have been intercepted, including some by U.S. persons inside the United States.[13]

The FISC must approve an order for programmatic surveillance if it finds that the government's certification "contains all the required elements" and the targeting and minimization procedures are consistent with the act and the Fourth Amendment. If the FISC does not grant the government's request for an order, it may appeal to the FISA Court of Review. Once the government's request is approved, the FISC does not supervise implementation of the targeting. The FISC does conduct a semiannual review of the programmatic surveillance it has authorized.

Beyond the risks of incidental collection, many Americans feared what the government might do with the information it gathered. The FAA requires that the Attorney General and the DNI certify that minimization procedures have been or will be submitted for approval to the FISC

13 Eric Lichtblau and James Risen, *Officials Say U.S. Wiretaps Exceeded Law*, NY Times, Apr. 6, 2009, at A1; James Risen and Eric Lichtblau, *Extent of E-mail Surveillance Renews Concerns in Congress*, NY Times, June 17, 2009, at A1.

prior to, or within seven days following, implementation.[14] However, the generic FISA minimization requirements were not modified in the FAA to accommodate the surveillance of individual targets through programmatic surveillance.[15] The FISC does not review the implementation of minimization procedures or practices for the programmatic surveillance it approves. Nor do statutory minimization rules require the government to discard communications of U.S. persons incidentally collected when the government is targeting someone abroad. The amended FISA permits the government to retain and disseminate information relating to U.S. persons so long as the government determines that it is "foreign intelligence information."[16] By implication, the government may compile databases containing foreign-intelligence information from or about U.S. persons, retain the information indefinitely, and then search the databases for information about specific U.S. persons. The combination of the government's use of the foreign-intelligence trump card to hold or disseminate information and the lack of judicial oversight of how private communications are filtered out leaves the minimization mechanism short of meeting its goals for programmatic FISA surveillance.

Although traditional FISA applications and orders may not comply with the Warrant Clause or traditional probable cause requirements, the substitution of individualized FISC review of applications and a specialized foreign intelligence-related probable cause have been construed by nearly every court that has considered their constitutionality as adequate for Fourth Amendment purposes. The programmatic orders are so dramatically different from the thirty-year FISA experience, however, that their suspicionless targeting procedures deliver us nowhere near meeting warrant or probable cause standards. Nor are the procedures reasonable

14 Foreign Intelligence Surveillance Act of 1978 Amendments Act of 2008, Pub. L. No. 110–261, § 702, 122 Stat. 2436 (codified at 50 U.S.C. § 1881a[3] [2008]).

15 *Id.*

16 50 U.S.C. § 1821(4)(B) (indicating that nonpublicly available information can be disseminated in a manner that identifies a U.S. person without their consent when such person's identity "is necessary to understand such foreign intelligence information or assess its importance").

in Fourth Amendment terms. Nor are any of the administrative officials required to find that the program targets are foreign agents, have or will engage in criminal activity, or are connected in any way with terrorism.

The programmatic title of FISA subordinates the FISC to the discretionary decisions of the Justice Department. Every FAA decision bearing on specific intelligence targets – except for the required FISC finding that a U.S. person outside the United States targeted for surveillance is a foreign power or agent of a foreign power – is made by executive branch officials and is not subject to review by the FISC or another judge. Prior identification of targets to a judge protects innocent third parties from being swept up in the surveillance and enforces the hallmark predicate for government surveillance – individualized suspicion. By focusing on what the collected information may be used for, FISA and the FISC (until the FAA) provided a useful, albeit opaque, mechanism to ensure the accountability of the collection scheme.

4. Shoring up the FISC as an Exceptional Court

The combined stresses of criminalizing terrorist activities and the digital revolution in communication and surveillance technologies have transformed the FISC from an effective model for an exceptional court that works into a clerk for executive branch investigators. Instead of doing what judges are good at – sifting facts and applying them to legal standards – the FISC spends much of its collective time on ministerial tasks. Unless reforms are made the special court may lose its independence and, over time, its legitimacy.

The original FISA procedure for reviewing applications for surveillance of foreign agents and lone wolves has served the nation well as a secondary, specialized system that serves discrete and important objectives. But the FISA experience shows in vivid ways the dangers that occur when a secondary system and its standards are mingled with those from the primary federal system, in this instance law enforcement and criminal prosecution in the federal courts. The byproduct of mingling the two is that the constitutional protections embedded in federal court prosecution are watered down and gradually eviscerated. Without FISA and the FISC, the federal courts would not have authorized electronic surveillance and physical searches absent probable cause of criminal activities or, in the event of exigent circumstances, on the basis of a finding of reasonableness. Employing the FISC, the government makes a less burdensome showing to the judge, and the target is never given notice of the application or the eventual surveillance. As ever more prosecutions related to terrorism are launched on the strength of FISA surveillance, the federal courts review the surveillance subject to permission already granted to the FISC by Congress. The courts do not undertake a de novo review of the surveillance application.

Because so many terrorism-related crimes now populate the criminal code in the United States it is unrealistic to expect any version of the wall that used to separate law enforcement and intelligence investigations to be rebuilt. The blending of the criminal and foreign-intelligence functions and personnel in the Justice Department, however, calls for reforms to protect the independence of the FISC and the integrity of the FISA process. One partial fix would be to create adversarial roles and processes. Both traditional FISA applications and certifications for programmatic surveillance orders are created, reviewed, critiqued, and presented entirely by Justice Department personnel, all with a singular objective to gain FISC approval of the applications and certifications. Congress or the FISC could create a straw adversary within the Justice Department to represent the interests of the described targets in an application or those likely affected by programmatic surveillance. The FISC could also be authorized by Congress to appoint cleared counsel to appear in connection with selected applications. Publicly released FISA Court of Review decisions demonstrate the shortcomings of insufficient procedures for those opposed to the government position to participate in the appeals process. Even where security concerns may require closing an argument or other session before the Court in part, an open session for cleared counsel to present arguments in opposition to the government would assist the FISC or FISA Court of Review in weighing legal arguments and enhance the legitimacy of the otherwise secret process in the eyes of the public.

Congress did not modify the traditional minimization requirements in FISA when it approved programmatic surveillance, and it is surely possible that extensive personal communications of innocent Americans will be retained in government databases for the foreseeable future. It would be possible for the FISC to make rules detailing specific minimization procedures in connection with programmatic orders. With the wall down and basket warrants enabling government access to vast stores of personal records, new rules protecting against abuses in retaining and misusing personal information would help restore confidence in the FISA system. As an Article III court, the FISC likely has authority to so regulate on its own, analogous to the role courts have played in defining other federal judicial rules.

One persistent problem with exceptional courts concerns their expertise. Courts such as the FISC are created to manage a highly secretive and factually nuanced system of surveillance, but the Article III judges eligible for the FISC have no special training in national security surveillance. Although some of those appointed to the FISC have had relevant military experience or have written scholarly articles on electronic surveillance, the FISC judges are not typically expert on the questions they are asked to review. Moreover, FISA itself seriously truncates the judicial role throughout the FISA processes. By and large, the FISC signs off on certifications from the government that collection of foreign intelligence is a significant purpose of the action at issue. The judges find probable cause, but only regarding the target's status as a foreign power, a foreign power's agent, or a lone wolf, and that the facilities targeted are used by the target. The FISC does not assess in any respect whether the approved surveillance will result in acquisition of the foreign intelligence sought. In effect, the FISC is a record keeper – is the government's paper application in order? Under the act as amended for programmatic surveillance, the FISC does even less in measuring the government's application for surveillance to a factual predicate. Instead of probable cause of foreign agency, for example, the FISC only determines that the target is or targets are reasonably believed to be outside the United States.

In programmatic surveillance the FISC may reject a certification only if does not "contain all the required elements," or the procedures "are not consistent with the requirements" of the act. The FAA does build in audits by inspectors general, and it provides for sharing some reporting information with congressional committees. The FISC, too, may review the programmatic surveillance procedures subject to "the need of the United States to obtain, produce, and disseminate foreign-intelligence information."[17]

Although the Supreme Court has not decided a FISA case – either on judicial review of a criminal conviction or a challenge to the FISC or its processes – all the lower courts that have heard challenges to the FISA architecture have upheld the scheme. The absence of adversarial proceedings and the use of ex parte processes do not violate the Article III case or controversy requirements, according to reviewing courts. Nor are challenges to FISA orders barred by the political question doctrine. As for substantive complaints, reviewing courts have found that FISA does not violate the Fourth Amendment, the Fifth Amendment's Confrontation Clause, or the First Amendment's free expression protections.[18]

Conclusions

The FISC remains an especially successful exceptional court. It was created to do a job that traditional Article III judges were reluctant to do and that the executive branch preferred be left to them. At the same time, the FISC was created at a time when surveillance abuses cast a shadow over the integrity of these important foreign-intelligence activities. In the years between creation of the court and the 9/11 attacks, the FISC

17 *Id.* § 1821(4)(A) (2010).

18 But see *Mayfield v. United States*, 504 F. Supp. 2d 1023 (D. Or. 2007) (finding Fourth Amendment violation), rev'd, 588 F. 3d 1252 (9th Cir. 2009).

developed some expertise in foreign-intelligence surveillance and the court gained considerable respect from observers inside and outside government. Although the secrecy of the FISC and its processes produced a measure of skepticism about what the court actually did behind closed doors, reviewing courts and others that followed the surveillance activities closely were assured that the FISC approved electronic surveillance only when its primary purpose was the collection of foreign intelligence.

The combination of the criminalization of many terrorist activities and the digital revolution in communications and surveillance capabilities altered the role of the FISC and, following the 2008 amendments to FISA, strained its credibility as an independent arbiter of lawful FISA surveillance. The use of FISA processes to build criminal cases is regrettable, in my view, but the lowering of the wall between law enforcement and intelligence-gathering has been supported by the FISA Court of Review and there is considerable momentum behind the use of FISA in building criminal cases. The programmatic surveillance now sanctioned by the FISC is more problematic, however, because the special court has assumed more of a clerical function than a judicial role. There remain opportunities to revise minimization rules, either through new legislation or FISC rulemaking, and to make government retention or dissemination of private information about innocent persons less likely. At the same time, if we must tolerate sweeping digital collection of our personal data, the FISC should have greater and more meaningful opportunities to oversee its collection – if not in advance, then after the fact.

Part II EXCEPTIONAL COURTS AND MILITARY COMMISSIONS ELSEWHERE

9 The Law Working Itself Pure? The Canadian Experience with Exceptional Courts and Guantánamo

Kent Roach

CANADA HAS NOT BEEN IMMUNE FROM THE USE OF exceptional courts or the legal and political controversies that often accompany their use. Canada did not use its newly enacted antiterrorism law to prosecute suspected terrorists in the ordinary criminal courts for three years after 9/11. Instead, it relied on administrative detention under immigration law that had not been used extensively before 9/11. Security certificates issued under immigration law are subject to review by specially designated judges of the Federal Court. Although the Federal Court is a regularly constituted superior court that hears civil and administrative claims against the federal government, it was an exceptional court in the context of security certificates because of the use of specially designated judges who examine secret evidence submitted by the government, but never disclosed to the detainee. The justifications offered for such use of the Federal Court are the familiar ones for exceptional courts: the need for secrecy; the expertise of specially selected judges trained in security matters; and the difficulties of criminal prosecutions in open court before juries. Security certificates have resulted in long-term and indefinite detention and have been politically and legally controversial. Indeed, some have criticized them as a milder Canadian version of Guantánamo. In any event, security certificates have been the subject of successful challenges under the Canadian Charter of Rights and Freedoms (hereinafter the Charter). In this way, the Canadian security certificate cases provide a case study of exceptional courts that have been successfully resisted and reformed.

Canada's second post-9/11 engagement with exceptional courts involves several indirect challenges to the detention and trial of Omar Khadr at Guantánamo Bay, Cuba. Khadr was fifteen years old when he was captured in Afghanistan. In October, 2010, he pled guilty before a military commission to murder, attempted murder, spying, conspiracy, and material support of terrorism. He received an eight-year sentence. The result for Khadr is far better than the forty-year sentence that the "jury" of military officers would have imposed on him after hearing testimony from a widow of an American soldier that Khadr admitted killing, and inflammatory but contested expert witness testimony about his continued dangerousness. At the same time, concerns lingered about the legitimacy of the guilty plea both in relation to the military commission's purported jurisdiction, especially over conspiracy and material support of terrorism offences, and a pretrial ruling by the military judge that Khadr's incriminatory statements were not tainted by threats that he would be raped in an American prison.[1] Former Guantánamo detainee David Hicks has argued that Khadr, like himself, only pled guilty in order to leave Guantánamo and because he was convinced that no military commission would render an acquittal.[2]

Khadr's lawyers fought numerous legal battles over Guantánamo in Canada, as well as in the military commission and before American courts. They won an injunction preventing Canadian security officials from continuing to travel to Guantánamo to interrogate Khadr, two Supreme Court of Canada decisions affirming that Canada had violated Khadr's rights under both the Charter and international law by interrogating him at Guantánamo in 2003 and 2004, and even an order requiring Canada to request his repatriation from Guantánamo. The latter order,

1 Order Denying Suppression Motions, CMCR 07–001 (2010), retrieved from http://www.defense.gov/news/D94-D111.pdf.

2 David Hicks, *Pressure to Plead Guilty*, 29(4) Hum. Rts. Defender (2010).

however, was overturned by the Canadian Supreme Court as interfering with Canada's diplomatic relations with the United States. Although Khadr won the vast majority of issues he litigated in Canada, he remained the only citizen of a Western democracy imprisoned at Guantánamo until his transfer to Canada in September 2012 to serve the remainder of his sentence in a Canadian prison. In this sense, his challenge to exceptional courts produced no effective remedy.

In this chapter, I argue that the use of exceptional courts will generally produce intractable legal and public relations quagmires, at least in healthy democracies committed to the rule of law. Exceptional courts should be avoided if at all possible for both due process and strategic reasons. In particular, exceptional courts that use secret evidence to facilitate intelligence gathering run a risk of condoning human rights violations and producing false positives that result in the detention of innocent persons. Exceptional courts will not have the legitimacy that regular courts have to punish and denounce terrorists. They may also undermine confidence in ordinary courts and lead to ordinary courts adopting problematic innovations made by exceptional courts.

I recognize that exceptional courts are used in many countries and have increased in popularity since 9/11.[3] Nevertheless, I do not think the story of largely successful legal and political resistance to exceptional courts told in this chapter is uniquely Canadian. It speaks to a healthy resistance that common law constitutionalism and vibrant democracies can provide to the use of exceptional courts. It also demonstrates the potential of "jurisdictional redundancy"[4] to provide multidimensional legal and political tools to resist exceptional courts. The Guantánamo process is not only a problem for American courts, but also for many other domestic and international courts.

3 For a discussion of how post- 9/11 practices have helped legitimate the use of exceptional courts in Egypt, Syria, Israel, and Singapore, *see* Kent Roach, The 9/11 Effect: Comparative Counter-Terrorism (2011) ch. 3.

4 Robert Cover, *The Uses of Jurisdictional Redundancy*, 28 Wm & Mary L. Rev. 639 (1981).

The first and longest part of this chapter examines Canada's use of security certificates subject to judicial review in the Federal Court as a form of exceptional court. It traces a process of the law working itself pure by examining successful legal challenges to the use of secret evidence and intelligence practices. It also suggests that the failure of exceptional courts to produce either legal or political legitimacy has resulted in a range of pathologies including more than 140 formal published judgments in security cases involving only five men in Canada. It has also produced political resistance and sympathy for the five men that have alarmed security officials. The last part of the chapter examines how lawyers acting for Omar Khadr used litigation in the Canadian courts to chip away at the legitimacy of his detention at Guantánamo, and how they may still use the Canadian legal process to attack the legitimacy of his guilty plea before an American military commission.

1. Canada's Security Certificates as a Form of Exceptional Court

Security certificates were introduced in Canadian immigration law in 1978 as a means to detain and remove noncitizens suspected of being a security threat. Three years after Canada suffered the deadliest act of aviation terrorism until 9/11 – the 1985 Air India bombing, killing 331 people – specific provisions were added to allow members of terrorist organizations to be detained under security certificates. Shortly after 9/11, additional amendments were enacted that contemplated that a person detained and removed under a security certificate could not be considered a refugee and could be deported to face a substantial risk of torture.[5]

Security certificates enable the ministers of immigration and public safety to declare that a permanent resident or foreign national is inadmissible to continue to remain in Canada on security grounds. Only twenty-seven security certificates have been issued in Canada since 1978,

5 Sharryn Aiken, *Of Gods and Monsters: National Security and Canadian Refugee Policy*, 14(2) Revue Quebecois de Droit International 1 (2001) (Can.).

most of them outside of the terrorism context. Security "offenses" are defined more broadly in Canadian immigration law than in Canadian criminal law. For example, the immigration-law grounds include being a member of a terrorist organization, which is not a crime in Canada. Moreover, the threat to national security can be established on a standard far less than the criminal-law standard of proof beyond a reasonable doubt. It can also be established on the basis of secret evidence that would never be accepted in criminal courts. A security certificate is subject to judicial review in the Federal Court to determine its reasonableness. Nevertheless, the executive signing of a security certificate preempts other proceedings, including applications for refugee status. Security certificates have been used in cases of suspected espionage and organized crime as well as in cases of suspected terrorism. The Supreme Court of Canada upheld the constitutionality of security certificates in a non-terrorist case in 1992, but stressed the importance of providing a summary of the secret evidence to the person named in the certificate.[6] The Supreme Court revisited security certificates in 2007, and declared the use of secret evidence that was not subject to adversarial challenge to be unconstitutional.[7]

From 2001 to 2003, the Canadian government issued security certificates under immigration law in order to detain and theoretically deport five noncitizens alleged to be involved with Al Qaeda. At the same time, it did not commence one criminal prosecution under the criminal law amendments of the 2001 Anti-Terrorism Act until 2004. The judges of the Federal Court appeared from their extrajudicial speeches to be divided on the appropriateness of the government's use of their court to hear secret evidence and intelligence. In 2002, Justice James Hugessen stated in an important and brave speech:

> [The judges of his court] do not like this process of having to sit alone hearing only one party and looking at the materials produced by only one party and having to try to figure out for ourselves what is wrong

6 *Chiarelli v. Canada*, (1992) 1 S.C.R. 711 (Can.).
7 *Charkaoui v. Canada*, (2007) 1 S.C.R. 350 (Can.).

> with the case that is being presented before us and having to try for ourselves to see how that witnesses that appear before us ought to be cross-examined.

The judge, who was first appointed to the bench in 1972, ended his speech with an extraordinary confession that he "sometimes feel[s] a little bit like a fig leaf"[8] in the absence of the usual benefits of adversarial challenge to the evidence presented to him in security-certificate proceedings.

Other Federal Court judges defended the legitimacy of their court in national security matters. In a 2005 speech, Chief Justice Alan Lutfy reminded his audience that the Federal Court had played a role in national security long before 9/11. With respect to security-certificate proceedings he stated, "Secret information is not taken at face value. Inquiries are made concerning sources, their numbers, their reliability and any corroborating or exculpatory information."[9] He defended what had been called the judicial management model[10] used in Israel and elsewhere where regular judges developed expertise and probed intelligence presented by the security service.

(a) Successful Challenges to the use of Secret Evidence

It took five years for Justice Hugessen's concerns about the problems associated with the use of secret evidence in security-certificate proceedings to be vindicated. In 2007, the Supreme Court of Canada held in *Charkaoui I*[11] that the absence of any adversarial challenge to the secret

8 James Hugessen, *Watching the Watchers: Democratic Oversight*, *in* TERRORISM, LAW AND DEMOCRACY, 386, 394 (D. Daubney et al. eds., 2002).

9 Honorable Justice Alan Lutfy, C. J., Federal Court, Keynote Speech at Norman Paterson School of International Affairs Seminar: Making National Security Accountable: International Perspectives on Intelligence Review and Oversight (May 18, 2005), retrieved from http://cas-ncr-nter03.cas-satj.gc.ca/portal/page/portal/fc_cf_en/Speech_18may05.

10 Daphne Barak-Erez and Mathew Waxman, *Secret Evidence and the Due Process of Terrorist Detentions*, 48 COLUM. J. TRANSNAT'L L. 1, 20–27 (2009).

11 *Charkaoui v. Canada*, (2007) 1 S.C.R. 350 (Can.).

evidence submitted to the judge violated the fair trial rights of the Charter. A unanimous Court stressed:

> [The fairness of the proceedings] rests entirely on the shoulders of the designated judge. Those shoulders cannot by themselves bear the heavy burden of assuring, in fact and appearance, that the decision on the reasonableness of the certificate is impartial, is based on a full view of the facts and law, and reflects the named person's knowledge of the case to meet... [because] the judge sees only what the ministers put before him or her. The judge, knowing nothing else about the case, is not in a position to identify errors, find omissions or assess the credibility and truthfulness of the information in the way the named person would be.[12]

The Court stressed limits to the judicial management model and held that the right to a fair hearing could only be satisfied by an adequate substitute for disclosure to the detainee and adversarial challenge to secret evidence.

The Court did not immediately release the three detainees who litigated the case or immediately strike down the security-certificate law. Rather, it provided the government one year to devise some system of adversarial challenge for the secret evidence. This followed practices used in other constitutional cases in Canada, but also erred on the side of the continued detention of the five men. The government opted for the system that maximized its interest in preserving secrecy. It created a British-style special advocate system that would generally restrict the ability of the special advocate to communicate with the detainee or others after having seen the secret evidence. The government, however, preserved the new legislation from successful Charter challenge by giving judges the discretion to authorize the special advocate to do what was required, including communicating with the detainee, in order to ensure the fairness of the proceedings. The new legislation also provides that reviewing Federal Court judges should only consider information that is reliable in security certificate proceedings and has not been obtained through torture

12 *Id.* at ¶ 63. *See generally* 42 Sup. Ct. L. Rev. (2d), 251–440 (2008).

or degrading treatment.[13] In this way, the new law moves security certificates closer to practices of ordinary courts and away from the paradigm of exceptional courts that accept secret and unreliable intelligence as evidence. Security-cleared special advocates created in the wake of the 2007 judgment have won successes in demonstrating that some secret evidence had been derived from unreliable human sources and torture.

(b) Successful Challenges to Intelligence Practices

Exceptional courts often use secret evidence produced by intelligence agencies. Litigants who resist exceptional courts will often challenge both secret evidence and the intelligence practices that produce such evidence. In 2008, the same security certificate detainee who won *Charkaoui I* won a second case in the Supreme Court over whether the Canadian Security Intelligence Service (CSIS) had a duty to retain the raw intelligence that was said to support their analytical conclusions and reports used as secret evidence in the security-certificate cases. The Court rejected a long-time CSIS policy that required the destruction of operational notes. This policy was consistent with a Cold War mentality that valued secrecy over prosecutions in the ordinary courts. The specially designated Federal Court judges had previously accommodated this mentality by often rejecting claims for disclosure of CSIS intelligence, sometimes without even examining the intelligence.[14]

13 *See* Immigration and Refugee Protection Act Amendments, S.C. 2008, c. 3 (Can.). The Canadian courts have subsequently held that the government must establish that the secret evidence is reliable and not obtained from torture or degrading treatment. *Re* Mahjoub (2010) F.C. 787 at ¶ 48 (Can.). This effectively places a higher standard on the government than in the United Kingdom, where a majority of a divided House of Lords required the applicant to establish that the evidence was obtained through torture. *A v. Secretary of State* (2005) UKHL 71.

14 Until 1982, national security claims of secrecy were unreviewable by Canadian courts, and even after that the Federal Court often deferred to them on the basis of concerns about the mosaic effect and Canada's status as a net importer of intelligence. Kent Roach, The Unique Challenges of Terrorism Prosecutions: Towards a Workable Relation Between Intelligence and Evidence 195–222 (2010).

The use of secret evidence protects the sources and methods of intelligence gathering from disclosure and allows countries to honor commitments not to allow the disclosure of foreign intelligence. At the same time, the use of secret evidence can also protect those gathering the secret evidence from criticism and embarrassment for the use of objectionable techniques in collecting the evidence. The use of secret evidence can draw the judges of exceptional courts into the secret world of intelligence agencies. Even if judges resolutely challenge the secret evidence, the fact that the challenge is conducted in secret may raise concerns about judicial independence. Although the Supreme Court in the *Charkaoui I* case concluded that the judges of the Federal Court remained independent and impartial even though they heard secret evidence submitted by the government, the very fact that such a challenge was made and seriously considered by the Supreme Court is telling.

In *Charkaoui II*, the Court stressed that original notes and raw intelligence would be more accurate sources of information for both the ministers who issue security certificates and reviewing courts. The Court concluded that "the consequences of security certificates are often more severe than those of many criminal charges."[15] This conclusion underlines a critical part of the thesis of this chapter: the use of exceptional courts as administratively expedient shortcuts around regular processes will often be the subject of successful challenge. In this case, the Supreme Court took a functional approach that effectively told Canada's intelligence agency that if its intelligence was going to be used as evidence to subject a person to long-term detention then it had better live up to similar evidentiary standards imposed by criminal courts on ordinary police forces.

CSIS appears not to have responded well to this judgment. A year after the judgment, Richard Fadden, the new head of CSIS, argued:

> [*Charkaoui II* had] turned one of our founding principles on its head. Our *Act* instructed us to collect/retain information that was "strictly

15 *Charkaoui v. Canada*, (2008) 2 S.C.R. 326 at ¶ 54 (Can.).

> necessary" in order to determine if a person was a threat. This was seen as *protecting* civil liberties. Now the highest court in the land has told us to do just the opposite. Retaining everything is now seen as the best defence of civil liberties.

He then issued an extraordinary and chilling warning:

> I am not sure if Canadians or even our national security community can foresee the full effects of this decision . . . I do predict, however, and I would be happy to talk about this in a few years, that within several years, someone will accuse us of acting like the Stasi because of the information we are now compelled to keep.[16]

These comments reveal resistance to judicial regulation of intelligence practices. They suggest that CSIS will indefinitely retain all targeted intelligence that it collects and may be prepared to blame any subsequent criticism that such holdings harm privacy on the Court's decision. Comparisons to the infamous East German intelligence agency, the Stasi, also ignore the fact that despite the Court's ruling on retention of intelligence, CSIS is still instructed by its enabling statute to collect only intelligence that is "strictly necessary"[17] to its statutory mandate in relation to reasonably suspected security threats.

The two *Charkaoui* cases were fundamental challenges to both security certificates and the workings of CSIS. Jim Judd, then head of CSIS, spoke publicly about "the judicialization of intelligence" as one of the major changes affecting intelligence agencies and complained in private that Canadian courts were treating his agency as if it were a police force.[18]

16 Richard Fadden, Director, Can. Sec. Intelligence Serv., Remarks to the Canadian Association for Security and Intelligence Studies Annual International Conference (Oct. 29, 2009), retrieved from http://www.csis-scrs.gc.ca/nwsrm/spchs/spch29102009-eng.asp.

17 Canadian Security Intelligence Service Act R.S.C. 1985, c.C-23 s.12.

18 Jim Judd, Director, Can. Sec. Intelligence Serv., Remarks at the Global Futures Forum Conference (Apr. 15, 2008), retrieved from http://www.csis-scrs.gc.ca/nwsrm/spchs/spch15042008-eng.asp. This speech is also consistent with a recent, more candid, WikiLeak in which Judd complained to American officials that the Canadian judges have an "'Alice in Wonderland' worldview" and have tied CSIS "in knots" and "left government security agencies on the defensive and losing public support for their effort

As a result of both *Charkaoui* decisions, the judicialization of intelligence that Judd astutely identified has increased in leaps and bounds. As a result of the increased disclosure requirements of raw intelligence in *Charkaoui II*, CSIS had to admit to the Federal Court in one shocking case that it had neglected to inform the Court about material in CSIS's holdings that cast doubt on the reliability of one of its human sources. Justice Noel, who like Chief Justice Lutfy had prided himself on the idea that judges acting alone could ensure fairness in security-certificate proceedings, wrote that this late disclosure cast doubt on the government's adherence to its duty to make full disclosure and the rule of law itself. Although he had previously been reluctant to disclose information relating to CSIS's human sources, he now held that "the rule of law requires no less"[19] than the disclosure of the full human source file to the security-cleared special advocates. This case suggests that judges who preside in exceptional courts may in the right circumstances begin to feel the gravitational pull of what my colleague David Dyzenhaus has called the "compulsion of legality."[20] Even if nothing so high-minded occurs, judges may simply become upset if they feel they have been misled and used by the government.

(c) Exceptional Courts and Rendition to Torture

Another element that makes security certificates in Canada exceptional is the possibility of deportation to a substantial risk of torture. The Supreme

to protect Canada and its allies," in part because, in Mr. Judd's view, the courts "inappropriately treated intelligence agencies like law enforcement bodies." U.S. Embassy Cable 2008–07-09, retrieved from http://www.nytimes.com/interactive/2010/11/28/world/20101128-cables-viewer.html#report/gitmo-08OTTAWA918. *See also* Kent Roach, *When Secret Intelligence Becomes Evidence*, 47 Sup. Ct. L. Rev. (2d) 247 (2009) (evaluating Canada's judicialization of intelligence).

19 *Re* Harkat, (2009) F.C. 553 at ¶ 14 (Can.). Note that subsequent to this ruling, Justice Noel held that CSIS's conduct in the case did not merit exclusion of evidence or a stay of proceedings on abuse of process grounds. *See Harkat v. Canada*, (2010) F.C. 1243 (Can.) (finding no abuse of process). This finding has been reversed on appeal. *Harkat v. Canada* 2012 F.C.A. 122 at para. 159.

20 David Dyzenhaus, *The Compulsion of Legality, in* Emergencies and the Limits of Legality 33 (Victor V. Ramraj ed., 2008).

Court held in *Suresh v. Canada*[21] that although the Charter will in most cases prohibit the deportation of a person to a substantial risk of torture, it may allow deportations to torture in undefined "exceptional circumstances." This regrettable decision was made early in 2002 and at a time when the fears created by 9/11 and expected second strikes were particularly intense.

The *Suresh* exception has rightly been subject to sustained international criticism. Despite urgings by the United Kingdom and other governments, the European Court of Human Rights has rejected it.[22] It was rejected both in the *Suresh* case itself – which involved an unsuccessful attempt to deport a person alleged to be a Tamil Tiger to Sri Lanka – and in another security-certificate case where Canada sought to deport a suspected terrorist to Egypt.[23] Nevertheless, the Canadian government has relied on the *Suresh* exception to justify continued detention and attempts to deport terrorist suspects who come from countries such as Egypt, Syria, Morocco, and Algeria. The *Suresh* exception thus has allowed the government to maintain that the security-certificate proceedings are still related to the immigration-law purpose of deportation, and are not being used pretextually as a form of administrative detention that avoids the demands of criminal prosecution. The *Suresh* exception demonstrates how governmental commitment to exceptional courts combined with fears of terrorism can produce a disturbing state of exception, albeit one that would be declared by the courts and not the executive. That said, the refusal by courts to employ the *Suresh* exception provides some grounds for concluding that the law may work itself pure in deed if not in word.

(d) The Security Certificate Cases

Six security certificates have been issued against men suspected of terrorism in the 2000s. The decision in *Suresh* did not result in his

21 Suresh v. Canada, [2002]1 S.C.R. 3 at ¶ 78 (Can.).

22 *Saadi v. Italy*, Eur. Ct. H.R. (2008), retrieved from http://www.echr.coe.int.

23 *Jaballah v. Canada*, (2006) F.C.1230 (Can.).

deportation to Sri Lanka, and he was released on light conditions that fell far short of house arrest. Mohamad Mahjoub, an Egyptian, was detained on June 26, 2000, allegedly for working for Osama bin Laden, but in 2007 he was released on strict conditions after a judge found that he could not be returned to Egypt within a reasonable amount of time and his controlled release would not threaten the security of Canada.[24] Mahmoud Jaballah, alleged to have terrorist ties with the Egyptian Al Jihad, was detained in August 2001. The government argued that he would not be tortured if deported to Egypt, or alternatively that deportation to torture was justified by the *Suresh* Court's exceptional circumstances ruling. Fortunately, the Federal Court has rejected both claims.[25] In 2007, he was released on a very strict form of house arrest.[26] Mohammed Harkat was detained on December 10, 2002, and was alleged to have ties to the Algerian Islamic Army Group. He was released in 2006 on strict conditions, but his security certificate was upheld at the end of 2010 as reasonable, although this finding has subsequently been overturned on appeal.[27]

Two security certificate cases have collapsed. Adil Charkaoui from Morocco was detained in May 2003 on suspicions of involvement with Al Qaeda. On his fourth detention review in 2005, he was released on strict conditions. In 2009, the government abandoned proceedings against him rather than follow a judge's ruling that more intelligence be disclosed to Charkaoui.[28] Hassan Almrei of Syria was detained on October 19, 2001. In 2005, he staged a hunger strike for more than sixty days in protest of his conditions of confinement in a remand center designed for prisoners awaiting trial. At the end of 2009, a judge quashed the security certificate as unreasonable, holding that while the certificate was reasonable in 2001

24 *Mahjoub v. Canada*, (2007) F.C. 171 (Can.).

25 *Jaballah v. Canada*, (2006) F.C. 1230 at ¶ 83 (Can.).

26 *Jaballah v. Canada*, (2007) F.C. 379 (Can.).

27 *Harkat v. Canada*, (2010) F.C. 1242 (Can.) rev'd in part 2012 F.C.A.122. Note that the appeal court upheld the trial judge's decision that the new special advocate system was constitutional and that the Supreme Court is scheduled to hear an appeal in this case in 2013.

28 *Charkaoui v. Canada*, (2009) F.C. 1030 (Can.).

given the available intelligence, there was no evidence that Almrei had engaged in terrorism, was a member of a terrorist group, or a threat to the security of Canada.[29] The judge also raised similar concerns as have been raised in *Harkat* about the reliability of CSIS's human sources in this case. Both Charkaoui and Almrei are free in Canada, but it is not known whether they are subject to continued surveillance by CSIS or the police.

(e) The Legal and Political Pathologies of the Security Certificate Cases

The prolonged legal proceedings in these cases reveal the legal pathologies that can be produced when exceptional courts are used in an otherwise healthy legal system. Courts that use secret evidence and are prepared to consider deporting someone to torture will attract rule-of-law antibodies. One measure of such legal resistance is the multiplicity of legal proceedings. Proceedings against Adil Charkaoui alone resulted in thirty-six separate written and published judgments from the Federal Court and two separate decisions in the Supreme Court from 2003 to 2009. The *Almrei* case resulted in fifteen reported decisions before the government abandoned the proceedings. The *Harkat* case has so far resulted in thirty-six reported judgments with more proceedings pending. The *Jaballah* case has so far resulted in thirty-four reported judgments, including those made on an earlier security certificate. Finally, the *Mahjoub* case has so far produced thirty-two reported judgments. Although some see such excessive litigation as a sign of too many rights and a "process that is so due that it seems due never to end,"[30] it reflects the problematic nature of the use of speculative and secret intelligence as evidence, indeterminate detention, and the difficulties of attempting to deport terrorist suspects to countries where they may be tortured. The length of these

29 *Almeri v. Canada*, (2009) F.C. 1263 (Can.).

30 Ed Morgan, *A Thousand and One Rights*, *in* The Security of Freedom: Essays on Canada's Anti-Terrorism Bill 412 (Ronald J. Daniels ed., 2001).

proceedings threatens to make them legally counterproductive, and no security certificate has been issued in a terrorist case since 2003.

Security certificates have been much more politically controversial than criminal terrorism prosecutions. Such controversy can be seen as a form of political pathology that mirrors the legal pathologies documented that have resulted in more than 140 published legal judgments in cases involving only five men. Richard Fadden, the head of CSIS, has complained:

> Suspected terrorists are given tender-hearted profiles, and more or less taken at their word when they accuse CSIS or other government agencies of abusing them. It sometimes seems that to be accused of having terrorist connections in Canada has become a status symbol, a badge of courage in the struggle against the real enemy, which would appear to be, at least sometimes, the government. To some members of civil society, there is a certain romance to this. This loose partnership of single-issue NGOs, advocacy journalists and lawyers has succeeded, to a certain extent, in forging a positive public image for anyone accused of terrorist links or charges.[31]

What Mr. Fadden seems unwilling or unable to understand, however, is that the sympathy that he sees is almost completely related to the unfair processes used against the security-certificate detainees. The leading Facebook site expressing support for the detainees does not express support for terrorism; it is called Stop Secret Trials in Canada.[32] Exceptional courts, at least in healthy democracies committed to the rule of law, will produce political and legal resistance that threatens to make them counterproductive.

Security certificates in Canada have failed as effective antiterrorism policy. The elected government and Parliament may be reluctant to devise an exit strategy from the security-certificate quagmire, but the independent courts are slowly taking such steps. The law in this respect

31 Fadden, *supra* note 16.

32 Facebook, retrieved from http://www.facebook.com/group.php?gid=2234830728 (last visited Mar. 26, 2012).

may eventually work itself pure and rid itself of reliance on security certificates as a form of antiterrorism law. Security certificates have failed as an effective antiterrorism strategy that commands public confidence. They have failed to protect secret intelligence from disclosure, and some of the disclosures have been most embarrassing to CSIS. Security certificates have been used as a form of indefinite detention and have morphed into a de facto and restrictive control order regime, both conditions never specifically authorized by Parliament. Since 2003, Canada has placed increased emphasis on criminal prosecutions in the ordinary criminal courts. To be sure, these proceedings have faced their share of legal challenges and have not always ended in convictions. There is, however, little sympathy in Canada for those convicted of terrorism offenses in ordinary criminal courts or even for those such as the two men who were acquitted of the Air India bombing in 2005.

Reliance on exceptional courts in the years after 9/11 may have distracted the Canadian government from some necessary reforms to the conduct of efficient but fair terrorism prosecutions. Such reforms would include allowing the ordinary criminal courts to examine classified information and determine if it has to be disclosed to the accused. Criminal courts in the United States and the United Kingdom perform this function, but in Canada it is only done by the same specially designated federal court judges who decide security-certificate cases.[33] In this sense, exceptional courts designed to maximize the state's interest in secrecy adversely influence the conduct of terrorism prosecutions in ordinary

33 The Supreme Court in *R. v. Ahmad* (2011) 1 S.C.R. 110 upheld the exclusive statutory jurisdiction of the Federal Court to make public-interest immunity determinations on national security grounds despite recognizing that the bifurcation of proceedings may be inefficient. The Court also stressed that trial judges in the ordinary criminal court might have to stay criminal prosecutions if they concluded that the accused's right to a fair trial might be jeopardized by a nondisclosure order made by the Federal Court. On the dangers of Canada's unique bifurcated approach to public interest immunity, *see* Commission of Inquiry into the Investigation of the Bombing of Air India Flight 182: A Canadian Tragedy (2010) vol. 3, chapters 5–7. For criticism of the Supreme Court's decision in *Ahmad*, *see* Kent Roach, *"Constitutional Chicken": Terrorism Prosecutions after Ahmad*, 54 Sup. Ct. L. Rev. 357 (2011).

criminal courts. Such extraordinary practices can produce a vicious circle that makes it more difficult to rely on the ordinary criminal courts.

2. Canada's Guantánamo Litigation

Although Omar Khadr's Canadian litigation did not secure his repatriation to Canada from Guantánamo, it did achieve significant successes. In 2005, a judge issued a temporary injunction that prevented Canadian intelligence officials from continuing to go to Guantánamo to question Khadr.[34] The Supreme Court twice held that Canadian interrogations of Khadr at Guantánamo in 2003 and 2004 violated both the Canadian Charter and international law.[35] In both cases, the Canadian court diplomatically based these conclusions on the U.S. Supreme Court's own decision in *Hamdan*.[36] The Canadian court focused on the 2003 and 2004 interrogations and did not attempt to opine on the dynamic and complex nature of the Guantánamo legal regime.

In its second *Khadr* decision, the Canadian Supreme Court stressed that the questioning of a youth held at Guantánamo at a time in 2003 and 2004 when there was no access either to counsel or courts "offends the most basic Canadian standards about the treatment of detained youth suspects."[37] These Canadian decisions, like similar British ones that make adverse comments about Guantánamo,[38] were part of widespread and continuing international criticisms of Guantánamo.

At the same time, the Canadian litigation did not provide Omar Khadr with an effective remedy. Although the Supreme Court in 2010 found that the violations of Canadian and international law had continuing effects, it reversed a lower court order that required Canada to request Khadr's

34 *Khadr v. Canada*, (2005) F.C. 1076 (Can.).

35 *Canada v. Khadr*, (2008) 1 S.C.R. 125 at ¶ 23 (Can.); *Canada* (Prime Minister) *v. Khadr*, (2010) 1 S.C.R. 44 at ¶ 16 (Can.).

36 *Hamdan v. Rumsfeld*, 548 U.S. 557 (2006).

37 *Canada v. Khadr*, (2010) 1 S.C.R. 44 at ¶ 25 (Can.).

38 *See, e.g., Abbasi v. Secretary of State*, (2002) EWCA (Civ) 1598, (62), (66) (Eng.); *Al Rawi v. Secretary of State*, (2006) EWHC (Admin) 972, (29) (Eng.).

repatriation to Canada on the grounds that the remedy interfered with the government's prerogatives over diplomacy.[39] The Canadian government responded to this decision with a diplomatic note requesting that the United States not use evidence obtained by Canadian officials, but some use was made of the videotaped interrogation in Khadr's pretrial military-commission proceedings. In subsequent Canadian litigation, a lower court concluded that Khadr had still not received an effective remedy. The judge indicated that he could, if necessary, order the government to request Khadr's repatriation should that be the only effective remedy.[40] The Canadian government successfully sought a stay of that judgment pending appeal, with the appeal's court judge who issued the stay expressing doubts whether courts could order the government to request Khadr's repatriation in light of the Supreme Court's 2010 decision overturning that remedy as not respectful enough of the government's prerogative with respect to diplomacy.[41] This appeal has now been found moot given Khadr's subsequent plea agreement.[42]

At one level, the failure of Khadr's litigation to secure his release reveals how Canada has capitulated to American hegemony and the United States's stubborn insistence even under President Obama on using military commissions and not closing Guantánamo. The Canadian government only asked for Khadr's return when asked to do so by the United States as part of a plea agreement that saved the Obama administration the embarrassment of placing a child soldier on trial. The Canadian government was likely motivated in part by the immense unpopularity of the Khadr clan, a self-professed "Al Qaeda family" that has abused its Canadian citizenship. At the same time, the Canadian government was motivated by a sense that it had best not waste its limited political capital with Washington on security matters regarding Khadr. Khadr was a very different case for Canadians than Maher Arar, another Canadian

39 *Canada v. Khadr*, (2010) 1 S.C.R. 44 at ¶¶ 27–47.
40 *Khadr v. Canada*, (2010) F.C. 715.
41 *Canada v. Khadr*, (2010) F.C. 199.
42 *Canada v. Khadr* (2011) F.C.A. 92.

who was subject to exceptional summary immigration proceedings in the United States and then rendered to Syria, where he was tortured before eventually being released. Canada did expend capital with the United States in vindicating Arar's claim of innocence. History will likely judge Canada's performance on Arar much more kindly than on Khadr.

The case of Omar Khadr may seem, at first blush, to be an exception to my thesis that exceptional courts will produce legal and political quagmires and ultimately fail in healthy democracies committed to the rule of law. After all, despite all his successful legal challenges, Khadr was imprisoned in Guantánamo until September 2012 and Guantánamo and its military commissions remain open for business. Khadr's plea agreement attempts to prevent him from bringing any legal claims in the United States or elsewhere in relation to his capture, detention, prosecution, conviction, or sentence.[43] Such provisions echo President Bush's November 2001 order attempting to preclude all judicial review of Guantánamo in any court in the world. It remains to be seen whether the attempt to preclude all subsequent litigation in any court in the world will fail, as the November 2001 order did. Both attempts reveal a lack of confidence in the ability of exceptional courts to withstand judicial scrutiny.

It is possible that Khadr will attempt to challenge his guilty plea and Guantánamo detention before Canadian courts, although that has not yet happened since his return to Canada. If made, such legal challenges may be settled, as they were in the United Kingdom, in order to avoid the disclosure of secret and embarrassing information. In any event, the legitimacy of Khadr's guilty plea is in doubt because of his successful Canadian litigation and the problematic nature of his unsuccessful attempts to obtain habeas corpus before the DC Circuit and his often unsuccessful attempts to litigate in his military-commission proceedings.[44] Today,

43 Pre Trial Agreement, CMCR 07–001 (2010), retrieved from http://www.defense.gov/news/Khadr%20Convening%20Authority%20Pretrial%20Agreement%20AE%20341%2013%20Oct%202010%20(redacted).pdf.

44 For a critical examination of Khadr's multiple unsuccessful attempts to seek habeas corpus in the District Court and his extensive and often unsuccessful litigation in his

exceptional courts can often be challenged in multiple legal fora – foreign, supranational and domestic – and through globalized media and civil society. The globalization of the legal and political order has intensified jurisdictional redundancy[45] well beyond that described by Robert Cover in 1981. It has increased the ability of those committed to the rule of law to relentlessly challenge exceptional courts. Exceptional courts may persist, but the controversy surrounding them will grow. It may make exceptional courts legally and politically counterproductive.

Conclusion

The Canadian experience suggests that the use of exceptional courts in terrorism cases will be both politically and legally controversial, and that in a globalized world populated with human rights-savvy lawyers, there will be prolonged litigation in many fora to contest the use of exceptional courts. To be sure, such litigation may not often be successful in terms of the ultimate remedy of shutting down exceptional courts or securing the release of those subject to their often pathological processes. Nevertheless, such litigation, especially when it is supported by a vibrant civil society, will challenge and undermine the legitimacy of exceptional courts. Three security-certificate cases in Canada currently drag on, but the use of such exceptional procedures in Canada has been a failure that has discredited the use of exceptional and secret trials. Although Omar Khadr only received limited remedies from Canadian courts, his multiple lawsuits opened up a northern front in the global critique of Guantánamo.

One argument for exceptional courts is that they might prevent the infection of the ordinary law and courts with emergency innovations in a manner similar to that posited in the extralegal measures model.[46]

military commission, *see* Kent Roach, *Uneasy Neighbors: Comparative American and Canadian Counter-Terrorism*, 38(5) William Mitchell L. Rev. 1701, 1759–1769 (2012).

45 Cover, *supra* note 4.

46 Oren Gross and Fionnuala Ní Aoláin, Law in Times of Crisis: Emergency Powers in Theory and Practice ch. 3–4 (2006).

The use of exceptional courts may, however, undermine confidence in the ordinary courts and deprive them of experience in difficult terrorism prosecutions. Canada might not have used terrorism prosecutions unless faced with the hard reality that it could not use security certificates against its own citizens. Similarly, there is widespread concern in the United States about the viability of criminal prosecutions as an alternative to Guantánamo despite many successful criminal prosecutions. An important lesson of 9/11 and terrorism in general is that we must not lose confidence in the ability of criminal prosecutions in the ordinary courts to justly punish, denounce, and incapacitate terrorists.The use of exceptional courts is a dubious method of preserving the purity of the ordinary courts. To be sure, ordinary criminal prosecutions will be difficult and sometimes they run the danger of acquitting the guilty and convicting the innocent. Nevertheless, they will resist the use of secret evidence that is so often the hallmark of exceptional courts and that erodes so much of the legal and political legitimacy of exceptional courts.

It is also possible that some of the practices of exceptional courts may migrate and infect those of the ordinary courts. One example is the way in which Canadian criminal law has expanded to embrace some of the intelligence-based concepts used in security-certificate cases, such as the deeming of a person's associations and political and religious beliefs as admissible forms of evidence.[47] Another is the continuing role of specially designated federal court judges in deciding public-interest immunity applications that would otherwise be decided by the ordinary criminal trial judges who conduct terrorism prosecutions. Restrictive conditions of release used in security-certificate cases may also inspire the use of control orders or peace bonds against all terrorist suspects. If he is eventually released in Canada, Omar Khadr may be placed under conditions such as house arrest similar to those imposed on security-certificate detainees. If so, he will have traded exceptional justice at Guantánamo for another

47 Kent Roach, *The Eroding Distinction Between Intelligence and Evidence*, *in* COUNTER-TERRORISM AND BEYOND (Nicola McGarrity et al. eds., 2010).

form of exceptional justice in Canada. The less harsh Canadian approach may in some ways be more dangerous because it is more easily normalized through our increased acceptance of various "pre-crime" interventions.[48] Once objectionable practices are introduced in exceptional courts, there is a real risk that they will spill over to ordinary processes, and this also undermines the idea that the exceptional can be contained in exceptional courts.

Exceptional courts will attract widespread and sustained political and legal challenges. Although the law may not work itself pure in the manner posited by Lord Mansfield[49] to effectively abolish exceptional courts, the political and legal legitimacy of exceptional courts will be undermined by multiple legal and political challenges to exceptional courts. Rule-of-law antibodies will attack exceptional courts and may bring them more in line with the practices of ordinary courts. In a battle against terrorism that is as much a contest of ideas as it is of arms, the political and legal controversies created by exceptional courts should be enough to discourage their use.

Exceptional courts are a particularly bad idea in terrorism cases because they avoid punishing terrorism as a crime.[50] The use of exceptional courts will infringe the due process rights of suspected terrorists while resulting in prolonged detention of suspected terrorists. They can elevate those detained without an ordinary trial into martyrs and objects of sympathy because of their unfair treatment. Almost everyone understands the injustice of secret evidence. Exceptional courts may incapacitate some terrorists, but they may also imprison the innocent. They can

48 *See* Lucia Zedner, *Preventive Justice or Pre-Punishment? The Case of Control Orders*, 60 Current Legal Probs. 174 (2007) (discussing the normalization of "pre-crime" measures). *But see* Judith Resnik, *Detention, the War on Terror and the Federal Courts*, 110 Colum. L. Rev. 579 (2010).

49 *Omychund v. Barker*, (1774) 26 Eng. Rep. 15 (P.C.).

50 For a defense of the use of criminal prosecutions in terrorism cases, *see* Kent Roach, *The Criminal Law and its Less Restrained Alternatives*, *in* Global Anti-Terrorism Law and Policy 191 (Victor Ramraj et al eds., 2d ed., 2012).

deprive detentions, guilty pleas, and verdicts of the full denunciatory and retributive force that should be reserved for those who are prepared to murder and maim civilians. Exceptional courts are a bad idea. They are an especially bad idea in terrorism cases. In systems committed to the rule of law, they should and will be resisted.

10 Vicious and Virtuous Cycles in Prosecuting Terrorism

The Diplock Court Experience

John Jackson

THE EVENTS OF 9/11 HAVE LED TO SUCH AN EXTENSIVE literature on the resort to emergency powers at both the national and international level that there has been a tendency to forget that before 9/11 a number of countries experienced their own forms of terrorism that in themselves led to a literature at the national level. September 11 globalized the so-called war on terror and put center stage questions about responses to terrorism that have in truth been going on for some time.[1] Contributors to this book, such as Steven Greer and Clive Walker, have made major contributions to the pre-9/11 literature on the exercise of emergency and terrorism powers in the United Kingdom and Ireland.[2]

One of the advantages of focusing on this literature is that with a longer focus and wider lens it can provide lessons on responses to terrorism over a longer period than simply since 9/11. Some have drawn attention to the truly horrific scale of the new global terrorism, differentiating it from the domestic terrorism of the past. Two differences are said

1 *See* Oren Gross and Fionnuala Ní Aoláin, Law in Times of Crisis: Emergency Powers in Theory and Practice (2006).

2 *See, e.g.*, Steven.C. Greer and A. White, Abolishing the Diplock Courts: The Case for Restoring Jury Trial to Scheduled Offences to Northern Ireland (1986); Clive Walker and Gerry Hogan, Political Violence and the Law in Ireland (1989).

to stand out: the scale of the threat – the fact that the global terrorist may strike anywhere with the potential to use weapons of mass destruction; and the fact that today's global terrorists are prepared to sacrifice their own lives. Consequently, it has been argued by Paul Kahn that the reaction of national states has been all the more punitive.[3] A vicious cycle has emerged whereby terror is followed by torture and principles such as the rule of law and human rights are sacrificed and replaced with talk of how we should respond to ticking time bombs. In an argument akin to Tony Blair's claim after the United Kingdom's 7/7 that the "rules of the game are changing,"[4] Kahn argues that 9/11 put an end to the narrative of the triumph of a global order on the basis of the rule of law that was holding sway at the end of the twentieth century – the idea that the new post–World War II legal order would progress from the UN Declaration of the Rights of Man to the more detailed covenant on Civil and Political Rights and finally to enforcement through the International Criminal Court. Instead terror reemerged, torture was resumed, and the politics of national sovereignty reasserted itself.

But if we take a step back to the pre-9/11 period of what Kahn calls the "familiar violence of domestic terrorist groups,"[5] it would be wrong to suggest that the threats were not as horrendous for those living within the regions where this violence has often been indiscriminately perpetrated. A number of questions then present themselves. Has the response to domestic terrorism always been met as severely as the war on global terror? Has terror always been matched by torture? Has there always been a space for sovereignty beyond the rule of law?

In this chapter I intend to focus on the specific case of prosecuting terrorism during the Northern Ireland conflict, and argue that after a number of false starts when terror was matched with security tactics that transgressed the rule of law – including the use of violence to obtain

3 Paul W. Kahn, Sacred Violence: Torture, Terror, and Sovereignty (2008).

4 C. Brown and M. Woolf, *Rights Laws to be Overhauled as Blair Says "The Game Has Changed,"* The Independent (London), 6 Aug., 2005.

5 Kahn, *supra* note 4, at 8.

confessions – a paradigm shift took place that led to greater emphasis on the rule of law and human rights. Exceptionality thus came to be replaced by normality. It will be argued that this normality has come at a price, however, as seemingly permanent antiterrorist measures have spilled over into the ordinary criminal justice system and indeed been exported to neighboring jurisdictions with a corresponding diminution in established rights that have long been part of the normal criminal landscape. These different cycles have been played out within the setting of the Diplock courts – the nonjury, single-judge courts recommended by the Diplock Commission and established by the British government in 1972 in an effort to move away from the previous strategy of dealing with political violence by means of detention or internment and replace it with a system of criminal prosecution.

1. Diplock Courts: The Vicious and Virtuous Cycles

The Diplock Commission (hereinafter the Commission) considered there were serious obstacles in the way of obtaining convictions under the ordinary criminal process. The usual method of obtaining convictions under the adversarial criminal process is by relying on witnesses who testify openly against defendants, but in the context of political violence the supply of witnesses can dry up because of the fear of intimidation. According to the Commission, the only kind of case in which convictions could be obtained by the ordinary processes of criminal law were ones in which there was sufficient evidence against the accused from one or more of three sources: oral evidence of non-civilian witnesses whose protection could be more readily ensured; physical evidence such as fingerprints; and an admissible confession, but there were problems with using these sources. Non-civilian witnesses could not be the direct source of information about paramilitary activity. Physical evidence was not always available and confessions under the common law were inadmissible unless they were given voluntarily by suspects, something that paramilitary suspects would not willingly provide. The difficulty in obtaining confessions under the common law was underlined by a decision of the Northern Ireland courts shortly before the announcement of the Commission, which excluded confessions in 1972 on the ground that they had been obtained in a detention center set up officially to obtain information from persons who would be less than willing to give it. Admissions obtained in this way failed to qualify as voluntary statements. Finally, the Commission referred to the problem of retaining juries in the existing climate of violence. The Commission was unable to point to particular cases of jury intimidation but considered that the jury system was under strain and likely to break down if it were not abolished in paramilitary trials.

In one sense the decision to move away from systems of internment toward the use of trials at all in the Northern Ireland conflict was a movement away from regarding the conflict as an emergency and a recognition of the need to establish a more normalizing framework for dealing with it. The Commission recognized this by accepting that the changes it recommended for terrorist trials had to meet the minimal human rights standards of the European Convention on Human Rights (ECHR). The changes it recommended therefore kept within this minimal baseline. First, the technical common law rules governing the admissibility of statements could be relaxed but only so long as they were not obtained by methods that fell foul of Article 3 of the ECHR, namely by torture or inhuman or degrading treatment. The requirement that confessions must be excluded where they have been obtained by torture has continued to endure as a fundamental principle of common law and international human rights law amid the contemporary war on terror.[6] Secondly, rules reversing the burden of proof in certain firearms cases and permitting the admissibility of witness statements in certain circumstances were recommended but within the parameters of the fair trial standards of Article 6. Finally, trial by jury could be replaced with trial by judge alone in cases involving political violence because Article 6 did not require a jury trial.

6 *See, e.g.*, John Jackson and Sarah Summers, The Internationalisation of Criminal Evidence 160–63 (2012).

This early affirmation of human rights standards was belied, however, by the Commission's continued support for the use of internment and the need therefore to continue to rely on Article 15 of the ECHR, which allows states to derogate from its obligations under the Convention "in time of war or other public emergency." In effect, the Commission endorsed an apparently contradictory twin-track policy of prosecution and criminalization along with a continuation of detention without trial, which did much to undermine the rule of law and respect for human rights. The emergency legislation that implemented the Commission's recommendations for the prosecution of terrorism also stretched the boundaries of respect for the rule of law and human rights by allowing for an extended period of questioning for suspected terrorists of up to seventy-two hours before being brought to a court, a period that was stretched further to seven days under UK-wide legislation one year later. This gave the green light to a coercive system of interrogation that did much to disfigure the reputation of the Diplock courts in their early days.

Although the Article 3 confessions test drew a boundary between acceptable and unacceptable interrogation, allegations of abuse emerged in the special interrogation centers set up for questioning terrorist suspects, who were held incommunicado without access to legal advice or friends and relatives. The opening of special interrogation centers at Castlereagh and Gough (designated terrorist detention centers) coincided with a major increase in the number of complaints of ill-treatment made against the police – 180 in 1975, 384 in 1976, and 671 in 1977.[7] These were backed up by the concerns of police medical doctors who made formal representations about the number of suspects who showed signs of physical ill-treatment. In November 1977 Amnesty International carried out an investigation into a number of cases of alleged ill-treatment, and in June 1978 it reported that it believed that maltreatment of suspected terrorists had taken place with sufficient frequency to warrant the establishment of a public inquiry.

7 Peter Taylor, Brits: The War against the IRA 81 (2001).

The Diplock courts became tainted with such allegations when they were seen to uphold the confessions that were obtained from the interrogation centers. Legal doctrine that at first betrayed some ambiguity over whether the new confessions standard proscribed physical violence, together with a legal process which in the absence of any authenticated version of police interviews made it difficult to determine how confessions were obtained, led to confessions being admitted and accepted under conditions that would not stand up to scrutiny under today's human rights law. In more recent times the Northern Ireland Court of Appeal has quashed a number of convictions stemming from this era, which has served to contrast the inability of the courts to offer protection to suspects during the early period of the emergency with their ability to offer much greater protection albeit ex post facto as the effect of the emergency has weakened and a degree of normalization has crept in.[8] The courts suffered a further blow to their reputation when – again, as a result of being held incommunicado – suspects were used to become informants ("supergrasses" as they were known) against their former paramilitary associates.[9] Suspects were rounded up on the word of these informants and detained for long periods pending trial. When judges began to convict them on this basis there were criticisms that the courts were merely a rubber stamp for security policies designed to take terrorist suspects out of circulation. A vicious cycle seemed to be emerging whereby security, if not torture, was the prevalent response to terrorism, to the detriment of human rights and the rule of law.

Then suddenly, just as the numbers of supergrasses and supergrass trials threatened to overwhelm the courts and engulf them in a major crisis of legitimacy, the cycle began to break. In a landmark case, the Lord Chief Justice Lord Lowry quoted Lord Atkin's famous dictum from a case involving executive power at the height of World War II, that in

8 For a review of these more recent decisions, *see* LAURIE ELKS, RIGHTING MISCARRIAGES OF JUSTICE?: TEN YEARS OF THE CRIMINAL CASES REVIEW COMMISSION 301 (2008).

9 STEVEN GREER, SUPERGRASSES: A STUDY IN ANTI-TERRORIST LAW ENFORCEMENT IN NORTHERN IRELAND (1995).

this country amid the clash of arms the laws are not silent.[10] They speak, he said, the same language in war as in peace; a war may be being waged by organizations that style themselves as armies, but such a war would not invade the courts. It would be wrong to characterize this judgment as marking a dramatic shift in judicial attitudes. Even in their darkest hour – during the confessions era of the late 1970s and the supergrass era of the early 1980s – statistics did not bear up the charge that the courts were a mere rubber stamp for security strategies.[11] But in the midst of the supergrass crisis the judges found a voice that put greater emphasis on the rule of law and delivered a clear message to the state authorities. The decision to use Lord Atkin's dictum to convey this message had a powerful symbolic effect. When this dictum is cited to reinforce the importance of the rule of law even in times of the gravest emergency, it is often forgotten that it was made in the course of a dissenting judgment over the interpretation to be given to a regulation that purported to give the executive the power to detain without trial. The record of the courts in times of emergency even in well-established democracies is far from unblemished. What the Chief Justice was doing in citing the dictum in the context of the ongoing threat to security in Northern Ireland was conveying the message that his courts at least would not succumb to executive pressure. His judgment marked an important turning point in beginning to rehabilitate the reputation of the Diplock courts at just the moment when their credibility was being questioned as never before. This judicial move prompts the interesting observation that the primacy of the rule of law or "business as usual" as far as the courts are concerned will only be reasserted in a situation of exceptionality when the exceptionality reaches such an acute point that it directly challenges the old normality.

Another virtuous turning point was marked by the increasing number of challenges that came to be brought on grounds of breach of the

10 *R v. Gibney and Others* (1983) 13 NIJB 7. Lord Atkin's dictum derives from *Liversidge v. Anderson* (1942) AC 206.

11 John Jackson and Sean Doran, Judge without Jury: Diplock Trials in the Adversary System 33–36 (1995).

European Convention on Human Rights before the European Court of Human Rights (ECtHR) located in Strasbourg, France. Until the passage of the Human Rights Act in 1998, which incorporated the ECHR into UK law, the domestic courts showed little inclination to enforce the ECHR, and remedies for breaches had to be sought in Strasbourg.[12] Although the Court took a cautious approach toward such challenges at first, the ECtHR gradually appeared to shift ground by giving less of a margin of appreciation to the state in setting the boundaries of human rights protection. For example, although the ECtHR was prepared to accept that the context of terrorism could be taken into account in determining how long the authorities may hold a suspect in custody without violating Article 5(3) of the ECHR, it did ultimately rule that a period of detention of four days and six hours was not permissible.[13] It took some considerable time for the United Kingdom to give effect to this decision, as it was blunted by the later decision of the ECtHR to uphold the United Kingdom's claim to derogate from Article 15 in a time of emergency.[14] These decisions nevertheless demonstrated that human rights were not mere aspirations of good faith but could be given teeth by a court of law to which states would have to respond.

Gradually then, the vicious cycle was replaced by a more virtuous cycle whereby human rights protections began to be introduced at the crucial stage of pretrial interrogation. Suspects were given a statutory right of access to legal advice for the first time in 1987, albeit this could be delayed up to forty-eight hours. Then in a landmark judgment in 1996, the ECtHR held that the concept of fairness enshrined in Article 6 required that an accused be given the benefit of legal assistance when warned that inferences could be drawn from a failure to answer questions.[15] After

12 For a comprehensive overview of the impact of the decisions of the ECtHR on the Northern Ireland conflict, see BRICE DICKSON, THE EUROPEAN CONVENTION ON HUMAN RIGHTS AND THE CONFLICT IN NORTHERN IRELAND (2010).

13 *Brogan v. United Kingdom*, App. No. 11209/84, 11 Eur. H.R. Rep. 117 (1988).

14 *Brannigan and McBride v. United Kingdom*, App. Nos. 14553/89, 14554/89, 17 Eur. H.R. Rep. 539 (1994).

15 *John Murray v. United Kingdom*, App. No. 18731/91, 22 Eur. H.R. Rep. 29 (1996).

this, new detention codes were introduced permitting legal advisers to sit in at interviews, requiring these to be audio and video recorded, and requiring judicial extension of detention after forty-eight hours. In 2002 the minimalist-confessions test was abolished and replaced by the test governing ordinary cases and the emergency detention regime gradually came to meet the standards that prevailed in other criminal cases. Today, in a post-conflict society, the Diplock courts remain intact and the security forces still retain wide powers to arrest and detain suspects, but they are questioned under a very different regime from the one that was in place ten years ago and the courts are prepared to apply rigorous scrutiny toward applications for detention to be extended.

2. Prosecuting Terrorism under the Rule of Law and Human Rights

On one view this progressive movement toward a prosecution regime, which is increasingly governed by the rule of law and human rights, would seem to contradict the argument that terrorism is necessarily linked to torture and politics beyond law. Although abuse of human rights was a hallmark of the emergency in the early days in the United Kingdom, gradually the normalization of the emergency meant that emergency powers began to merge into the ordinary criminal justice landscape and were brought more under the control of the rule of law and human rights. I have argued elsewhere that the gradual normalization of the Diplock system, making it less distinguishable from conventional criminal courts, is attributable to two factors: the ideology of the participants who were subject to it; and the ideology of human rights.[16] Although the maltreatment of paramilitary suspects in the 1970s and the subsequent supergrass strategy in the early 1980s showed that the Diplock system was capable of succumbing to those intent on gaining convictions no matter what, ultimately the rule-of-law ideology of the lawyers and judges

16 John Jackson, *Many Years On in Northern Ireland: The Diplock Legacy*, 60(2) N. Ir. Legal Q. 213 (2008).

saved it from becoming totally discredited as a mere tool of antiterrorist policy. A number of factors appear to have reinforced this ideology: the professionalism of the advocates – some of whom acted for both prosecution and defense; the independence of the judges whose previous training at the Bar gave them a strong sense of professional identity that was separate from the state; and the increasing accountability that was brought to bear on judges as their rulings came under the intense scrutiny not only of international courts and organizations but "well-informed and potentially hostile critics," as well.[17] In a sense then, the Diplock solution of devising a trial system that would deal with paramilitary offenders while staying within minimum human rights norms worked because the protagonists made it work. Lawyers and judges were able to keep the trial system pure enough to withstand fundamental human rights challenges even though challenges continued to be made to the emergency powers.[18] As a result, the Diplock courts began to obtain a foothold of legitimacy that was sustained as time went on.

Whereas the lawyers and judges did much to keep the trial system immune from executive pressure, they did little themselves to halt human rights abuses in the interrogation centers. Instead, it was left to human rights organizations to expose these abuses and take cases to the ECHR. So it was the ECtHR, not the Northern Ireland courts, which ruled on the length of time suspects could be held in custody before being brought before a court, and established the right of lawyers to have access to their clients in the detention centers. The Northern Irish courts have more recently applied these new standards by reversing convictions from the early Diplock era.[19]

It may be argued that this growing emphasis on the rule of law and human rights is attributable to the post-conflict landscape and did not

17 *See* Lord Lowry, *National Security and the Rule of Law*, 26 Israel L. Rev. 117, 131.

18 *See* Fionnuala Ní Aoláin, *Transitional Emergency Jurisprudence: derogation and transition*, *in* Transitional Jurisprudence and the ECHR: Justice, Politics and Rights (M. Hamilton and A. Buyse Eds., 2011).

19 *See, e.g.*, *R v. Hanna and Hindes* (2005) NICA 36; *R v. Adams* (Robert) (2006) NICA 6; *R v. Mulholland* (2006) NICA 32.

assert itself when the levels of violence were at their worst. Campbell has argued that international courts are more prepared to scrutinize alleged human rights violations in post-conflict periods of transition toward peace than in periods of war or intense conflict. He has illustrated that during the period of the conflict considerable deference was shown by the ECtHR to government claims arising out of the Northern Ireland conflict while the violence continued.[20] After 1994, however, when the conflict showed signs of coming to an end, a number of violations were found on the part of the state. A similar analysis could be applied to the Diplock courts themselves. But it is notable that even before signs of the conflict came to an end, it was the judges and lawyers themselves who brought an end to the supergrass system, and the first signs of the need for changes to be made to the interrogation centers as a result of human rights pressure occurred when a judicial inquiry – the Bennett Inquiry – recommended certain changes in 1979.[21] Although these fell short of the safeguards available to suspects in ordinary cases, the pressure continued throughout the 1980s, leading to access to a solicitor after forty-eight hours in 1987, and in the early 1990s to delays in granting access being significantly reduced – again, all before the conflict showed signs of ending. Far from human rights organizations having minimal effect at times of acute terrorism, the Northern Ireland experience would seem to point to their relevance when there are enough domestic and international mechanisms in place to enable their concerns to be raised.

This virtuous narrative may be used to point to a wider lesson that when a culture of legal independence is combined with a commitment to human rights, much can be done to withstand the pressures that can lead to a complete subservience to state security in times of emergency. The narrative needs to be qualified, however, in at least two respects. First, such forces may not be able to withstand such pressures in the

20 Colm Campbell, *"Wars on Terror" and Vicarious Hegemons: The UK, International Law and the Northern Ireland Conflict*, 54 INT'L & COMP. L.Q. 321 (2005).

21 *See* COMMITTEE OF INQUIRY INTO POLICE INTERROGATION PRACTICES IN NORTHERN IRELAND REPORT, 1979, Cm. 7497.

beginning stages of an emergency when the very survival of the state itself may appear to be at stake. In its early days the Diplock courts quickly gained a reputation for succumbing to executive pressures, which took some time to shake off. Paradoxically, however, extreme measures which directly threaten the independence of the courts may act as the catalyst for the legal establishment to reassert the importance of the rule of law. Secondly, however, the mere assertion of independence and the rule of law is not enough in itself to halt human rights abuses. As McEvoy has shown, lawyers succumbed to an ethos of "quietism" during the Northern Ireland conflict, which did little to arrest the abuses that took place.[22] Had there been a greater willingness by the legal profession to join forces with human rights organizations, such abuses might have been prevented or countered more effectively. Notwithstanding such quietism, however, the fact remains that challenges were able to be made to such abuses and the Diplock system endured into the post-conflict era.

There is another darker narrative about the Diplock experience, which is reflected in the fact that under today's post-conflict conditions of relative peace a number of changes that were justified as a result of the conflict have become regular features of the criminal justice landscape, not just in Northern Ireland but in neighboring jurisdictions where these features have been successfully exported. Up until the supergrass trials the Diplock courts were identified with particular strategies that marked them out very clearly from normal trials. The heavy reliance on confession evidence followed by the heavy reliance on supergrasses made it easy for these courts to be characterized as exceptional courts for exceptional times. After the collapse of the supergrass system, however, the courts became less identified with any one particular strategy and went through a period of normalization that made it harder to differentiate them so clearly from ordinary courts. This did not mean that the conflict between the security forces and the paramilitaries became any less intense, but it was a conflict that would be played out in a clandestine manner behind

22 See Kieran McEvoy, *What Did Lawyers Do During the "War"? Neutrality, Conflict and the Culture of Quietism*, 4 MODERN L. REV. 350 (2011).

the scenes rather than in the full panoply of the courts or even in interview rooms. Instead of the courts being used as an instrument of policy, they reverted to their more traditional role of adjudicating on evidence that directly implicated paramilitary activists in offenses which informants told their "minders" were going to happen.

The security forces continued to call for measures that would assist in the fight against terrorism, but the changes called for began to take on a different guise. Instead of being justified on the basis that they were needed to deal with an emergency, they were justified as a necessary part of the criminal justice balance in the changed order of dealing with the seemingly permanent specter of terrorism. The best example of this was the call for changes to the right of silence. Although these were called for by security forces who claimed they were met with a "wall of silence" when they interviewed paramilitary suspects, they were introduced not as an emergency measure but under the normal Order in Council procedure which applied to ordinary criminal legislation in Northern Ireland.[23] The curtailment of the right of silence to permit triers of fact to draw inferences from silence was a radical departure from previous practice, but by being introduced across the entire criminal justice system, it was able to be represented as an ordinary piece of criminal legislation, which in time came to be exported to the neighboring jurisdiction of England and Wales.[24] Indeed, it was these very changes that led the ECtHR to issue its judgment in *John Murray v UK* requiring that terrorist suspects have the same opportunity of access to legal advice when they were cautioned about the consequences of remaining silent as ordinary suspects are allowed under normal legislation.

While the changes to the right of silence led to a narrowing of the gap between ordinary and emergency procedures in the police station, trial procedures within the Diplock court and other courts became almost

23 *See* The Criminal Evidence (Northern Ireland) Order, 1988, H.L. For a detailed review of the introduction of this legislation and the impact it had, *see* J. JACKSON, M. WOLFE, AND K. QUINN, LEGISLATING AGAINST SILENCE: THE NORTHERN IRELAND EXPERIENCE (2001).

24 *See* Criminal Justice and Public Order Act, 1994, §§34–37.

identical when the confessions test was changed to conform to the test applied in ordinary courts.[25] One of the features of the Diplock system from its inception was the degree to which it drew on the ordinary courts for its offenses, procedures, and personnel – both judges and lawyers. There were, of course, special scheduled offenses peculiar to the Diplock system, and there were some special procedures such as the rule on confessions, but the bulk of offenses were also triable in ordinary trials – common law offenses, for example, such as murder, manslaughter, kidnapping, false imprisonment, and assault occasioning actual bodily harm. Very similar rules of evidence applied, and the judges and lawyers who populated Diplock courts also appeared in ordinary trials. The Diplock courts were therefore easy to institutionalize within the ordinary criminal justice system, and as time moved on they increasingly became part of that ordinary system. No longer viewed as special courts associated with an emergency, they became more like an ordinary court with a mode of trial that has become a seemingly permanent feature of the criminal justice landscape, although technically having to be renewed periodically by parliament.[26]

This process of normalization has been aided by a change to the scheduling system that has served to reduce the numbers of cases being tried in the Diplock system, but at the same time has had the effect of extending its reach beyond the emergency context that occasioned its introduction. The old system – whereby scheduled offenses were automatically triable in the Diplock courts subject to the attorney general certifying them out where there was no connection to the emergency – has been replaced by a new system, where cases have to be certified for Diplock trial by the Director of Public Prosecutions (DPP) where he or she suspects that one of a number of conditions is met and is satisfied that there is a risk the administration of justice might be impaired if the trial were conducted with a jury.[27] The conditions go beyond the emergency

25 *See* Terrorism Act 2000 (Cessation of Effect of Section 76) Order, 2002 (Eng.).

26 *See* Justice and Security (Northern Ireland) Act, 2007.

27 *See id.* §1.

context to include the fact that the offense was committed as a result of or in response to religious or political hostility and the fact that the defendant is an associate of a member of a paramilitary organization even if not directly involved in one. Furthermore, the certification process is no longer an extraordinary process carried out by the attorney general, who exercised discretion in favor of the individual accused. Instead, it is carried out by the DPP, the officer who is now responsible for all prosecution decisions in Northern Ireland since the introduction of a new public prosecution system in 2005.[28] The DPP also makes other mode of trial decisions when deciding, for example, if a case is more appropriately tried summarily in the magistrates' court or on indictment in the Crown Court. More worrying is the fact that Section 1 of the 2007 Justice and Security Act specifically states that the DPP's decision to issue a certificate cannot be questioned in any court of law except on the ground of dishonesty, bad faith, or other exceptional circumstances. Effectively, the DPP has been given an unreviewable power to make decisions on the mode of trial.

3. Addressing the Adversarial Deficit in Judge-Only Trials

None of this would matter so much if the criteria that the DPP had to apply were clear and predictable and the Diplock mode of trial was one that was specifically adapted to deal with the threat of terrorism. No one objects to the DPP making mode-of-trial decisions between the Crown Court and the magistrates' court. The point is not that the Diplock mode of trial should not be employed to deal with the threat of terrorism – despite tremendous progress being made in moving Northern Ireland toward a more peaceful society, there is still a dissident terrorist threat that will require an interface with the due process of law.[29] Nor is the point that this mode of trial is necessarily an inferior one or one that necessarily disadvantages defendants as compared with trial by jury – defendants

28 *See* Justice (Northern Ireland) Act, 2002.

29 Police Service of Northern Ireland, Annual Report of the Chief Constable, 2010, Statistical Report, pt. 5.

may have a better chance of contesting certain issues successfully before a judge than a jury.[30] The point is rather that a mode of trial that has not been traditionally employed to deal with serious cases in the common law context has been employed and indeed extended beyond the limits for which it was originally designed without any thought being given as to whether the ordinary trial procedures employed for jury trial are suited to its needs. The process of normalization has meant that conventional procedures adapted for jury trial have been transferred to a juryless mode of trial without considering whether the absence of the jury calls for a more root-and-branch change to trial procedure.

This makes no concession to the fact that the withdrawal of the jury and substitution of a professional trier of fact for lay triers of fact irredeemably alters the structure of the trial. It is not just that the professional trier will inevitably occupy a more dominant position over the parties than if a jury were present. It is the fact that the bifurcated nature of judge-and-jury trial has been replaced by a unitary court consisting solely of a professional judge, with the result that it is no longer possible to shield the trier of fact from inadmissible or confidential information that comes to the attention of the judge. This kind of information is particularly prevalent in terrorism trials where, on the one hand, the defense often allege that evidence was improperly obtained by state officials overreaching themselves and, on the other hand, state authorities often wish to keep certain kinds of information secret from the defense to protect their sources of information. The question that then arises is whether judges are able to put this information out of their minds when they act in their new role as triers of fact. There are different views as to how successful judges can be in managing this feat, but there is inevitably a sense that they have become tainted by exposure to such evidence. The sense of unfairness is compounded when the defense is unaware of the information the judge has become privy to. Under human rights law, if the prosecution wish to conceal any material evidence from the defense

30 *See, e.g.*, Jackson and Doran, *supra* note 16, at 295.

on grounds of public interest such as national security or the need to protect witnesses, it must make a claim for public interest immunity (PII) before the judicial authorities.[31] Under disclosure rules, judges have to make rulings on whether information for which PII is claimed should be disclosed to the defense, and in the consequence of this become privy to matters that are prejudicial to the defense. The difficulty about these hearings is that they invariably take place in the absence of the defense, with the result that the defense is not given an opportunity to rebut the information that the judge has heard. This can potentially give rise to fair-trial challenges, as it falls foul of the principle of equality of arms and adversarial procedure.[32]

To meet this problem, the Diplock courts have developed a practice whereby a separate judge is appointed to decide issues of PII where either the prosecution or defense suggest that the material in question may be prejudicial to the defense.[33] This practice has itself been controversial, for as the independent reviewer on terrorism has pointed out, there is a continuing obligation to review disclosure decisions in the context of the evidence that emerges during the course of the trial. This is an example of the difficulties that set in when trial procedures designed for a bifurcated trial have to be made to work in a unitary context. The vital checks and balances that the jury brings to the trial can no longer be employed, and there has been no root-and-branch examination of what procedures are best suited in the new environment.

These difficulties, of course, afflict any unitary tribunal in any procedural context, whether it be a military commission or a bench trial. It is sometimes suggested that the requirement that reasons be given for findings of fact can compensate for any exposure that the tribunal

31 See *Rowe and Davis v. United Kingdom*, App. No. 28901/95, 30 Eur. H.R. Rep. 1 (2009).

32 *See, e.g.*, *Edwards and Lewis v. United Kingdom*, App. Nos. 39647/98, 40461/98, 40 Eur. H.R. Rep. 24 (2005); M. Bisgrove, *Judges as Tribunals of Fact: To What Extent Do the Provisions for a Defendant to be Tried on Indictment by a Judge Sitting without a Jury Conflict with the Defendant's Right to a Fair Trial Where Issues of PII Are Present*, Crim L. Rev. 702 (2010).

33 *See R v. Harper*, (1994) N.I. 199; *R v. McKeown*, (2005) N.I. 301.

has had to tainted or unchallenged evidence. Written reasons have been compared favorably to the sphinx-like unreasoned general verdict that the jury pronounces.[34] At another level, however, the defense is given no formal opportunity before the judgment to respond to the court's views on the weight of the evidence. Of course, there is no such opportunity available in a jury trial, either. But it may be argued that here at least the decision makers go into closed session and deliberate together on evidence that has been properly admitted. An argument has been made that rather than requiring the judge to deliver a verdict and judgment "package," there is some attraction in the idea that he or she should be obliged at the close of evidence to issue a provisional statement of reasons for his or her conclusion.[35] Counsel would then be given the opportunity to challenge those reasons in advance of the judge's final decision. It is again not intended to make a detailed argument here for what would be a radical break with the procedures that apply in jury trials, but simply to make the point that such deviations from jury procedure have not been fully investigated and considered. Instead, the default position has been adopted whereby procedures should deviate as little as possible from what happens in a jury trial without any consideration as to how safeguards promoted by jury trial – such as the non-exposure to inadmissible or confidential information – might be properly compensated. The lack of safeguards associated with the jury trial may become particularly telling in terrorist trials where judges may become privy to large quantities of inadmissible or confidential material that the accused is unable to respond to, despite facing charges of the utmost gravity and facing penal consequences of the most severe kind if convicted of them.

Bench trials are not, of course, unknown in the common law world, but they have more commonly been instigated at the election of the defense or the parties.[36] It is different when such trials are imposed on

34 *See, e.g.*, *Taxquet v. Belgium*, App. No. 926/05, Eur. Ct. H.R. (2nd section) (2009), (Grand Chamber) (2010).

35 Jackson and Doran, *supra* note 16, at ch. 9.

36 *See* Sean Doran and John Jackson, *The Case for Jury Waiver*, Crim. L. Rev. 155 (1977).

the defense without an examination of what compensatory mechanisms might be put in place to deal with the adversarial deficit that arises in them. But far from being confined to specific terrorist contexts, this is a mode of trial that is being exported and imposed in ordinary cases, as well. In a further example of exceptionality creeping into normality, there is now a mechanism in England and Wales – and ironically, alongside Diplock trials in Northern Ireland, as well – whereby applications can be made for nonjury trial where there is evidence of a real and present danger of jury tampering, and there are examples of such trials having taken place. In the Republic of Ireland the use of the Special Criminal Court – the three-judge nonjury court that has existed for some time alongside Diplock courts in Northern Ireland to deal originally with terrorist trials – has recently been extended to deal with organized crime, as well.[37]

Conclusion

The Diplock experience suggests it is possible to bring normal prosecutions for terrorism on the basis of the rule of law and human rights even in times of acute crisis, provided there is a strong ideological commitment to these values among the different professionals responsible for delivering justice and forums available both domestically and internationally for voicing concerns and exerting pressure. Seen in these terms the Diplock courts moved from a vicious cycle of reliance on dubious confession and supergrass evidence in their early days toward the more virtuous cycle we see today. As the trials have become more acceptable in terms of human rights, however, they have also become a normal part of the criminal justice landscape without the recognition that for all their normalcy they remain an exceptional mode of trial for serious offenses within the common law tradition, and the procedures that have traditionally evolved for jury trials may not suit the nonjury contexts. We have been effectively sleepwalked into accepting a mode of trial without a rigorous review of

37 *See* Criminal Justice (Amendment) Act (Northern Ireland), 2009.

the circumstances when it may be justified with a built-in mechanism for challenging its application in a particular case, and without a rigorous examination of what procedures are best suited for such a mode of trial when it is justified.

The Diplock experience may thus be presented as a refutation of the scenario painted by Kahn at the beginning of the chapter where terrorism fills a space for sovereignty and politics beyond the rule of law. But when we abandon long-established traditions such as jury trials in order to make terrorist trials effective, we need to recognize that we have, albeit by default, created exceptional procedures and not succumb to the more natural inclination to think that we can continue with business as usual in their absence. In particular, we should recognize that trial by a professional judge is a distinct mode of proceeding rather than perpetuate the fiction that a jury-oriented process is easily adapted to a juryless tribunal.

11 Terrorism Prosecution in the United Kingdom

Lessons in the Manipulation of Criminalization and Due Process

Clive Walker

CONSISTENT WITH HIS "WAR ON TERROR" PARADIGM, President George W. Bush asserted that "it is not enough to serve our enemies with legal papers."[1] Resonant with this view, although also reflecting its own rich legal history of counterterrorism, the United Kingdom's primary legal focus in the immediate aftermath of 9/11 was weighted more toward executive interventions than court-based criminal prosecution. The immediate emanation of "executive intervention" was the detention without trial of foreign terror suspects, a measure characteristic of executive intervention in that it was on the basis of the evaluation of future risk by a government minister rather than exhaustive proof of a past crime before a court. However, this vying between executive action and criminal prosecution never pitched as decisively in favor of executive action as in the United States and is now fading in United Kingdom domestic law.[2] The first part of this chapter will examine the foundations for the reinvigoration of the criminal justice paradigm. This aspect advances this book's inquiry into

1 President George Bush, State of the Union Address (Jan. 20 2004), retrieved from http://georgewbush-whitehouse.archives.gov/news/releases/2004/01/20040120-;7.html.

2 Although reference is made to the United Kingdom, the focus is on England and Wales. Neither regional variations, principally in Northern Ireland, nor foreign military interventions are considered here, but for details on those topics see CLIVE WALKER, TERRORISM AND THE LAW chs. 4, 11 (2011).

exceptional courts, as it posits the alternative approach that regular models of criminal justice can and should predominate in counterterrorism. Next, this chapter will explore the salient implications to date for British criminal justice, particularly questioning the extent to which the delivery of criminal justice has remained "regular" or whether elements of exceptionality have insinuated themselves within the process. The final part of this chapter will reflect on the future implications, followed by wider reflections.

1. The Primacy of Criminal Prosecution

The then-Home Officer Minister Tony McNulty stated in 2008 that "prosecution is – first, second and third – the government's preferred approach when dealing with suspected terrorists."[3] The British government might further assert that the primacy of criminal prosecution has been assured as a policy aspiration ever since the Diplock Report plotted a path out of internment without trial and military predominance in Northern Ireland. According to that report, "exceptionality" means departures from human rights norms to an extent that can only be justified by a notice of derogation, such as a state of emergency, under Article 15 of the European Convention on Human Rights. Yet state practices between 2001 and 2005 appeared to amount to a denial of this prosecution-based strategy. Detention without trial reappeared under the Anti-terrorism, Crime and Security Act 2001, succeeded by control orders under the Prevention of Terrorism Act 2005. Control orders are another instance of "executive intervention," allowing for a government minister to impose obligations – such as curfews and restrictions on association and communication – on terrorism suspects.[4] The London bombings of July 7, 2005,

3 472 PARL. DEB., H.C. (6th ser.) (2008) 561 (U.K.). *See also* JOINT COMMITTEE ON HUMAN RIGHTS, COUNTER-TERRORISM POLICY AND HUMAN RIGHTS, PROSECUTION AND PRE-CHARGE DETENTION, 2005–6, H.L.240, H.C. 1576, ¶ 28.

4 *See* Clive Walker, *Keeping Control of Terrorists without Losing Control of Constitutionalism*, 59 STAN. L. REV. 1395 (2007).

aggravated this hostility to criminal justice, and the warning of then-Prime Minister Tony Blair that "the rules of the game are changing"[5] certainly attained traction against foreign suspects, who were subjected to new measures relating to deportation, exclusion, and nationality. However, one paradoxical development on the domestic front, which has grown in importance because of the trend of homegrown "neighbor terrorism"[6] – the recognition that most terrorists now are British citizen neighbors and not aliens – has been a reversion to criminal prosecution. Whether this reversion involves the simple adoption of the same rules as for the "ordinary decent criminal"[7] will be determined in the next section of this chapter. The point here is to confirm a shift in underlying policy and rhetoric.

This domestic trend may be evidenced by three indicators. One is that recent editions of antiterrorism legislation have avoided primary reliance on executive measures. The break can be seen starkly in the Terrorism Act 2006, which concentrates on the delivery of new offenses – such as incitement of terrorism and preparation of terrorism – or new police investigative powers, notably, twenty-eight-day detention. Within the Counter-Terrorism Act 2008, its administrative innovations of notification and foreign travel restriction in Part IV are dependent on criminal convictions, and Part III enhances post-conviction sentencing powers.

The second indicator is the dearth of executive orders. Despite the apocalyptic analysis in 2007 of Jonathan Evans – the director of the security service – that 2,000 suspects pose a threat to national security,[8] there

5 Prime Minister Tony Blair, Remarks at Press Conference (Aug. 5, 2005), retrieved from http://webarchive.nationalarchives.gov.uk/+/http://www.number10.gov.uk/Page8041.

6 Clive Walker, *Know Thine Enemy as Thyself: Discerning Friend from Foe under Anti-Terrorism Laws,* 32 MELB. U. L. REV. 275 (2008). Another consequence is an emphasis on social control through prevention. *See* Clive Walker and J. Rehman, *Prevent Responses to Jihadi Extremism, in* GLOBAL ANTI-TERRORISM LAW AND POLICY (Victor V. Ramraj, Michael Hor, Kent Roach, and George Williams eds., 2d ed. 2011).

7 *See* REVIEW OF THE OPERATION OF THE NORTHERN IRELAND (EMERGENCY PROVISIONS) ACT 1978, 1984, Cmnd. 9222 at ¶ 136 (U.K.).

8 Jonathan Evans, Dir. Gen., Sec. Serv., Address to the Society of Editors Conference: A Matter of Trust (Nov. 5, 2007), retrieved from https://www.mi5.gov.uk/output/intelligence-counter-terrorism-and-trust.html.

were just 8 control orders in force at the end of 2010. This modest usage is not for a want of customers but arises more because these executive measures are perceived as less cost effective, legally certain, or legitimate compared to criminal prosecution.

The third indicator is a statistical regathering of pace for criminal prosecution, evidenced by returns around 2006/07. Compared to the period in the aftermath of 9/11, there have been relatively high rates of charges and low rates of "other action."[9]

Moving from factual analysis to ethical evaluation, is regular criminal prosecution preferable to executive measures as a response to terrorism in countries such as the United Kingdom and the United States? In favor of criminal prosecution is that it prizes individual responsibility through the requirement of mens rea, whereas collective risk to public or state security predominates in executive measures. The individuation of crime might thus be esteemed as an affirmation of the values of human autonomy and equality. There are also gains for system legitimacy through a more open affirmation of public accountability and due process than is commonly embedded in executive measures. Some of these benefits will, of course, be compromised the more that crimes and criminal processes are modified in pursuance of the goal of criminalization – a modified or exceptional criminal process may not be as morally pristine as an exceptional system.

Among the downsides of a priority for criminal justice is the lesser ability of prosecution to incapacitate in anticipation of a terrorism event no matter how catastrophically deadly or damaging. Thus, the threat to life and political stability from terrorism may justify a different response than, say, in the case of normal crimes such as murder, most of which in the United Kingdom arise from a narrow domestic setting and pose no political threat. As the then-Director of the Security Service Dame Eliza Manningham-Buller warned in 2005: "We may be confident that an individual or group is planning an attack but that confidence comes

9 Home Office, Statistics on Terrorism Arrests and Outcomes Great Britain 11 September 2001 to 31 March 2008 (2009) (U.K).

Date	Arrest	Charges				Convictions			Other Action
	Arrest – Total	Release without Charge	Terror Offence	Other Crimes	Total (% of Arrest)	Terror Offence	Other Crime	Total (% of Charge)	Total (% of Arrest)
2001/02	108	58	22	16	38 (35%)	6	6	12 (32%)	13 (12%)
2002/03	275	141	64	30	94 (34%)	9	25	34 (36%)	39 (14%)
2003/04	191	81	52	38	90 (47%)	6	15	21 (23%)	21 (11%)
2004/05	168	109	35	12	47 (28%)	2	16	18 (38%)	13 (8%)
2005/06	285	193	50	25	75 (26%)	24	14	38 (51%)	16 (6%)
2006/07	213	101	81	22	103 (48%)	33	12	45 (44%)	10 (5%)
2007/08	231	136	55	19	74 (32%)	22	6	28 (38%)	19 (8%)
Total	1471	819	359	162	521 (35%)	102	94	196 (38%)	131 (9%)

from the sort of intelligence I described earlier, patchy and fragmentary and uncertain, to be interpreted and assessed. All too often it falls short of evidence to support criminal charges to bring an individual before the courts, the best solution if achievable."[10]

The next problem with proof in criminal prosecution arises from the disclosure of secret sources, techniques, and data. The beauty of executive procedures is that they can handle "intelligence information, whose disclosure may involve unacceptable risks."[11] The final drawbacks relate to potential negative perceptions of the courts protecting the state and not victims, allied with the appearance of judges being co-opted into the work of the executive, resulting in damage to their reputation for impartiality and independence. The danger is that minority communities, on whom the legislation unevenly impacts, will feel distrust leading to less cooperation.[12] Authentication of this phenomenon is, however, disputed.[13]

2. The Challenges Faced in Criminal Prosecution

Although a priority for criminal prosecution may be warranted either in principle or because of tactical benefits, account must be taken of attendant costs and problems. The high security and prolonged imprisonment of dozens of convicted terrorists is a very direct cost, both for those held and the taxpayer. More generally, both criminal offenses and criminal processes might be affected by the precautionary logic of neutralizing risk rather than punishing sustained misdeeds. The potential arises for

10 Retrieved from http://www.mi5.gov.uk/output/director-generals-speech-to-the-aivd-2005.html.

11 Review of the Operation of the Prevention of Terrorism Acts 1974 and 1976, 1978, Cmnd.7324 at ¶ 52 (U.K.).

12 *See*, for example, House of Commons Home Affairs Committee, Terrorism and Community Relations (2003–04 HC 165).

13 For the most comprehensive survey, *see* Defence Science and Technology Laboratory, What Perceptions Do the UK Public Have Concerning the Impact of Counter-Terrorism Legislation Implemented since 2000? (2010).

the manipulation of both offenses and processes, with further damage to system legitimacy and therefore the achievement of goals such as deterrence and community support.

(a) Challenges in Criminal Processes

The enduring compromises within the traditional criminal justice process caused by coping with terrorism are illustrated above all in the United Kingdom by the juryless Diplock courts in Northern Ireland, which were instituted following the Diplock Report as a bespoke shift toward criminalization.[14] Because the focus of this chapter is on England and Wales, these courts will not be examined further, but the question of whether there has been any reproduction of a special trial or pretrial process regime elsewhere within the United Kingdom will be explored. The greater the movement to these regimes the less convincing will be the rhetoric in favor of normality.

Some modifications to criminal justice processes have occurred. Section 16 of the Terrorism Act 2006 ensures that preparatory hearings are mandatory in terrorism cases. The objective is to ensure that enhanced and experienced judicial management is applied to every terrorism case on indictment. This change has been underlined by the Protocol on the Management of Terrorism Cases issued by the president of the Queen's Bench Division.[15] The Protocol ensures that all indictable terrorism cases will be managed via the "terrorism cases list" by the presiding judges of the South Eastern Circuit and other nominated judges of the High Court and will be tried by a nominated judge of the High Court.[16] This attention to detail and the imposition of senior-judicial active involvement is

14 *See*, Justice and Security (Northern Ireland) Act 2007; John Jackson, *Vicious and Virtuous Cycles in Prosecuting Terrorism: The Diplock Court Experience*, in this volume.

15 See http://www.judiciary.gov.uk/publications-and-reports/guidance/index/mgt-terrorism-case.

16 See http://www.judiciary.gov.uk/publications-and-reports/guidance/index/mgt-terrorism-case.

generally to be welcomed, but it potentially dilutes the principle of trial by peers and could threaten further if concerns about cost and delay become overweening. In *R v. Omar Khyam*,[17] it was alleged that the judges appeared so concerned about delays and costs that that they were asked to recuse themselves. The arrangement could also be perceived as creating too cozy a relationship between judges and prosecutors and reducing the assigned judges' healthy exposure to interaction with counsel and brethren in normal cases. The ring-fencing of national security cases could also pave the way for more drastic changes in the future, although for now these criticisms are somewhat overblown as very few judges experience national security as a majority or significant proportion of their workload.

In addition, there are pressures on the equality of arms through defense resources not matching those of the police and prosecution, especially in the employment of experts.[18] In addition, the construction of the defense case may be hampered by high security conditions.[19] Defendants also face the danger of media prejudice, which is encouraged by extravagant talk from police and politicians.[20]

Moreover, there is an impetus toward secrecy that is manifested in two ways. First, there is the proliferation of special advocates. These legal counselors perform a key role in executive-based processes such as control order proceedings under Paragraph 7 of the Schedule to the Prevention of Terrorism Act 2005. Their role, first appearing in the context of the Special Immigration Appeals Commission Act 1997 to assist litigation about deportation for the public good on national security grounds, is to

17 *R v. Omar Khyam*, [2008] EWCA (Crim) 1612, [2008] All E.R. (D) 312 (Jul) (Eng.).

18 *See* Ali Naseem Bajwa, *Learn by Trial and Terror,* 151 Solic. J. 7(2007).

19 For an extreme example, *see R v. Benbrika* (2008) Vic 80 (Austl.).

20 *See R v. McCann and Others*, [1991] 92 Cr. App. Rep. (S). 239; Lord Carlile, Home Office, Operation Pathway ¶ 40 (2009). But judges have now taken a robust attitude to recognizing publicity as an abuse of process. *See R v. Barot*, [2006] EWCA (Crim) 2692, (31) 2007] All E.R. (D) 246 (May) (Eng.); *R v. Abu Hamza*, [2006] EWCA (Crim) 2918 (92); *R v. Meziane*, [2004] EWCA (Crim) 1768, (47), [2004] All E.R. (D) 293 (Jun) (Eng.).

"represent the interests" under section 6(1) of a relevant party in control order proceedings where that party and his legal representative are excluded from the proceedings because of the sensitivity of the information. Their role will comprise not only testing the government's case to the full (although without instructions in regard to the secret evidence), but also testing the very need for closed sessions and evidence, and determining that the fullest material evidence has been made.[21] Their impact in the context of control orders and others remains controversial. For example, Lord Steyn has declared that "the special advocate procedure undermines the very essence of elementary justice,"[22] although the European Court of Human Rights has expressed some cautious approbation.[23] The House of Lords has ventured that special advocates would be unobjectionable in principle for criminal proceedings.[24] But the later precedent of *R v. Davis* strongly suggests that the courts will prefer a statutory foundation to succumbing to the "melancholy truth" of function creep.[25]

The next unwelcome aspect of the trend toward secrecy in process is the secrecy of judgments of the public criminal courts. This is evidenced by the judgment in *R v. Omar Khyam*, parts of which were redacted. *Redaction* means that these transactions cannot be the subject of public comment or inquiry, thereby betraying the principle of open justice. The trial concerned a fertilizer bomb plot that had relied heavily on interventions by the security services as part of Operation Crevice, which was a

21 *See* Constitutional Affairs Committee, The Operation of the Special Immigration Appeals Commission (SIAC) and the Use of Special Advocates, 2004–05 H.C. 323-I, ¶61 (U.K.).

22 *R v. Roberts*, [2005] UKHL 45, (88) (appeal taken from Eng.). *See also* David Bonner, Executive Measures, Terrorism and National Security ch. 8 (2007); Justice, Secret Evidence pt. IV (2009); Martin Chamberlain, *Update on Procedural Fairness in Closed Proceedings*, 28 Civ. Just. Q. 448 (2009); John Ip, *The Rise and Spread of the Special Advocate,* Pub. L., 2008, at 717; Gus Van Harten, *Weaknesses of Adjudication in the Face of Secret Evidence*, 13 Int'l J. Evidence & Proof 1, 15–17 (2009).

23 *A and Others v. United Kingdom*, App. No. 3455/05, Eur. Ct. H.R. ¶¶ 219–20 (2009).

24 *R v. H*, [2004] UKHL 3, (22), [2004] 2 A.C. 134 (appeal taken from EWCA (Crim)). But no usage has occurred. Justice, *supra* note 22, at ¶ 315.

25 *Al Rawi v. Security Service*, [2010] EWCA (Civ) 482, (69), [2010] 4 All E.R. 559 (Eng.).

major investigation by the police and security services into a group of British citizens with links to Al Qaeda in Pakistan who were plotting to make fertilizer-based bombs to attack shopping centers, nightclubs, and utility installations. Their trial for explosives and other offenses included evidence from a former accomplice who was held by the Federal Bureau of Investigation (FBI), lasted thirteen months, and involved a record twenty-seven days of jury deliberations. The police had arrested the men in 2004 but had not then tracked all their contacts, including Mohammad Sidique Khan and Shehzad Tanweer, who would later be involved in the July 7, 2005, London-transport suicide bombings. However, a Canadian contact, Mohammed Momin Khawaja, was convicted.[26]

Probably without precedent, virtually all of the judgment in the acquittal on appeal of Danny Morrison has been suppressed.[27] Morrison, a leader of Sinn Féin, had been convicted of being an accomplice in the kidnapping of a police informant. On appeal, the prosecution conceded that nondisclosure undermined the conviction but would not reveal the facts, which were speculated to point toward the presence of IRA double agents who had managed events to ensnare Morrison.

Moving from mode of trial and trial processes to evidentiary features, the rules of evidence have not been altered substantially in recent British terrorism prosecutions, in contrast to past experience in Northern Ireland.[28] Critics might argue that the damage has already been done and that changes to the right to silence and hearsay have been sustained in normal laws.[29] Problems with admission and disclosure do, however, persist. The suppression of evidence through public interest immunity claims have been handled tolerably well, with the exception that it is envisaged that the future admissibility of intercept data as evidence pursuant to the Chilcot Report requires special rules to nullify any "quixotic" judge who

26 *R v. Kh*awaja, [2008] 4 F.C.R. 3 (Can.).
27 R v. Morrison, [2009] NICA (Crim) 1.
28 *See* Terrorism Act 2000, 2000, c. 11, § 76 (U.K.); Terrorism Act 2000 (Cessation of Effect of Section 76) Order 2002, 2002 S.I. 2141 (U.K.).
29 *See* Criminal Justice and Public Order Act 1994, 1994, c. 33, §§ 34–39 (U.K.); Criminal Justice Act 2003, 2003, c. 44, pt. XI (U.K.).

creates a "material risk" to security.[30] There remain dire warnings about the expense and practicability of the process, although intercept data is often crucial evidence in terrorism prosecutions elsewhere.

Another category of potential evidence that causes discomfort in terrorism cases concerns the admissibility of evidence obtained from torture.[31] A ringing rejection of such evidence was sustained in *A v. Secretary of State for the Home Department (no.2)*, but the exclusion embodies important limits. Its emphasis on torture belies an indulgence toward inhuman and degrading treatment, thereby ignoring the evil design of regimes such as Guantánamo.[32] Furthermore, whereas the victim need only advance some plausible evidence to raise the issue of torture, leaving it to the prosecution or tribunal to inquire as to the specifics, where the tribunal is left in a state of suspicion about whether torture was used the evidence can still be admitted, which could be seen as giving the benefit of the doubt to torturers. Another gray area where the courts have not perhaps been sufficiently strict concerns a continuum in joint operations with foreign states, notably Pakistan, whereby "collaboration" might arise from briefings or even regular relations with unwholesome regimes.[33]

Another source of evidence that has historically proven problematic in terrorism cases concerns agents and informants. Recent examples have included O'Farrell, Rafferty, and McDonald, who were convicted in May 2002 of attempting to acquire weaponry for the Real IRA after being lured into a meeting in Slovakia with British Security Service agents

30 Privy Council, Review of Intercept as Evidence: Report to the Prime Minister and the Home Secretary, 2008, Cm.7324, at ¶ 63 U.K.). Intercept evidence is deemed inadmissible in criminal proceedings. Regulation of Investigatory Powers Act 2000, 2000, c. 23, § 17 (U.K.).

31 *See R v. Omar Khyam*, [2008] EWCA (Crim) 1612, [2008] All E.R. (D) 312 (Jul) (Eng.).

32 Forms of "deep interrogation" have continued to be used by the British military despite a ban in 1972. Ministry of Defence, An Investigation into Cases of Deliberate Abuse and Unlawful Killing in Iraq in 2003 and 2004 ¶ 19 (2008). The 1972 policy was reaffirmed by Ministry of Defence. JDN 3/05 'Tactical Questioning, Debriefing and Interrogation' (London, 2005), *Joint Doctrine Publication 1–10* (London, 2006) para 209.

33 This more expansive notion of collaboration was rejected in *R v. Ahmed and Ahmed* [2011] EWCA Crim 184, retrieved from http://www.bailii.org/ew/cases/EWCA/Crim/2011/184.html.

pretending to represent the Iraqi government.[34] The handling of agents and informants to combat state crimes is an ancient problem, especially in the Irish context. Section 29 of The Regulation of Investigatory Powers Act 2000, which imposes more formal administrative controls over "covert human intelligence sources," may curtail some excesses but does not impose regular independent oversight. In addition, the fact that the informants against jihadi terrorism may be run by overseas agencies, such as the Central Intelligence Agency, is a new twist that again casts doubt on the effectiveness of either administrative or judicial accountability.

Despite the manifold challenges outlined in this section, Lord Diplock's policy of criminalization – the primacy of criminal prosecution by processes which satisfy at very least the due process demands of Article 6 of the European Convention on Human Rights – remains valid. That approach has secured convictions in trials involving complex evidence and multiple defendants and by processes which, compared to exceptional justice or executive interventions, will better secure due process for the suspect and attain a more legitimate result as far as the public are concerned. Nevertheless, the criminal processes in terrorism cases must bear extra pressure to be speedy and produce the "right" result. Each failure to convict will bring pressures to compromise. Thus, acquittals on the principal charges in Operation Overt, following the first Airline Liquid Bomb trial in September 2008, elicited the complaints from law enforcement. Specifically, police Chief Peter Clarke complained that the jury failed to sustain convictions "despite strong evidence," although he also conceded that there is "no need for military commissions or the juryless Diplock courts of Northern Ireland."[35] But the very mention of that agenda shows that normal trials are themselves on trial as modes of counterterrorism. As a result, it would be naïve to assume that the principled arguments adduced here against exceptional criminal process

34 *R v. McDonald and Others*, [2005] EWCA (Crim) 1945, [2005] All E.R. (D) 220 (Jul) (Eng.).

35 Peter Clarke, *The 'Surveillance Society' Has Led to Many Terrorists Being Imprisoned,* THE TIMES, Sept. 9, 2008, at 7.

will necessary prevail if there is perceived to be any serial faltering in the delivery of convictions. Counterterrorism policy and legislation has often been driven by the amplification of emotion in response to the vividness of terrorism,[36] and these arguments can be readily channeled by politicians into criticisms of judges who are out of touch with the reality of terrorism and scornful of victims.

(b) Challenges in Criminal Offenses

The design of criminal offenses within antiterrorism legislation evinces several signs of adaptation to the precautionary dynamic of risk aversion. Three consequent problems can be identified: net widening; guilt by association; and reverse burdens of proof. Taken together, the greater the departure from the ordinary criminal norm the more the delivery becomes in reality the exceptional form of criminal justice that the rhetoric has claimed to shun.

Net widening of the criminal law first arises through the use of the term terrorism, as defined by Section 1 of the Terrorism Act 2000. It is not intended here to analyze at length the meaning of that term. For present purposes, it can probably be accepted by supporters and critics alike that it deliberately exceeds in some way the bounds of any single offense, although overall it remains grounded within the notion of criminality.[37] There is no offense of terrorism per se, but the foremost special offenses are dependent on the concept of terrorism, including membership offenses under Part II of the Terrorism Act 2000, and offenses of the possession of preparatory materials or information relevant to terrorism under Sections 57 and 58 of the Terrorism Act 2000.[38]

36 *See* Frank Furedi, Invitation to Terror (2007); Cass R. Sunstein, Worst-Case Scenarios (2007); Oren Gross, *Chaos and Rules: Should Responses to Violent Crisis Always Be Constitutional?*, 112 Yale L. J. 1011 (2003); Eric A. Posner and Adrian Vermeule, *Emergencies and Democratic Failure*, 92 Va. L. Rev. 1091 (2006).

37 *Brogan v. United Kingdom*, App. Nos. 11209, 11234, 11266/84, 11386/85, Eur. Ct. H.R. ¶ 50 (1988).

38 *See* Walker, *supra* note 2, at ch. 5.

Their broad range reduces the chances that threatened terrorism plots cannot ground any prosecution. At the same time, a foundation in terrorism criminalizes the commitment to political motives as much as the conjuring of violence.

A second aspect of net widening is the encompassing of *foreign terrorism* – terrorism committed outside the United Kingdom and aimed against foreign regimes. This step was taken most comprehensively by the Terrorism Act 2000, which adopted the policy of countering all terrorism threats and not primarily those arising from conflicts in Ireland. A number of changes ensued. First, by Part II of the Terrorism Act 2000, the power of proscription of terrorist organizations has been extended beyond the Irish context, and most of the listed organizations are now non-Irish and relate to jihadi terrorism.[39] The Terrorism Act 2000 also reformulated the definition of terrorism in section 1(4)(d) expressly to encompass actions directed against foreign governments. In addition, there is a growing trend of according extraterritoriality on the specialist terrorism offenses, such as by Section 17 of the Terrorism Act 2006. The danger is that prosecutions become viable when terrorism is plotted against foreign tyrannies. A recent rash of cases about Libya is testament to these dangers.[40]

Two principal responses have allayed the problems of net widening. The most potent is a welcome degree of reticence on the part of the police to utilize the powers theoretically available to them. Indulgence continues to be shown to the likes of the Partiya Karkerên Kurdistan (PKK), Hamas, and Tamil demonstrators, with very few recorded prosecutions. The next response has been to impose the filter of consent by a law officer to prosecution for many of the offenses under the antiterrorism legislation,[41] although this filter does not reverse the chilling effect.

39 *See* Walker, *supra* note 2, at ch. 8.

40 *See R v. F*, [2007] EWCA (Crim) 243, [2007] 2 All E.R. 193 (Eng.).

41 Terrorism Act 2000, 2000, c. 11, § 117 (U.K.); Terrorism Act 2006, 2006, c. 11, § 37 (U.K.); Counter-Terrorism Act 2008, 2008, c. 28, § 29 (U.K.).

Guilt by association through offenses of membership of proscribed organizations, such as the Irish Republican Army and Al Qaeda, under Part II of the Terrorism Act 2000 is the next problem engendered by the criminalization of terrorism. As operated in Britain at least, the main answer to the danger of guilt by association has again been a very low rate of prosecutions – there were no convictions from 1990 to 2001 and just fifty-five charges between 2001 and 2007. Consequently, the membership offense primarily serves the purpose of symbolic denunciation rather than individual sanction.

The third issue that has tainted criminal law concerns the deployment of reverse burdens in special precursor offenses. The problem is relevant to membership offenses just described, but it has become acute and recurrent in connection with offenses of possession of articles and information relevant to terrorism, in violation of Sections 57 and 58 of the Terrorism Act 2000.[42]

The judicial responses to these features have been complex. As regards membership and possession offenses, the courts have ensured that the switch in burden of proof is interpreted as evidentiary and not legal. In this way, the defendant need only raise as a realistic issue, for example, that the membership has lapsed or possession of the article was for reasonable purposes. At that point the burden of proof beyond a reasonable doubt switches back to the prosecution. This point is confirmed in Section 118 of the Terrorism Act 2000. Various other efforts have been made to curtail the impact of the special offenses of possession,[43] and the courts have thereby halted a trend whereby Sections 57 and 58 of the Terrorism Act 2000 were becoming akin to offenses of the possession of terrorism fantasy literature.[44] However, even after these limiting

42 *See* Walker, *supra* note 2, at ch. 5.

43 *See R v. AY*, [2010] EWCA (Crim) 762, [2010] All E.R. (D) 194 (Apr) (Eng.); *R v. F*, [2007] EWCA (Crim) 243, [2007] 2 All E.R. 193 (Eng.).

44 *R v. Malik*, [2008] EWCA (Crim) 1450, [2008] All E.R. (D) 201 (Jun) (Eng.); *R v. Zafar*, [2008] EWCA (Crim) 184, [2008] 2 W.L.R. 1013 (Eng.).

interpretations, these offenses remain top of the list for specialist charges, and 32 percent of terrorist-offense charges fall under Section 57 alone.

The overall impact is that more drastic alterations have been sustained to criminal offenses than criminal processes. Two questions thereby arise. The first is why the government and legislature should feel more confident about intervention into the first area than the second. No certain answer can be given, save perhaps that judicial response to procedural changes has often been fiercer because it concerns an issue where the judges claim expertise and control.[45] Judges may be more relaxed about criminal offenses because the signal given by them, reflecting the provided statistics, is more directed to the police than the courts. The second question concerns the overall impact in terms of the spectrum between normal and exceptional justice. Taking these criminal offenses in isolation, it cannot be said that they transform the whole system from ordinary criminal justice into exceptional justice. That depiction would exaggerate the degree of change and ignore the fact that very similar trends have occurred in other areas of criminal justice, affecting serious fraudsters, sex offenders, drug traffickers, and organized gangsters.[46]

3. Future Manipulation in Criminalization

The positioning of the United Kingdom on the spectrum between normal and exceptional criminal justice has varied considerably over time, and

45 *See* International Transport *Roth GmbH v. Secretary of State for the Home Department*, [2002] EWCA (Civ) 158, (85)–(86), [2003] Q.B. 728 (Eng.) ("[G]reater deference will be due to the democratic powers where the subject-matter in hand is peculiarly within their constitutional responsibility, and less when it lies more particularly within the constitutional responsibility of the courts.... There are no tanks on the wrong lawns.").

46 *See* Criminal Justice Act 1987, 1987, c. 38 (U.K.); Drug Trafficking Act 1994, 1944, c. 37 (U.K.); Youth Justice and Criminal Evidence Act 1999, 1999, c. 23, pt. II (U.K.); Serious Organised Crime and Police Act 2005, 2005, c. 25 (U.K.).

despite the current rhetoric, the challenges now posed by terrorism have produced significant adjustments to criminal offenses, although more modest changes to criminal processes. Because, as emphasized at the close of the discussion of criminal processes, the situation remains fluid, the final section of this chapter will address potential future manipulations that might be canvassed so that criminalization can continue to take a prime counterterrorism role. For offenses, pressures might build in three directions.

The first is to continue to extend jurisdiction, so as to prosecute foreign attackers, whether motivated by the wish to respond to British victims abroad – such as those injured in Mumbai in 2008 – or more generally to demonstrate international solidarity. However, much has already been achieved, and the more pressing problems relate to the effectiveness of international police cooperation and the ability to rely on evidence gathered abroad. In addition, the transformation of United Kingdom terrorism offenses into offenses of universal jurisdiction would lack legitimacy insofar as they are not sanctioned by international law,[47] and so might hamper the cooperation necessary for progress. Going beyond the bounds of international law may also result in the attempted imposition of British standards within overseas conflicts where violent resistance may be warranted.[48]

The second pressure is to adopt ever-wider precursor offenses. One precedent, admired by some, is in the French Penal Code, article 421.2.1 – the charge of *association de malfaiteurs en relation avec une entreprise terroriste*, but there is already an offense of engaging in conduct in preparation of terrorism in Section 5 of the Terrorism Act 2006. Any advance in the French formulation can reside only in "a minimum of objective, independent evidence and a maximum of speculation, innuendo and

47 For example, the UN Convention for the Suppression of Terrorist Bombings as enforced by the Terrorism Act 2000, and applied in *R v. McDonald and Others*, [2005] EWCA (Crim) 1945, [2005] All ER (D) 220 (Jul) (Eng.).

48 438 Parl. Deb., H.C. (6th ser.) (2005) 1045 (U.K.).

inference, some of which is supplied by sources of questionable impartiality and integrity."[49]

The third pressure might be to revive offenses against the state, such as treason, in order to achieve a more ringing form of denunciation. But much of the drive behind this idea dissipated when the death penalty was removed from treason in 1998. The woeful British experiences of miscarriages of justice in terrorism cases[50] as well as the technicalities surrounding the crime of treason have muted official enthusiasm for any revival.

As for criminal processes, pressures are being felt to migrate to the lowest common denominator of the key due process standards in Article 6 of the European Convention on Human Rights,[51] so as to solve the prosecutor's terrorism dilemma; namely, the need for intervention prior to the point where, in a non-terrorist case, there might have been a tipping point between bad thoughts and bad deeds. The level of that lowest common denominator has been explored mainly within the executive system of control orders, which are designed deliberately to exploit the boundaries between lower civil and higher criminal standards. In response, the judges have refused to be sidelined by recognizing non-justiciability, but have asserted that the lowest common denominator demands that "the controlee must be given sufficient information about the allegations against him to enable him to give effective instructions in relation to those allegations."[52] The frequent judicial interventions have themselves created a major impetus against executive control orders and thereby favor prosecution. The government has responded to this rebalancing by establishing an inquiry into the rules relating to secrecy in the legal process that may not reduce the prominence of

49 Michael McColgan and Alessandro Attanasio, France: Paving the Way for Arbitrary Justice 35 (1999). *See also* Human Rights Watch, Preempting Justice: Counter-Terrorism Laws and Procedure in France pt. III (2008).

50 *See* Clive Walker and Keir Starmer, Miscarriages of Justice ch. 2 (1999).

51 These standards are incorporated into United Kingdom law by the Human Rights Act 1998, 1998, c. 42 (U.K.).

52 *Re* AF (no 3), [2009] UKHL 28, [59], [2010] 2 A.C. 269.

criminal justice solutions but may affect their fairness in relation to disclosure.[53] The other evidential issue yet to be settled concerns the future admission of intercept evidence, with ongoing studies seeking to find solutions that are palatable to the intelligence agencies, at the same time warning that any reform will not augment prosecution to any marked degree.[54]

National security courts are not on the United Kingdom counterterrorism agenda, thereby avoiding the thorny problems of choice of jurisdiction and discrimination – who would be selected for trial before such courts and for which offenses. Juries largely survive in Britain, aside from the isolated examples of the special nonjury Scottish trial in the Netherlands of those accused of the Lockerbie bombing[55] and aside from the allowance of judge-only trials subject to a high level of proof of jury intimidation under Section 44 of the Criminal Justice Act 2003.[56] Further incursions into jury trials have been mooted for coroners' inquests but were finally defeated in the context of Clause 11 of the Coroners and Justice Bill 2008–09. The arguments for juryless courts would be distinct to those in Northern Ireland. Bias is not a prominent predicament,[57] so the main arguments will turn on complexity and cost – that juries cannot appreciate the evidence and society cannot afford the luxury of forensic education. The Airline Liquid Bomb trials were the most expensive in British history, although a third trial did result in three convictions for conspiracy to murder.

53 *See* 513 Parl. Deb., H.C. (6th ser.) (2010) 175 (U.K.).

54 *See* Advisory Group of Privy Counsellors, Intercept as Evidence, 2009, Cm. 7760 (U.K.); Privy Council, Review of Intercept as Evidence, 2008, Cm. 7324, at ¶¶ 53, 58 (U.K.); Lord Carlile, Home Office, Third Report of the Independent Reviewer Pursuant to Section 14(3) of the Prevention of Terrorism Act 2005 ¶ 38 (2008).

55 *See* High Court of Justiciary (Proceedings in the Netherlands) Order, 1998, S.I. 1998/2251 (U.K.); *HM Advocate v. Al-Megrahi* 2002 J.C. 99 (Scot.).

56 *See R v. JSM*, [2010] EWCA (Crim) 1755, [2010] All E.R. (D) 244 (Jul) (Eng.); *R v. KS*, [2010] EWCA (Crim) 1756, [2010] All E.R. (D) 243 (Jul) (Eng.); *R v. Twomey*, [2009] EWCA 1035, [2009] All E.R. (D) 192 (Jun) (Eng.).

57 Jury vetting is enhanced in terrorism cases. Attorney-General's Guidelines, *Exercise by the Crown of its Right of Stand-By*, [1989] 88 Cr. App. R. 123 (Eng.).

If one reaches the conclusion – contrary to the findings of this chapter – that normal criminal courts do not measure up to the enormity of the multiple difficulties created by notorious terrorists, then internationalization rather than militarization might offer a more promising avenue to avoid the easy charge of "victor's justice."[58] The compromises to the Lockerbie trial processes and ongoing challenges to their verdicts demonstrate some of the downsides to a nationalistic approach in extreme circumstances.

Conclusions

The resurgence after early 2005 of criminal justice solutions to terrorism and the partial displacement of executive interventions is a welcome trend. In British jurisdictions, this trend has not yet necessitated resort to exceptional "terrorist courts" or "terrorist criminal processes" involving any systematic catalog of changes or any derogation notice to excuse fundamental compromises to rights. Nevertheless, the fundamental paradox of proof beyond doubt in a climate of precautionary risk management has encouraged a slide toward minimum standards of due process. To arrest any further slide, the criminal justice agencies must assert their own values and expertise. Thus, the Crown Prosecution Service should treat the extra funding for its counter terrorism division as a signal of confidence in its independence and values. In addition, the judges must continue to develop their jurisprudence of national security and not be deflected by those who advise deference to the executive in the application of policy to individuals.

The United Kingdom experience illustrates several wider points. First, it suggests that a willingness to engage in reflection and reform can produce positive as well as negative counterterrorism legal developments. The policy has been subject to frequent inquiry as to the appropriate

58 *See* Geoffrey Robertson, *Fair Trial for Terrorists?*, *in* HUMAN RIGHTS IN THE "WAR ON TERROR" 169 (Richard A. Wilson ed., 2005).

legal strategy, ranging from the Diplock Report to the Macdonald Report in 2011, which recommends the amendment and curtailment of control orders so that "where people are involved in terrorist activity, they must be detected and, wherever possible, prosecuted and locked up . . . [as] a primary purpose of public policy."[59] The second point is that the British experience underlines the plasticity of normal and special in criminal justice. There is plasticity in the normal criminal justice system's ability to recalibrate what is normal, as illustrated by sweeping changes to the right to silence in the Criminal Justice and Public Order Act 1994 and the rules of hearsay in the Criminal Justice Act 2003, as well as the specialist non-terrorist procedures mentioned. This chapter has demonstrated equal plasticity in the realm of the special, ranging from a Diplock system in Northern Ireland through to the more piecemeal features encountered in terrorism trials in England and Wales. These varied adaptations, which are replicated in many other jurisdictions, suggest that it is legitimate to examine how criminal justice might adapt to the special challenges of terrorism, and that it is wrong to treat criminal justice as a sacrosanct monolith.

In conclusion, the vital questions regarding the criminalization of terrorism are not so much about exceptionalism or specialism. Those concepts are not in reality susceptible to being defined as ideal types, nor in the case of specialism may its features necessarily cross normative boundaries. Rather, the legal system must first assess whether the new format addresses the problem of terrorism effectively and distinctly and second, whether it does so in a way that maintains legitimacy by reflecting the cherished values of that society, including the rights to life, liberty, and due process of victims as well as suspects, rather than causing damage to them. Finally, the primacy of criminal prosecution should not become an obsession but should be positioned within a continuum of other social interventions. Alternative social interventions should be

59 Home Department, Review of Counter-Terrorism and Security Powers, 2011, Cm. 8803, at 9 (U.K.).

triggered especially for those on the threshold of political violence, some of whom are now prosecuted for precursor specialist crimes. Just as war crimes and de-Nazification were not pursued to their logical degree in Germany after 1945, the same forgiveness can surely apply to persons who are merely at risk of committing terrorism. The Home Office has latterly recognized the need to apply a layered approach to counterterrorism. A prime example is Project Channel whereby responsible citizens in Muslim communities provide an early warning system for the identification of extremists. Social interventions in the forms of counseling and engagement in approved activities are then applied. Some of our neighbor terrorists should face prosecution, but a range of other tactics such as assessment, counseling, and assimilation should be developed to achieve a harmonious life with our unruly and sometimes nasty neighbors.

12 Trying Terrorists

The Israeli Perspective

Emanuel Gross

WHAT IS THE PROPER FORUM IN WHICH SUSPECTED terrorists are to be tried? For the purpose of examining this question, this chapter focuses on the processes that the State of Israel has adopted and contrasts those with the American military commissions. I will argue that despite the great differences between Israel and the Unites States, primarily regarding the structure of the judiciary and the circumstances surrounding the need of each to face this question, a snapshot of today's standpoint reveals that processes in both the United States and Israel produced roughly the same end consequences.

The first part of this chapter discusses the establishment of military courts in the West Bank soon after its occupation by Israel during the Six-Day War in 1967 and the developments and processes that have accompanied the military courts since then. This chapter addresses the central legislation governing the trials and detentions of suspected terrorists and the judicial review led by the Israeli Supreme Court regarding these issues. The second part reviews the resemblance and differences between the United States and Israel, emphasizing the different circumstances that brought about the establishment of military commissions and military courts in the first place, and arguing that these circumstances are inevitably the main cause for the divergence.

1. Military Courts in the Occupied Territories

Israeli military courts were established in the Gaza Strip and the West Bank (both hereinafter referred to as the Area) following the 1967 Six-Day, War under Military Proclamation No. 2.[1] The establishment of the military courts was in compliance with articles 64 and 66 of the fourth Geneva Convention, regarding the authority of the occupying power to legislate and establish military courts in the occupied territory.[2] The military proclamation also endowed the Area commander with full legislative, executive, and judicial authorities over the Area and declared that the law in force prior to the occupation remained in force as long as it did not contradict new military orders.

Exercising this authority, in 1970 the military commander issued the Security Provisions Order (hereinafter the Order),[3] which constitutes the jurisdiction of the military courts, the laws governing arrest and detention, the definition of offenses and the determination of penalties for offenders, and the establishment of legal procedures in the military courts of the Area. The Order, a primary legislation in the Occupied Territories, has been elaborated over the years and amended more than ninety times.[4] In 2009, the Order was consolidated with all other orders and proclamations applied in the Area into the Security Provisions Order of 2009 (2009 SPO).[5] One such amendment was a revision regarding the requirements of military judges' legal training. Until 2004, it was required that of a three-judge panel only the presiding judge had to have legal training; the

1 Military Proclamation No. 2 Concerning Regulation of Authority and the Judiciary (West Bank) (1967). Article 3 of the Military Proclamation endowed the Area commander with full legislative, executive, and judicial authorities over the Area and declared that the law in force prior to the occupation remained in force as long as it did not contradict new military orders.

2 Fourth Geneva Convention of August 12, 1949, Relative to the Protection of Civilian Persons in Time of War, 6 U.S.T. 3316, T.I.A.S. No. 3365, 75 U.N.T.S. 287.

3 Security Provisions Order (West Bank) (No. 378) (1970).

4 Netanel Benisho, *Criminal law in the West Bank and Gaza*, 18 IDF L. Rev. 293, 297 (2005).

5 Security Provisions Order (consolidated version) (West Bank) (No. 1651), 2009.

two other judges could be ordinary military officers. The 2004 amendment provided that all judges of a military court must have legal training.[6] Another example of an amendment pertains to the courts' jurisdiction. Soon after the 1967 war the military courts abstained from hearing cases that lacked any territorial link with the Area.[7] In the *Akrash* case, a military court ruled that in order to construct jurisdiction over extraterritorial offenses, a statute that expressly granted the military court this jurisdiction was needed.[8] Following this judgment, the military commander inserted an extraterritorial section to the SPO, authorizing military courts "to try... anyone who committed an act outside the Area which would constitute an offence had it been committed within the Area and the act harmed or was designed to harm the security of the Region or public order therein."[9] Through this and other jurisdictional provisions, a considerable range of offenses concerned with assistance to commission of offenses, attempt, incitement, conspiring, and membership of unlawful organizations became triable by the military courts.[10]

Perhaps the most important development was the establishment of an appellate tribunal to hear appeals in cases decided by military courts. Until the late 1980s, the military-court system had no mechanism of judicial review of the decisions of military courts. A controversial procedure that had been activated during those years was that decisions of the military courts were brought before the military commander for his approval. After the ruling of the Israeli Supreme Court in *Arjub*,[11] a Military Court of Appeals was established in 1989.[12]

6 Amendment No. 89 to Article 4 of the SPO (Order No.1550) (2004). *See also* Amos N. Guiora, *Where are Terrorists to be Tried: A Comparative Analysis of Rights Granted to Suspected Terrorists*, 56 Cath. U. L. Rev. 805, 818 (2007).

7 *E.g.*, Ramallah (RAM)/160/68, *The Military Prosecutor v. Wildman*, 1 SJMC 377; RAM/78/69, *The Military Prosecutor v. Bakir*, 1 SJMC 450.

8 RAM/78/69, *The Military Prosecutor v. Akrash*, 1 SJMC 450.

9 Order No. 517 (Amendment No. 7 to the SPO) (1973).

10 *See also* Zvi Hadar, *The military courts*, *in* Military Government in the Territories Administered by Israel, 1967–1980: The Legal Aspects 193 (Meir Shamgar ed., 1982).

11 HCJ 87/85, *Arjub v. The Military Commander in the West Bank*, 42(1) PD 353 (1988).

12 *Id.* Although the Supreme Court rejected petitions that sought to obligate the military commander to establish a court of appeal under the notion that applicable international

The military commander, on the basis of a decision by a judge selection committee, appoints military judges. The military court of first instance hears cases before a single judge or a panel of three judges, depending on the severity of charges. A single judge is competent to impose a punishment of up to ten years imprisonment; a three-judge panel may impose the maximum punishment carried by the offense. The Military Court of Appeals usually hears appeals in panels of three judges.

The defendant has a fundamental, legally guaranteed right to be present at all the proceedings in the military court, with no exceptions other than his or her own behavior in the courtroom. The right of the defendant to be represented is also expressly provided by the 2009 SPO. The legal representation is provided by either a Palestinian or Israeli civilian lawyer. Representation is mandatory in grave offenses, (i.e., offenses that are punishable by ten or more years' imprisonment). If the accused cannot afford a lawyer, the military court will appoint him one at no cost. In cases in which no obligatory representation is required the military court may still appoint a lawyer if the accused cannot afford one.

(a) Administrative Detentions

Israel applies a two-track approach to Palestinians suspected of having committed acts of terrorism.[13] The first track is a criminal trial by a military court that is regulated by the 2009 SPO. The other track, and the one we shall now turn to, is that of administrative detention.

Administrative detentions by the occupying power are permitted in accordance with article 78 of the fourth Geneva Convention, which states:

> If the Occupying Power considers it necessary, for imperative reasons of security, to take safety measures concerning protected persons, it may, at the most, subject them to assigned residence or to internment.

law does not contain any provision regarding courts of appeal compelling them to be established in the Occupied Territory, the High Court of Justice strongly recommended the initiation of an appellate instance.

13 Guiora, *supra* note 6, at 817–18.

> Decisions regarding such assigned residence or internment shall be made according to a regular procedure to be prescribed by the Occupying Power in accordance with the provisions of the present Convention. This procedure shall include the right of appeal for the parties concerned. Appeals shall be decided with the least possible delay. In the event of the decision being upheld, it shall be subject to periodical review, if possible every six months, by a competent body set up by the said Power.

Consequently, the power of the Israeli government to detain administratively is governed by three acts. First, the Emergency Powers (Detentions) Law of 1979, which replaced the arrangement regarding administrative detention set forth in the Defense (Emergency) Regulations of 1945;[14] second, the Order regarding Administrative Detention (ADO),[15] which is part of the military legislation applying in the Area; and third, the Incarceration of Unlawful Combatants Law (IUCL),[16] which was enacted in 2002. The ADO and the IUCL are the key statutes regulating administrative detention.

The ADO empowers the military commander to order the detention of a person when the commander has "reasonable basis to believe that the security of the Area or public security" requires so.[17] Administrative detentions, unlike the criminal process, are not punitive.[18] An individual may be detained if available intelligence information indicates that he or she is involved in the preparation of a future terrorist act. When the individual order of administrative detention is about to expire the military commander may extend it for a period that does not exceed six months.[19] There is no statutorily determined time period limiting

14 Article 85 of the Defence (Emergency) Regulations, 1945.

15 Order Regarding Administrative Detention (Temporary Order) (Combined Version) (Judea and Samaria) (No. 1591), 5767 – 2007, retrieved from http://www.btselem.org/download/administrative_detention_military_order_1591_eng.pdf.

16 The Incarceration of Unlawful Combatants Law, 2002.

17 ADO, § 1(a).

18 Guiora, *supra* note 6, at 819.

19 ADO, § 1(b).

the number of detentions, hence the detention for six months may be indefinitely renewable. Nevertheless, renewability requires a showing that the detainee continues to present a viable security threat each and every time.[20] The ADO consists of an apparatus of judicial review. Within eight days from the day the person is detained or from the day the detention order is extended, the detainee must be brought before a military judge holding the rank of at least major to determine if the detention is justified. The judge may approve or cancel it or shorten the period of detention specified in the order. Both the detainee and the military commander can appeal the judge's decision to the Military Court of Appeals. In hearings of both the lower and appellate court, the judge is not bound by the regular rules of evidence. Section 7 of the ADO provides that "it shall be lawful to deviate from the rules of evidence if the judge is satisfied that this will be conducive to discovery of the truth and just handling of the case." In particular, a judge may "admit evidence also not in the presence of the detainee or his representative, or without revealing it to them," if he is convinced that disclosure of the evidence is liable to "harm the security of the Area or public security." The judge may also admit hearsay evidence.

The IUCL gives the authorities power to detain "unlawful combatants" as defined in section 2 of the Law (i.e. persons who participate, directly or indirectly, in hostile acts or who are members of forces that carry out hostile acts against the State of Israel and who do not meet the criteria for prisoner of war status under the third Geneva Convention). The IUCL was intended to prevent these persons from returning to the cycle of hostilities against the state.[21] From the language of section 2 it is clear that it is not essential for someone to take part in hostile acts against the state. His membership in a "force perpetrating hostile

20 However, the Supreme Court put a limit on the indefinite detention by imposing the rule of proportionality. *See* Further Hearing 7048/97, *Anon. v. Minister of Defense*, 54(1) PD 721; Emanuel *Gross, Human Rights, Terrorism and the Problem of Administrative Detention: Does a Democracy Have the Right to Hold Terrorists as Bargain Chips?*, 18 ARIZ. J. INT. & COM. L. 721 (2001).

21 CrimA 6659/06, *Anonymous v. State of Israel*, *infra* note 37.

acts" (i.e., a terrorist organization) may include that person within the definition of unlawful combatant. Like the ADO provision regarding the authority of the military commander to order the detention of a person, section 3 of the IUCL regarding the internment of unlawful combatant provides the following: "Where an officer at the rank of minimum a Captain has reasonable cause to believe that a person brought in front of him is an unlawful combatant, he may issue an order directing his temporary internment, until a decision regarding the issuing of an internment order [by the Chief of Staff] will be provided." Consequently:

> [W]here the Chief of Staff has reasonable cause to believe that a person being held by state authorities is an unlawful combatant and that his release will harm state security, he may issue an order under his hand, directing that such person be interned at a place to be determined; an internment order shall include the grounds for internment, without prejudicing state security requirements.

Section 7 of the IUCL provides a rebuttable presumption whereby the release of a person who satisfies the conditions of the definition of unlawful combatant is presumed to harm the security of the state as long as the hostile acts against it have not ceased.

Another fundamental law that is most relevant to administrative detention is Israel's Basic Law: Human Dignity and Liberty (hereinafter Basic Law),[22] which anchors in law the right to freedom as a basic, constitutional, and fundamental right. Section 5 of the Basic Law provides: "There shall be no deprivation or restriction of the liberty of a person by imprisonment, arrest, extradition or otherwise." Section 8 of the Basic law, known as the Limitation Clause, provides the exception: "There shall be no violation of rights under this Basic Law except by a Law befitting the values of the State of Israel, enacted for a proper purpose, and to an extent no greater than is required, or by regulation enacted by virtue of express authorization in such Law."

22 Basic Law: Human Dignity and Liberty (S.H. 1992, No. 1391, p. 150) (1992).

(b) Judicial Review of the Supreme Court

Soon after the military courts began to operate, Palestinian residents of the Area submitted petitions to the Israeli Supreme Court, sitting as a High Court of Justice, in which they challenged the legality of the military courts' actions and decisions.[23] A threshold question was whether the Court had jurisdiction to hear the petitions.[24] In the *Jam'iat* case,[25] the Court concluded:

> It seems that there is no longer cause to doubt the rule that the Supreme Court, sitting as the High Court of Justice, is authorized to exercise judicial review over the actions of the military government in Judea, Samaria and the Gaza Strip. True, the issues was initially left for further review . . . [but] over the years, the status of the military government has been clarified and now there is no doubt that . . . this court is entitled to the right of review. The reason for this is that the military commander and those under his command are public servants who serve a public function in accordance with the law.[26]

After the Court's ruling in *Jam'iat*, its jurisdiction to review IDF actions in the Area and specifically proceedings in the military courts was no longer in doubt. Since then thousands of petitions submitted by Palestinians have been reviewed by the Supreme Court.

The case of *Al-Harub*[27] is an example of the application of the first track taken against suspected terrorists. A military court convicted Al-Harub of membership and activity in the Hamas terrorist organization and a deliberate attempt to cause death.[28] He was sentenced to life imprisonment and his appeal to the military appellate court was denied.

23 HCJ 302, 306/72, *Abu Hilu v. State of Israel*, 27(2) P.D. 169.

24 *See, e.g.*, *Abu Hilu*, *supra* note 23; HCJ 390/79, *Dawikat v. State of Israel*, 34(1) P.D. 1; HCJ 802/79, *Samara v. The Commander of Judea and Samaria*, 34(4) P.D. 1.

25 HCJ 393/82, *Jam'iat Iscan Al-Ma'almoun Al-Tha'auniya Al-Mahduda Al-Mauliya v. Commander of the IDF Forces in the Area of Judea and Samaria*, 37(4) P.D. 785.

26 *Id.* paras. 32, 33–34.

27 HCJ 7932/08, *Al-Harub v. Commander of the Military Forces in the Judea and Samaria Area* (unpublished, judgment of 29 December 2009). retrieved from http://www.hamoked.org/files/2011/113450_eng.pdf.

28 Al-Harub had a dominant role in dispatching a suicide bomber to a café in Jerusalem.

After his verdict was handed down, Al-Harub filed for a petition to the Supreme Court sitting as High Court of Justice, challenging the reasonableness of security legislation in the Area and claiming that in contravention of the principle of penal uniformity, legislation in the Area allows the imposition of a life sentence for a deliberate attempt to cause death, whereas in Israel the maximum penalty for attempted murder is a twenty-year prison sentence.[29] Al-Harub argued that the disparity between the penalties discriminates criminal defendants who are tried in the Area vis-à-vis defendants tried in Israel. He argued that courts both in Israel and the Area confront the phenomenon of terrorism and thus there was no factual justification for the different penal levels. The Supreme Court rejected Al-Harub's arguments and ruled that the existence of a discrepancy between the law in the Area and Israel does not, of itself, constitute grounds for judicial intervention. The Court concluded that, generally speaking:

> The law in the Area differs from the law in Israel and there is no fault in this per se. This notwithstanding, the military courts in the Area have discretion and must use it, in the appropriate cases, while taking into consideration the law and maximum penalty inside Israel among the other circumstances relating to a specific defendant and the unique security situation in the Area.[30]

The Supreme Court has stated repeatedly that under Article 78 of the fourth Geneva Convention, administrative detention may only be used as a forward-looking preventive measure against a person who poses an individual threat to the security of the state or the Area and may not be used as punishment for past acts.[31] In the *Sajadiya* case, the Supreme

29 According to the principle of penal uniformity, identical penalties should be imposed for identical offenses, including when they are heard for different instances.

30 Al-Harub, *supra* note 27, at para. 13. Regarding Al-Harub specifically, the Court found that the penalty imposed on him was reviewed in the previous proceeding and was warranted.

31 HCJ 7015/02, *Ajuri v. IDF Commander*, 56(6) P.D. 352, para. 24 ("We have held repeatedly that the measure of administrative internment – which is the measure considered by Art. 78 of the Fourth Geneva Convention together with assigned residence – may be adopted only in the case of a 'danger presented by the acts of the petitioner

Court held that administrative detention is intended to thwart a security danger resulting from acts that the detainee is likely to commit where it is not reasonably possible to prevent them by taking regular legal measures or by an administrative measure that results in less serious harm to the individual's rights and liberties.[32]

The *al-Ma'maleh* case[33] came before the Supreme Court after the enactment of the Basic Law: Human Dignity and Liberty. The case concerned a situation where an administrative detention order was issued against al-Ma'maleh by the military commander, al-Ma'maleh appealed to the military court, and the military judge shortened the period of detention. A day before the date of release as decided by the military judge, the military commander signed an order extending al-Ma'maleh's detention. There was no dispute that the military commander had the authority to extend the detention, but in the circumstances, he did so after a military judge found that there had been no grounds to allow a long period of detention, therefore shortening the detention time. The Supreme Court elucidated that administrative detention limited one's liberty in the most restrictive way: an individual's liberty is deprived not by court, but by an administrative authority (the military commander); not by judicial procedure, but by an administrative decision; often not on the basis of disclosed evidence that the detainee can contest, but on the basis of confidential material. The Court further stated that the deprivation of liberty is even graver in light of the fact that the same administrative authority that was authorized to issue the arrest was also authorized to extend it from time to time.[34] The Court clarified that the decision of the judge hearing an

to the security of the Area.'"); HCJ 7709/95, *Sitrin v. IDF Commander in Judaea and Samaria* (unpublished); HCJ 1361/91, *Mesalem v. IDF Commander in Gaza Strip*, 45(3) IsrSC 444, 456; HCJ 554/81, *Beransa v. Central Commander*, 36(4) IsrSC 247, 250; HCJ 814/88, *Nasrallah v. Commander of Military Forces in the West Bank*, 43(2) P.D. 271; HCJ 3239/02, *Marab v. IDF Commander in Judaea and Samaria*, 57(2) P.D. 349, 367 (2003).

32 HCJ 253/88, *Sajadiya v. Minister of Defense*, 42(3) P.D. 801, 821.

33 Administrative Detention Appeal (ADA) 2320/98, *al-Ma'maleh et al. v. Commander of Military Forces in the West Bank et al.*, 52(3) P.D. 346.

34 *Id.* para. 2.

administrative detention case always prevailed over the decision of the military commander: "The liberty of the individual is too precious to be placed in the hands of the military commander alone. Therefore, the law subordinates the commander to the judge, thus the detention order is subject to judicial review. Judicial review is the defense line of the detainee liberty, and must be carefully safeguarded." The Court concluded:

> In a dispute between the military commander and the judge regarding the danger posed by the detainee, when the same material is placed before both of them, the opinion of the judge prevails. This conclusion is dictated by the purpose of the Detentions Order, by the essence of the judicial review, and by the need for a proper balance between security and individual liberty.[35]

In the case at hand, the Court ruled that the military commander was not permitted to issue an order extending the detention.[36]

Although the IUCL came into force in 2002, its constitutionality was not considered by the Supreme Court until 2007, in the *Anonymous* case.[37] In *Anonymous* the appellants challenged their detention under the IUCL, claiming that it was unlawful, and raising fundamental questions concerning the interpretation of the IUCL provisions, its adherence to international humanitarian law, and the constitutionality of the arrangements prescribed in it. The appellants had been placed under administrative detentions[38] that were extended from time to time by the military commander and upheld on judicial review by a military court. The Tel-Aviv-Jaffa District Court heard the judicial review on the issuing

35 *Id.* para. 10.

36 The Court noted two exceptions to this rule: (1) when new information of substantial weight is obtained regarding the danger posed by the detainee; and (2) when the judge's decision to shorten the detention is intended only to require the military commander to reconsider if further detention is necessary, prior to the completion of the period originally specified in the order. In this case, the decision is referred to as a non-substantive reduction.

37 CrimA 6659/06, *Anonymous v. State of Israel* (unpublished, judgment of June 11, 2008).

38 By virtue of the Order regarding Administrative Detentions (Temporary Order) (Gaza Strip Region) (no. 941), 5748 – 1988, containing the same provisions as the ADO.

and extending of the detention orders and, on the basis of the information presented to it, found the appellants to be "major activists in the Hezbollah organization who would very likely return to terrorist activities if they were released now, and that their release was likely to harm state security." Accordingly, it upheld the decisions to further detain them. The detainees appealed the decision to the Supreme Court arguing, inter alia, that the IUCL in its present format violated the rights to liberty and dignity enshrined in Basic Law: Human Dignity and Liberty, in a manner that did not satisfy the conditions of the limitation clause of that law. The appellants also claimed that the Basic Law was inconsistent with the law of war that it purported to realize. The Supreme Court held that the purpose of the IUCL was to remove from the cycle of hostilities a person who belonged to a terrorist organization or who participated in hostile acts against the State of Israel. To that end, the law could only be activated against combatants and not against innocent civilians.[39] The Court rejected the appellants' argument that applying the law of war, the category of unlawful combatant, was invalid as provided for in Section 2 of the IUCL.[40] Rather, the court found that the term unlawful combatants did not constitute a separate category, but rather constituted a subcategory of civilians recognized by international law. Consequently it held that the ICUL merely determined special provisions for the detention of civilians who were unlawful combatants.[41] It followed that for the purposes of internment under the IUCL, the state was required to provide clear and convincing evidence that even if the prisoner had not taken a substantial direct or indirect part in hostile acts against the state, he belonged to a terrorist organization and contributed to the cycle of hostilities in the broad sense of the term.[42] The Supreme Court further held that the IUCL was in compliance with Basic Law: Human Dignity and Liberty.[43] The Court concluded that the IUCL was "intended to

39 CrimA 6659/06, *Anonymous v. State of Israel*, *supra* note 37, para. 6.

40 *Id.* paras. 10–14.

41 *Id.* para. 14.

42 *Id.* para. 23.

43 *Id.* paras. 28–49.

prevent persons who threaten the security of the state due to their activity or their membership in terrorist organizations that carry out hostile acts against the State of Israel from returning to the cycle of hostilities," and that on this basis its legislative purpose was a proper one.[44] The Court was also satisfied that the IUCL met the proportionality test that was required by the limitation clause of the Basic Law and that violations of the human rights concerned were not excessive. In determining the proportionality of a statutory act that violates a constitutional human right, the Court uses three subtests: first, the rational connection test, whereby the legislative measure violating the constitutional right and the purpose that the Basic Law is intended to realize must be compatible; second is the least harmful measure test, which requires that the legislation violate the constitutional right to the smallest degree possible in order to achieve the purpose of the Basic Law; and third is the test of proportionality in the narrow sense, according to which the violation of the constitutional right must be commensurate with the social benefit it bestows.[45] Notably, in applying the rational connection test (between the measure and its purpose) the Court found that administrative detention that prevented an unlawful combatant from returning to the cycle of hostilities against the State of Israel realized the legislative purpose and satisfied the purpose that the Basic Law was intended to realize.[46] The Court was particularly concerned with the question of whether there existed alternative measures that would involve a lesser degree of violation of the constitutional right. The Court engaged in careful assessment and evaluation of different measures identified by the appellants in their briefs as able to constitute viable alternatives to administrative detention, but concluded that these suggested measures did not realize "[t]he purpose of the internment of [IUCL] and therefore they cannot constitute a suitable alternative measure to internment in accordance with the Law."[47] The

44 *Id.* para. 30.

45 *See, e.g.*, HCJ 2056/04, *Beit Sourik Village Council v. Government of Israel*, P.D. 58(5) 807 (2004); HCJ 7052/03, *Adalah Legal Centre for Arab Minority Rights in Israel v. Ministry of the Interior* (2006) (unpublished).

46 CrimA 6659/06, *Anonymous v. State of Israel*, *supra* note 37, para. 32.

47 *Id.* para. 48.

Court held that "the arrangements prescribed in the IUCL do not, per se and irrespective of the manner in which they are implemented, violate the right to personal liberty excessively, and they fall within the bounds of the room for constitutional maneuver granted to the legislature."[48] The Court found that the IUCL did not allow the internment of innocent civilians who had no real connection to the cycle of hostilities and that it established mechanisms whose purpose was to ameliorate the violation of the detainees' rights, including a cause of detention that was on the basis of a threat to state security and the conducting of a hearing and preliminary and periodic judicial reviews of internment under the Basic Law.[49] On the basis of these provisions, the Supreme Court concluded that the IUCL satisfied the third subtest of the requirement of proportionality.[50] The underlying rationale of the Supreme Court's ruling in *Anonymous* is, therefore, that "the Internment of Unlawful Combatants Law satisfies the conditions of the limitation clause, and there is no constitutional ground for [the Court's] intervention."[51]

It should be noted that the IUCL was enacted in the first place following a judicial review by the Supreme Court regarding Lebanese nationals held in detention as "bargaining chips" by virtue of administrative detention orders issued from time to time by the Israeli minister of defense.[52] In that case, applying similar judicial proportionality and limitation tests, the Supreme Court held that the state did not have authority to hold Lebanese nationals in detention by virtue of administrative detention orders if the sole reason for their detention was to hold them as bargaining chips in order to obtain the release of captives and missing servicemen.[53]

48 *Id.*
49 *Id.* para. 49.
50 *Id.*
51 *Id.*
52 CrimFH 7048/97, *Anonymous v. Minister of Defence*, 44(1) P.D. 721 (2000).
53 *See also* CrimA 6659/06, *Anonymous v. State of Israel*, *supra* note 37, para. 6; Emanuel Gross, *Human Rights, Terrorism and the Problem of Administrative Detention in Israel: Does a Democracy Have the Right to Hold Terrorists as Bargaining Chips?*, 18 ARIZ. J. INT'L & COMP. L. 721 (2001).

In August 2008, two months after the judgment in *Anonymous* and despite the Supreme Court's upholding the constitutionality of the IUCL, the IUCL was almost entirely revised. Many provisions were added and existing provisions – such as those pertaining to the imprisonment and procedure and circumstances regarding the issuing of the detention order, judicial review provision, and right to meet with a lawyer – received further detailing.

2. Comparative Dimensions

A starting point of comparative analysis is to address the fundamental distinction between the circumstances leading to the establishment of the military commissions in the United States and those leading to the creation of their military-court counterparts in Israel. The specificity of circumstances has a crucial impact on the salient differences between the two systems. Whereas the Israeli military courts were established in an occupied territory, the military commissions were established by the United States as means to an end, the means being the military commissions and the end being the nontraditional War on Terror.

Second, the military courts established in the Occupied Territories were created as the main ordinary criminal courts in the Territories and were thus oriented from the very beginning to try all individuals, committing all criminal offenses, whether or not involving terror-related acts. Conversely, the United States's military commissions were established for the very narrow purpose of dealing with suspected terrorists.

Third, the Israeli military courts are a mature system, in comparison to the contemporary military commissions. Although Israel is a "young" country compared with the United States, it had to deal with terrorism from its very first days, whereas the terrorist attacks of 9/11 presented the United States with what had been considered by many to be a new challenge of international terrorism. The American system developed quickly and with great intensity, whereas the development process of the military courts in the Occupied Territories was slower and steadier.

The major differences between the two systems are due, to a large extent, to the different political realities in each country drawing from the specificity of the fight against terrorism, which projects on the enactments of laws, issuing of orders, and governing of different procedures. However, the key to a legal, constitutional, and effective mechanism to try suspected terrorists in and by a democratic state is the continuous availability of judicial review and ability of ordinary courts to implement sustained oversight on the functioning of exceptional judicial bodies.

13 Exceptional or Not? An Examination of India's Special Courts in the National Security Context

Jayanth K. Krishnan and Viplav Sharma

HOW IS THE INDIAN GOVERNMENT, UNDER ITS CONSTITUTIONALLY democratic system, dealing with the suspected terrorists that it captures and detains? That is the core question this chapter seeks to address. In Part 1, we offer a brief summary on the structure of the regular Indian criminal justice system. As India's regular courts are considered by many to be broken and incapable of providing justice in a timely manner, the state has opted to construct alternative fora to dispose of criminal matters more expeditiously, including, for our purposes, terrorism-related cases. In Part 2, we provide background on how special courts established under different antiterrorism statutes in India have evolved over the years, including a discussion of the Terrorism and Disruptive Activities (Prevention) Act (TADA) of 1985 and the 2002 Prevention of Terrorist Activities Act (POTA). As we suggest, the special courts under these laws were in fact not so special.[1] Because the lawyers, judges, norms, and even physical facilities were frequently the same as found in the regular courts, there was a great blurring between these two fora. Eventually, both

1 *See* Jayanth K. Krishnan, *India's PATRIOT Act: POTA and the Impact on Civil Liberties in the World's Largest Democracy*, 22 L. & INEQ. 265 (2004). On this point of lack of specialness, we also draw on throughout: Menaka Guruswamy, *Countering Terror on Terrorising the Law*, SEMINAR 599, 2–5 (July 2009) (commenting on the set of newer antiterrorism laws passed).

TADA and POTA were repealed, with the latter occurring in the fall of 2004.

In Part 3, we discuss how the 2008 Mumbai terror attacks reignited the call for sweeping measures to be enacted. The result was the passage of two statutes, the Unlawful Activities (Prevention) Act (UAPA) and the National Investigation Agency Act (NIAA), both of which helped establish the most recent set of NIAA special courts, which we analyze in detail. Finally, in Part 4, we outline the challenges these latest courts present to India's democracy. We rely on various cases and data that show a conflation and tension among these NIAA courts, other denoted special courts, the regular judiciary, and India's democratic system of government. We conclude by arguing that in order for special terrorism courts to serve a constructive purpose in India, there must be clarification on the jurisdiction of these fora, which, we believe, would strengthen the government's justification for maintaining such institutions.

1. Contextualizing Special Courts within India's Regular Criminal Court System

To understand how India's special terrorism courts fit within the judiciary, it is important first to explain the structure of the regular criminal courts. The courts of first resort in this system are divided between magistrates courts and sessions courts. Typically, an accused is arraigned in front of a judicial magistrate. Depending on the magnitude of the crime, those accused of lesser offenses are tried in magistrates courts and those charged with more serious crimes are held over for trial in sessions courts. Charges brought against defendants normally emanate from the Indian Penal Code, which dates back to 1860.

Under the Indian Code of Criminal Procedure from 1973, the defendant has the right in a sessions court to appeal both interlocutory and final rulings to an appellate state high court, and then to the Indian Supreme Court. Magistrate defendants have the same right, but must appeal to a sessions court first. However, there is an important exception to this appeals process. Under the Indian Constitution, where a defendant has been arrested and believes there is a violation of his or her constitutionally protected fundamental rights, a writ petition may be made directly in the state's high court or even in the Indian Supreme Court to evaluate the merits of the case.[2]

There is a general contemporary consensus that the Indian criminal justice system is plagued by massive delays in adjudication at all levels within this institutional hierarchy.[3] These delays are caused by a variety of factors, including a lack of qualified judges to hear cases, procedural difficulties in disposing of currently pending cases, strategic litigation maneuvers by both private and governmental lawyers, and the manner in which private lawyers collect their fees, which is often per court appearance. Thus, to bypass the log-jammed regular judicial process, over the past three decades there has been a proliferation of alternative fora that would more quickly dispose of cases, such as fast-track courts, "jail adalats,"[4] more informal police bodies to hear certain criminal matters, and, for our purposes, special terrorism courts. We now analyze the details of this last set of fora.

2. Terrorism Statutes and Their Accompanying Courts: A Snapshot[5]

The roots of antiterrorism statutes in India date back to pre-independence times, with the 1919 Rowlatt Act perhaps the most infamous of India's

2 For a discussion of forum shopping, *see* Jayanth K. Krishnan, *Lawyering for a Cause and Experiences from Abroad*, 94 CAL. L. REV. 575 (2006).

3 On delays and backlog, *see generally* Marc Galanter and Jayanth K. Krishnan, *Bread for the Poor: Access to Justice and Rights of the Needy in India*, 55 HASTINGS L. J. 789 (2004); Jayanth K. Krishnan and C. Raj Kumar, *Delay in Process, Denial of Justice: The Jurisprudence & Empirics of Speedy Trials in Comparative Perspective*, 42 GEO. J. INT'L L. 747 (2011).

4 This term refers to "jailhouse courts." Galanter and Krishnan, *supra* note 3.

5 This section will rely on Krishnan, *India's PATRIOT Act* (2004), *supra* note 1. For a summary of India's various antiterrorism statutes, *also see* Bhanu Pratap Singh, *Recent Anti-Terror Changes in Criminal Justice Administration*, August 2009, retrieved from http://papers.ssrn.com/sol3/papers.cfm?abstract_id=1458279.

British statutory legacy.[6] The Rowlatt Act provided the legal basis for the colonial regime to arrest, detain, try, and convict persons suspected of terrorism. Indeed, the harshness of the law prompted widespread demonstrations, led most notably by Mohandas Karamchand Gandhi, who charged that the colonial action classified Indians as inferior individuals within their own homeland. Following independence, a series of antiterrorism statutes were passed in order to address threats found in various regions of India.[7]

With respect to the UAPA – India's antiterrorism statute currently in force – it is the latest incarnation of this same-named law that originally emerged in 1967. Before discussing it, however, two other important pieces of legislation require analysis, the first of which is TADA. TADA was passed following the assassination of Prime Minister Indira Gandhi by extremists in 1984. The law contained a number of provisions enhancing the state's power to combat terrorism including allowing the police to conduct arrests on the basis of mere suspicion and detaining suspected terrorists for up to one year without bail.[8]

In terms of the special, or what were called "designated courts" under TADA, the statute gave these fora a mixture of regular court and exceptional powers. For example, as with regular sessions courts, defendants in TADA courts could be tried in absentia.[9] Further, in terms of staffing, a TADA court judge was required to have the status of a sitting regular sessions judge.[10] (Practically speaking, in areas of the country that faced higher terrorist threats, the docket of TADA court judges was mainly restricted to only TADA-based cases, whereas in less troubled areas,

6 On the Rowlett Act, *see* Anil Kalhan, Gerald Conroy, Mamta Kaushal, Sam Scott Miller, and Jed S. Radkoff, *Colonial Continuities: Human Rights, Terrorism and Security Laws in India*, 20 Colum. J. Asian L. 93, 128–36, 153, 171 (2006).

7 Krishnan, *supra* note 1, at n.12. For a detailed discussion, *see* Ujjwal Kumar Singh, The State, Democracy, and Anti-Terrorism Laws in India (2007).

8 For a discussion of this point and of the statute, *see* Krishnan, *supra* note 1, at 267–69. *See generally* Manoj Mate and Adnan Naseemullah, *State Security and Elite Capture: The Implementation of Antiterrorist Legislation in India*, 9 J. Human Rts. 262 (2010).

9 *See* The Terrorist and Disruptive Activities (Prevention) Act, No. 28 of 1987, India Code (1987), § 14(5), *amended by* Act 43 of 1993.

10 *Id.* § 9(6).

judges wore two distinct hats, those dealing with terrorism matters and those dealing with regular sessions courts cases.)

The overlap, however, also caused confusion. Under Section 12 of TADA, TADA courts could try defendants not only under the statute but also under provisions found within the regular Indian criminal law.[11] So a defendant charged with an offense of terrorism could also be charged with attempted murder under a regular Indian penal statute. The consequence of Section 12 then was extraordinary, because the protections given to defendants in TADA courts were far fewer than those provided by the sessions courts. For instance, the TADA trials could be held in camera, and admissions made under police custody – although not admissible in regular courts – were admissible in the TADA courts.[12] In addition, interlocutory appeals, although permissible in regular sessions courts, were prohibited by TADA.[13] In TADA courts, terrorist suspects had the burden of disproving their guilt to authorities – rather than having their innocence presumed. This standard contravened the fundamental rights of the Indian constitution. Eventually, these reactionary provisions, together with public outrage and the government's own rather critical assessment, led to the law's demise in 1995.[14]

In the intervening years between the end of TADA and POTA's passage in 2002, two important antiterrorism bills came before the Indian

11 *Id.* § 12. *See also* Krishnan, *supra* note 1, at 267–69.

12 *Id.* § 15. *See also* Krishnan, *supra* note 1, at 267–69.

13 The Terrorist and Disruptive Activities (Prevention) Act § 19(1–2). Although final judgments in a TADA court could be appealed within thirty days to the Supreme Court as a matter of right both on law and facts. Krishnan, *supra* note, at 267–69.

14 Consider, for example, that during the ten-year TADA regime approximately 76,000 people were detained "with only about one percent of these detainees ever being convicted of any crime." *See* Krishnan, *supra* note 1, at 269 (drawing on COMMONWEALTH HUMAN RIGHTS INITIATIVE, SUBMISSIONS TO THE REVIEW COMMITTEE ON POTA, retrieved from http://www.humanrightsinitiative.org/artres/pota_submission.pdf). Furthermore, between 1985 and 1995, when TADA was in force, there were high levels of what were called police encounters. These incidents manifested in two ways: one whereby suspects were killed by officers upon capture; the other, where after arrest, the defendant was killed in a staged attack by the police. The motivation for these encounters was an underlying belief that under TADA gaining convictions in court were remote and often an inordinately lengthy exercise.

Parliament. The first, the Criminal Law Amendment Bill, sought to reinstitute much of TADA's language, but it never mustered sufficient support to pass. The other, the Prevention of Terrorism Ordinance, which later became POTA – the Act – contained provisions that the government cited as reasons for why this new law was rights-enhanced relative to TADA. For example, American Miranda-type safeguards were contained in POTA.[15]

But despite pronounced ameliorations, there remained a number of provisions within POTA violating basic individual rights and freedoms. For example, by not clearly defining the word "terrorism" and its implications, the statute chilled who might associate with one another and with what organizations. The implementation of POTA also resulted in disparate treatment by the state toward particularly vulnerable communities – with politically, religiously, and socioeconomically disadvantaged groups suffering disproportionately.[16] Further, as with TADA, POTA established a set of special courts to deal with suspected terrorists: Sections 23–26 of POTA adopted TADA's positions regarding how the special courts were created; how the benches were staffed; the jurisdiction of the special courts; and the powers of the special courts with respect to non-POTA offenses.[17] POTA special court proceedings also provided a statutorily based, presumptive faith standard toward police-produced evidence and police testimony.[18] The POTA courts, like the TADA courts, prohibited interlocutory appeals and heard cases in camera.[19]

15 Note that prohibitions against police coercion of detainees and the right to appeal existed, as well. Krishnan, *supra* note 1, at 269–73.

16 *Id.* at 273–77.

17 *See* Prevention of Terrorist Activities Act, Act No. 15 of 2002, India Code (2002), §§ 23–26.

18 In a country where the police have been cited repeatedly as hostile – if not overtly derisive, dishonest, and corrupt – toward detained suspects, such a preexisting power imbalance did not auger well for defendants who contemplated exercising their right to remain silent or who sought due process in their trials. *See* Krishnan and Kumar, *supra* note 3.

19 On the proceedings being police-favored and in camera, *see* Krishnan, *supra* note 1, at 283–88. On the right to appeal and political motivation, *see id.*, at 288–98.

Although POTA courts overlapped with their predecessor courts, they shared commonalities with the regular criminal courts, as well. For example, the qualification requirements and selection processes for prosecutors were the same for both POTA and regular criminal courts.[20] Moreover, notwithstanding the preclusion of interlocutory appeals, POTA's appellate process conformed more with the regular courts, allowing for defendants to appeal final judgments to the state high court. Finally, POTA allowed for regular sessions courts to hear POTA cases, where there was yet to be "constituted"[21] an actual "Special Court."[22]

At the same time, the POTA courts did possess certain distinctive features. For instance, the POTA courts did not have the ability to determine which cases they could hear. Instead, these powers were placed with the executive branch. These courts also gave defendants only intermittent access to their lawyers.[23] Additionally, under Section 8 the statute allowed the POTA courts to seize the property of suspected terrorists, even absent an actual trial.[24]

Thus, the picture of the POTA courts was complex. On the one hand, they possessed distinctive qualities of their own; on the other hand, they contained substantive overlap with TADA and the regular sessions courts. In 2004, after journalists, policymakers, human rights activists, and scholars uncovered various abuses,[25] POTA was revoked following the election of the Congress Party-led government. Although India faced subsequent terrorist threats and attacks, it was not until after the 2008 Mumbai tragedy that two major pieces of legislation were passed into law – the UAPA and the NIAA. The next section evaluates these laws and their contribution to the latest set of special courts.

20 Prevention of Terrorist Activities Act § 28.

21 *Id.* § 35.

22 *Id.*

23 Information on the jurisdictional stripping and basic structure doctrine come from Krishnan, *supra* note 1, at 280–83. On the lawyers point, *see id.*, at 277–80. *See also* Prevention of Terrorist Activities Act §§ 27, 33, and 34(4).

24 Prevention of Terrorist Activities Act § 8.

25 For a discussion of this point, *see* Krishnan, *supra* note 1.

3. More (or Less) of the Same? UAPA

Following the repeal of POTA, the 1967 UAPA, which was still on the books, was amended in 2004 to include many provisions similar to those in POTA.[26] The UAPA was amended again in 2008 after the Mumbai attacks. The pattern here of retooling and reverting to the continued use of exceptional provisions is important to note across political regimes and contexts. However, there are distinguishing features between the 2008 UAPA and POTA that deserve attention.[27] In Section 4 of the UAPA,

26 Perhaps the most infamous provisos of POTA are also part of UAPA, including the statutory acquiescence of a six-month pre-charge and pretrial detention period of suspected terrorists, thirty days of which may be served in pure police custody. In addition, and also following from POTA, under UAPA a suspected terrorist defendant has the onus of proving his or her innocence – even for purposes of bail hearings. In fact, under UAPA the charges are deemed to be prima facie true against the defendant in such a bail proceeding (UAPA, sec. 43(D)(5). Add to the mix that the offences listed in UAPA are classified as cognizable under 43(D)(1) – meaning that the police may arrest those they believe are terrorists on grounds of suspicion alone – and the outcome is a law that looks very similar to POTA. *See* Nehal Bhutal, *Back to the Future*, Human Rights Watch, July 27, 2010, retrieved from http://www.hrw.org/en/node/91967/section/7. *Also see* Singh, *supra* note 5; Kalhan et al., *supra* note 6 at 153–73 (for a discussion of pre-2008 UAPA), UAPA, sec. 43(f); and *see* Ravi Nair, *Unlawful Activities (Prevention) Amendment Act 2008: Repeating Past Mistakes*, ECON. & POLITICAL WEEKLY, 10–14, Jan. 24, 2009; UAPA Retains Most of POTA's Stringent Provisions, TIMES OF INDIA, Dec. 17, 2008, retrieved from http://timesofindia.indiatimes.com/India/UAPA_retains_most_of_POTAs_stringent_provisions/articleshow/3847843.cms; and Rajeev Dhavan, *India's Unlawful Activities Prevention Act (UAPA): The Return of POTA & TADA*, SOUTH ASIAN CITIZENS WEB, Dec. 19, 2008, retrieved from http://www.allvoices.com/s/event-2057931/aHR0cDovL3d3dy5zYWN3Lm5ldC9hcnRpY2xlNDI5Lmh0bWw. Finally, there are court-based similarities between POTA and UAPA in terms of UAPA's Sections 25, 26, and 28 being similar to Sections 7, 8, and 10 of POTA.

27 One writer has even noted that the 2004 UAPA statute is comparatively "a more moderate instrument." Stella Burch Elias, *Re-thinking 'Preventive Detention' from a Comparative Perspective: Three Frameworks for Detaining Terrorist Suspects*, 41 COLUM. HUM. RTS. L. REV. 99, n.381 (2009). As support for this position, there is the assertion that the highly criticized approach of POTA special courts accepting police confessions as admitted evidence was prohibited by the 2004 UAPA. Note, this UAPA provision falls into line with the Indian Criminal Procedure Code section 173. The 2008 UAPA also included allowing a new National Investigation Agency (NIA) to enforce the statute's provisions. The NIA has as its mission in the streamlining, consolidating,

for example, the statute authorizes a "Tribunal."[28] The tribunals are one-member benches, and can be created "as and when necessary . . . by the Central Government,"[29] which gives these bodies a rather ad hoc nature. Under UAPA, before the government seeks to categorize an individual or organization as one that participates in terrorist-related activities, it must receive certification from the tribunal. During this proceeding the charged defendant has the ability to rebut the allegation.[30] Once a determination is made, however, it is final and non-appealable.[31]

The statute also states that the UAPA tribunal can create its own procedural rules.[32] But curiously, when conducting investigations, the tribunal is simultaneously and statutorily bound by the same procedural rules that govern the regular courts.[33] There is another perplexing component: assuming that there is terrorist certification granted by the tribunal, the statute mandates that a civil-servant collections officer assess all of the property of the defendant that might be used for "unlawful purposes."[34] Somewhat similarly to POTA, such property may be seized thereafter by the police while legal proceedings against the defendant are pending. However, confusingly, under the UAPA the accused has the ability to challenge the tribunal forfeiture proceedings in – of all places – a regular court.[35]

and prioritizing of information in order to provide the appropriate responses to deal with domestic and foreign terrorist threats. UAPA defenders also point to the Indian government's passage of the 2005 Right to Information Act, which they argue promotes full transparency and allows every Indian the right to seek status updates on matters involving the government's detention of suspected terrorists.

28 Unlawful Activities (Prevention) Act, No. 37 of 1967, India Code (1967), § 4.

29 *Id.* § 5(1). Note, the one-member bench must be a sitting member of a state high court. *Id.*

30 *Id.* § 4.

31 *Id.* § 9. For a recent and important discussion of UAPA, *see* Sudha Setty, *What's in a Name? How Nations Define Terrorism Ten Years After 9/11*, 33 U. Penn J. Int'l. L. 1, 51–55 (2011).

32 *Id.* § 5 (5).

33 *Id.* § 5 (6)(7).

34 *Id.* § 8 (2)(3).

35 *Id.* § 8 (8). Another irony here is that the district court is to follow the criminal procedure code under Section 9. But, under Section 9 there cannot be an appeal from this

The complications are further enhanced by the relationship UAPA has with the NIAA. The latter permits the formation of NIAA courts to handle legal matters relating to the protection of national security and cases prosecuted under UAPA.[36] As with the POTA courts, these NIAA fora allow judges to be chosen by the central government, although one difference is that the National Investigation Agency (NIA) may play a role in the selection process, as well.[37] There are other similarities to POTA courts regarding jurisdiction, naming of prosecutors, hearings being held in camera, and limitations on appeals. The central and state governments may create these courts at will, as well.[38] Moreover, the practice of discovery – a key tenet of the criminal justice process particularly for defense lawyers – is again not incorporated within these latest NIAA courts.

district court, and notwithstanding this entire discussion, Section 47 generally bars the regular courts from reviewing the actions by the central government. Unlawful Activities (Prevention) Act. For more discussion on UAPA, *see* Sudha Setty, *Comparative Perspectives on Specialized Trials for Terrorism*, 63 ME. L. REV. 131, 164–70 (2010).

36 *See* Guruswamy, *supra* note 1. Included within the ambit of these special courts' jurisdiction (within its appendix [i.e., "schedule"] are the following specifically-listed offenses:

> 1. The Atomic Energy Act, 1962 (33 of 1962); 2. The Unlawful Activities (Prevention) Act, 1967 (37 of 1967); 3. The Anti-Hijacking Act, 1982 (65 of 1982); 4. The Suppression of Unlawful Acts against Safety of Civil Aviation Act, 1982 (66 of 1982); 5. The SAARC Convention (Suppression of Terrorism) Act, 1993 (36 of 1993); 6. The Suppression of Unlawful Acts Against Safety of Maritime Navigation and Fixed Platforms on Continental Shelf Act, 2002 (69 of 2002); 7. The Weapons of Mass Destruction and their Delivery Systems (Prohibition of Unlawful Activities) Act, 2005 (21 of 2005); 8. Offences under – (a) Chapter VI of the Indian Penal Code (45 of 1860) [sections 121 to 130 (both inclusive)] and (b) Sections 489-A to 489-E (both inclusive) of the Indian Penal Code (45 of 1860).

See National Investigation Agency Act, Schedule 2008. For a discussion of the UAPA and NIAA, *see* Singh, *supra* note 5. *Also see* Ranbir Singh, *Critiques of Recent Legislations from Human Rights Perspective in India: Do We Need Special Laws?* 8 J. NAT'L. HUMAN RTS. COMM'N. 7 (2019).

37 National Investigation Agency Act, No. 34 of 2008, INDIA CODE (2008), §§ 3(1) and 11(4)(5).

38 National Investigation Agency Act §§ 11, 13–17, and 21–22.

Additionally, the NIAA courts are allowed to hear regular criminal cases, and conversely, UAPA-related cases need not be tried exclusively in NIAA special courts.[39] This blurring of the lines between the NIAA courts and regular courts is further illustrated by the fact that the individuals who serve as judges in the two fora are often the same people – whereby the role they play ultimately depends on the hat they wear.[40] Therefore, the question that then arises is under what conditions will a defendant's case be placed in an NIAA special court, as opposed to a regular sessions court? This is the query we address in the next section.

4. Forum Selection and the Implications of Special Courts for Democratic India

Within the scholarly literature and public policy circles exists an ongoing debate as to how suspected terrorists – particularly in the post-9/11, Madrid, London, and Mumbai eras – should be treated by prosecuting states. There are those who believe that such individuals must be afforded the same rights as any other defendant and thus subscribe to the view that the regular criminal justice process is the proper venue for terrorism-related trials.[41] In contrast, those on the opposite side argue that because defendants charged with terrorism pose a unique risk to the national security of the state, military tribunals that rely on military law are most appropriate.[42] Then there are a range of commentators who fall

39 *See* Unlawful Activities (Prevention) Act § 2(1)(d) (noting regular sessions courts can also hear UAPA-based cases).

40 There is immunity for prosecutors and NIA officials. National Investigation Agency Act § 18.

41 For a discussion of this debate, *see* BENJAMIN WITTES, LAW AND THE LONG WAR: THE FUTURE OF JUSTICE IN THE AGE OF TERROR (2008); Daphne Eviatar, *Gitmo Prisoners Pose Thorny Problem for Obama*, WASH. INDEP., Nov. 11, 2008, retrieved from http://washingtonindependent.com/19390/national-security-courts.

42 *See id.*; also for a discussion of the relevant case law in the United States, *see* *Boumediene v. Bush*, 553 U.S. 723 (2008); *Hamdan v. Rumsfeld*, 548 U.S. 557 (2006); *Hamdi v. Rumsfeld*, 542 U.S. 507 (2004); *Rasul v. Bush*, 542 U.S. 466 (2004). For a concise, insightful discussion on the evolution of this area of the law, *see* BENJAMIN

in between, with different versions of special national security courts offered. In the United States, one of the more well-known, self-described "bipartisan solution[s]"[43] comes from Jack Goldsmith and Neal Katyal, who have proposed creating "a comprehensive system of preventive detention that is overseen by a national security court composed of federal judges with life tenure."[44] In the Indian context, the tension associated with the presence of special courts has been highlighted, as well. Venkat Iyer documents how the Indian government has, through de jure and de facto means, abusively swept into special court proceedings individuals and groups that otherwise should have been protected by the regular judicial process.[45]

This entire discussion evidences a dilemma, more generally, for democratic states. The question centers on how best to safeguard aggregate security interests while at the same time ensuring that the civil liberties of individuals are not unduly hindered. Iyer's historical work illustrates a justified fear among today's rights activists that non-terrorist defendants may be absorbed into Indian special courts, but there is a converse issue, as well. As discussed, Indian prosecutors can charge terrorism suspects with both UAPA-related and Indian Penal Code (IPC) crimes – within

Wittes, Robert Chesney, and Rabea Benhalim, the Emerging Law of Detention: The Guantánamo Habeas Cases as Lawmaking (2010), retrieved from http://www.brookings.edu/~/media/Files/rc/papers/2010/0122_guantanamo_wittes_chesney/0122_guantanamo_wittes_chesney.pdf.

43 Jack L. Goldsmith and Neal Katyal, *The Terrorists' Court,* NY Times, July 11, 2007, retrieved from http://www.nytimes.com/2007/07/11/opinion/11katyal.html%_r=1.

44 *Id.* Such courts, according to these two scholars, would adopt certain aspects of the regular process (such as prohibiting unjustifiable pretrial detention periods, allowing for appeals, and treating noncitizen and citizen terrorism defendants alike), recognizing the challenges that confront states in this age of terrorism. As such, they argue, American national security courts might permit: interrogations of suspects without lawyers, extended periods of detention in certain cases, closing trials to the public, and broadening prosecutorial scope and evidence-gathering methods. *See generally* Jack L. Goldsmith, *Long Term Terrorist Detention and Our National Security Court* (Brookings Inst., Working Paper, Feb. 4, 2009), retrieved from http://www.brookings.edu/~/media/files/rc/papers/2009/0209_detention_goldsmith/0209_detention_goldsmith.pdf.

45 *See* Venkat Iyer, States Of Emergency: The Indian Experience (2000).

the delay-ridden regular criminal courts, which are often seen as being heavily favorable to prosecutors and hostile to defendants' rights. In some cases prosecutors will even tack on other charges from various state and local criminal laws, as well as from more narrowly tailored laws that have been passed by the central or state government.[46]

Perhaps no better known case interweaving UAPA, the IPC, and other narrowly tailored laws within a sessions court is that of Ajmal Amir Kasab, the lone surviving shooter in the November 2008 Mumbai attacks. A total of eighty-six counts were filed against Kasab, with the prosecution accusing the defendant of being directly responsible for murdering 72 people and injuring more than 100. Among the more prominent laws that Kasab was charged with violating were:

Sections 34 and 120 of the IPC that relate to criminal conspiracy;

Section 121 of the IPC that criminalizes waging war on the Indian state;

Section 302 of the IPC that criminalizes murder; and

the Arms Act, Explosives Act, and Passport Act.

With respect to UAPA, Kasab was charged under Section 15, which explicitly prohibits committing any terrorist acts. Kasab was also charged under UAPA with murder, conspiracy to commit murder, and waging war against the Indian government.[47] Ultimately, in a nearly 1,600-page opinion in *State of Maharashtra v. Kasab* that was delivered in May of 2010, Kasab was found guilty on all eighty-six charges brought against him, receiving the death penalty on five of these charges.[48] In February

46 On narrowly tailored laws, *see* Krishnan and Kumar, *supra* note 3. A group of special laws that have been particularly used in conjunction with UAPA are the Indian Arms Act, the Indian Customs Act, the Indian Explosive Substances Act, and the Indian Foreign Exchange and Passport Acts.

47 *See Man's Trial Starts in Mumbai Attack, with Pakistan Accused*, NY TIMES, Apr. 17, 2009, retrieved from http://www.nytimes.com/2009/04/18/world/asia/18mumbai.html?ref=ajmal_kasab; Rahi Gaikwad, *Kasab Pronounced Guilty of Waging War against India*, THE HINDU, May 3, 2010, retrieved from http://www.thehindu.com/news/national/article419894.ece.

48 One of these five capital convictions fell under UAPA's jurisdiction, that of being found guilty for engaging in terrorist activities. (The others were part of the IPC.) *See*

of 2011, the Bombay High Court upheld the verdict, and then in August of 2012 the Supreme Court of India affirmed the ruling, as well. Kasab was subsequently hanged on November 21, 2012.

The case of Kasab highlights a crucial point. The matter did not unfold in an official UAPA tribunal or NIAA special court; it started and concluded within a sessions court. To be sure, the latest version of UAPA and the NIAA were formally passed into law only at the end of 2008 in response to the Mumbai attacks. But the Kasab trial did not begin until early 2009, which provided sufficient time for the government to try him in an NIAA forum – especially if all that was needed was for a sessions judge to don NIAA robes and apply the new law to the case at hand.

However, the case was brought in a sessions court. In press accounts there was frequent mention made to this being a special court; however, this specialness was because of the fact that the proceedings took place not in a traditional courtroom, but instead – for security purposes – in a makeshift room within the famous Arthur Road Jail in Mumbai where the defendant was being detained.[49] Another reason the court

State of Maharashtra v. Kasab, (2009) Sessions Case No. 175, retrieved from http://www.scribd.com/doc/31991360/Kasab-Trial-Court-Judgment. *See generally* Vikas Bajaj, *Mumbai Gunman Sentenced to Death*, NY Times, May 6, 2010, retrieved from http://www.nytimes.com/2010/05/07/world/asia/07mumbai.html?scp=6&sq=kasab&st=cse; *26/11: Kasab Guilty; Ansari, Sabauddin Sheikh Acquitted*, Times of India, May 3, 2010, retrieved from http://timesofindia.indiatimes.com/india/26/11-Kasab-guilty-Ansari-Sabauddin-Shaikh-acquitted/articleshow/5885540.cms; *Mumbai Celebrates Kasab's Death Sentence*, One India News, May 6, 2010, http://news.oneindia.in/2010/05/06/mumbaicelebrates-kasabs-deathsentence.html; *Kasab Gets Death Sentence on 5 Counts, Life on 5 Counts*, NDTV, May 6, 2010, retrieved from http://www.ndtv.com/news/india/kasab-gets-death-sentence-on-4-counts-life-on-5-counts-23619.php.

49 Although, note the Kasab court could be viewed as a special court for another reason: a regular sessions court may take on the role of a special court for trials that involve prosecutions relating to the NIAA or national security statutes, such as, for example, the UAPA. National Investigation Agency Act § 22. Furthermore, where a sessions court wears such a special court hat, all other cases "shall . . . remain in abeyance." National Investigation Agency Act § 19(1). For these reasons, the argument is that the judge's court functioned as a special court. However, this argument does not carry the day, given that the Kasab trial was public and few features of a special court were in place, in the vein of past POTA or TADA courts.

was deemed special was because the sessions court judge who heard the matter had his docket reduced to one – that of the Kasab case. However, it was essentially a regular criminal court – rather than a separate terrorist forum or military tribunal – that heard the landmark Kasab case. This fact only underlines our argument that, in India, even in the highest profile terrorism case since independence, special courts play an unexceptional and not-so-prominent role in the adjudication process.

Another recent high-profile case offers a similar conclusion. In *Chhattisgarh Government v. Binayak Sen* the defendant, a well-known doctor and member of the People's Union of Civil Liberties, was charged with violating state, IPC, and UAPA offences, mainly as they related to the aiding and abetting of an outlawed terrorist group known as the Naxalites. Although Sen vigorously denied committing any crime, the state government branded him a Naxal terrorist. Because this case began prior to the establishment of the NIAA courts and after POTA was repealed, it is understandable why Sen would have been placed in the regular criminal justice process.

Subsequently, however, a series of strange procedural developments began to unfold. Sen's case started in a sessions court in August 2007, then was transferred to one of the mentioned fast-track courts a month later, but then was moved back to the sessions court in October 2009.[50] At the time that Sen's case returned to the regular court, the NIAA fora were available to hear his matter, but the prosecution refrained from filing the case there. After having his case languish for more than three years, Sen was convicted in 2010. He is now appealing the judgment.[51]

Both the *Kasab* and *Sen* cases raise the fundamental question of why the NIAA courts were not used to prosecute the respective defendants. If any two cases might appear to present a golden opportunity to employ

50 *Chhattisgarh Government v. Piyush, Sen, and Others* (2007) Sessions Case No. 182.

51 *See Binayak Sen v. State of Chhattisgarh*, Petition for Special Leave to Appeal (2011) Supreme Court of India Crl. Nos. 2053/2011. In April of 2011, the Supreme Court allowed Sen to post bail as the appeals process moves forward, and on April 17, 2011, Sen was released from custody.

Table 1. *Cases Prosecuted in Courts on Charge-Sheets Filed by the National Investigation Agency (as of the end of 2011)*

Prosecutions Occurring	No. of Cases	Various Statutes under Which Defendants Have Been Charged
NIAA special courts	11	The Indian Penal Code, 1860; The Unlawful Activities (Prevention) Act, 1967 (as amended 2008); The Arms Act, 1959; The Explosive Substances Act, 1908; The Prevention of Damage to Public Property Act, 1984.
Other special courts	4	The Indian Penal Code, 1860; The Unlawful Activities (Prevention) Act, 1967 (as amended, 2008); The Arms Act, 1959; The Explosive Substances Act, 1908; Maharashtra Control of Organized Crime Act, 1999
Charge-sheet filed but unclear in what forum case is	10	The Indian Penal Code, 1860; The Unlawful Activities (Prevention) Act, 1967 (as amended, 2008); The Arms Act, 1959; The Explosive Substances Act, 1908; Maharashtra Control of Organized Crime Act, 1999; The Prevention of Damage to Public Property Act, 1984.

these special courts, it would seem to be these two. Furthermore, if cases like *Kasab* and *Sen* are not being heard in the NIAA courts, then which ones, if any, are? Conversely, are there other terrorism-related cases that are being tried in the regular criminal courts rather than in these established special fora? To answer these questions, we examined the current set of terrorism cases being investigated by the country's main antiterrorism agency – the NIA. In India, when investigating officials believe cases should proceed to trial, the investigators will draft what is called a "charge-sheet" and then consult with prosecutors. At that point, prosecutors will determine whether to actually go forward in court. As Table 1 shows, the data drawn directly from the NIA's own Web site are both revealing and curious for a few reasons.

First, between 2009 and the end of 2011, there were twenty-five NIA charge-sheeted cases filed within the entire country.[52] Moreover, the table highlights the point made regarding how defendants in both the NIAA courts and other courts – in Table 1 referred to by the government as "special courts" – can face overlapping charges that derive from the regular penal code, UAPA, and other narrowly tailored laws. But again, there is confusion about the government's process. What are these other special courts? What is their jurisdiction? Are they courts that formally (say, on certain days of the month) serve as regular criminal courts, but on other days operate as special antiterrorism courts? It is also unclear why the NIAA courts do not hear only cases that relate to terrorism or, more specifically, that are within their statutory authority, and why these other special criminal courts have terrorism cases pending before them at all.

Otherwise put, there does not appear to be a uniform rationale for when prosecutors will bring cases to the NIAA courts or to these other special courts or to the regular courts. Our hypothesis is that much of the decision-making process has to do with which actual courts are present within a particular jurisdiction that is trying the defendant. Again, if it is simply a matter of a sessions court judge wearing a NIAA hat and then calling the court an NIAA court, why that could not be done in all jurisdictions is unclear; further empirical work is required on this front. One point of information that the table does not provide is the extent to which state-level police officials are charge-sheeting defendants with UAPA offenses in regular sessions courts. As discussed, this was the approach in the government's case against Binayak Sen, but broader patterns in this regard also require further empirical research.

Hence, this discussion underscores a conflation between – and confusion within – various types of courts in India. Under previous antiterrorism statutory regimes, such as POTA and TADA, the government

52 In our data analysis, we found thirteen cases (from central headquarters and at the regional level – Guwahati and Hyderabad) that were categorized as being under further investigation by the NIA and thus not yet charge-sheeted.

created special courts to hear and try cases against suspected terrorists. These alternative courts, as discussed, suffered from a host of problems, not the least of which was their lack of transparency and ad hoc manner in which they functioned. With the UAPA and NIAA working in conjunction with one another to create yet another iteration of special courts, the thought was that a new process would finally emerge, one that would result in fairer, more efficient justice for defendants and victims of terrorism-related activities. However, the outcome to date has been that only a limited number of cases have gone before the NIAA courts, with, ironically, the most high-profile terrorism trials placed within the regular criminal justice process.

Conclusion

This chapter has surveyed India's different antiterrorism laws, with an emphasis on special courts and trial processes both before and after the 2008 Mumbai attacks. Special courts in India have been incorporated into different pieces of legislation for decades. As we have argued, however, the statutory language creating these courts, as well as how they function in practice, are blurred together with the regular criminal justice courts. This obscuration has important ramifications. Particularly with the NIAA courts, there appears to be an inherent arbitrariness in which cases enter these fora and which ones are filed in the regular criminal courts. To some extent the selection process may be because of the fact that certain jurisdictions simply do not have NIAA courts present, and thus because the legislation allows for terrorism cases to be tried in the regular criminal courts, there is a practical need to shunt them into these latter venues. But this lack of availability argument is belied by data from the NIA, which shows that there are thirty-five NIAA courts spread throughout the country.[53]

53 *See* National Investigation Agency Web site, retrieved from http://nia.gov.in/niasplcourts.aspx.

Another reason for directing terrorism cases into the regular criminal process may relate to an affirmative choice by the state that, in most situations, justice is best rendered by civilian courts. The Indian Home Minister noted after the *Kasab* trial that because that process worked so well, no expansion of the current UAPA law was needed.[54] To many, such prosecutorial decisions might appear laudable, but consider an alternative explanation: because the regular criminal courts, with all their pathologies and delays, are already so heavily tilted against the defendant prosecutors may see these fora as decidedly advantageous to try terrorism cases. After all, prosecutors know these regular courts best and are familiar with the other actors working within them as well as the statutory procedures, evidentiary standards, and governing norms. Empirical verification of this proposition is required, but that the government brought two of its most high-profile terrorism cases, *Kasab* and *Binayak Sen,* in non-NIAA courts gives this hypothesis certain plausibility.

Thus, it remains unclear what accounts for whether cases are tried in regular criminal courts or special courts. In our view neither of the options serves as an optimal forum for defendants suspected of and charged with acts of terrorism. In the broken regular criminal court system defendants languish, prosecutors delay, and outcomes are not determined until well into the future. The history of special courts in India also shows that the safeguards within them are few, transparency is minimal, and abuses are common. That both sets of courts have overlapping jurisdictions, not to mention overlapping actors, only further complicates the relationship. As the analysis reveals, the special courts and regular criminal courts both suffer from serious foundational problems that need immediate remedy if the interests of justice are to be truly served. In sum, rather than being exceptional or special, India's terrorism courts, as we have shown, in reality are ultimately – and sadly – more ordinary than not.

54 *See Conviction Came without Anti-Terror Law: Chidambaram*, THE HINDU, May 6, 2010, http://www.thehindu.com/news/national/article423365.ece.

Part III INTERNATIONAL LAW, EXCEPTIONAL COURTS, AND MILITARY COMMISSIONS

14 The Right to a Fair Trial in an Extraordinary Court

David S. Weissbrodt and Joseph C. Hansen

THE RIGHT TO A FAIR TRIAL IS A FUNDAMENTAL HUMAN RIGHT. This chapter begins by summarizing the basic components and protections of a fair trial as established by international human rights standards. It next examines how fair-trial standards apply to extraordinary courts by looking at both their theoretical and practical application. The essay concludes by suggesting that extraordinary courts present a serious, recurring risk of denying a fair trial to those persons subject to trial and that more must be done to address the gap between norms and practice.

This chapter uses the terms "extraordinary" and "special" interchangeably. Precisely defining an extraordinary court is an elusive task and one that interpretive bodies have largely avoided. The broadest definition of a special court, as Amnesty International uses the term, is that *special courts* are those procedures that try categories of people on the basis of special legal status (such as juveniles or suspected terrorists) or particular categories of offenses.[1] Another potential definition characterizes special courts as those tribunals that lack certain guarantees of independence and impartiality.[2] It would, however, be circular reasoning

1 Amnesty International, Fair Trials Manual 151 (1998).

2 *Cf.* Laura A. Dickinson, *Using Legal Process to Fight Terrorism: Detentions, Military Comissions, International Tribunals, and the Rule of Law*, 75 S. Cal. L. Rev. 1407, 1422 (2002) (stating that a "military commission run by members of the military without any recourse to a civilian judicial body" cannot satisfy the requirement of independence).

to define a legal proceeding as lacking impartiality and independence and then to evaluate those same procedures for their independence and impartiality. This chapter uses the terms extraordinary and special courts more narrowly to describe domestic courts specifically created to try offenses related to state security (broadly conceived), the use of military courts to try civilians, or where governments themselves categorize the procedures as special. Many of these courts suffer from procedural defects, including a lack of such fundamental attributes as independence and impartiality.

1. The Right to Fair Trial

One of the basic human rights is the right to a fair trial.[3] The right to a fair trial ensures that no person is deprived of liberty without due process of the law.[4] We first detail the procedural components of the right to a fair trial and the breadth of their application.

To define and ensure a fair trial, human rights instruments have delineated several substantive protections. For example, Article 14 of the International Covenant on Civil and Political Rights guarantees, inter alia, equality before the courts; a fair and public hearing by a competent, independent, and impartial tribunal established by law; the right to be presumed innocent; the right to have legal assistance and the ability to communicate with counsel; the right to be tried without undue delay; the right to be tried in one's own presence; the right to examine witnesses; and the right to appeal a conviction to a higher tribunal.[5] Other international instruments, such as the European Convention for the Protection of Human Rights and Fundamental Freedoms, the American Convention

3 *See, e.g.*, Universal Declaration of Human Rights art. 10, G.A. Res. 217 (III) A, UN Doc. A/RES/217(III) (Dec. 10, 1948).

4 International Covenant on Civil and Political Rights art. 9(1), Mar. 23, 1976, 999 U.N.T.S. 171.

5 *Id.* art. 14. For a review of the historical development of fair trial rights, *see* David Weissbrodt, The Right to a Fair Trial: Articles 8, 10 and 11 of the Universal Declaration of Human Rights 1–110 (2001).

on Human Rights, and the African Charter on Human and Peoples' Rights, parallel these procedural protections, ensuring a fair trial.

The right to a fair trial is also protected in situations of armed conflict. During non-international armed conflicts, Common Article 3 of the Geneva Conventions assures "all the judicial guarantees which are recognized as indispensable by civilized peoples" within a regularly constituted court.[6] In situations of international armed conflict, the third Geneva Convention provides a list of trial rights by which the state detaining a prisoner of war must abide, essentially requiring that the trial be at least as procedurally secure as a court-martial.[7] The first Additional Protocol to the Geneva Conventions further requires, for situations of international armed conflict, "an impartial and regularly constituted court respecting the generally recognized principles of regular judicial procedure" and subsequently elaborates such recognized principles, including the rights to be informed of the offense charged and all trial rights; not be convicted for ex post facto violations; be presumed innocent until proven guilty; be tried in one's presence; not be compelled to testify against oneself; examine witnesses; be free from double jeopardy; have the judgment pronounced publicly; and be advised of further remedies.[8] This dual protection across times of peace and armed conflict underscores the importance of procedural and due process rights in a trial context.

Moreover, the statutes of the International Criminal Court, the International Criminal Tribunal for the Former Yugoslavia, the International Criminal Tribunal for Rwanda, and the Special Court for Sierra Leone all list the deprivation of a fair trial as a war crime.[9]

6 Geneva Convention Relative to the Treatment of Prisoners of War art. 3, Aug. 12, 1949, 6 U.S.T. 3316, 75 U.N.T.S. 135 (hereinafter Geneva Convention III).

7 *See id.* art. 102.

8 Protocol Additional to the Geneva Conventions of 12 August 1949, and Relating to the Protection of Victims of International Armed Conflicts (Protocol I) art. 75(4), June 8, 1977, 1125 U.N.T.S. 3.

9 Rome Statute of the International Criminal Court art. 8(2)(a)(vi), 8(2)(c)(iv), July 17, 1998, 2187 U.N.T.S. 90; Statute of the International Criminal Tribunal for the Former Yugoslavia art. 2(f), S.C. Res. 827, UN Doc. S/RES/827, May 25, 1993, 32 I.L.M. 1192; Statute of the International Criminal Tribunal for Rwanda art. 4(g), S.C. Res. 955, UN

Finally, a state cannot circumvent fair-trial protections by simply detaining a person indefinitely and denying the detainee any form of judicial process. International instruments generally require being informed promptly of reasons for arrest, being brought promptly before a judge, and being entitled to a trial within a reasonable time or release. Additionally, those deprived of their liberty have the right to judicial proceedings to challenge the lawfulness of their detention. Indeed, the American Convention prohibits states from suspending this right under any circumstances, including a state of emergency.[10] Equally important, although international instruments do not expressly prohibit incommunicado detention, decisions interpreting various treaties have found that it frequently leads to violations of the prohibitions on torture, ill-treatment, and disappearances; can constitute cruel, inhuman, or degrading treatment in itself; and violates the required prompt access to legal counsel.

In short, the uniformity of fair-trial protections and the breadth of situations in which they apply – even during armed conflicts – strongly suggest that the right to a fair trial is non-derogable.[11] Nonetheless, fair-trial protections developed over the past sixty years have clashed in recent years with issues of terrorism and national security. We now turn to examine the application of fair-trial rights to extraordinary courts, given the inherent strains between a regime devoted to individual rights and a paradigm emphasizing national security.

2. The Right to a Fair Trial in Extraordinary Courts

Most human rights instruments do not prohibit per se the existence of special courts, but the entire panoply of fair-trial rights guaranteed by

Doc. S/RES/955, Nov. 8, 1994, 33 I.L.M. 1598; Statute of the Special Court for Sierra Leone art. 3(g), Jan. 16, 2002, 2178 U.N.T.S. 138.

10 *See* Judicial Guarantees in States of Emergency, Advisory Opinion OC-9/87, Oct. 6, 1987, Inter-Am. Ct. H.R. (ser. A) No. 9 (1987).

11 Weissbrodt, *supra* note 5, at 93.

various human rights instruments apply to them.[12] According to the Human Rights Committee:

> The provisions of article 14 [of the Civil and Political Covenant] apply to all courts and tribunals within the scope of that article whether ordinary or specialized, civilian or military.... While the Covenant does not prohibit the trial of civilians in military or special courts, it requires that such trials are in full conformity with the requirements of article 14 and that its guarantees cannot be limited or modified because of the military or special character of the court concerned.[13]

Other human rights bodies, such as the Inter-American Commission, go further to prohibit outright the trial of civilians in extraordinary courts.

The requirement for a public hearing may be the single permissible exception among the procedural guarantees of the right to a fair trial. International instruments have left states some flexibility to decide whether to hold proceedings in public, provided that states can justify a private proceeding. Relevant to special courts and issues of terrorism, states may justify a private proceeding on grounds of national security or the *ordre public* (a grave threat to public order). These exceptions must be construed narrowly, and any judgment must be made public. Nonetheless, this exception is not specific to special courts, as it may also apply for cases related to family issues (for example, matrimonial disputes and guardianship), morality (for example, excluding the press in cases involving sexual offenses), and where publicity may prejudice the interests of justice. In other words, the right to a public hearing, although generally considered a basic component of a fair trial, may be slightly less strictly applied than other protected trial rights.

12 *See* UN Human Rights Comm., General Comment No. 32, ¶ 22, UN Doc. CCPR/C/GC/32 (2007) (hereinafter General Comment 32); *see also* David Weissbrodt and Andrea W. Templeton, *Fair Trials? The Manual for Military Commissions in Light of Common Article 3 and Other International Law*, 26 L. & Ineq. 353, 358 (2008).

13 General Comment 32, *supra* note 12.

The right to a fair trial therefore theoretically applies no differently to extraordinary courts than it does to regular courts. Nonetheless, extraordinary courts consistently raise concerns over the right to a fair trial, particularly concerning independence and impartiality.

(a) Independence and Impartiality

Perhaps the central issue in ensuring fair trials in an extraordinary court is whether the court is independent and impartial. Ensuring compliance of extraordinary courts with legal standards is at the core of an independent and impartial tribunal.

Independence and impartiality are distinct concepts. *Independence* refers to the structural arrangement ensuring that both the judiciary and individual judges can make decisions free from interference.[14] Numerous aspects ensure independence, but they can be loosely drawn into two categories: separation of powers and conditions of service.[15] Concerning separation of powers, the judicial branch must be structurally independent from other governmental branches or institutions.[16] Moreover, the judiciary must be free from inappropriate interference with the judicial process by external actors (including prosecutors), and must have exclusive jurisdiction over issues within its competence. Further, judges should only be subject to suspension or removal for reasons of incapacity or unfit behavior. There must also be a protected realm of internal judicial matters, such as court administration and case assignment. Regarding

14 Office of Democracy and Governance, U.S. Agency for International Development, Guidance for Promoting Judicial Independence and Impartiality 5 (rev. ed. 2002).

15 *See* General Comment 32, *supra* note 12, ¶ 19 (identifying the issue of conditions of service as an important element in "protect[ing] judges against conflicts of interest and intimidation").

16 For an overview of basic principles necessary to ensure the integrity of the judiciary, *see* United Nations Congress on the Prevention of Crime and the Treatment of Offenders, Milan, It., Aug. 26–Sept. 6, 1985, *Basic Principles on the Independence of the Judiciary*, UN Doc. A/CONF.121/22/Rev. 1 (Sept. 6, 1985) (hereinafter Basic Principles).

conditions of service, factors such as the selection and appointment of judges, term of office, security of office, adequate remuneration, promotion, tenure, pension, and age of retirement must be secured by law in a manner that protects judges from threats to their personal or professional security. These requirements are rigorous, and special courts often raise questions of structural independence, in particular because they are frequently connected to the executive branch or military. Under these circumstances, the job security of judges in special courts may be linked to the disposition of cases; there may be direct pressure to convict when the judges adjudicate charges against opponents of the military or government that employs them.

Impartiality refers to the biases of a particular judge. Individual biases derive from external influences (such as bribes or threats) and internal pressure (such as psychology or morality). Although realistically no judge acts without some level of partiality, cases and academic commentary have highlighted two basic tests for the impartiality demanded by legal instruments. Impartiality may be violated both subjectively – if a judge has an actual bias against a party to the case – or objectively – if an objective observer would find the appearance of bias.[17] In the situation of objectively perceived bias, even if the judge concludes he can act impartially, he nonetheless should recuse himself "to preserve the integrity of his court and the concept of law."[18] In extraordinary courts, military judges – tasked with deciding cases of persons captured and prosecuted by the military – may not appear objectively impartial,

17 Suzannah Linton, *Safeguarding the Independence and Impartiality of the Cambodian Extraordinary Chambers*, 4 J. Int'l Crim. Just. 327, 328 (2006). For the latter, the appeals chamber in the ICTY stated that the appearance of bias may manifest itself in two ways: either the judge has a financial or proprietary interest in the outcome of the case or "the circumstances would lead a reasonable observer, properly informed, to reasonably apprehend bias." *Prosecutor v. Furundzija*, No. IT-95–17/1-A, Judgment, ¶ 189 (July 21, 2000).

18 Theodor Meron, *Judicial Independence and Impartiality in International Criminal Tribunals*, 99 Am. J. Int'l L. 359, 366 (2005).

and they often possess sole discretion over whether to recuse themselves. Moreover, trials with "faceless judges," where the accused cannot know the identity of the judge, will likely fail the objective impartiality test.[19]

Independence and impartiality both seek to address the same concern: guaranteeing a fair trial by providing parties a tribunal in which the outcome is not predetermined. It is perhaps for this reason that the two concepts have been intertwined since the drafting of the Universal Declaration of Human Rights.[20] Nonetheless, the two concepts identify different issues in ensuring a fair trial. On the one hand, although conceptually distinct, independence and impartiality are functionally related and often overlap. Tribunals without structural independence can hardly be perceived to be objectively impartial.[21] For example, the Human Rights Committee determined that special courts in Turkey and Peru were not structurally independent and, consequently, that the accused had been denied a fair trial.[22] On the other hand, whereas some interpretive bodies or courts simply consider whether a previous proceeding violated the right to an independent and impartial tribunal without meaningfully differentiating the two,[23] others, such as the Human Rights Committee, clearly distinguish the two concepts.[24] Even if the reviewing court does not question the independence of the tribunal system, it may still need to examine whether the specific trial was conducted impartially (both subjectively and objectively).

19 General Comment 32, *supra* note 12, ¶ 23.

20 *See* Weissbrodt, *supra* note 5, at 12–15.

21 *See, e.g.*, Linton, *supra* note 17, at 328 ("It is only where there is an independent judiciary that a judge can adjudicate impartially, because the Rule of Law requires that he or she should not be apprehensive of repercussions or retaliation from outside influences.").

22 *See generally* Richard Wilson, *Can the U.S. Courts Learn from Failed Terrorist Trials by Military Commission in Turkey and Peru?*, 11 Hum. Rts. Brief 11–13 (2003).

23 *See* Stefan Trechsel, Human Rights in Criminal Proceedings 50 (2005) ("It appears that the European Court of Human Rights itself does not attach much importance to the distinction [between independence and impartiality].").

24 *See* General Comment 32, *supra* note 12, ¶¶ 19, 21.

In the case of extraordinary courts, as will be discussed, guaranteeing the theoretical protections of a fair trial – especially an independent and impartial tribunal – becomes particularly troublesome.

(b) The Difference between Norms and Practice: (The Lack of) Fair-Trial Protections in Extraordinary Courts

International human rights courts and similar bodies have refused to find military courts per se incapable of achieving impartiality and independence.[25] After all, the third Geneva Convention refers to court-martial proceedings as the standard of military justice for prisoners of war.[26] In regular U.S. court-martial proceedings, for example, military officers who serve as judges, prosecutors, and defense counsel enjoy considerable independence from the command structure. The military officers who serve as judges and juries in the court-martial system are generally not handpicked to achieve pro-prosecution results in particular cases. Further, all trial participants are protected against higher officers who seek to exercise undue command influence. Ordinary soldiers in a nation's service who are subject to court-martial enjoy a concern for their welfare as part of a well-ordered and disciplined force. Such a concern for achieving a well-ordered military force is not, however, the concern of a Prisoner of War (POW) court-martial. Nonetheless, the traditions and procedures of courts-martial are presumed by the third Geneva Convention to be sufficiently preserved to be used as a system of justice for POWs from the opposing army.

When military courts are used to try civilians or persons charged with terrorism, there is less reason for confidence in their capacity to protect the fair-trial rights.[27] When nations afford procedures in military and other extraordinary courts that do not reach the fair trial protections traditionally afforded in courts-martial, there is significant reason

25 *See, e.g., id.* ¶ 22.

26 Geneva Convention III, *supra* note 6, art. 102.

27 *See* Amnesty International, *supra* note 1, at 155–56.

to reject the results of such proceedings as violating international human rights. Similarly, special courts handpicked for particular cases or particular categories of cases often lack the independence and impartiality of regular courts or courts-martial.[28] International human rights courts and similar institutions have carefully scrutinized the conduct of military and police officers selected to serve as judges or lawyers in extraordinary courts.[29] Indeed, even in a structurally independent tribunal system, the simple presence of such judges will almost assuredly raise valid concerns over their objective impartiality.[30] Hence, although military courts trying civilians and other extraordinary courts are not per se violations, they rarely pass muster because they fail to achieve the independence, impartiality, and judicial guarantees required by human rights and humanitarian law.

To provide a few examples, India established special courts to handle cases brought pursuant to its Prevention of Terrorism Act (passed in 2002 and repealed in 2004).[31] These courts granted the central government, not the judiciary, the power to determine jurisdiction, and each judge was a central government appointee with broad power to draw adverse inferences against defendants. Spain's counterterrorism policies were widely applied following 9/11 and allowed the magistrate of the Audiencia Nacional, a special court for terrorism cases, to request

28 *See, e.g.*, Weissbrodt and Templeton, *supra* note 12, at 365.

29 *See, e.g.*, UN Working Group on Arbitrary Detention, Dec. No. 40/1995 (Turkey), ¶ 14, UN Doc. E/CN.4/1997/4/Add.1 (1996).

30 Courts considering violations of the right to an independent and impartial tribunal in the context of extraordinary courts have generally found such courts to be both non-independent and partial. The African Commission on Human and Peoples' Rights, without analyzing independence (Article 7[1] of the African Charter only ensures trial by an impartial court), has found that the presence of military and police officers as judges in special tribunals by "its composition alone creates the appearance, if not actual lack of impartiality." *Constitutional Rights Project v. Nigeria*, Comm'n No. 87/93, African Comm'n H.P.R., ACHPR/RPT/8th/Rev.I (1995), retrieved from http://www1.umn.edu/humanrts/africa/comcases/87-93.html.

31 Jayanth K. Krishnan and Viplav Sharma, *Exceptional or Not? An Examination of India's Special Courts in the National Security Context*, in this volume.

secret proceedings barring defense access to prosecutorial evidence.[32] The African Commission on Human and Peoples' Rights determined Nigeria had breached fair-trial protections in its military tribunals by denying access to counsel, conducting the trial in camera, and allowing an appeal only to a military council that entertained the various roles of complainant, prosecutor, and judge.[33] The European Court of Human Rights held that Turkey's State Security Court violated the right to a fair trial both because of doubts about the court's independence and impartiality and because of a wide variety of procedural inadequacies.[34]

In a cogent analysis of the difficulties of ensuring fair trials in special courts, the Inter-American Court of Human Rights found that convictions by "faceless" Peruvian military courts of civilians accused of terrorist activities violated the right to a fair trial.[35] Peru defended its military courts, arguing that it had legally established them, that their independence and impartiality were guaranteed under the national constitution, and that given the danger of terrorism, it was necessary to try the civilians in a military court. The Court rejected Peru's arguments, stating that "military tribunals are not the tribunals previously established by law for civilians."[36] According to the Court, "A basic principle of the independence of the judiciary is that every person has the right to be heard by regular courts" and the very act of trying a civilian in an extraordinary military court for a matter that a regular court should hear violated the individual's right to an independent tribunal.[37] Moreover, the Court concluded that the military judges were not independent or impartial, and that the military courts also violated various other fair-trial protections.

The case is notable because despite Peru's undisputed position that it had "scrupulously complied with the procedural guarantees established

32 *See* Amos N. Guiora, *Transnational Comparative Analysis of Balancing Competing Interests in Counter-Terrorism*, 20 Temp. Int'l & Comp. L.J. 363, 391 (2006).

33 *See* Diane Marie Amann, *Guantánamo*, 42 Colum. J. Transnat'l L. 263, 331–32 (2004).

34 *Öcalan v. Turkey*, 41 Eur. Ct. H.R. 45 (2005).

35 *Castillo Petruzzi v. Peru*, Judgment, Inter-Am. Ct. H.R. (ser. C) No. 52, *passim* (1999).

36 *Id.* ¶ 128.

37 *Id.* ¶ 129.

in Peruvian law,"[38] the Court determined that the procedures established under national law nonetheless violated the basic right to a fair trial as provided under the American Convention. Consequently, the Inter-American Court extended the protections of independence beyond separation of powers and judicial conditions of service by declaring that trying a civilian in an extraordinary court – even one with formal, constitutionally ensured independence – for a matter that should be heard by a regular court facially violated the right to an independent tribunal. Following 9/11, the Inter-American Commission produced a report consistent with this holding, stating the right to a fair trial "generally prohibits the use of ad hoc, special, or military tribunals or commissions to try civilians for terrorist-related or any other crimes."[39]

The Peru case highlights a recurring problem of extraordinary courts: governments facing the prospect of trying individuals for acts of terrorism face practical challenges, such as determining how and where to try individuals who blur boundaries between civilian and military spheres. The worldwide consensus of human rights instruments and bodies, however, is that such challenges do not present sufficient justification to suspend the core right of a fair trial, absent a formal state of emergency. Indeed, there is little justification to relax basic protections in the face of practicality concerns, as any subsequent result from a biased tribunal will suffer from concerns of legitimacy.

Ultimately, although the right to a fair trial applies to extraordinary courts, such courts almost uniformly fail to provide an accused with a fair trial. The independence and impartiality – the cornerstone of any fair trial – of extraordinary courts is particularly problematic because of the structural makeup of such tribunals (for example, allowing unlawful command influence or improper jurisdiction over civilians) and the frequent presence of military or police officers as judges. Moreover, extraordinary courts usually employ procedural shortcuts that fall short of those

38 *Id.* ¶ 171.

39 Inter-Am. Comm'n H.R., Report on Terrorism and Human Rights, OEA/Ser.L/V/II.116, Doc. 5 rev. 1 corr., exec. summ. ¶ 18 (2002).

guaranteed by the right to a fair trial. In sum, an accused standing before an extraordinary court holds little chance of receiving a fair trial.

3. Addressing Fair Trial Deprivations in Extraordinary Courts

The likelihood of special courts violating fair-trial standards should come as no surprise: in the words of the Human Rights Committee, "[Q]uite often the reason for the establishment of such courts is to enable exceptional procedures to be applied which do not comply with normal standards of justice."[40] Given that in practice extraordinary courts often disregard fair trial rights, what approaches should be taken to ensure this right is respected?

As a starting point, all courts must be established by law. According to the Inter-American Court, military tribunals are not the courts previously established by law for trying civilians; under that logic, no civilian should be tried in an extraordinary court for a matter the regular court could hear.[41] Similarly, the United Nations' Basic Principles on the Independence of the Judiciary prohibits the creation of special courts that do not use the duly established procedures of the legal process and displace the jurisdiction of ordinary courts.[42] Even in situations of non-international armed conflict, Common Article 3 of the Geneva Conventions assures a regularly constituted court.[43]

Nonetheless, because a special court may still be established by law and other international bodies have not gone as far as the Inter-American Court in outright prohibiting the trial of civilians by extraordinary courts, the main approach to address fair-trial violations by special courts has

40 UN Human Rights Comm., General Comment No. 13, ¶ 14, UN Doc. HRI/GEN/1/Rev.1 (1994) (replaced by General Comment 32, *supra* note 12).

41 *Castillo Petruzzi v. Peru*, Judgment, Inter-Am. Ct. H.R. (ser. C) No. 52, ¶ 128 (1999).

42 Basic Principles, *supra* note 16, art. 5.

43 Geneva Convention III, *supra* note 6, art. 3. For example, in 2006, the U.S. Supreme Court held in *Hamdan v. Rumsfeld* that the President lacked congressional authorization for the military commissions (although Congress later responded by authorizing their creation). 548 U.S. 557, 594–95 (2006).

been to try and discourage their use, especially for the trial of civilians. The Human Rights Committee has noted "that the trial of civilians in military or special courts may raise serious problems as far as the equitable, impartial and independent administration of justice is concerned." Further, the Committee has stated that trials should be "limited to cases where the State party can show that resorting to such trials is necessary and justified by objective and serious reasons, and where with regard to the specific class of individuals and offences at issue the regular civilian courts are unable to undertake the trials."[44] The Inter-American Commission has similarly discouraged the use of special courts for the trial of civilians.

Beyond discouraging resort to special courts, however, there remains much to be desired. Whether because of the risk of a non-independent judiciary or partial judges, an inability to be present at trial, a lack of independent counsel, a refusal to allow cross-examination of adverse witnesses, or a denial of the right to appeal, special courts employ procedural "shortcuts" to bypass fair-trial safeguards.

A notable consequence of the procedural bypasses of extraordinary courts is that with each procedural shortcut, a court is perceived as less legitimate, both domestically and abroad. Examples across jurisdictions abound, casting doubt on the legitimacy of the results obtained as a result of the lack of procedural safeguards employed. For example, the procedural irregularities of the U.S. military commissions in Guantánamo Bay underlie a strongly held viewpoint that any convictions obtained will have been achieved illegitimately. In this sense, fair-trial protections are more than academic interests; they legitimize the totality of the judicial-criminal process. Accordingly, if governments seek results perceived as legitimate, it is in their interest to ensure that extraordinary courts comport with universally accepted fair-trial protections.

Courts and interpretive bodies have consistently held that fair-trial rights apply to all types of tribunals. What remains to be addressed is

44 General Comment 32, *supra* note 12, ¶ 22.

the gap between the practice of extraordinary courts and the principles that have been codified in human rights treaties and declared by human rights bodies. In their effort to combat terrorism while maintaining legitimacy in the public eye, governments would do well to provide the basic components of a fair trial in extraordinary courts, when the resort to the exception is sought in extreme times.

15 Approaches and Responses of the UN Human Rights Mechanisms to Exceptional Courts and Military Commissions

Alex Conte

THE CHALLENGES POSED BY THE USE OF EXCEPTIONAL COURTS and military commissions have been considered, in various contexts, by many of the human rights mechanisms of the United Nations (UN). As stated by Gross and Ní Aoláin in their introduction to this collection, the use of exceptional courts as a means of responding to violent challengers is not a new phenomenon. This is borne out by the long record of action taken by UN human rights mechanisms on the subject, dating back to well before the military commissions scheme established by former U.S. President George W. Bush. This chapter provides an overview of the approaches of and responses to the use of such courts and commissions as they relate to international human rights law. Consideration is given to the views and findings of a range of UN human rights mechanisms, clustered on a thematic basis to reflect on issues of competence and jurisdiction, independence and impartiality, equality of arms, and procedural and evidentiary issues. The conclusions and recommendations considered relate to universal fair trial obligations and standards, as well as their application to country-specific contexts from throughout the world, including Algeria, Bahrain, Brazil, Cameroon, Chile, Colombia, Equatorial Guinea, Ethiopia, Guatemala, Ireland, Israel, Lebanon, Mexico, Peru, Slovakia, Turkey, and the United States of America.

Pertaining to the UN human rights treaty bodies, reference is made to General Comments, Concluding Observations on State party periodic reports, and Views on individual communications, as adopted by the Human Rights Committee (HRC), the Committee against Torture, and the Committee on the Rights of the Child. The approaches of independent human rights experts of the Human Rights Council, known as Special Procedures, are examined, including those of the Special Rapporteur on human rights and counterterrorism; the independence of judges and lawyers; torture, extrajudicial, summary and arbitrary executions; and the Working Group on arbitrary detention. Reference to the work and resolutions of political offices and bodies is also made, namely the UN Human Rights Council and its predecessor the Commission on Human Rights, and of the High Commissioner for Human Rights.

1. Jurisdictional Competence of Exceptional Courts and Military Tribunals

International instruments, including the International Covenant on Civil and Political Rights (ICCPR), do not prohibit the establishment of exceptional courts or military tribunals. UN human rights mechanisms have nevertheless found that recourse to such courts or tribunals is restricted by certain fundamental human rights obligations and guarantees, particularly in the case of jurisdiction over civilians and in respect of alleged violations of human rights. In light of the increased use since 9/11 of military commissions with jurisdiction over nonmilitary personnel, and of numerous serious allegations and findings of human rights violations perpetrated by military and security services in operations under the so-called War on Terror, these approaches by the UN mechanisms – although not new – are evermore important.

(a) Jurisdiction over Civilians

One of the key jurisdictional issues for international human rights law concerning the use of exceptional courts and military tribunals is the trial of civilians. Because of the different operation of military courts, and their establishment as mechanisms to deal with military discipline and the conduct of military personnel during operations abroad, their use to try civilians invokes issues of due process and the overarching right to a fair trial by ordinary courts established by law, particularly as this pertains to the independence and impartiality of the fact finders. The same very often also applies to, and is generally exacerbated in the context of, the trial of civilians by exceptional courts.

Although the ICCPR does not explicitly prohibit the trial of civilians by military or specialized courts, the HRC – the treaty-monitoring body established under Article 28 of the ICCPR – has repeatedly called on states parties to the ICCPR to ensure that the jurisdiction of military courts is restricted to offences of a strictly military nature committed by military personnel.[1] This is also the case with reports of the Committee against Torture, established under Article 17 on the Convention against Torture and other Cruel, Inhuman or Degrading Treatment or Punishment.[2] The general position in favour of jurisdiction over civilians by ordinary civilian courts is further reflected in the updated Set of Principles for the Protection and Promotion of Human Rights through

1 *See, e.g.*, UN Human Rights Comm., Concluding Observations on the Situation of Civil and Political Rights in Equatorial Guinea, ¶ 7, UN Doc. CCPR/CO/79/GNQ (July 30, 2004); UN Human Rights Comm., Concluding Observations: Third Periodic Report of Cameroon, ¶ 21, UN Doc. CCPR/C/79/Add.116 (Nov. 4, 1999); UN Human Rights Comm., Concluding Observations: Initial Report of Slovakia, ¶ 20, UN Doc. CCPR/C/79/Add.79 (July 30, 1997); UN Human Rights Comm., Concluding Observations: Second Periodic Report of Lebanon, ¶ 14, UN Doc. CCPR/C/79/Add.78 (Apr. 7, 1997). *See also* UN Human Rights Comm., Draft Principles Governing the Administration of Justice through Military Tribunals, Principles 3, 8, UN Doc. E/CN.4/2006/58 (Jan. 13, 2006); UN Human Rights Comm., Draft Universal Declaration on the Independence of Justice, Principle 5(f), UN Doc. E/CN.4/RES/1989/32 (Mar. 6, 1989).

2 *See, e.g.*, UN Comm. Against Torture, Concluding Observations: Third Periodic Report of Turkey, ¶ 5(c)(iii), UN Doc. CAT/C/TUR/CO/3 (Jan. 20, 2011); UN Comm. Against Torture, Concluding Observations: Initial Report of Ethiopia, ¶ 14(d), UN Doc. CAT/C/ETH/CO/1 (Nov. 2010); UN Comm. Against Torture, Concluding Observations: Fifth Periodic Report of Chile, ¶ 14, UN Doc. CAT/C//CHL/CO/5 (June 23, 2009); UN Comm. Against Torture, Concluding Observations: Initial Report of Peru, ¶ 66, UN Doc. A/50/44 (July 26, 1995).

Action to Combat Impunity.[3] Added to this, the UN Basic Principles on the Independence of the Judiciary, endorsed by the General Assembly in its Resolutions 40/32 (1985) and 40/146 (1985), and more recently by Human Rights Council resolution 19/31 (2012), reiterate in Principle 5: "Everyone shall have the right to be tried by ordinary courts or tribunals using established legal procedures. Tribunals that do not use the duly established procedures of the legal process shall not be created to displace the jurisdiction belonging to the ordinary courts or judicial tribunals."

In its General Comment on the right to a fair trial under Article 14 of the ICCPR, the HRC has explained that the trial of civilians by military or special courts and tribunals should only take place on an exceptional basis, limited to cases where the state can show that the trial of a civilian by a military or specialized court is necessary and justified by objective and serious reasons, such as during military occupation, and where the civilian courts are unable to try the person because of the specific class of individual and offence(s) at issue.[4] This position is underpinned, according to the former Special Rapporteur on the independence of judges and lawyers, Leandro Despouy, by the fact that civilians cannot commit offences of a military nature.[5] Where states have been unable to demonstrate that the regular civilian courts are unable to try an individual, or that other forms of special or high-security civilian courts are inadequate, the HRC has adopted views in individual communications brought

3 Independent Expert to Update the Set of Principles to Combat Impunity, *Updated Set of Principles for the Protection and Promotion of Human Rights through Action to Combat Impunity*, Principle 29, UN Doc. E/CN.4/2005/102/Add.1 (Feb. 8, 2005) (by Diane Orentlicher).

4 UN Human Rights Comm., General Comment 32 – Article 14: Right to Equality Before Courts and Tribunals and to a Fair Trial, ¶ 22, UN Doc. CCPR/C/GC/32 (2007). *See also* Special Rapporteur on the Promotion and Protection of Human Rights and Fundamental Freedoms while Countering Terrorism, *Promotion and Protection of Human Rights and Fundamental Freedoms while Countering Terrorism*, ¶ 28, UN Doc. A/63/223 (Aug. 6, 2008).

5 Special Rapporteur on the Independence of Judges and Lawyers, *Civil and Political Rights, Including the Questions of Independence of the Judiciary, Administration of Justice, Impunity*, ¶ 26, UN Doc. A/61/384 (Sept. 12, 2006) (by Leandro Despouy).

before it that the rights under Article 14 of the ICCPR have been violated.[6]

In the context of the use of exceptional courts as a means of responding to violent confrontations, the Special Rapporteur on the promotion of human rights and fundamental freedoms while countering terrorism, Ben Emmerson, has stated in his 2012 report to the UN Human Rights Council that the ordinary rules for criminal law and procedure should also apply to individuals suspected of involvement in terrorist acts, and that this implies that the trial of such individuals must meet international standards for a fair and public hearing before an independent and impartial civilian court.[7] This is a position also taken by the current and former UN High Commissioners for Human Rights.[8] The former Special Rapporteur on the independence of judges and lawyers, Leandro Despouy, has also expressed that the "regrettably common practice" of using military or emergency courts to try civilians in the name of national security runs counter to all international and regional standards and established case law.[9]

6 *See, e.g.*, *Madani v. Algeria*, Judgements UN Human Rights Comm., ¶ 8.7, UN Doc. CCPR/C/89/D/1172/2003 (2007); *Kavanagh v. Ireland*, Judgements UN Human Rights Comm., ¶¶ 10(2), 10(3), 11, UN Doc. CCPR/C/71/D/819/1998 (2001).

7 Special Rapporteur on the Promotion and Protection of Human Rights and Fundamental Freedoms while Countering Terrorism, *Framework Principles for Securing the Human Rights of Victims of Terrorism*, ¶¶ 34, 68(b), UN Doc A/HRC/20/14 (June 4, 2012) (by Ben Emmerson). *See also* Special Rapporteur on the Promotion and Protection of Human Rights and Fundamental Freedoms while Countering Terrorism, *Mission to Peru*, ¶33, UN Doc. A/HRC/16/51/Add.3 (Dec. 15, 2010) (by Martin Scheinin); Special Rapporteur on the Promotion and Protection of Human Rights and Fundamental Freedoms while Countering Terrorism, *Mission to Egypt*, ¶ 32, UN Doc. A/HRC/13/37/Add.2 (Oct. 14, 2009) (by Martin Scheinin); UN Doc. A/63/223, *supra* note 4, ¶28.

8 *See, e.g.*, Report of the United Nations High Commissioner for Human Rights on the Protection of Human Rights and Fundamental Freedoms while Countering Terrorism, Human Rights Council, 8th Sess., June 8, 2008, ¶42, UN Doc. A/HRC/8/13 (June 2, 2008).

9 Special Rapporteur on the Independence of Judges and Lawyers, *Civil and Political Rights, Including the Questions of Independence of the Judiciary, Administration of Justice, Impunity*, ¶ 60, UN Doc. E/CN.4/2004/60 (Dec. 31, 2003) (by Leandro Despouy).

The 2006 Decaux Principles reiterate that military courts should not have jurisdiction to try civilians and that states must, in all circumstances, ensure that civilians accused of a criminal offence of any nature are tried by civilian courts. The Commentary to Principle 5 notes that the existence in many countries of military or special tribunals that try civilians can present serious problems as far as the equitable, impartial, and independent administration of justice is concerned. It opines that "[q]uite often the reason for the establishment of such courts is to enable exceptional procedures to be applied which do not comply with normal standards of justice."[10] This observation is reflected in the findings of other Special Procedures. In a report focusing on the right to a fair trial in the fight against terrorism, the former Special Rapporteur on human rights and counterterrorism, Martin Scheinin, expressed his concern about the lower fair-trial guarantees that in practice often characterize military and special courts because of prolonged periods of pre-charge and pretrial detention, with inadequate access to counsel, intrusion into attorney-client confidentiality, and strict limitations on the right to appeal and bail.[11]

Similar concerns have been raised by the Special Rapporteur on the independence of judges and lawyers, Gabriela Knaul, including in the case of the trial of human rights defenders by a military court in Bahrain. Concluding that there were serious allegations of a lack of due process, the Special Rapporteur expressed concern over apparent restrictions to the right to counsel, the making of confessions under duress, and the use of evidence obtained by torture and ill-treatment.[12] Concerns about the right to counsel, appeal, and the principle of equality before the law were also noted by the former Special Rapporteur on the independence of judges and lawyers, Leandro Despouy, in his 2005 consideration of

10 UN Doc. E/CN.4/2006/58, *supra* note 1, ¶ 20.

11 UN Doc. A/63/223, *supra* note 4, ¶¶ 27, 45(b).

12 Press Release, Office of the High Commissioner for Human Rights, Bahrain: UN Human Rights Experts Urge Immediate Release of Abdulhadi Al-Khawaja (Apr. 13, 2012), retrieved from http://www.ohchr.org/en/NewsEvents/Pages/DisplayNews.aspx?NewsID=12056&LangID=E.

antiterrorism laws in the United States.[13] The UN Working Group on arbitrary detention has also taken a very clear position against the trying of civilians in military courts, warning that "one of the most serious causes of arbitrary detention is precisely the existence of such courts, virtually none of which respects the guarantees of the right to a fair trial."[14]

As indicated in the introduction to this chapter, the use of exceptional courts and military tribunals as a means of responding to violent challengers is not a new phenomenon. The increased attention paid to them by the UN human rights mechanisms in the past ten years is partly symptomatic, however, of the corresponding increase in recourse to such courts and tribunals since 9/11. UN mechanisms have taken a consistent approach, one that has not, incidentally, been the result of any internal effort to achieve cohesion between the mechanisms that, although often referring to each other's work, operate independently of each other. The message concerning the jurisdiction of such courts and tribunals over civilians is clear: they are not to be used in such a way. They are in violation of the overarching right to a fair and public hearing by a competent, independent, and impartial tribunal established by law, and they often involve the use of measures and procedures that undermine both the right to a fair trial and various other related human rights guarantees.

(b) Jurisdiction over Cases of Human Rights Abuses

Restricted jurisdiction also applies to the subject matter of jurisdiction given to exceptional courts or military tribunals. Over the past twenty

13 Special Rapporteur on the Independence of Judges and Lawyers, *Civil and Political Rights, Including the Questions of Independence of the Judiciary, Administration of Justice, Impunity*, ¶¶ 18–19, UN Doc. E/CN.4/2005/60 (20 Jan., 2005) (by Leandro Despouy).

14 UN Human Rights Comm., Report of the Working Group on Arbitrary Detention, ¶ 67, UN Doc. E/CN.4/2004/3 (Dec. 15, 2003).

years, the HRC has expressed its concern in a large number of situations where jurisdiction has been conferred to military courts to try cases concerning allegations of human rights violations. This has in practice involved the use of military courts to put military personnel on trial, and sometimes civilians, concerning allegations that such persons have violated human rights, including allegations of torture and ill-treatment, summary executions, and enforced disappearances. In 1992, when issuing its Concluding Observations on the examination of the second periodic report of Colombia, the Committee stated:

> The measures that have been taken do not seem to be sufficient to guarantee that all members of the armed forces who abuse their power and violate citizens' rights will be brought to justice and punished. Military courts do not seem to be the most appropriate ones for the protection of citizens' rights in a context where the military itself has violated such rights.[15]

On the basis of this rationale, the Committee recommended that Colombia limit the competence of its military courts to matters of internal issues of discipline within the armed forces, and similar matters, so that any allegation of human rights violations having been perpetrated by the military be dealt with by ordinary courts, rather than by the military itself.[16] In its 2010 Concluding Observations on the examination of the fifth periodic report of Mexico, the Committee observed that Mexico's military courts have jurisdiction to try cases of alleged human rights violations committed by military personnel in cases where the victim is a civilian. Noting that all victims of human rights violations must have access to effective remedies – as guaranteed by Article 2(3) of the ICCPR – the HRC recommended that Mexico amend its Code of Military Justice to ensure that the jurisdiction of military courts does not extend to cases of

15 U.N. Human Rights Comm., Concluding Observations: Third Periodic Report of Colombia, ¶ 393, U.N. Doc. ccpr/c/79/Add.2 (Sept. 25, 1992). *See also* Comm. on the Rights of the Child, Concluding Observations: Third Periodic Report of Colombia, ¶ 44, U.N. Doc. CRC/C/COL/CO/3 (June 8, 2006).

16 UN Doc. CRC/C/COL/CO/3, *supra* note 15.

human rights violations.[17] The former Special Rapporteur on torture and other cruel, inhuman, or degrading treatment or punishment, Sir Nigel Rodley, arrived at the same conclusions and recommendations following his 1998 report on his official country mission to Mexico.[18] Considering the similarly wide jurisdiction of military courts in Guatemala, the HRC noted that the power of such courts to decide cases that belong to the ordinary courts contributed to the impunity enjoyed by military personnel in Guatemala and prevented their punishment for serious human rights violations.[19] The former Special Rapporteur on human rights and counterterrorism expressed similar concern about the potential for military courts in Peru to adjudicate cases concerning excessive use of force or human rights violations against civilians.[20]

Reflecting these concerns, and building on Resolution 1994/67 of the former Commission on Human Rights, Principle 9 of the Decaux Principles provides: "In all circumstances, the jurisdiction of military courts should be set aside in favour of the jurisdiction of the ordinary courts to conduct inquiries into serious human rights violations such as extrajudicial executions, enforced disappearances and torture, and to prosecute and try persons accused of such crimes." In the context of the right of all persons to be protected against enforced disappearance, it is notable that Article 16(2) of the Declaration on the Protection of all Persons from Enforced Disappearance – adopted by the UN General Assembly in 1992 – provides that all acts of enforced disappearance "shall be tried only by the competent ordinary courts in each State, and not by any other

17 UN Human Rights Comm., Concluding Observations: Fifth Periodic Report of Mexico, ¶ 18, UN Doc. CCPR/C/MEX/CO5 (May 17, 2010). *See also*; UN Doc. CCPR/C/79/Add.78, *supra* note 1; UN Human Rights Comm., Concluding Observations: Initial Report of Brazil, ¶ 315, UN Doc CCPR/C/79/Add.66 (July 24, 1996).

18 Special Rapporteur on the Question of the Human Rights of all Persons Subjected to any Form of Detention or Imprisonment, in Particular: Torture and other Cruel, Inhuman or Degrading Treatment or Punishment, *Visit to Mexico*, ¶ 88(j), UN Doc E/CN.4/1998/38/Add.2 (Feb. 11, 1998).

19 UN Human Rights Comm., Concluding Observations: Second Periodic Report of Guatemala, ¶ 20, UN Doc. CCPR/CO/72/GTM (Aug. 27, 2001).

20 UN Doc A/HRC/16/51/Add.3, *supra* note 7, ¶ 33.

special tribunal, in particular military courts."[21] The UN Working Group on enforced disappearances has likewise emphasized the need for all persons accused of having committed acts of enforced disappearances to be tried only by competent civilian courts.[22] The former Special Rapporteur on extrajudicial, summary, and arbitrary executions, Philip Alston, has similarly recommended that all cases of alleged extrajudicial executions should be dealt with by the ordinary courts, and not by military tribunals.[23]

Bearing in mind the danger for perpetuating a culture of impunity posed by military jurisdiction over human rights violations, an updated Set of Principles for the Protection and Promotion of Human Rights through Action to Combat Impunity (Principles to Combat Impunity) was presented to the former Commission on Human Rights in 2005.[24] Principle 29 declares that the jurisdiction of military tribunals must be restricted to the exclusion of human rights violations. According to the former Special Rapporteur on the independence of judges and lawyers, Leandro Despouy, this notion is founded on the fact that military functions do not, and cannot, include the commission of gross human rights violations.[25] Like the HRC and Principle 29 of the Principles to Combat Impunity, Despouy has also noted that military jurisdiction over allegations of human rights violations constitutes a serious obstacle for many

21 *Compare* Declaration on the Protection of all Persons from Enforced Disappearance, G.A. Res 47/133, UN Doc. A/RES/47/133 (Dec. 18, 1992), *with* International Convention for the Protection of all Persons from Enforced Disappearances, art. 11(3), G.A. Res. 61/177, UN Doc. A/RES/ 61/177 (Jan. 12, 2007) (providing that any person tried for an offence of enforced disappearance must benefit from a fair trial "before a competent, independent and impartial court or tribunal established by law").

22 UN Human Rights Comm., Report of the Working Group on Enforced or Involuntary Disappearances, ¶ 375, UN Doc. E/CN.4/2005/65 (Dec. 23, 2004).

23 Special Rapporteur on Extrajudicial, Summary or Arbitrary Executions, *Mission to Colombia*, ¶¶ 89–90, UN Doc. A/HRC/14/24/Add.2 (Mar. 31, 2010) (by Philip Alston); Special Rapporteur on Extrajudicial, Summary or Arbitrary Executions, *Mission to Mexico*, ¶ 107(f), UN Doc. E/CN.4/2000/3/Add.3 (Nov. 25, 1999) (by Asma Jahangir).

24 UN Doc E/CN.4/2005/102/Add.1, *supra* note 3.

25 UN Doc A/61/384, *supra* note 5, ¶ 26.

victims of human rights violations in their quest for justice.[26] Alston has likewise concluded that "subjecting allegations of human rights abuse to military jurisdiction often leads to impunity."[27]

The views and recommendations of the UN mechanisms is again consistent, this time concerning the use of the military to try its personnel concerning allegations of human rights violations, and in some cases also to try civilians. The approach, one that opposes such use of military courts, is on the basis of the danger that the military will not find its own to be violators of human rights and will therefore fail to be impartial in such matters, thus undermining the need for accountability of perpetrators of human rights violations and access to justice for the victims of such violations.

(c) Compliance with Fair Trial Standards

In cases where it is permissible to establish special courts, or to try civilians under military courts or commissions, the requirements of Article 14 of the ICCPR must still be complied with. As expressed by the HRC, it is important in such circumstances "to take all necessary measures to ensure that such trials genuinely afford the full guarantees stipulated in article 14."[28] Although Article 14 of the ICCPR is not included in the list of non-derogable rights under Article 4(2) of the Covenant, states derogating from normal procedures in circumstances of a public emergency threatening the life of the nation must ensure that such measures are temporary, namely that they apply only during a state of emergency and no longer than this. States must also make certain that they do not exceed restrictions that are strictly required by the exigencies of the actual situation. The Committee has explained that deviating from the fundamental principles of a fair trial is prohibited at all times, and that

26 UN Doc E/CN.4/2005/60, *supra* note 13, ¶44.

27 Special Rapporteur on Extrajudicial, Summary or Arbitrary Executions, *Civil and Political Rights, Including the Questions of Disappearances and Summary Executions*, ¶ 37, UN Doc E/CN.4/2006/53 (Mar. 8, 2006) (by Philip Alston).

28 UN Doc. CCPR/C/GC/32, *supra* note 4, ¶ 22.

the guarantees of a fair trial may never be made subject to derogating measures if this would circumvent the protection of non-derogable rights, such as the right to life and the prohibition against torture in Articles 6 and 7 of the ICCPR.[29] This position is further reflected in the view of the HRC that although reservations to particular clauses of Article 14 may be acceptable, a general reservation to the right to a fair trial would be incompatible with the object and purpose of the ICCPR.[30]

In his summary introduction to the updated set of Principles Governing the Administration of Justice through Military Tribunals, the Special Rapporteur of the former Sub-Commission on the Promotion of Human Rights, Emmanuel Decaux, similarly spoke of the need to situate military justice as "an integral part of the general judicial system."[31] The full application of fair trial rights to military and special courts has also been reiterated by the UN General Assembly in its adoption of the Basic Principles and Guidelines on the Right to Remedy and Reparation for Victims of Violations of International Human Rights and Humanitarian Law,[32] by the Human Rights Council and its predecessor the Commission on Human Rights, and by the Special Procedures of the Council and the former Commission.[33] It is against this background that

29 *Id.* ¶ 6.

30 UN Doc. CCPR/C/GC/32, *supra* note 4, ¶ 5; Human Rights Comm., General Comment 29 – States of Emergency: Article 4, ¶ 16, UN Doc. CCPR/C/21/Rev.1/Add.11 (2001); Human Rights Comm., General Comment 24 – Issues Relating to Reservations Made upon Ratification or Accession to the Covenant of the Optional Protocols Thereto, or in Relation to Declarations under Article 41 of the Covenant, ¶ 8, UN Doc. CCPR/C/21/Rev.1/Add.6 (1994).

31 UN Doc. E/CN.4/2006/58, *supra* note 1. *See also* Human Rights Council Res. 19/3, ¶ 8, Integrity of the Judicial System, UN Doc. A/ HRC/RES/19/31 (Mar. 18, 2012).

32 Basic Principles and Guidelines on the Right to a Remedy and Reparation for Victims of Gross Violations of International Human Rights Law and Serious Violations of International Humanitarian Law G.A. Res. 60/147, UN Doc. A/RES/60/147, Principle 23(b) (Mar. 21, 2006).

33 *See* UN Doc. A/ HRC/RES/19/31, *supra* note 31, ¶ 8; UN Doc. A/61/384, *supra* note 5, ¶ 19; UN Commission on Human Rights Res. 2005/30, Integrity of the Judicial System, E/CN.4/RES/2005/30 (Apr. 19, 2005); UN Commission on Human Rights Res. 2004/32, Integrity of the Judicial System, E/CN.4/RES/2004/32 (Apr. 19, 2004); UN Commission on Human Rights Res. 2003/39, Integrity of the Judicial System,

this chapter now turns to consider some of the substantive elements of the right to a fair trial.

2. Independence and Impartiality

One of the primary challenges faced by the use of special courts established outside the ordinary justice system is that of independence and impartiality. This pertains to both the institutional independence of such mechanisms from the executive branches of the state, as well as to the ability of the finders of fact to act impartially in matters that may personally affect them or their peers. Connecting both is the need for objective impartiality so that justice is not only done but also appears to be done. In respect of both criminal and noncriminal proceedings, every person has the right to a hearing by an independent and impartial tribunal established by law, a right reflected in Article 10 of the Universal Declaration of Human Rights, Article 14(1) of the ICCPR, and in respect of criminal proceedings against minors, in Article 40(2)(b)(iii) of the Convention on the Rights of the Child.[34] As a central pillar of the right to a fair trial, independence and impartiality require, in general terms, that tribunals should be free from any form of direct or indirect influence, that they treat all persons under their jurisdiction on the same basis, and that judicial officers exercise their functions without personal bias or prejudice and in a manner that offers sufficient guarantees to exclude any legitimate doubt of their impartiality. These requirements are absolute and may not be subject to any exception. They are especially important in times of crisis when the dangers of lack of independence and impartiality are increased and may lead to continued discontent and instability rather than sustainable transition and respect for the rule of law.

Concerning the independence of courts and tribunals, the HRC has explained that the functions and competencies of judicial officers and the

E/CN.4/RES/2003/39 (Apr. 23, 2003). *See also* UN Human Rights Comm., Situation of Detainees at Guantánamo, ¶ 31, UN Doc. E/CN.4/2006/120 (Feb. 15, 2006).

34 *See also* UN Doc. E/CN.4/2006/58, *supra* note 1, Principle 13.

executive branch of government must be clearly distinguishable, and that the executive must not be capable of controlling or directing the court or tribunal.[35] This position has been reiterated by the former Special Rapporteur on human rights and counter-terrorism.[36] Scheinin also expressed serious concerns about the independence and impartiality of military and specialized courts because of the cumulative effect of "simplified provisions for dismissal of judges sitting in military or special courts, the lack of security of tenure of judges, the fact that often judges are serving (military) officers appointed by the executive, and the broad discretional power of the executive to refer cases to such courts."[37]

The former Special Rapporteur of human rights and counterterrorism has also considered the use of military courts in Israel and the occupied Palestinian territory, concluding that "[w]hile the Special Rapporteur makes no judgment as to the impartiality or otherwise of individual military judges, the fact remains that military courts have an appearance of a potential lack of independence and impartiality, which on its own brings into question the fairness of trials."[38] In April 2012, the spokesperson of the Office of the High Commissioner for Human Rights, Rupert Colville, referred to the use of Israeli military courts to try civilians from Gaza as a practice that seriously undermines fair trial guarantees.[39]

3. Access to and Equality before the Courts and Tribunals

Equality in the administration of justice lies at the heart of the rule of law and demands that justice be administered in a way that achieves

35 UN Doc. CCPR/C/GC/32, *supra* note 4, ¶ 19.

36 UN Doc A/63/223, *supra* note 4, ¶ 25.

37 *Id.*

38 Special Rapporteur on the Promotion and Protection of Human Rights and Fundamental Freedoms while Countering Terrorism, *Mission to Israel, Including Visit to Occupied Palestinian Territory,* ¶ 29, UN Doc. A/HRC/6/17/Add.4 (Nov. 22, 2007) (by Martin Scheinin).

39 Press Release, Office of the High Commissioner for Human Rights, Press Briefing Notes on Gaza and Belarus, (Apr. 20, 2012), retrieved from http://www.ohchr.org/EN/NewsEvents/Pages/DisplayNews.aspx?NewsID=12071&LangID=E.

fairness for all parties, regardless of their identity or the nature of the proceedings.[40] At the international level, this is a principle that finds its roots in the early development of human rights instruments and was borne, in part, out of the atrocities during the Second World War. In the current context this implies, according to the HRC, that there be objective and reasonable grounds to justify the application of exceptional criminal procedures or specially constituted courts or tribunals.[41] Even in the context of the trial of terrorist suspects, the former Special Rapporteur on human rights and counterterrorism, Martin Scheinin, has called for caution in allocating such cases to military, special, or specialized courts.[42] This further strengthens the presumption against the trial of civilians by military or special courts, and reinforces the primacy of the ordinary criminal justice system. It has been noted by Scheinin that access to and equality before courts and tribunals is not limited to citizens of the states, but must be available to all individuals, regardless of their nationality or statelessness, and whatever their status.[43] He has further emphasized that in cases involving serious charges and where the accused is denied bail, the accused "must be tried in as expeditious manner as possible, even in bona fide emergency situations where there is a serious terrorist threat."[44]

Equal treatment also involves "equality of arms," pursuant to which the procedural conditions at trial and sentencing must be the same for all parties. It calls for a fair balance between the parties, whether the accused and her or his counsel or the prosecution, such that each party is afforded a reasonable opportunity to present the case under conditions that do not place the party at a substantial disadvantage vis-à-vis the opponent. Equality of arms is fundamental to safeguarding a fair trial and engages various aspects of the right to a fair trial. The former Special Rapporteur on human rights and counterterrorism has commented that

40 UN Doc. CCPR/C/GC/32, *supra* note 4, ¶ 2. *See also* International Convention on Civil and Political Rights, art. 3, Mar. 23, 1976, 999 U.N.T.S. 171.

41 UN Doc. CCPR/C/GC/32, *supra* note 4, ¶ 14.

42 UN Doc A/63/223, *supra* note 4, ¶ 24.

43 *Id.* ¶ 14.

44 *Id.* ¶ 17.

the disproportionate aggregation of resources between the prosecution and defence in terrorism cases "is a matter that strikes at the heart of the principle of equality of arms required in the safeguarding of a fair trial."[45] This is one of the numerous issues affecting the equality of arms in military and exceptional proceedings, as illustrated in the discussion of the U.S. Military Commissions Act 2006 that follows.

4. The U.S. Military Commissions Act 2006

In May 2007, the former Special Rapporteur on human rights and counterterrorism undertook an official country mission to the United States of America. This was part of the Special Rapporteur's mandate to undertake country missions in order to give context to the work undertaken by his mandate, particularly important given the U.S.-proclaimed "war on terror" and in light of the role that the United States has paid in post–September 11 operations and mechanisms to counter terrorism. In the course of that mission, he paid special attention to the enactment by Congress of the Military Commissions Act of 2006 (MCA). Although the findings and recommendations of the Special Rapporteur are not final words on that subject, and recognizing also that the military commissions scheme has been subject to amendment since that time, the conclusions of the Special Rapporteur illustrate a number of the issues mentioned thus far, as well as referring to additional issues specific to the MCA. The intention here is to provide some context-specific illustrations of the issues involved, as approached by one of the Special Procedures of the Human Rights Council.

Concerning the jurisdiction of the military commissions, three points were raised by the Special Rapporteur. The first concerned the question of the possible trial of civilians,[46] and the very need to establish the

45 *Id.* ¶ 35.

46 Special Rapporteur on the Promotion and Protection of Human Rights and Fundamental Freedoms while Countering Terrorism, *Mission to the United States of America*, ¶ 30, UN Doc. A/HRC/6/17/Add.3 (Nov. 22. 2007) (by Martin Scheinin). For a more recent report on aspects of military trials in the United States, *see* Special Rapporteur

commissions as an alternative to the ordinary courts. On the latter point, the Rapporteur concluded that it was incorrect for the United States to say that its ordinary civilian courts were unable to handle the trial of persons on charges such as conspiracy and terrorism. He cited in this regard the civilian court prosecutions, in absentia, of Osama bin Laden concerning the bombing of the U.S. embassies in Kenya and Tanzania in 1998, the 2000 Grand Jury indictment of bin Laden concerning attacks on the *USS Cole*, as well as the Miami District Court trial and conviction in 2007 of José Padilla and others on charges of conspiracy to provide material support to terrorists.[47] Secondly, the Special Rapporteur challenged the MCA jurisdiction over offences that go beyond war crimes and the laws of war, thus beyond the proper scope of jurisdiction to be granted to military courts-martial.[48] Also concerning jurisdiction, Scheinin concluded that the offences listed in Section 950v(24)–(28) of the MCA were not covered by the law applicable at the time that the alleged acts were committed, thus involving the retroactive application of criminal law in breach of Article 15 of the ICCPR and universally acknowledged general principles of law.[49]

On the subject of independence and impartiality, the Special Rapporteur expressed serious concerns, including: the individual selection of judges and members in a military commission, compared with the appointment by lottery of military judges in courts martial; the fact that the convening authority is employed by the Department of Defense, undermining the appearance of impartial selection of members of individual commissions; the lack of prohibition against the selection of members of a commission who fall within the same chain of command; and the ability of the convening authority to intervene in the conduct of trials.[50]

on Extrajudicial, Summary or Arbitrary Executions, *Follow-Up to Country Recommendations – United States of America*, UN Doc A/HRC/20/22/Add.3 (Mar. 30, 2012) (by Christof Heyns).

47 UN Doc. A/HRC/6/17/Add.3, *supra* note 46, ¶ 21.

48 *Id.* ¶ 20.

49 *Id.* ¶ 21.

50 *Id.* ¶¶ 24–25. *See also* UN Doc E/CN.4/2006/120, *supra* note 33, ¶ 32.

The Special Rapporteur expressed concern over reports that the distribution of resources was such that military defence counsel were significantly under-resourced as compared to military trial counsel, matters striking at the heart of the principle of equality of arms.[51] He also considered the use and availability of evidence in proceedings before military commissions, including: the classification of evidence and its nondisclosure to trial counsel, including evidence that may be exculpatory or otherwise beneficial to the defence case; the ability of a military judge to admit into evidence information obtained by coercion, exacerbated by the fact that an accused may not be aware of such coercion where interrogation techniques are classified; and the potential admissibility of hearsay evidence.[52] Scheinin also noted with concern the ability of a military commission to determine charges in respect of which the death penalty may apply, in circumstances where there has been less than a full and rigorous guarantee of fair trial rights, and that the acquittal of a person by a military commission did not result in a right of release.[53]

Concluding that the composition and operation of military tribunals under the MCA involved multiple incompatibilities with the ICCPR, the Special Rapporteur recommended that these commissions be disestablished and that, wherever possible, ordinary civilian courts be used to try terrorist suspects. In the case of persons charged with war crimes identified in the Rome Statute of the International Criminal Court, he opined that military courts martial could try such persons, provided:

> Safeguards are in place to check against the exercise of bias or executive interference, including rights of appeal to civilian courts. In any such proceedings, the security classification of information should not interfere with the presumption of innocence or the equality of arms, nor should evidence obtained by any form of torture or cruel, inhuman or degrading treatment be admitted in proceedings. The United States should take steps to ensure that any person acquitted of charges is released upon acquittal, or in the case of a person convicted of an

51 UN Doc. A/HRC/6/17/Add.3, *supra* note 46, ¶ 29.

52 *Id.* ¶¶ 26–28.

53 *Id.* ¶¶ 31–32.

offence, that release occurs upon completion of the sentence imposed. The Special Rapporteur further recommends that the imposition of the death penalty be excluded for military tribunals or courts martial.[54]

Conclusions

The UN human rights mechanisms have dealt with various aspects of the challenges posed to international human rights law and the rule of law by the use of exceptional courts and military commissions. The starting point has consistently held that such courts, tribunals, and commissions must operate in a way that genuinely affords the full guarantees of the right to a fair trial, as well as relevant rights that may be affected, including the right to life and the prohibition from torture. These are rights to be afforded to all persons regardless of their nationality or statelessness, and whatever their status. Exceptional and military proceedings must thus be situated as an integral part of the general judicial system.

Concerning the jurisdictional reach of military or specialized courts, it is also the consistent approach of the UN human rights mechanisms that the trial of civilians by such courts and tribunals should only take place on an exceptional basis. Reflecting the primacy of the ordinary criminal justice system, this must be limited to situations where the regular civilian courts are unable to try an individual, or where other forms of special or high-security civilian courts are inadequate. Failing this, the trial of civilians by exceptional or military courts will result in a violation of Article 14 of the ICCPR as well as of corresponding international fair-trial standards. Jurisdiction is also limited with respect to subject matter, namely that military courts should not be able to conduct inquiries into, or try alleged perpetrators of, human rights violations. The presumption against military jurisdiction is an absolute one in the case of the trial of persons suspected of acts of enforced disappearance. The HRC, the former Special Rapporteur on the independence of judges and lawyers; the

54 *Id.* ¶¶ 60.

former Special Rapporteur on extrajudicial, summary, and arbitrary executions; and the updated Principles to Combat Impunity express concern that military jurisdiction over human rights violations presents serious obstacles to accountability and access to justice.

A common concern of the UN mechanisms has related to the unspoken reasons for, but often inevitable effects of, the establishment of exceptional courts and tribunals, namely to enable exceptional procedures to be applied that do not comply with normal standards of justice. The UN mechanisms have concluded that military and special courts and tribunals have in practice often involved prolonged periods of pre-charge and pretrial detention, arbitrary detention, limitations on the right to bail, inadequate access to counsel, intrusion into attorney-client confidentiality, the making of confessions under duress, the use of evidence obtained by torture or other ill-treatment, general issues of equality before the law and between the parties to proceedings, and strict limitations on the right to appeal. The independent and impartial functioning of military and special tribunals has also been of common concern to the UN human rights mechanisms. Such courts and tribunals often involve simplified provisions for the appointment and dismissal of judges, accompanied by a lack of security of tenure and the concurrent holding of military office while serving as judicial officers. The latter feature has been concluded to give the appearance of a potential lack of independence and impartiality, which is by itself inconsistent with the requirements of a fair trial. In the examination by the former Special Rapporteur on human rights and counterterrorism of the U.S. MCA, several grave deficiencies were identified, all of which point to the establishment of such commissions as a means of applying procedures that do not comply with the normal standards of justice.

16 Exceptional Courts and the European Convention on Human Rights

Steven Greer

WHAT IS A COURT OF EXCEPTIONAL, SPECIAL, OR EXTRAordinary jurisdiction, and how can it be distinguished from a normal or regular court, or one with merely a particular or specific jurisdiction? Answering these questions in the context of contemporary Europe is complicated by the fact that, in spite of the homogenization of public institutions since the end of the Cold War, various legal traditions continue to flourish. As a result, there is no uniform structural or procedural model of a normal court against which those with particular, special, exceptional, or extraordinary jurisdiction might easily be compared.[1] Furthermore, although the specialization of professional functions, an inherent feature of modernity, has ramifications for European and other modern legal processes, the emergence of tribunals with specific jurisdiction – over, for example, family, juvenile, maritime, election, commercial, immigration, military, employment, and antiterrorist matters – is not just a recent or one-way trend. Courts with special, extraordinary, or specific jurisdiction were also a feature of premodern Europe. Some tribunals, such as ecclesiastical courts, have also either disappeared or greatly diminished in significance as the

1 *See generally* SARAH SUMMERS, FAIR TRIALS: THE EUROPEAN CRIMINAL PROCEDURAL TRADITION AND THE EUROPEAN COURT OF HUMAN RIGHTS (2007) (arguing that there is a distinctive European criminal procedural tradition, but not considering how this applies to special courts).

"contemporary European institutional model"[2] has become both deeply and widely institutionalized.

The constitutions of some democratic European countries expressly provide for the creation of the kind of exceptional courts on which this collection focuses, namely those established to deal with security or public order crises. For example, Article 38(3)(1) of the Irish Constitution of 1937 states: "Special courts may be established by law for the trial of offenses in cases where it may be determined in accordance with such law that the ordinary courts are inadequate to secure the effective administration of justice, and the preservation of public peace and order." By contrast, Article 101 of the German Basic Law bans extraordinary courts, but does not define what they are. In the UK, special, exceptional or extraordinary courts can be established by legislation whenever Parliament deems it necessary to meet a particular perceived need, as in the case of the Diplock courts discussed further in this chapter and elsewhere in this collection. The European Convention on Human Rights (the Convention or ECHR) – presided over by the European Court of Human Rights (ECtHR) and the (now-defunct) European Commission of Human Rights and binding on forty-seven of Europe's forty-eight states – fails even to mention exceptional courts and their synonyms. It cannot, therefore, be said to prohibit them. The core issue therefore is not whether special or extraordinary courts ought to exist in contemporary European democracies fully committed to the rule of law and human rights. It lies rather in establishing the conditions under which they are legitimate. This depends, as it does for all courts, not only on their effective integration with national democratic constitutional processes, but also on their adherence to the ECHR. The Convention's main contribution is to require all courts to comply with the fair-trial standards provided by Article 6, which concern both how they are constituted and the

2 Steven Greer, The European Convention on Human Rights: Achievements, Problems and Prospects 317 (2006).

procedures they follow.[3] Article 5 of the ECHR also provides, among other things, a set of pretrial due process standards – including those relating to arrest, detention, and charging with a criminal offense – relevant to all criminal courts, including those with special jurisdiction.

Three types of exceptional court germane to the central theme of this collection have featured in the Strasbourg jurisprudence: courts staffed by military judges trying civilians for crime; courts staffed by a mixture of military and nonmilitary judges trying civilians for crime; and special antiterrorist criminal courts staffed by nonmilitary judges trying civilians for terrorist offenses. In Europe, the trial of civilians by military judges or a combination of military and nonmilitary judges has effectively been an issue only in Turkey, where their independence and impartiality have been contested. The compliance of some special civilian antiterrorist criminal courts with the right to fair trial has been considered by the Strasbourg institutions in relation to Ireland and the United Kingdom. The Strasbourg institutions do not appear ever to have considered whether or not the Convention permits the trial by military tribunals of alleged foreign enemy combatants seized on the battlefield in foreign wars. Before considering these three types of exceptional court in more detail some discussion of context is required.

1. The European Convention on Human Rights

The ECHR, the most celebrated achievement of the Council of Europe, was established by ten western European liberal democracies in 1949 to serve four principal objectives at the onset of the Cold War. First, it provided a statement of common values contrasting sharply with Soviet-style communism, hence the ECHR's almost exclusive focus on civil and political rights. Second, it was intended to contribute to the prevention of

3 For a discussion of the idea of fair criminal trial as a human right, see Ian Langford, *Fair Trial: The History of an Idea*, 8 J. HUM. RTS. 37 (2009); SUMMERS, *supra* note 1; David Harris, *The Right to a Fair Trial in Criminal Proceedings as a Human Right*, 16 INT'L & COMP. L.Q. 352 (1967).

another war between Western European states and, third, to reenforce a sense of common identity should the Cold War become an active armed conflict. Fourth, it established an "early warning" device by which a drift toward authoritarianism in any member state could be detected via complaints from other states to independent transnational judicial institutions in Strasbourg. This function was also itself inextricably linked to the prevention of war, since the slide toward World War II suggested the rise of authoritarian regimes in Europe made the peace and security of the continent more precarious. By the 2000s, all but one of Europe's forty-eight states (Belarus) had become members of the Council of Europe. Twenty-seven, including several former communist states, now also belong to the European Union, the principal function of which is to encourage economic integration.

The ECHR opened for signature in 1950. Since then fourteen Protocols have either added further rights, optional for member states, or, with one temporary exception, universal changes in procedure. The most significant development over the past half-century has been the eclipsing of the interstate process by individual applications. Although there have been only two dozen or so of the former in the Convention's entire history,[4] individual applications, 95 percent of which are rejected as inadmissible, now exceed 65,000 a year.[5] More than 90 percent of the Court's judgments result in a finding of at least one violation,[6] and between 1959

4 *See, e.g.*, Protocol No. 14 to the Convention for the Protection of Human Rights and Fundamental Freedoms, Amending the Control System of the Convention: Explanatory Report, ¶ 11, May 13, 2004, C.E.T.S. 194.

5 For example, out of the total number of applications allocated to a judicial formation between November 1998 and December 2010, only 4 percent were declared admissible, European Court of Human Rights, Annual Report 2010, 155, available at http://www.echr.coe.int/NR/rdonlyres/CCA6D671-912C-4EBD-89F8-58852F783A76/0/2010_Rapport_Annuel_EN.pdf; European Court of Human Rights, Annual Report 2012 – Provisional Version, 154, available at http://www.echr.coe.int/NR/rdonlyres/9A8CE219-E94F-47AE-983C-B4F6E4FCE03C/0/2012_Rapport_Annuel_EN.pdf.

6 European Court of Human Rights, *Violation by Article and by State 1959-2011*, available at http://www.echr.coe.int/NR/rdonlyres/2B783BFF-39C9-455C-B7C7-F821056BF32A/0/TABLEAU_VIOLATIONS_EN_2011.pdf; Annual Report 2012,

and 2011, some 45 percent of judgments in which a violation was found concerned breaches of the right to fair trial under Article 6.[7]

The jurisprudence of the Strasbourg institutions, which now includes nearly 16,000 judgments, has several distinctive characteristics. First, it is limited to declaring whether or not the ECHR has been violated and does not annul offending domestic law or policy. Although compensation may be awarded, the Court cannot otherwise remedy the consequences of violation, for example by overturning convictions. Nor does it generally specify how the breach should be corrected. However, in recent years, "pilot judgments" have increasingly done so for systemic violations affecting thousands of potential victims, albeit in very general and schematic terms.[8] The lack of a doctrinal tradition and formal doctrine of precedent, together with the fact that complaints range across forty-seven legal systems, make the Court's judgments highly fact- and state-specific. Finally, a degree of discretion ("margin of appreciation"), which varies according to Convention provision and context, is permitted to states in implementing Convention rights.

Article 6 of the ECHR is the principal provision for present purposes. Article 6(1) provides that, in the determination of civil rights and obligations or any criminal charge, everyone is entitled to a fair and (subject to some limited exceptions) public hearing, within a reasonable time by an independent and impartial tribunal established by law. Article 6(2) provides that everyone charged with a criminal offense has the right to be presumed innocent until proven guilty according to law. Article 6(3) provides a set of minimum due process rights, including a right to be informed promptly and in an intelligible language of the nature

153, *ibid*. 'Judgments on the merits' refers to 'Judgments finding at least one violation' plus 'Judgments finding no violation'.

7 European Court of Human Rights, *Overview 1959–2011*, 5, available at http://www.echr.coe.int/NR/rdonlyres/8031883C-6F90-4A5E-A979-2EC5273B38AC/0/APERCU_19592011_EN.pdf.

8 Philip Leach, et al., Responding to Systematic Human Rights Violations: An Analysis of "Pilot Judgments" of the European Court of Human Rights and their Impact at National Level (2010).

and cause of the accusation, to adequate time and facilities to prepare a defense, and to call, examine, and cross-examine witnesses under the same conditions as those of the prosecution. Other implicit rights have been derived from express Article 6 rights, such as the right to equality of arms and the right not to be tried on unfairly obtained evidence.[9] Under the derogation provision in Article 15, any or all of these guarantees can be suspended "in time of war or other public emergency threatening the life of the nation . . . to the extent strictly required by the exigencies of the situation," provided such measures are not inconsistent with a given state's other obligations under international law.

The jurisprudence of the Strasbourg institutions on exceptional courts has largely been concerned with their independence and impartiality. In *Campbell and Fell v. United Kingdom*[10] (not itself a case concerning such courts), the ECtHR held that in determining whether a court is independent of both the executive and the parties, consideration must be given to the manner by which members are appointed, the duration of their term of office, the existence of guarantees against outside pressures, and whether there is also an appearance of independence. Independence and impartiality are interwoven concepts, but are arguably not as sharply distinguished in the Strasbourg jurisprudence as they might be. "Independence" refers to the character of the judicial system and denotes its structural separation and the appearance of separation from other public institutions, particularly the executive. Because it would be neither possible nor desirable for courts to be entirely insulated from other public institutions, including the government, it is, however, a relative rather than an absolute characteristic. For example, although the ECtHR generally does not approve of renewable terms of judicial office – since they create possible opportunities subtly to influence career-conscious judges – appointment by the executive is permitted provided judges are

9 David Harris et al., Law of the European Convention on Human Rights 246–71 (2d ed. 2009).

10 7 Eur. H.R. Rep. 165, para. 78 (1985).

free from interference when carrying out their functions. Judicial independence also hinges on the provision of effective practical guarantees against outside pressure (although not necessarily formally prescribed by law), immunity from dismissal at executive discretion, protection from being subject to governmental instruction about how adjudication should be conducted, the exclusion of the executive from the sentencing tariff, and the capacity to make decisions binding even on government. "Impartiality," on the other hand, refers to the integrity of the judicial process and the need to avoid the risk of actual and/or apparent personal judicial bias toward either party. Unlike independence, impartiality is, therefore, an absolute standard as not even the slightest whiff of partisanship is tolerable. Therefore, although impartiality is compromised by a lack of judicial independence, a structurally independent tribunal may nevertheless fail to be impartial for other contingent reasons.

2. Criminal Trials of Civilians by Military Judges in Turkey

In the Council of Europe, criminal trials of civilians by military courts staffed by military personnel or a mixture of military and nonmilitary judges effectively existed only in Turkey, until the practice was abolished at the beginning of the twenty-first century.[11] These courts derived from the unique history and profile of the Turkish armed forces in national public life. While every other Council of Europe state regards its armed forces as a threat to the integrity of the state and democratic politics unless kept under strict civilian control, Turkey's armed forces see themselves, and are seen by the secular political establishment, as the ultimate custodians of these very values. This is the result of a uniquely authoritarian,

11 In *Martin v. United Kingdom*, the ECtHR condemned as a violation of Article 6 the trial for murder of a civilian by a military court. At the material time, the accused had been living in Germany with his family including his father, a solider serving with the British army. In accordance with the North Atlantic Treaty Organization Status of Forces Agreement 1951, he was subject to Army jurisdiction rather than that of the German courts. 44 Eur. H. R. Rep. 652 (2007).

centralist, and militaristic process of modernization and democratization following the dismemberment of the Ottoman empire in the aftermath of the First World War. At its inception in 1924, the modern Turkish constitutional vision was expressed by the "six arrows of Kemalism" – nationalism, secularism, republicanism, populism, statism, and reformism – which the armed forces generally still take to be their particular responsibility to preserve and protect.[12]

(a) Trial of Civilians by Courts Staffed Exclusively by Military Personnel

The criminal trial of civilians by military courts in peacetime was abolished in Turkey on July 30, 2003, prior to being condemned by the ECtHR in *Ergin*.[13] The applicant was a newspaper editor who, in September 1997, published an article critical of the ceremony marking the departure of conscripts on military service. He was charged with incitement to evade military service, tried, found guilty, and sentenced by two military judges and an army officer on the General Staff Court. Having had his appeal dismissed by the Military Court of Cassation in February 1999, the applicant complained to Strasbourg that his right to freedom of expression under Article 10 of the ECHR had been breached, and that his right to fair trial under Article 6 had been violated because the trial court had not been independent or impartial. The ECtHR unanimously upheld the petition on both grounds.

In considering the Article 6 complaint, the Court reiterated the familiar *Campbell and Fell* criteria outlined earlier. Impartiality had to be considered objectively, which meant ascertaining if sufficient guarantees had been afforded to eliminate suspicion that the tribunal that tried the applicant lacked this element. Although the trial of civilians by

12 Chris Rumford, *Resisting Globalization? Turkey-EU Relations and Human and Political Rights in the Context of Cosmopolitan Democratization*, 18 INT'L SOC. 379, 381–83 (2003).

13 *Ergin v. Turkey* (No. 6) 47 Eur. H. R. Rep. 829, (2008).

military judges alone does not appear to have been upheld in any case in the Strasbourg jurisprudence, the ECtHR nevertheless stated that the Convention does not absolutely prohibit it in all circumstances. In *Ergin*, the ECtHR also noted that international developments over the previous decade confirmed a trend toward the exclusion of criminal jurisdiction by military judges over civilians, and that the constitutional position of the military in democratic states must be limited to national security matters since judicial power is normally an attribute of civil institutions. As such, it held that criminal jurisdiction of military courts over civilians requires particularly careful scrutiny, can only be justified in very exceptional circumstances, and demands compelling justifications in addition to a clear and foreseeable legal basis substantiated in each case. It is not sufficient for national law to allocate certain offenses to military courts in abstracto. The ECtHR added that trial of civilians by military judges for offenses against the army itself could, as in this case, give rise to particular concerns about the impartiality of the proceedings because judges could readily identify with one of the parties. As the applicant (a civilian) had no duty of loyalty to the army, any apprehensions he might have had about appearing before military judges were understandable and he might legitimately have feared partisanship on the part of the General Staff Court. Ultimately, therefore, the applicant's doubts about independence and impartiality were objectively justified and his right to fair trial had been breached.

However, despite the substantive result in *Ergin*, it is not clear in what circumstances criminal trials of civilians by courts staffed entirely by military personnel could be justified in contemporary Europe. It is difficult to imagine anything short of derogation under Article 15 sufficing. But even in such circumstances it would be difficult both to envisage how the "strictly required by the exigencies" test would be satisfied and to identify the added value such a court would bring to the proceedings. Even 9/11 and its aftermath have not produced a crisis in Europe that credibly fulfills these requirements.

(b) Trial of Civilians by Courts Staffed by Military and Nonmilitary Judges

Turkey was also effectively the only state in Europe to conduct trials of civilians for terrorist and non-terrorist offenses by mixed National (or State) Security Courts (NSCs), staffed by a military and two nonmilitary judges. In 1999, following constitutional and legislative amendments, the military judge was replaced by a civilian judge, and in 2004 NSCs were abolished entirely. In *Incal v. Turkey*,[14] the ECtHR considered the compatibility of the pre-1999 arrangements with the ECHR. Local leaders of the Izmir section of the People's Labor Party, including the applicant, were prosecuted, tried, and convicted by the Izmir NSC for spreading separatist propaganda capable of inciting crime and resistance to the government through racist language. An application had been made for permission to distribute leaflets criticizing a local authority for allegedly intending to "drive the Kurds out of the cities" by cracking down on small-scale illegal trading and the spread of squatters' camps. The court rejected the prosecution's submission that these were offenses to which the Prevention of Terrorism Act applied. The applicant petitioned the ECtHR, which unanimously held that his right to freedom of expression under Article 10 ECHR had been breached, and, by a majority of twelve to eight, that Article 6(1) had also been violated.[15]

The Turkish government cited the expertise of military judges in law enforcement against organized crime and armed groups as a justification for their inclusion on NSCs. However, the majority of the ECtHR held that this was not the issue. It had to consider instead whether the applicant had been accorded a fair trial. Public confidence was also at stake. But although the applicant's opinion about the fairness of his trial was

14 *Incal v. Turkey* 29 Eur. H. R. Rep. 449 (2000).

15 This verdict has been confirmed in a string of subsequent cases against Turkey. In *Öcalan v. Turkey*, for example, a majority of the Grand Chamber of the ECtHR held that the applicant's right to a fair trial had been violated by the participation of a military judge in the preliminary stages of his trial by an NSC even though this judge had been replaced by a nonmilitary judge thereafter. 41 Eur. H. R. Rep. 985 (2005).

important, it was not decisive. The critical question was whether doubts about the impartiality and independence of the tribunal in question were objectively justified.

Declaring that the questions of independence and impartiality would be decided together, the ECtHR also distinguished two tests with respect to impartiality. The first concerned the personal convictions of a particular judge; the second required guarantees to be offered sufficient to exclude any doubts about his or her impartiality. There was no dispute that only the second of these was relevant here, nor about the independence and impartiality of the nonmilitary judges. The ECtHR noted that NSCs had first been lawfully established in 1973 to deal with offenses affecting the country's territorial integrity and national unity, its democratic regime, and its internal and external security. The independence and impartiality of military judges serving on these courts were guaranteed by the constitution and law, and they had the same training as civilian judges. No public or other authority could direct or seek to influence them in the discharge of their judicial functions. They sat on NSCs as individuals, were generally not removable from office, and could not be forced to take early retirement. Their rights and obligations, together with their relationship with the military authorities, were also regulated by law.

The majority of the ECtHR, however, identified some features of the role and position of military judges on NSCs raising doubts about their independence and impartiality. As military service personnel, they were part of the service chain of command ultimately taking orders from the executive. They were subject to military discipline and assessment reports, and served on NSCs for four years subject to renewal. Decisions pertaining to their appointment were to a great extent taken by the army's administrative authorities and the Court of Cassation did not have full jurisdiction over NSC verdicts. The majority of the ECtHR therefore held that these factors undermined the appearance of independence and public confidence and the applicant had legitimate cause to fear that the NSC that tried him might have been unduly influenced.

The eight judges dissenting on the Article 6(1) complaint noted that, in other cases, the ECtHR had accepted that the domestic law of many European states legitimately permitted experts, whose knowledge was desirable or necessary, to sit alongside professional judges provided independence and impartiality were maintained. They also pointed out that judges on any court are subject to assessment and appointment decisions by nonjudicial authorities. Nor, they argued, did the term of office of military judges on NSCs give cause for concern. The ECtHR had held in other circumstances that three-year judicial terms may be sufficient and, at the end of an unrenewed four-year term, military judges on NSCs remained military judges for the remainder of their careers. As there were also constitutional safeguards, the minority concluded that there was no objective justification for whatever doubts there may have been about the independence and impartiality of military judges on NSCs.

The core issue in the debate over the legitimacy of the criminal trial of civilians by military or mixed military-civilian courts concerns the added value a military background brings. As a matter of principle there can be no objection to courts with a precise, legally defined, special, or extraordinary jurisdiction. Every modern legal system distinguishes between civil, criminal, and administrative courts and in most there are also more specialized tribunals. It cannot be denied, therefore, that judges who staff any court should have expertise appropriate to its jurisdiction, possibly requiring particular experience and/or training. There is also a clear trend in modern, democratic systems that all professional judges should be drawn from a pool of legal professionals with a common, general legal training before specialization. If this is true of both military and civilian judges, the distinction between them may matter less than might first appear. However, it is not clear what distinctive technical expertise legally trained military judges bring to the trial of the kind of offense of which the applicant in *Incal* was convicted. Although military judges may have a distinctive technical expertise relevant to antiterrorist policing, it is not at all clear what they bring to antiterrorist adjudication. At the very least, how such adjudication differs in technical respects, particularly from the adjudication of other kinds of serious organized crime, has not been clearly specified.

3. Trials of Civilians by Special Antiterrorist Criminal Courts Staffed by Nonmilitary Judges

In the 1970s and 1980s, Germany, Italy, Turkey, and France experienced ideological terrorism from the far left and far right, while from the 1970s to late 1990s, secessionist or nationalist terrorism also occurred in Southeastern Turkey, the United Kingdom (particularly in Northern Ireland), the Republic of Ireland, and Corsica. Despite several cease-fires, the most promising announced in September 2010, it is not yet clear if the violent campaign conducted since the early 1970s by the Basque separatist organization Euskadi Ta Askatasuna (ETA) is finally over. In addition to the trial of terrorist and other offenses in Turkey by NSCs, special civilian antiterrorist courts were also introduced in Northern Ireland, the Republic of Ireland, Spain, France, and to a more limited extent in Germany.[16] Although some pretrial elements of antiterrorist law enforcement in these states were condemned as incompatible with the ECHR by the judicial institutions at Strasbourg, their antiterrorist courts were not.[17] Since the early 2000s, European states have also been exposed to Al Qaeda-type terrorism.

The Strasbourg institutions have considered special civilian antiterrorist courts in cases brought against the Republic of Ireland and the United Kingdom with respect to Northern Ireland. As already indicated, Article 38(3) of the Constitution of Ireland 1937 empowers the legislature to establish special courts with wide-ranging powers when "the ordinary courts are inadequate to secure the effective administration of justice

16 ANTONIO VERCHER, TERRORISM IN EUROPE: AN INTERNATIONAL COMPARATIVE LEGAL ANALYSIS 336, 341–50 (1992).

17 *See generally* Mary Arden, *Meeting the Challenge of Terrorism: The Experience of English and other Courts*, 80 AUSTL. L.J. 818 (2006); Colin Warbrick, *The Principles of the European Convention on Human Rights and the Response of States to Terrorism*, 3 Eur. Hum. Rts. L. Rev. 287 (2002).

and the preservation of public peace and order." The Special Criminal Court (SCC), established by §35(2) of Ireland's Offences Against the State Act 1939 (OASA), is operationalized when the government publishes a proclamation that, as the Constitution also requires, the ordinary courts are "inadequate to secure the effective administration of justice and the preservation of public peace and order." Section 39 of the OASA provides for the constitution of SCCs, which were introduced for the first time in 1939 and remained in existence until 1962, then lapsed for a decade before being revived in 1972 in response to "the Troubles" in Northern Ireland. Since 1984, a panel of nine judges, which may include an officer of the Defense Forces not below the rank of commandant, is appointed by the government. There must be an uneven number of no less than three judges on the bench for any given trial, but since 1972, all judges serving on SCCs have in fact been judges or former judges of the ordinary courts.[18]

The European Commission of Human Rights considered the compatibility of the SCC with the ECHR in two applications. Although *X and Y v. Ireland*[19] was ruled inadmissible for reasons largely unconnected with the character of the court in question, the Commission nevertheless accepted the government's submission that it was an independent and impartial tribunal established by law. However, having failed to persuade the domestic courts that the SCC that tried them was not independent, and that the OASA was unconstitutional, the applicants in *Eccles, McPhillips and McShane v. Ireland*[20] complained to the Commission that their right to fair trial under Article 6(1) of the ECHR had been breached. They argued that SCC judges lacked independence, both because they were removable by the government at will and because their salaries were at the discretion of the Minister for Finance.

18 *See* Fergal F. Davis, The History and Development of the Special Criminal Court: 1922–2005 133 (2007); Seosamh O. Longaigh, Emergency Law in Independent Ireland: 1922–1948 (2006).

19 App. No. 8299/78, 22 Eur. Comm'n H.R. Dec. & Rep. 51 (1981).

20 App. No. 12839/87, 59 Eur. Comm'n H.R. Dec. & Rep. 212 (1988).

The application was, however, ruled inadmissible on the grounds of being "manifestly ill founded." In explaining how it reached this conclusion, the Commission began with the familiar observation that the test was not the independence of SCCs in the abstract, but whether the applicants had been tried by an independent and impartial court. Citing the familiar *Campbell and Fell* criteria, the Commission stated that the inability of the executive to remove judges during their term of office was a corollary of independence. Moreover, it observed that because the SCC is not a permanent court, the rotation of judges was inevitable and unobjectionable provided it was for administrative and not improper reasons. The Commission accepted that there was no evidence that the government improperly used the power of removal to interfere with trials by SCCs. The replacement of five members of the court in 1986, one of whom (Mr. Flynn) had been a judge in the applicants' case, was intended to ensure that the SCC was staffed by judges from ordinary courts. Moreover, Mr. Flynn was over the normal retirement age. The Commission also attached importance to the fact that the SCC that tried the applicants had been composed of experienced judges, namely the President of the High Court, a Circuit Judge, and a former President of the District Court. It observed that the SCC applied the same rules of evidence as ordinary criminal courts and that its judgments could be appealed in the same way. In the Commission's opinion, there was no evidence of any attempt to influence the SCC or undermine its independence by abuse of the remunerative discretion and, in any case, any attempt to do so would have been open to restraint as unlawful, ultra vires, or unconstitutional by the regular higher Irish courts. Regrettably, the Commission did not consider whether or not the SCC retained the appearance of independence.

In 1973, as part of its response to the violent conflict there, the British government introduced to Northern Ireland special antiterrorist, single-judge, nonjury "Diplock" courts – named after the British judge whose inquiry recommended them – to deal with the perceived problems of juror intimidation and risk of improper acquittals of Protestant/unionist defendants by predominantly Protestant/unionist juries, and also to provide an alternative to internment without trial.[21] Because the Convention does not provide a right to trial by jury, the absence of the jury from the Diplock courts could not directly raise a compliance issue. The ECtHR has also confirmed that the Diplock courts do not otherwise inherently violate the Convention. In *Murray (John) v. United Kingdom*,[22] the applicant complained that his right to fair trial had been breached by having been deprived of legal advice for forty-eight hours while in police custody, and by the fact that the convicting Diplock judge had, as authorized by statute, drawn an adverse inference from his silence in police questioning and at trial. The ECtHR upheld the first of these complaints by a majority of twelve to seven, and the second – the most relevant to the issues under discussion in this chapter – by a majority of fourteen to five. It was pointed out that the right to silence, although an integral part of the general right to a fair trial under Article 6(1), and the privilege against self-incrimination under Article 6(2), are not absolute. In the circumstances of a given case a balance had to be struck between basing guilt solely on silence and not drawing any inferences from it at all. The ECtHR noted that refusing to answer police questions or to testify were not in themselves offenses, that there was other strong evidence against the applicant, and the Diplock trial system provided safeguards against unfairness stemming from such silences and refusals to testify. These included, but were not limited to, police and judicial warnings about the possible adverse effects of remaining silent; the need for a prima facie case independent of silence; the fact that guilt could not be based on silence alone; that, in addition to his or her silence the other evidence against the accused called for an explanation; that only common sense inferences from silence could properly be drawn at the judge's discretion;

21 Northern Ireland (Emergency Provisions) Act 1973, c. 53, §2; *see also* John Jackson, *Vicious and Virtuous Cycles in Prosecuting Terrorism: The Diplock Court Experience*, in this volume; Steven Greer and Anthony White, Abolishing the Diplock Courts: The Case for Restoring Jury Trial to Scheduled Offences in Northern Ireland (1986).

22 22 Eur. H.R. Rep. 29 (1996).

and that the trial was conducted by an experienced judge required to give reasons, including for inferences drawn from silence and the weight attached to them. None of the dissenters doubted the independence and impartiality of the trial court.

In a 1984 study, Dorff acknowledged that "in many respects trials in the 'Diplock' courts are in accordance with . . . fundamental principles safeguarding the right to fair trial," but expressed concern about the impact of certain pretrial features of the wider Diplock system, particularly pressures on suspects to confess to the police.[23] Some of these have been tested in Strasbourg,[24] but because they are not integral to the character of the Diplock courts, they are not considered further here. National debates about the Diplock courts and the Irish SCCs have, in any case, focused less on the Convention conception of fairness and much more on alleged weaknesses in the justifications for their establishment and the impact the removal of the jury has on the complex (mostly common law) rules of evidence and procedure that generally assume jury trial. Concerns have also been expressed that trials of terrorist offenses by judge(s) alone are less publicly accountable than trial by jury.

In the ECHR context, four conclusions germane to the present discussion can be drawn about special antiterrorist criminal courts staffed by nonmilitary judges. First, they are not inherently a violation of the right to fair trial under Article 6, nor are they, by nature, incompatible with the Convention in any other respect. Second, they can, therefore, be introduced without an Article 15 derogation. Third, Strasbourg's judicial institutions have, however, required the independence and impartiality of such courts to be guaranteed by safeguards alternative to the more regular ones that their establishment tends to bypass. Finally, even the

23 Douwe Korff, The Diplock Courts in Northern Ireland: A Fair Trial? 93–100 (1984).

24 *See, e.g.*, *McVeigh, O'Neill and Evans v. United Kingdom*, 25 Eur. Comm'n H.R. Dec. & Rep. 15 (1981); *Fox, Campbell and Hartley v. United Kingdom*, 13 Eur. H.R. Rep. 157 (1991); *Brogan v. United Kingdom*, 11 Eur. H.R. Rep. 117 (1989); *Brannigan v. McBride*, 17 Eur. H.R. Rep. 539 (1994).

fulfillment of this requirement does not entirely settle the debate about the legitimacy of such courts, as the grounds for their creation, their operation – particularly in common law systems – and whether or not (in the case of the SCC) they preserve the appearance of independence may not have been adequately considered in Strasbourg.

Conclusion

Several conclusions can be drawn from this brief study. First, because the ECHR does not mention special, extraordinary, or exceptional courts, it cannot obviously be said to prohibit them. However, all courts must comply with Article 6 fair-trial requirements unless these are suspended under a valid Article 15 derogation. Broadly speaking, Article 6(1) requires courts to be established by law and to be independent and impartial, while the procedure they follow in criminal proceedings must also adhere to the due process guarantees provided by Articles 6(2) and (3). Impartiality is an absolute standard in that no judicial partisanship can be tolerated. But independence is variable and context-specific because no court can be totally isolated from its surrounding political environment. Determining whether the other constituents of fairness have been met is not an objective matter, either. As the Strasbourg institutions themselves have repeatedly made clear, however, their responsibility is confined to deciding if the court that tried a given applicant, rather than the type of which it may be a specific example, complies with the Article 6 requirements. The main Convention-related complaints about exceptional courts established for the criminal trial of civilians have concerned their independence and impartiality. Cases heard by the Strasbourg institutions have not conclusively established that courts staffed entirely by military judges for this purpose will always fail these tests, even without derogation. However, there is no known case of such a tribunal having been found Convention-compliant. The difference of opinion between the majority and minority in *Incal* over the criminal trial of civilians by mixed courts staffed by military and nonmilitary personnel is also no longer of any practical significance, as Turkey's NSCs – effectively the only such courts in a Council of Europe state – have been abolished. However, the minority view lacks credibility, not least because of its failure to specify the contribution a military judge adds to the proceedings that could not be equally provided by a civilian counterpart. The fact that military and mixed courts trying civilians have disappeared from contemporary Europe is itself testimony to the difficulty of finding an adequate justification. The United Nations Human Rights Committee similarly requires that, where states seek to try civilians by military court or other special tribunal, objective reasons must be provided to explain why nonmilitary courts could not be used, and to confirm that the due process standards of Article 14 of the International Covenant on Civil and Political Rights are observed.[25]

Special criminal courts staffed by nonmilitary judges for the trial of civilians charged with terrorist offenses have been established in the UK, Ireland, Spain, France, and Germany. Not all of these have been tested for Convention compliance by the Strasbourg institutions and most are now obsolete. Two issues relating to the fairness of all types of special court considered here – their rationales and whether they can be considered as fair as the courts they effectively replace – have, however, not been fully considered in the limited Strasbourg jurisprudence on special antiterrorist criminal courts staffed entirely by nonmilitary judges. It is prima facie plausible that, in some circumstances, such courts may be necessary because of the threat terrorist organizations would otherwise pose to ordinary criminal courts trying such offenses. But the empirical basis of this claim needs to be critically evaluated on a country-by-country basis, and, if they can be justified, such courts must be as fair as possible, particularly as far as distinguishing clearly between terrorist and

25 *See* Evelyne Schmid, *A Few Comments on a Comment: The UN Human Rights Committee's General Comment No. 32 on Article 14 of the ICCPR and the Question of Civilians Tried by Military Courts*, 14 INT'L J. HUM. RTS. 1058 (2010).

non-terrorist offenses is concerned. Ultimately, determining whether a special antiterrorist criminal court staffed entirely by nonmilitary judges is fair will depend on how the ECtHR interprets Article 6 standards in the specific national contexts, a question of fine judgment rather than objective determination.

17 The Legitimacy Deficit of Exceptional International Criminal Jurisdiction

Yuval Shany

AD HOC INTERNATIONAL CRIMINAL TRIBUNALS HAVE BEEN resorted to with increased frequency in the last eighteen years. Following the early precedents set by the creation of the International Criminal Tribunal for the Former Yugoslavia (ICTY) and the International Criminal Tribunal for Rwanda (ICTR), the international community has supported the creation of hybrid tribunals – staffed by both international and domestic personnel and applying both international and domestic law – with relation to crimes that occurred in Sierra Leone, Cambodia, and Lebanon. Internationalized criminal tribunals were also created in connection with the international community's involvement in East Timor, Bosnia and Herzegovina, and Kosovo. In all of these cases, the international response has been exceptional in nature: institutions were created alongside the ordinary judicial system for a limited period of time, in response to special catastrophic events, for the purpose of handling a select category of past crimes, which were removed, fully or partly, from the ordinary criminal jurisdiction of national courts.

Although constituting a permanent forum of criminal adjudication, the International Criminal Court (ICC) also exercises its jurisdiction in an "episodic" manner – following a Security Council referral or the referral of situations by the territorial or national states, in other words the states in whose territory the crimes have occurred or whose nationals committed them. Hence, it operates in some respects in ways not dissimilar to the manner of operation of special ad hoc or hybrid international criminal tribunals, which are similarly established pursuant to a Security Council resolution or with the consent of the territorial or nationality state. Even the exercise of universal jurisdiction by individual states has strong features of "special" jurisdiction, as the actual practice of states in this field tends to be highly exceptional in nature.[1] Given the irregular and less-than-universal coverage of international criminal jurisdiction, the initiation of international criminal procedures through new or existing judicial institutions is likely to continue to pose attributes of exceptionality in the foreseeable future.

In this chapter, I argue that the exceptional exercise of jurisdiction by international criminal tribunals raises a number of legitimacy concerns (Part 1). The exceptional nature of such procedures may lead to actual or perceived selectivity in criminal law application that might be motivated by political rather than legal considerations. In some cases, the unexpected invocation of international criminal adjudication may also generate retroactivity problems. In Part 2, I explain how these legitimacy problems may adversely affect the effectiveness of international criminal tribunals – in particular, limit state cooperation with them and erode their ability to trigger parallel national proceedings. As a result, I propose in Part 3 that ad hoc international criminal tribunals and other exceptional international criminal jurisdictions consider embracing two corrective strategies that may reduce their legitimacy deficit: a robust application of the principle of complementarity and a prudent application of substantive international criminal law. Both strategies will underscore the last-resort nature of exceptional international criminal jurisdiction, and may render

1 *See, e.g.*, Rudolph E. Brandes, *Who's afraid of Universal Jurisdiction? The Fujimori Case*, 15 Sw. J. L. & Trade Am. 123, 137 (2008) ("Finding cases where universal jurisdiction has been applied successfully is generally very rare"); Christopher "Kip" Hale, *Does the Evolution of International Criminal Law end with the ICC? The "Roaming ICC": A Model International Criminal Court for a State-Centric World of International Law*, 35 Denv. J. Int'l L. & Pol'y 429, 439 (2007) ("Extremely rare is the situation where a State uses universal jurisdiction to gain jurisdiction over a defendant in order to apply an international law exclusively").

its application more effective. In the long run, improving the of international criminal adjudication through reducing its legitimacy deficit may facilitate the strengthening of regular judicial institutions, such as the ICC. Such institutions would then be able to utilize their powers more effectively even in borderline cases, where the facts, law, or need for international judicial intervention are open to a serious challenge.

1. The Legitimacy-Deficit Problem

The exceptional exercise of jurisdiction by special international criminal tribunals may raise difficult due process challenges from the point of view of the individuals put on trial before such fora. Because the substantive norms employed by ad hoc international criminal tribunals and other forms of exceptional international criminal jurisdiction derive typically from customary international law – often codified only in a partial manner when the alleged crimes have occurred – problems of legal uncertainty and compatibility with the *nullum crimen sine lege* principle may arise.[2] In addition, the procedural rules governing the criminal process before special international tribunals often differ in critical respects from those governing criminal trials in the defendant's own local legal system, and may deviate, by implication, from local perceptions of procedural fairness. Moreover, some international criminal trials, conducted by both exceptional and ordinary tribunals, are plagued by a variety of logistical problems that complicate the tribunals' ability to access certain crime scenes and secure the testimony of all relevant witnesses. Consequently, the truth-finding and ascertaining capacity of international criminal tribunals may be circumscribed.[3] The combination of a new body of law

2 *See, e.g.*, Robert Cryer, Prosecuting International Crimes: Selectivity and the International Criminal Law Regime 238–40 (2005); Susan Lamb, Nullum Crimen, Nulla Poena Sine Lege in *International Criminal Law*, in 1 The Rome Statute of the International Criminal Court: A Commentary 733 (Antonio Cassese et al. eds., 2002).

3 *See, e.g.*, Charmeyne de los Reyes, *State Cooperation and its Challenges for the International Criminal Tribunal for Rwanda*, *in* From Human Rights to International

and an unfamiliar judicial process, as well as suboptimal fact-gathering facilities may lead key constituencies to question the adequacy of the international criminal process and raise particularly strong criticism of the legitimacy of exceptional international criminal procedures.[4]

To be clear, some of the legitimacy concerns associated with the operation of ad hoc international criminal tribunals and other exceptional exercises of international jurisdiction are common to any attempt to prosecute individual suspects before exceptional criminal courts – be they national or international in nature. In particular, the very resort to exceptional substantive norms and trial procedures raises concerns of unfairness and selectivity.[5] Still, there are some unique features attendant to exceptional international criminal adjudication. Such unique features may, in fact, cut in both directions – some exacerbating and some mitigating the international procedure's legitimacy deficit.

As a consequence of the underdeveloped state of international criminal-law doctrine, the substantive criminal law and procedural norms applied by international criminal tribunals tends to be vaguer and less predictable than those applied by national courts including exceptional criminal courts.[6] This constitutes, of course, a legitimacy-detracting attribute,

CRIMINAL LAW 55, 61 (Emannuel Decaux et al. eds., 2007); Nancy Amoury Combs, *Testimonial Deficiencies and Evidentiary Uncertainties in International Criminal Trials*, 14 UCLA J. INT'L L. & FOREIGN AFF. 235 (2009).

4 *See, e.g.*, GERD OBERLEITNER, GLOBAL HUMAN RIGHTS INSTITUTIONS 39 (2007); Carrie Gustafson, *International Criminal Courts: Some Dissident Views on the Continuation of War by Penal Means*, 21 HOUS. J. INT'L L. 51 (1998); Dominic McGoldrick, *Criminal Trials before International Tribunals: Legality and Legitimacy*, *in* THE PERMANENT INTERNATIONAL CRIMINAL COURT: LEGAL AND POLICY ISSUES 9 (Dominic McGoldrick et al. eds., 2004).

5 *See, e.g.*, Robert S. Litt and Wells C. Bennett, *Better Rules for Terrorism Trials, in* LEGISLATING THE WAR ON TERROR: AN AGENDA FOR REFORM 124, 143 (Benjamin Wittes ed., 2009); Gregory S. McNeal, *Institutional Legitimacy and Counterterrorism Trials*, 43 U. RICH. L. REV. 967, 1005 (2009); Michael A. Newton, *Some Observations on the Future of US Military Commissions*, 42 CASE W. RES. J. INT'L L. 151, 162 (2009).

6 *See, e.g.*, Kai Ambos, *Remarks on the General Part of International Criminal Law*, 4 J. INT'L CRIM. JUST. 660, 662 (2006) (discussing the underdeveloped stage of international criminal law's rule of attribution); Antonio Cassese, *The ICTY: A Living and Vital Reality*, 2 J. INT'L CRIM. JUST. 585, 590 (2004) ("This need [for law development and interpretation] is all the more notable in the area of international criminal law – a

which exacerbates the fairness and retroactivity problems associated with exceptional criminal adjudication. At the same time, the broad international support that international criminal tribunals enjoy, and the limited jurisdictional reach of the ICC – the "ordinary" international criminal procedure to which the ad hoc international tribunals should have constituted an exception – may counter some of the suspicion and distrust, which attaches to the operation of exceptional tribunals at the domestic level.[7] In a legal system such as international law, where ordinary criminal courts underperform, resort to exceptional criminal tribunals may be more understandable – in fact, inevitable – and would consequently tend to attract greater legitimacy from relevant constituencies.[8]

There is, however, another aspect of the exceptionality of international criminal adjudication: The relationship between the special international criminal process and particularly affected states. Although international criminal tribunals target individuals for prosecution, the dividing line between allegations of individual criminal responsibility and allocation of state responsibility for violating international law is often vague. This blurring of responsibilities is accentuated by the tendency of international criminal tribunals to focus almost exclusively on top-level decision makers, effectively rendering the criminal proceedings an indirect form of legal assessment of important state policies.[9]

corpus of rules that is still unclear and underdeveloped"); Mark Drumbl, *A Hard Look at the Soft Theory of International Criminal Law, in* THE THEORY AND PRACTICE OF INTERNATIONAL CRIMINAL LAW: ESSAYS IN HONOR OF M. CHERIF BASSIOUNI 1 (Leila Nadya Sadat and Michael P. Scharf eds., 2008)

7 *See, e.g.*, Jeffrey S. Becker, *A Legal War on Terrorism: Extending* New York v. Quarles *and the Departure from Enemy Combatant Designations*, 53 DEPAUL L. REV. 831, 871; (2003); Katherine Flanagan-Hyde, *The Public's Right of Access to the Military Tribunals and Trials of Enemy Combatants*, 48 ARIZ. L. REV. 585, 607 (2006); Frédéric Mégret, *Justice in Times of Violence*, 14 EUR. J. INT'L L. 327, 335 (2003).

8 *See* John M. Bickers, *Too Little, Too Late? Why President Obama's Well-Intentioned Reforms of the Military Commissions May not be Enough to Save Them*, 31 WHITTIER L. REV. 381, 417 (2010) ("In a regime without a regular court, all trials must by definition be conducted in ad hoc 'special' tribunals.").

9 For a discussion, *see* Yuval Shany, *Two Sides of the Same Coin? Judging Milošević and Serbia before the ICTY and ICJ*, in The MILOŠEVIĆ TRIAL – AN AUTOPSY (Timothy Waters ed., 2013) (forthcoming).

For the state concerned, the application of international criminal jurisdiction over one or more of its nationals, without its consent, might be regarded as an infringement of important legal rights attendant to notions of state sovereignty. When such criminal proceedings take place before a foreign domestic court, exercising universal or other form of extraterritorial jurisdiction, the principle of *par in parem non habet imperium* may be infringed,[10] and when the proceedings occur before an international tribunal, the consensual basis of international adjudication may be eroded.[11]

In addition, the seemingly selective decision-making process leading to the establishment of ad hoc tribunals – such as the ICTY – as well as the Security Council referral of cases to the ICC – such as in the case of Sudan – in response to some atrocious situations only exposes exceptional international criminal procedures to accusation of politicization and the application of double standards.[12] Similar concerns have been raised with regard to the selective in appearance exercise of jurisdiction by international criminal tribunals over the conduct of just some actors operating in the covered crime scene. For example, ICTY jurisdiction was applied to acts taken by local actors in the Balkans, but not NATO actors. Similarly, the ICTR applied jurisdiction over Hutu, but not Tutsi suspects. This perceived selectivity detracts from the legitimacy of

10 *See, e.g.*, Kenneth Henley, *Human Rights and the Rule of Law: Sovereignty and the International Criminal Court, in* UNIVERSAL HUMAN RIGHTS: MORAL ORDER IN A DIVIDED WORLD 173, 183 (David A. Reidy and Mortimer N. S. Sellers, eds., 2005); Mugambi Jouet, *Spain's Expanded Universal Jurisdiction to Prosecute Human Rights Abuses in Latin America, China, and Beyond*, 35 GA. J. INT'L & COMP. L. 495, 514–15 (2007).

11 For a discussion, *see* Dapo Akande, *The Jurisdiction of the International Criminal Court over Nationals of Non-Parties: Legal Basis and Limits*, 1 J. INT'L CRIM. JUST. 618, 634–40 (2003); David J. Scheffer, *Staying the Course with the International Criminal Court*, 35 CORNELL INT'L L.J. 47 n.68. (2002).

12 *See, e.g.*, M. Cherif Bassiouni, *Perspectives on International Criminal Justice*, 50 VA. J. INT'L L. 269, 307 (2010); Silvia A. Fernández de Gurmendi, *The Role of the Prosecutor, in* THE INTERNATIONAL CRIMINAL COURT: THE MAKING OF THE ROME STATUTE: ISSUES, NEGOTIATIONS, RESULTS 175, 178 (Roy S. Lee ed., 1999); Brad R. Roth, *Coming to Terms with Ruthlessness: Sovereign Equality, Global Pluralism, and the Limits of International Criminal Justice*, 8 SANTA CLARA J. INT'L L. 231, 237–38 (2010).

special international criminal procedures in the eyes of target states and key constituencies therein.[13]

These legitimacy concerns are further exacerbated by the structural limits on the independence of exceptional international criminal procedures. Because international criminal tribunals lack independent enforcement powers, their operations critically depend on state cooperation for access to evidence and witnesses and arrest and transfer of suspects. Hence, the price they could pay for upsetting the interests of certain strategically situated states could be extremely high.[14] In the same vein, the precarious budgetary situation of most international criminal tribunals leads them to de facto dependency on key funding states and UN organs, such as the Security Council. Hybrid courts are also less than fully independent in this sense because they rely on the intensive cooperation and budgetary contribution of the host state, or of the international administration of the relevant territory in which they operate. These apparent limits of the independence of special international criminal tribunals render the aforementioned concerns of selectivity, politicization, and lack of fairness more plausible and thus more harmful to the tribunals' perceived legitimacy.

In sum, it looks as if international criminal adjudicatory bodies suffer from a serious legitimacy deficit (as do other institutions of international governance).[15] It also seems that this deficit expands when international

13 *See, e.g.*, Eric D. Gordy, *Post War Guilt and Responsibility in Serbia: The Effort to Confront it and the Effort to Avoid It, in* SERBIA SINCE 1989: POLITICS AND SOCIETY UNDER MILOŠEVIĆ AND AFTER 166, 175 (Sabrina P. Ramet and Vjeran Pavlaković eds., 2005); Benjamin N. Schiff, *Universalism Meets Sovereignty at the International Criminal Court, in* NEGOTIATING SOVEREIGNTY AND HUMAN RIGHTS: ACTORS AND ISSUES IN CONTEMPORARY HUMAN RIGHTS POLITICS 59, 74 (Noha Shawki and Michaelene Cox eds., 2009).

14 For a discussion of the limits on the independence of the ICTY and ICTR vis-à-vis NATO and Rwanda, *see* Yuval Shany, *Judicial Independence as an Indicator of International Court Effectiveness: A Goal-Based Approach, in* THE CULTURE OF JUDICIAL INDEPENDENCE: CONCEPTUAL FOUNDATIONS AND PRACTICAL CHALLENGES 251 (Shimon Shetreet and Christopher Forsyth eds., 2011).

15 For a discussion of the legitimacy deficit associated with international governance, *see, e.g.*, ERIKA DE WET, THE INTERNATIONAL CONSTITUTIONAL ORDER 20–21 (2005); Daniel

criminal jurisdiction is exercised in an ad hoc or selective manner, raising concerns of high levels of politicization. As the next part of this chapter illustrates, the practical implications associated with this state of affairs in international law are somewhat different from those relating to the operation of exceptional criminal courts in the domestic sphere: whereas at the domestic level critics are primarily concerned with assessing the justice and fairness of special criminal proceedings, at the international level one should also be concerned with the impact of perceived legitimacy deficits on judicial performance. Legitimacy deficits may actually hinder the ability of international criminal tribunals to effectively perform the tasks they were entrusted with, such as ending impunity or promoting national reconciliation.[16]

2. Implications of Legitimacy Deficits for Judicial Performance

The centrality of notions of legitimacy in sustaining the effectiveness of international criminal tribunals is tied to two serious limitations afflicting their work: lack of independent enforcement powers and restricted prosecuting capacity. The lack of enforcement powers was already noted in a different context – the dependency of international criminal tribunals on states and international organizations. Arguably, cooperation with international criminal tribunals and support of their work hinges not only on a good degree of compatibility between the expected performance of such tribunals and the interests of relevant states and international organizations, it also assumes a good degree of perceived legitimacy that would "pull" key states and important international organizations toward

C. Esty, *Good Governance at the Supranational Scale: Globalizing Administrative Law*, 115 Yale L.J. 1490, 1515 (2006); Eric Stein, *International Integration and Democracy: No Love at First Sight*, 95 Am. J. Int'l L. 489, 490–91 (2001); Rüdiger Wolfrum, *Legitimacy in International Law from a Legal Perspective: Some Introductory Considerations*, *in* Legitimacy in International Law 1, 5 (Rüdiger Wolfrum and Volker Röben eds., 2008).

16 For a discussion, *see* Yuval Shany, *The Role of National Courts in Advancing the Goals of International Criminal Tribunals*, 103 Am. Soc'y Int'l L. Proc. 210 (2009).

cooperation and support of international criminal adjudication.[17] Thus, international criminal tribunals must walk a fine line between dependence and independence. Their ability to generate cooperation and support and to attract compliance with judicial decisions would be compromised by failure to accommodate important state interests, but also by attributing excessive weight to such interests at the expense of their perceived adherence to general principles of law, fairness, and justice – the building blocks of judicial legitimacy.[18]

Another important explanation of the unique role of legitimacy for special international criminal tribunals stems from their restricted prosecuting capacity. Given the length and high costs of international trials, even the best-funded international criminal tribunals can only simultaneously handle a handful of cases (and even this limited workload depends on the tribunals' ability to secure the detention and transfer of the accused). In fact, although the number of international criminal tribunals has grown exponentially in recent years, the number of indictments per crime scene or country situation has actually been on the decline[19] – a phenomenon that can be explained in part by the combined effect of mounting adjudication costs and "donor fatigue."[20] The number of cases per situation addressed by the ICC and foreign courts exercising universal jurisdiction is also, typically, very low. The upshot of this may

17 For a discussion of the relationship between perceptions of legitimacy and the compliance pull of international norms and institutions, *see* Thomas Franck, The Power of Legitimacy Among Nations 112 (1990).

18 For a discussion of the notion of constrained independence as potentially reflecting such a compromise formulation, *see* Laurence R. Helfer and Ann-Marie Slaughter, *Why States Create International Tribunals: A Response to Professors Posner and Yoo*, 93 Cal. L. Rev. 899, 942–44 (2005).

19 Whereas the ICTY prosecuted 161 individuals, the ICTR has tried less than half of that number (81; 10 additional suspects were indicted and not tried), the SCSL has tried 10 individuals (out of 13 indicted), and the ECCC has indicted and tried 5 individuals. The Special Tribunal for Lebanon has not tried anyone to date.

20 For a discussion, *see* Ralph Zacklin, *The Failings of Ad Hoc International Tribunals*, 2 J. Int'l Crim. Just. 541, 543 (2004); United Nations Office of the High Commissioner for Human Rights, *Rule-of-Law Tools for Post-Conflict States: Prosecution Initiatives* 7 (2006).

be that the practical importance of international criminal proceedings is mainly symbolic and catalytic: by sending a strong message of international condemnation of the atrocities that occurred, articulating the international community's demand for legal accountability, and threatening to prosecute criminal suspects in the events of state inaction they may trigger or nurture domestic and international legal and political processes that could lead to the punishing of past criminals and prevention of future crimes.[21]

The limited enforcement and prosecution capacities of international tribunals underscore the role of domestic courts – in particular, the domestic courts of states directly involved in international crimes – in combating impunity through legal means. Indeed, the philosophy underlying the operations of the ICC and completion strategy of the ICTY and ICTR is one of positive complementarity the necessity of fostering and encouraging the exercise of criminal jurisdiction by domestic courts, as a critical division-of-labor strategy. But in order to make a positive impact at the domestic level –to either directly trigger and support local trials or influence the background legal and political conditions that would eventually make such trials possible, the operation of international criminal tribunals needs to enjoy some degree of legitimacy in the eyes of the domestic constituencies.

Arguably, the legitimacy problems associated with exceptional international criminal proceedings – in particular, questions surrounding their fairness and independence– may erode the symbolic value of international criminal adjudication and decrease its long-term impact.[22]

21 *See, e.g.*, Iain Cameron, *Jurisdiction and Admissibility Issues under the ICC Statute, in* The Permanent International Criminal Court: Legal and Policy Issues 65, 93 (Dominic McGoldrick et al. eds., 2004); Laurie F. Damrosch, *Enforcing International Law Through Non-Forcible Measure*, 269 Recueil des Cours 9, 241–42 (2007); Marieke Wierda et al., *Early Reflections on Local Perceptions, Legitimacy and Legacy of the Special Tribunal for Lebanon*, 5 J. Int'l Crim. Just. 1065, 1079 (2007).

22 *See, e.g.*, Laura Bingham, *Strategy or Process? Closing the International Criminal Tribunals for the Former Yugoslavia and Rwanda*, 24 Berkeley J. Int'l L. 687, 716 (2006); Lana Ljuboja, *Justice in an Uncooperative World: ICTY and ICTR Foreshadow ICC Ineffectiveness*, 32 Hous. J. Int'l L. 767, 792 (2010).

Domestic actors seeking to promote local mechanisms of legal accountability might be prevented from relying on decisions of international criminal tribunals if the latter are perceived locally as politically biased.[23] Moreover, international proceedings afflicted by serious perceived flaws would not serve as a good model for domestic courts to follow.[24] As a result, the ability of exceptional international tribunals to prod or inspire their national counterparts to exercise complementary jurisdiction – a key condition for an effective, coordinated fight against impunity – might be impaired by their perceived legitimacy deficit.

3. Corrective Strategies: Robust Complementarity and Restrictive Law Application

The need to bolster the legitimacy of exceptional international criminal procedures in the eyes of the domestic constituencies in the societies implicated in the alleged international crimes may require international tribunals to address both procedural and substantive legitimacy aspects. It is worth mentioning in this regard that these two aspects of legitimacy may point in different directions. As noted by Thomas Franck in *Fairness in International Law and Institutions* with regard to fairness, which Franck considered to be one of the building blocks of legitimacy: "These two aspects of fairness – the substantive (distributive justice) and the procedural (right process) – may not always pull in the same direction, because the former favors change and the latter stability and order. The tension between stability and change, if not managed, can disorder the system."[25]

23 *See, e.g.*, Christoph Burchard, *The Nuremberg Trial and its Impact on Germany*, 4 J. Int'l Crim. Just. 800, 806 (2006); Andrew T. Guzman, *International Tribunals: A Rational Choice Analysis*, 157 U. Pa. L. Rev. 171, 207 (2008).

24 *See, e.g.*, Larissa J. van den Herik, The Contribution of the Rwanda Tribunal to the Development of International Law 62 (2005); Göran Sluiter, *Atrocity Crimes Litigation: Some Human Rights Concerns Occasioned by Selected 2009 Case Law*, 8 Nw. U. J. Int'l Hum. Rts. 248 (2010).

25 Thomas M. Franck, Fairness in International Law and Institutions 7 (1998).

As noted, the application of criminal law in exceptional international procedures challenges the existing legal order: it erodes the principle of nullum crimen sine lege and introduces a vertical judicial mechanism to indirectly monitor and enforce state compliance with certain international norms without necessarily securing the relevant states' consent. This "legal change" project – which already suffers in Franckian terms from a legitimacy deficit associated with its lack of adherence to a rule hierarchy, which may give expression to basic principles of state consent and, as noted, generate substantive due process concerns[26] – is further open to accusations of selectivity and politicization in the way the project is executed. Policy considerations relating to the need to sustain the effectiveness of special international criminal tribunals may therefore support the proposition that such judicial bodies ought to operate with some awareness of their legitimacy deficit, and apply their legal-change tools with a degree of caution. A cautious approach to international criminal adjudication may compensate exceptional international tribunals for some of their legitimacy shortcomings.

It may be noted, however, that international criminal tribunals that exercise jurisdiction with the support of those relevant states whose policies are subject to indirect judicial review – for example the ICC when exercising self-referral jurisdiction or hybrid criminal courts operating with the cooperation of the host government – have more leeway than their counterparts exercising more contested jurisdictional titles. Hence, international criminal tribunals enjoying the support of the territorial state or the accused's state of nationality may adopt more aggressive legal-change strategies than tribunals operating without such consent.[27] Another relevant factor in the equation may be the capacity of international criminal tribunals to attain their goals without the cooperation

26 *Id.* p. 193.

27 *See, e.g.*, Etelle R. Higonnet, *Restructuring Hybrid Courts: Local Empowerment and National Criminal Justice Reform*, 23 Ariz. J. Int'l & Comp. L. 347, 361 (2006); Claus Kress, *"Self-Referrals" and "Waivers of Complementarity,"* 2 J. Int'l Crim. Just. 944, 948 (2004).

of local constituencies and institutions. Arguably, where strong external enforcement capabilities are available, the relative importance of legitimacy in the eyes of local constituencies as a generator of cooperation and compliance may decline. If, however, local consent to the exercise of exceptional international criminal jurisdiction is lacking, and external enforcement possibilities are scarce, international criminal tribunals should at least consider the adoption of measures designed to mitigate their perceived legitimacy deficit. One corrective strategy available to international criminal tribunals applying special adjudicatory powers is a robust application of the principle of complementarity. By affording deference toward the local courts of the state in which the alleged crimes have occurred, or that had some other form of direct involvement in their commission, the image of international criminal adjudication as an extraordinary measure of last resort is reinforced, and conflicts with notions of state sovereignty and the principle of nonintervention are reduced.[28] A strong principle of complementarity, which supports the application of international jurisdiction only where the response of the local legal systems are clearly inadequate, could therefore strike a better balance between the need to respect national sovereignty and the strong preference for domestic choice of accountability measures that it entails and fighting impunity. Note that a robust application of complementarity may also be supported by additional efficiency and due process policy arguments: It can help in alleviating the caseload of international tribunals and limit the number of cases removed from their more "natural" fora, whose procedural and substantive laws are typically more readily available to the defendant.[29]

If I am right, then in cases involving a good faith, yet perhaps suboptimal local response to the alleged crimes, special international criminal

28 *See, e.g.*, Federica Gioia, *State Sovereignty, Jurisdiction, and "Modern" International Law: The Principle of Complementarity in the International Criminal Court*, 19 Leiden J. Int'l L. 1095, 1115 (2006); R.B. Philips, *The International Criminal Court Statute: Jurisdiction and Admissibility*, 10 Crim. L. F. 61, 63–64 (1999).

29 For a general argument against the fairness of international criminal adjudication, *see* George P. Fletcher, *Against Universal Jurisdiction*, 1 J. Int'l Crim. Just. 580 (2003).

tribunals should be hesitant to exercise their jurisdiction, particularly if such exercise of jurisdiction is objected to by the state in question and few possibilities for enforcing the law against that state exist. International judicial intervention would be of limited utility in circumstances where (a) the need for external intervention is reduced, as some accountability measures such as truth commissions or lustration systems have already been set up by the domestic polity; and (b) the success prospects of the external intervention are low because of its legitimacy deficit and lack of enforcement powers. Positive or proactive complementarity measures designed to gradually spur national courts into action may be more suitable in such situations – the threat of prosecutions may primarily serve as a potential "stick" designed to induce more state action.[30]

It is interesting to note that in the context of their "completion strategy," both the ICTY and ICTR have ceased opening new cases, and have transferred their remaining investigation files to the local authorities in the Balkans and Rwanda, respectively.[31] The ICTY has also made a significant use of its Rule 11 bis authority to transfer pending cases back to the local jurisdictions where the crimes have occurred. The recently established International Residual Mechanism for Criminal Tribunals will similarly be expected to direct cases, first and foremost, to national courts. Thus, it could be argued that the de facto substitution of the primacy principle contained in the ICTY and ICTR Statutes, with a complementarity-based approach, is indicative of the latter's superior long-term sustainability. Such a move to complementarity confirms the centrality of international criminal tribunals' catalytic role vis-à-vis

30 *See* William W. Burke-White, *Proactive Complementarity: The International Criminal Court and National Courts in the Rome System of International Justice*, 49 Harv. Int'l L.J. 53, 57 (2008).

31 *See, e.g.*, Erik Møse, *The ICTR's Completion Strategy: Challenges and Possible Solutions*, 6 J. Int'l Crim. Just. 667, 672 (2008); David Tolbert and Aleksander Kontic, *The International Criminal Tribunal for the Former Yugoslavia: Transitional Justice and the Transfer of Cases to National Courts, and Lessons for the ICC, in* The Emerging Practice of the International Criminal Court 135, 145–49 (Carsten Stahn and Göran Sluiter eds., 2009).

national courts, and is consistent with the strong version of complementarity advocated here.

The tentative decision of the ICC prosecutor to refrain, for the time being, from initiating cases arising out of Colombia, and to monitor the operation of the local Justice and Peace Law – notwithstanding its controversial elements, in particular the low maximum sentences it prescribes – may also be regarded as supportive of a reading of the principle of complementarity that prefers partial and imperfect local proceedings to better, but possibly under-effective, international adjudication.[32] Again, such a preference may be less appropriate in circumstances where the local authorities show no interest or ability in prosecuting at all or in establishing legal accountability through other means, or consent expressly to international criminal adjudication of a given case or situation.[33]

A second corrective strategy addressing the legitimacy deficit of exceptional international criminal adjudication may involve the prudent application of substantive international criminal law by international tribunals, relying primarily on those normative parts featuring high degrees of determinacy, and thus endowed with Franckian legitimacy.[34] The notion that only clear violations of clear international law norms should lead to international prosecution by international criminal tribunals – if factual and legal determinacy exists – assists such tribunals in underscoring the exceptionality of resorting to international justice and deflecting some accusations of politicized law interpretation and application. Although a selective application of the law can nonetheless be justified on principled grounds, an allegedly selective and tendentious reading

32 For a discussion of the Colombia situation, *see, e.g.*, KAI AMBOS, THE COLOMBIAN PEACE PROCESS AND THE PRINCIPLE OF COMPLEMENTARITY OF THE INTERNATIONAL CRIMINAL COURT: AN INDUCTIVE SITUATION REPORT (2010); Jennifer S. Easterday, *Deciding the Fate of Complementarity: A Colombian Case Study*, 26 ARIZ. J. INT'L & COMP. L. 49(2009).

33 *See Prosecutor v. Katanga*, Case No. ICC- 01/04–01/07, Decision of (25 Sept. 25, 2009 (ICC Appeals Chamber; admissibility) (finding that prosecutorial inaction by the DRC and its decision to surrender a suspect to the ICC renders moot the question of complementarity vis-à-vis the DRC).

34 FRANCK, *supra* note 25, at 52.

of the law or facts may imply the total subjugation of legal to political considerations – a conclusion leading to exacerbation of the existing legitimacy deficit of ad hoc international tribunals and other exceptional international criminal procedures. Note that a prudent substantive law-application approach is also supported by general criminal-law principles, such as reasonable doubt as a basis for acquittal and the need to strictly construe criminal law norms and interpret ambiguous terms in favor of the accused. It is also supported by the expectation that international criminal tribunals focus their efforts on prosecuting the most serious violations of international criminal law.[35]

The reluctance of the ICTY Office of the Prosecutor to indict NATO service members for violating the principle of proportionality during the Kosovo campaign of 1999, and more broadly, the reluctance of the ICTY Chambers to press in other cases for convictions for excessive collateral damage, may be illustrative of prudence in law application in the sense described. Arguably, the perceived legitimacy deficit associated with using open-ended standards such as lack of proportionality or excessiveness as the basis for criminal convictions has had an inhibiting effect on the ICTY's prosecutorial policies and jurisprudence, especially when faced with the strong opposition of powerful states.

At the same time, the Report of the Human Rights Council Fact-Finding Mission to Gaza – analogous in its operation in some respects to the exercise of exceptional international criminal jurisdiction, as it entailed an ad hoc quasi-judicial review of individual and state policies – has attracted considerable criticism due in part to its allegedly liberal law-application tendencies. The Report pronounced grave conclusions on the basis of indeterminate facts and vague legal standards, such as lack of proportionality or failure to exercise due caution.[36] This detracted

35 Statute of the International Court of Justice, preamble, June 26, 1945, 33 U.N.T.S. 993 ("Determined . . . to establish an independent permanent International Criminal Court in relationship with the United Nations system, with jurisdiction over the most serious crimes of concern to the international community as a whole").

36 For a discussion of some of the more problematic legal constructions employed in the Goldstone report, *see, e.g.*, Michael N. Schmitt, *Military Necessity and Humanity in*

further from the legitimacy of the Mission's findings in the eyes of Israel, the unwilling reviewed state, and its allies, which perceived the very establishment of the Mission as tainted with selectivity and political bias.[37] This perception appears to have limited the report's effectiveness; to date, very few minor war-crimes prosecutions have taken place in Israel or elsewhere with relation to the events addressed in the report – a fact that is perhaps indicative of the report's limited success in triggering national proceedings.[38]

Conclusion

Exceptional international criminal tribunals and other tribunals exercising special international criminal jurisdiction may suffer from a legitimacy deficit as a result of the problems of retroactivity, selectivity, and politicization that sometimes allegedly characterize their work. Such problems, which are almost inextricably linked to exceptional criminal adjudication, are exacerbated when the substantive law applied by international

International Humanitarian Law: Preserving the Delicate Balance, 50 VA. J. INT'L L. 795 (2010); Yuval Shany, *Human Rights and Humanitarian Law as Competing Legal Paradigms for Fighting Terror, in* INTERNATIONAL HUMAN RIGHTS AND HUMANITARIAN LAW: COLLECTED COURSES OF THE ACADEMY OF EUROPEAN LAW (Orna Ben Naftali ed., 2011). Interestingly enough, Goldstone himself acknowledged that some of the report's findings were untenable. Richard Goldstone, *Reconsidering the Goldstone Report on Israel and War Crimes*, WASH. POST, Apr. 1, 2011.

37 *Goldstone Report: Interview with PM Netanyahu* (Israel TV Channel 2 broadcast Sept. 17, 2009), retrieved from http://www.mfa.gov.il/MFA/Government/Speeches+by+Israeli+leaders/2009/Goldstone_Report_Interviews_PM_Netanyahu_17-Sep-2009 ("This game was fixed. This was a field trial the result of which was known in advance").

38 *See, e.g.*, UN Human Rights Council, *Report of the Committee of Independent Experts in International Humanitarian and Human Rights Laws to Monitor and Assess any Domestic, Legal or other Proceedings Undertaken by both the Government of Israel and the Palestinian Side, in the Light of General Assembly Resolution 64/254, Including the Independence, Effectiveness, Genuineness of these Investigations and Their Conformity with International Standards*, UN Doc. A/HRC/15/50(2010).A/HRC/15/50 (Sept. 21, 2010), retrieved from http://www2.ohchr.org/english/bodies/hrcouncil/docs/15session/A.HRC.15.50_AEV.pdf.

criminal tribunals is perceived as indeterminate, incoherent, and conflicting with traditional notions of state sovereignty.

As a result of these difficulties, the operation of exceptional international criminal procedures may encounter resistance not only from targeted individuals and their allies; it is also subject to criticism by those very states or groups of states whose policies are being indirectly reviewed through the criminal process, especially if they have never consented to the process to begin with. Such resistance and delegitimization attempts may lead to under compliance with international judicial decisions and a limited impact of international tribunals on their national counterparts in those states in whose name or territory the alleged crimes have occurred.

As corrective measures to the perceived legitimacy deficit of special international criminal tribunals I suggested two judicial strategies of restraint: first, a strong presumption in favor of complementarity, reducing confrontational interventions by special international criminal tribunals to obvious cases of inability or unwillingness on the part of the "natural forum" states to impose legal accountability. Second, a more prudent application of international criminal law by special international criminal tribunals may be needed – leading them to focus on "clear-cut" serious violations of law, where the applicable law and relevant facts are relatively noncontroversial.

Although the approach proposed here may admittedly result in the under enforcement of international criminal law, it reflects awareness to the legitimacy problems associated with international judicial institutions at their present stage of development, which relies to a considerable extent on exceptional adjudicatory procedures. Once the international community develops a more routinized system of adjudication supported by stronger enforcement powers, the existing legitimacy deficit may shrink and with it the need for significant judicial restraint. But as long as the international criminal project remains in a fragile state of growth and maturation, I believe that prudence in application of jurisdiction and law is called for.

Index